A Nation Changed?

A Nation Changed?

The SNP and Scotland Ten Years On

Edited by
GERRY HASSAN and SIMON BARROW

Luath Press Limited
EDINBURGH
www.luath.co.uk

In Memory of Roanne Dods

First published 2017

ISBN: 978-1-912147-16-8

Printed and bound by Bell & Bain Ltd., Glasgow

Typeset in 11 point Sabon by Lapiz

Contents

Acknowledgements

A book project like this is by necessity a collective effort and the product of many suggestions and ideas. First and foremost, we would like to thank the stellar range of contributors who gave their time, insights and ideas. We often asked the impossible in terms of briefs, and in each and every case were met with assistance and encouragement.

Indeed, many of our contributors made helpful suggestions for the direction and content of the book, and even more, made us feel that we were taking part in a genuinely politically and intellectually engaged exercise. We would like to humbly thank each and every one of our contributors and trust they found it as worthwhile and stimulating as we did.

Second, the original brief was to produce a book that marked the anniversary of the SNP's ten years in office, assessing its record, the terrain it operates on, and its future prospects. Its genesis as an idea was as a companion to an earlier volume, *The Modern SNP: From Protest to Power*, published by Edinburgh University Press in 2009. It has by dint of the scale and ambition of the project become a much more authoritative and far-reaching study covering most aspects of the SNP in office and public life. The inspiration for this has ended up coming closer to the volumes of analysis which contemporary historian Anthony Seldon has produced studying the Thatcher, Major, Blair and Cameron administrations. We do hope this volume will be seen as both about politics now, and as a serious contribution to contemporary Scottish history.

Our sincere thanks are due to the numerous people who gave time and advice in shaping this book, its contents and contributors, including Alan Sinclair, Jim McCormick, Libby Brooks, Philip Schlesinger, Iain Macwhirter, Angela Haggerty, Willie Sullivan, Isabel Fraser, Douglas Fraser, Madeleine Bunting, Mike Small, Nigel Smith, Katherine Trebeck, Robin McAlpine, Joe Lafferty, Lesley Thomson, Gordon Guthrie, Beth Bate, Kenny MacAskill, Kirsty Hughes, Ian Dommett, Gehan Macleod, Jordan Tchilingirian, Bob Thomas, Michael Marten and Carla J Roth. A big thanks to Andrew Conway for the graphs and tables at the back of the book, and to Allistair Burt for working with us to come up with a cover which didn't invoke the usual images of just the Scottish Parliament and politicians.

We would also like to acknowledge our debt of gratitude to Luath Press and to Gavin MacDougall and all his staff. They have been passionate about this book from the outset and we would like to celebrate the wider contribution that Gavin and Luath have made to the political and intellectual life of this country. Their contribution in the last few years to ideas, politics and current affairs, has made Scotland and our debates richer and more fully informed, and we thank Gavin and everyone at Luath for this.

A project such as this has many eyes and supporters who make it possible, and this book could not have happened without the insights and abilities of Rosie Ilett who assisted in the latter stages of production.

Finally, in the period producing this book one of Scotland's most inspiring cultural practitioners – Roanne Dods – died after a short illness. Roanne was a force for good, an inspiration to everyone who met her, and mixed intellectual curiosity with practical action. In bringing this book together we can think of no finer model of the kind of Scotland, its politics, culture and ideas, than the one Roanne represented in everything she did.

Gerry Hassan   Simon Barrow

gerry@gerryhassan.com   simon.barrow@ekklesia.co.uk

The SNP, Modern Scotland and Power in Transition

Gerry Hassan and Simon Barrow

THE SNP HAS shaped and dominated Scottish politics over the past ten years. Besides that, it has emerged as a powerful force – in parliamentary terms as the third force – in British politics.

It hasn't been all plain sailing. There have been many bumpy moments, reverses and defeats. Initially the SNP did not experience devolution as hospitable or friendly territory, finding it difficult to adjust to the new environment in the early years. But then this was true for Labour, too. Eventually, when Alex Salmond came back as leader in 2004, the party discovered a voice and strategy which contributed to its narrow victory in May 2007. This was an election that turned out to be a watershed, beginning the process of the SNP establishing itself as the dominant party of Scottish politics.

From today's vantage point it looks as if the current state of affairs was always meant to be. But there was nothing inevitable about the impressive position the SNP found itself in at the beginning of 2017, and this needs to be remembered. Politics is made up of numerous unpredictable variables. Equally, the SNP's seemingly impregnable position is not as unassailable and hegemonic as some seem to assume (something now more obvious after the 2017 local and UK elections). Further powerful challenges are coming to Scotland, the UK and the global order. This is an age of disruption, involving inevitable surprises and populist revolts, from which no nation, Scotland included, is immune.

The SNP's recent rise was aided by a number of contingent factors, as well as long-term shifts, including elements of those regular, critical ingredients for success: luck and timing. Long-term factors aided the SNP, such as the hollowing out and implosion of both Scottish Labour and 'Labour Scotland', alongside the decline of the Scottish Conservatives over the last 50 years and, in recent decades, their portrayal as a pariah party – which may have just come to an end with the 2017 UK election result in Scotland. In the short-term, the SNP's victory in 2007 was assisted by the demise of Tommy Sheridan's Scottish Socialist Party, which polled respectably in 2003 and collapsed by 2007. Then, following the election, the decision of the Liberal Democrats not even to consider coalition discussions with the SNP created the conditions for minority, single party government.

Perhaps the biggest factor in all this was the SNP's changing of itself. None of the external factors would have been sufficient if the party had not been transformed, even compared to the Scottish Parliament elections of 1999 and 2003. Instead, it professionalised, became disciplined and most importantly, had a will and desire to succeed by gaining power. Prior to 2007 the SNP had never 'won' a national election – meaning finishing first in the popular vote. This meant that elements in the party lacked that hunger to win which all successful parties need; an example being the British Conservatives' electoral record over the 20th and early 21st centuries.

This desire to win, combined with the change in SNP strategy, tone and attitude which occurred in 2006-7, affected how Alex Salmond and the senior leadership presented their case. They emphasised the positive attributes of self-government, rather than the negatives of Scotland in the union. This drew on the academic discipline of positive psychology. It was translated into how the party campaigned, entered office and, subsequently, governed. A secondary effect over this period was that it disorientated the SNP's main opponents, Labour, who still combated the older, predictable version of 'the Nationalists', failing to adapt to the newer, more positive version.

A decade in office is a significant milestone – one at which it is possible to assess the SNP record in government and, just as critically, how Scotland has changed and not changed over that period. This is the purpose of this book. It aims to offer a wide-ranging analysis of the SNP's record in power and its impact across wider society. It does so by offering informed scrutiny, rejecting the twin cul-de-sacs of either giving a straight pass to the party, or damning everything the SNP and the Scottish Government does.

How do we seriously measure the effectiveness of a political party and the government it shapes? One indicator would be electoral support and on this the SNP scores impressively, winning 32.9 % of the constituency popular vote in 2007 and 46.5 % nine years later in 2016. This is the highest vote share by any party in a Scottish devolved election. How does the retreat of the 2017 UK election to 36.9 % fit into this picture and how should it be judged?

Another measure is examining levels of public trust in how the Scottish Government looks after Scottish interests. These have consistently been higher over the course of the SNP in office than the previous Labour-Liberal Democrat administration. The figure of 65 % in 2016 represented a falling back from a peak of 73 % in 2015. This is still hugely ahead of the UK Government's trust ratings in Scotland, which were 25 % in 2016 and 23 % in 2015 (Scottish Social Attitudes Survey, 2017).

In terms of policy achievements, the SNP saw significant keynote policies implemented early on, with previous Labour-Lib Dem achievements parcelled into a Scottish 'social compact'. But longevity in office brings accumulated pressures. In recent years, with public spending cuts and constraints to the Scottish budget, it has been more difficult for the SNP to maintain the same momentum. Growing challenges in education and health, local government cuts, and falling Further Education college numbers have all been used by opposition parties to depict the SNP administration, after ten years, as presiding over a Scotland going in the wrong direction.

At the same time, there have been many achievements from the SNP in office. Significantly, there has been a profound shift in Scottish formal political institutions, their roles, and how Scotland itself is seen from within and without. First, there has been the emergence of the Scottish Government as the primary political institution of power in the country: a move beyond simple rebranding, but rather one recognised by Westminster and legislation, which carries with it increased popular expectations. Second, the nature of the post of First Minister has become that of the uncontested leader of the country. This is a far cry from its diminutive role under Labour previously. Third, and just as important, modern Scotland has arrived on the international stage – initially with the release of Abdelbaset al-Megrahi, and then, more substantially, through the long first independence referendum campaign.

Overall, then, the SNP's decade of dominance has been characterised by a mixture of both continuity and change. The former has been exhibited in the defensive nature of the party's social democracy. On the other hand, the SNP has undoubtedly changed as a party over this period. Its electoral support has increased, with party membership increasing dramatically after the 2014 referendum.

Through all this change the party has maintained an ethos that exhibits a sense of togetherness and comradeship which can be described as that of family. Before the 2014 independence referendum, the SNP's membership experienced numerous life-defining events as friends and extended family – births, deaths, marriages and even the occasional divorce. Positive aspects of these were publicly marked and celebrated in the 2011 SNP manifesto, which contained photos and references to some of the high profile personal events of the previous four years (SNP, 2011). This gave a loud message from the SNP to its members and to the public: this is a real community that embraces a familial set of bonds.

The family dynamic has in turn given the party a 'big tent', cross-national appeal, and has taken it into every region, area and social group in Scotland, making it truly 'the Scottish National Party'. But this level of success also involves inherent constraint. The SNP now knows that every decision made in government creates winners and losers, inspires and generates new supporters, and contains the prospect of disappointing others. This breadth of support does not give absolute freedom. Instead it can reinforce a politics of caution and conservatism in policy and governing practice.

In this respect, there are striking similarities between the SNP at its peak and Scottish Labour at its own height. Diverse national appeal reinforces a politics of safety first and a leaning towards the status quo. If left unchecked as happened in Labour's case, this will eventually lead to stasis and decline. The example of what happened to Scottish Labour is a warning to the SNP about what occurs when complacency overcomes creativity. Labour's decline from its 49.9 % peak in 1966, to less than one-fifth of the popular vote now, is one of the most dramatic declines of any centre-left party in the developed world (with only the Greek PASOK party, in unprecedented national crisis, experiencing a sharper decline).

The SNP has been changed by power in numerous ways. Take the Scottish Parliament. In 2016 the SNP elected 63 MSPs. Currently, 23 are ministers, which along with the chief whip and 11 Parliamentary Liaison Officers (PLOs) gives a total 'payroll' vote of 35. This leaves a mere 28 – less than half the parliamentary party – as backbenchers (SPICE, 2017).

Similarly, the election of an unprecedented 56 SNP MPs to Westminster in May 2015 gave the party access to resources and platforms which have transformed it as a parliamentary force. Combine these changes with the introduction of the Single Transferable Vote (STV) system for Scottish local government elections from 2007 onward, and Labour's inbuilt First Past the Post advantage disappeared overnight. This produced a double shift, as Labour lost the councillor class which had traditionally been the backbone of its organisation, and enabled the SNP to elect representatives and form groups the length and breadth of the country.

Which Scotland Has Changed and Who Has Gained?

Scotland has been characterised in the devolution era by language and intentions such as social justice, inclusion and fairness. Yet, over this period, and in particular the SNP's tenure of office, it is important to probe beyond such rhetoric and ask how power has shifted in Scotland as a result of devolution and the SNP's period in office. Who has gained and who has not gained? Who are the insiders and outsiders?

In particular, do individuals and communities believe that they have more power and a stronger voice? The evidence is that most people do not think they have a real say or real power. The 2015 Scottish Household Survey showed that

23.6 % believed they could influence decisions affecting their area: the highest level recorded since the question was first asked in 2007, and 19.6 % answered in the positive (Scottish Household Survey, 2016). This indicator shows a consistent and widespread sense of disempowerment over the past decade. Not all of that can be laid at the door of the SNP, of course. There is a wider public disaffiliation from political institutions at play. But the party has not managed to reverse that trend, despite its growing influence and power.

One positive piece of evidence for democratic engagement was the experience of the 2014 independence referendum, producing an unprecedented 84.6 % turnout. Sizeable parts of Scotland, forgotten and marginalised by politics in previous decades, were galvanised. This was 'the missing Scotland' and 'the missing million'. It drew on US political experience of the truncated electorate, as older, more affluent voters increasingly dominate politics, with all the distortions that entails (Hassan, 2014; 2016).

It is necessarily sobering to reconsider romantic myths about the 2014 referendum. The contours of the result showed that No areas and affluent, middle class voters still turned out in larger numbers than Yes areas and poorer voters – but with this important caveat: something fundamental still shifted. Take the example of Glasgow. It had the lowest turnout in Scotland at 75 %; something which independence campaigners bemoaned. But to put that in perspective, in the 2011 Scottish Parliament elections the turnout was 40.8 % (Herbert *et al*, 2011). So this was a huge upsurge of participation. However, part of the engagement of the referendum has proven to be more a one-off spike than a watershed. Turnout in subsequent elections in Glasgow returned to the previous trend: with 47.4 % participation in the 2016 Scottish elections (Aiton *et al*, 2016). A glimpse of real change for some people disappeared with the referendum defeat, it seems. The return to 'politics as usual' was not a welcome one.

So what has the SNP fundamentally changed in contemporary Scotland, in relation to everyday lives, opportunities, and the voice and power people feel they have? Asking a random group of Scottish voters (SNP, non-SNP, pro- and anti-independence, undeclared or don't know) via Facebook in April 2017, as the ten year anniversary approached, found a rich mix of views.

There is, for many, respect for the SNP, their intentions and some of their achievements. Yet this is often posed in a defensive way. It is about protecting Scotland from the rightward lurch of British politics. One person commented: 'Their greatest achievement is shielding [the] Scottish population from the worst privations of the Tories.' Another said that 'all radical change in [the] last decade has actually emanated from Westminster, e.g. welfare reform, austerity, Brexit.'

But there was for many SNP and independence supporters a sense of disappointment about specific policies such as 'community empowerment ... both an achievement and a disappointment' and 'knowing who owns our land is one thing, but intervening to give communities control over it would offer Scotland so much more.' Increasing centralisation and the expansion of state powers is viewed by some with suspicion: one person commented about 'lack of respect for freedom for the individual.' Another declared that 'my trust in the state has been ruined.'

Yet others spoke of the absence of widening life chances and any redistribution to those on lower incomes. 'The poor are still poor', said one. 'Where we have seen least success is in alleviating poverty in the peripheral urban areas' and 'not implementing progressive tax powers', said others. A contrary view was that 'the poorest are better off in Scotland' than the rest of the UK, thanks to efforts of the Scottish Government.

Many commented on the SNP 'having good intentions' and 'wanting the best for Scotland', but there was also a weariness that comes with a decade in government, such as 'they talk a good game, but where is the delivery?' One voter talked of the independence referendum 'lifting people's heads up, but now things are returning to the way they have always been'; another of the problem of conformity, identifying 'shutting down valid criticism' as 'doing down the goal of independence' and being ultimately counter-productive. Another distinctive strand was concern over whether the disadvantaged, powerless and outsiders feel that they have greater power than they did prior to the SNP taking office. One activist said: 'There has been too much rhetoric, but not enough action'; another that, 'if you live on a council estate you are left behind Scotland' (Facebook, 4 April 2017).

These are anecdotal and subjective testimonies. But the battering ram of change which emerged in the referendum of 2014, and which lost the vote, while altering society and enveloping Scotland in the subsequent 'tartan tsunamis' of 2015 and 2016, cannot endure forever. To state the obvious, the post-referendum wave translated into support for the SNP, which is much narrower and more restrictive than the energy and spirit of the referendum. It is also true that the cross-class appeal of the referendum, with all its contradictions, could not be held together permanently with the same enthusiasm – mixing, for example, SNP, Greens, Labour and ex-Labour supporters, Scottish Socialists, and numerous people desperate for social change in the immediate (one example being the punitive experience of Westminster welfare changes and the widespread use of sanctions).

The winners from the devolution era and the SNP in office are often to be found in insider Scotland, networked and professional groups, and movers and shakers of alphabet soup Scotland (CBI, SCDI, SCVO, etc.). Previous studies have shown that the people the Scottish Government and Parliament talk to most in formal consultations are themselves. This represents a circular, closed, self-re-inforcing cycle of activity. For all the good intentions and words this has not substantially altered in any major way under the SNP.

The Boo Words: Thatcherism and Blairism and Modern Scotland

The above taps into the overriding drivers of Scottish politics and its oft-de-clared centre-left characteristics. These have been shaped by numerous factors, but one significant influence had been opposition to the direction of British politics over the last 35 to 40 years.

Thatcherism, and opposition to it, has become one of the foundation stories of modern Scotland. This is characterised in simple, emotional terms by recall-ing selected symbolic events of the era – mass unemployment, council house sales, privatisation, the poll tax, the 'Sermon on the Mound', and Ravenscraig (actually closed post-Thatcher by John Major in 1992). Yet what the preva-lence of anti-Thatcherite rhetoric disguises is the extent to which Thatcherism has nevertheless shaped political discourse and mainstream politics. Alex Sal-mond inadvertently revealed this when he said, in a 2008 interview with Iain Dale, about how Scotland saw Thatcherism: 'It didn't mind the economic side so much. We could see the sense in some of that. But we didn't like the social side at all.' He said in the same interview: 'The SNP has a strong social conscience, which is very Scottish in itself. One of the reasons Scotland didn't take to Lady Thatcher was because of that' (*Total Politics*, September 2008; quoted in Dale, 2010: 8).

It was a fascinating quote, illustrating the difference within Salmond between his economic and social priorities, and it caused a stir by breaking one of the golden rules in contemporary Scottish politics: always profess allegiance to anti-Thatcherism, no matter your beliefs. The next day Salmond felt he had to phone up the BBC to say: 'I was commenting on why Scots, in particular, were so deeply resentful of Thatcher... That doesn't mean the nation liked her economic policies, just that we liked her lack of concern for social consequences even less' (BBC *Scotland*, 22 August 2008, quoted in Torrance, 2009: 258).

This twin-track approach is also seen in relation to attitudes towards Blairism and New Labour. Tony Blair once won three UK elections, had a Brit-ish-wide 93 % satisfaction rating in 1997, and was in the early days widely popular in Scotland. Now, across the UK and Scotland, he is viewed in toxic terms. In February 2017, when he called for opposition to Brexit, Blair had a

14 % satisfaction rating across the UK – lower even than current Labour leader, Jeremy Corbyn at that time.

Anti-Blairite rhetoric in Scotland has become as commonplace as anti-Thatcherism. It is possibly even more potent, because it defines what supposedly happens to centre-left politicians when they 'sell out' and become 'red Tories', or subject to the distortions of 'London Labour'. One example of how pivotal this has become was when then Scottish Labour leader Johann Lamont made, in 2012, what became known as her 'something for nothing' speech – about some of the big-ticket items of the SNP, such as free care for the elderly and no student tuition fees. Critics responded to it by calling it Thatcherite and Blairite in equal measure. In truth it was a calculated if clumsy attempt to re-open a complex debate about universalism and particularism in social security.

So anti-Thatcher and anti-Blair rhetoric can easily be used to camouflage complex realities and the abiding influence of Blairite principles across the political mainstream. David Torrance claimed recently. 'The irony is that the modern SNP – its spin, triangulation and whatever-works centrism – is thoroughly Blairite' (Twitter, 17 February 2017). This caused former SNP candidate and ex-Labour member Gordon Guthrie to respond: 'This is clearly nonsense – if the SNP triangulated it would have triangulated *away* from independence' (Twitter, 18 February 2017). Nevertheless, beyond the independence question, the SNP in government has embraced a politics that can be argued to have been influenced and shaped by some of the main tenets of Blairism, while professing like everyone else in Scottish politics a deep-seated rejection of all things Blairite. Such pronouncements about Thatcher and Blair police the boundaries of what is seen as permissible debate, allow people to stress their supposedly radical credentials, while avoiding a critique of the continuing conservatism of much of our political landscape, the SNP included.

The Limits of Official Stories about Modern Scotland

The dominant popular accounts of devolution and SNP Scotland are far removed from the terrain we have explored so far. Iain Macwhirter explained why he had supported Yes in the independence referendum as follows:

> My support for what the SNP has done in Scotland is almost entirely because of their social democratic policies and their commitment to social justice, nuclear disarmament, racial integration, open borders, increased immigration and the defence of public services.
>
> (Macwhirter, 2014: 105)

This view was combined with a damning portrayal of the nature of the union that is the United Kingdom and portrayal of the British state which some would say came close to 'othering'. This approach was given succour by such prominent voices as historian Tom Devine, who when he declared for independence in the latter stages of the campaign, described the attachment to the union in Scotland as running on near to empty, saying that there was 'very little left in the union except sentiment, history and family.' Immediately after the vote he called the UK 'a failed state' – a palpably over-the-top statement in the context in which that term is normally used (Devine 2014; BBC, 2014).

Such comments are, now, for many, the official stories of modern Scotland: a confident, competent social democracy, increasingly asserting the politics of difference from the rest of the UK, as the British state sinks below a mass of prejudice, xenophobia and plutocratic capture. This view informed the left-wing case for independence in the 2014 referendum made by the likes of the Radical Independence Campaign (RIC) and Common Weal. In the midst of a campaign such progressive populism is understandable; but as a substitute for deeper and more subtle analysis, it leaves much to be desired.

There are numerous shortcomings in easy political sentiment. First, social democratic aspiration can readily fall into wish-fulfilment. Take Macwhirter's first assertion: 'their commitment to social justice'. The SNP have done many progressive things and have good intentions in this area, but their concept and advancement of social justice has also to be seen as lacking. For over a decade, there has been no significant redistribution of wealth towards those who are poorer, and little conscious effort to shift public opinion towards a more radical notion of social justice. Instead, the SNP have gone with the grain of Scottish society, telling a good story to us of ourselves: of our fairness, decency and egalitarianism, without engaging in any substantial follow-through, for example on taxation. In this there is quite a lot of similarity between the SNP at its peak and British New Labour at its height.

Second, talk of 'racial integration, open borders [and] increased immigration' underline the inclusive nature of Scottish nationalism. That has been an absolute and a constant of the SNP and of wider civic nationalism in Scotland. However, it is easy to overstate Scotland's sense of difference on this compared to recent debates in England. In particular, opinion polls and surveys have shown that people in Scotland can have just as hard views on immigration and open borders as the rest of the UK, and that in many respects, our tolerance, commitment to diversity, and perhaps, even our anti-racism, just hasn't been tested in the way it has in parts of England.

Third, Devine's description of the union and the UK reinforces the degree to which the idea of Britain has become problematic north of the border. However, leaving aside the over-the-top rhetoric, the British state is increasingly seen as synonymous with a virulent, right-wing policy agenda – a perspective subsequently aided by Brexit, the triumphalist English nationalist rhetoric of some Brexiteers, and what *The Economist*'s Bagehot column has called 'a McCarthyite mood in the Brexiteer press' (Bagehot, 2017).

This tendency to caricature the British state in exclusively negative terms informs the left-wing drive for Scottish independence which parcels up the excesses of Thatcherism, Blairism, the poll tax and Iraq war, along with other sins. There is often an overt moral dimension to this, distinctively Scottish in character. Yet its version of the British state is too simple, amounting at times to little more than a stereotype, a Nairnite-style critique which has never read Tom Nairn's magnum opus *The Breakup of Britain*, and which is too dismissive of the impact of 30 years of post-war Labour Governments (Nairn, 1977). On this basis, Scottish politics is presented as being more virtuous, ignoring any shortcomings – usually blamed on Westminster and/or the Tories. Hence, our scandalous records on child poverty, health inequalities, or working class exclusion from higher education; or the SNP and mainstream Scotland's thin concepts of social justice and social democracy in these accounts, pass without major comment – either the fault of someone else, or worse, inconvenient truths to be ignored.

It says something about how deep such sentiment is in Scotland that a historian as eminent as Tom Devine should add his voice to them. But in this he is a follower, not a trendsetter. Moreover, all this informs a historical pattern of how Scotland has done politics for a large part of its history: which is by buying into and reinforcing serial, single stories which in turn reinforce the dominant political party or social group. We have been here many times before, with the power of the Kirk, the Liberals in the 19th century, imperial Empire Scotland, the Labour Party in the second half of the 20th century, and now neo-nationalist Scotland.

Here we have privileged stories presented as inclusive: attempting to incorporate or exclude the numerous counter-stories that always will and should exist. For example, the 50 year dominance of Scottish Labour saw it attempt to delegitimise the progressive nationalist counter-story as eccentric, irrelevant to modern society, and at the time, tainted by anti-Englishness and dangerous tribalism. Slowly these charges became less plausible, until more and more people beyond the Labour tribe itself stopped believing or even listening to them. Today, neo-nationalist Scotland accounts attempt to do the same to Labour and Tories: presenting both as holding Scotland's potential back, not standing up for Scotland, and ultimately being beholden to London. This has worked with the former and the power of the moniker 'London Labour', but less with the Tories, as they have found a new appeal post-2014 referendum. All politics involves attempting to define your opponents, but Scotland has had a historical pattern of dominant single stories which can lead to a groupthink version of the country: one which, if it remains entrenched, will ultimately prove increasingly questionable, undermining the SNP and revealing itself unsuited to the challenges which will emerge in any future independent Scotland.

Scotland Today: Brexit, IndyRef2/ScotRef and Challenges Ahead

This brings us to the political environment in 2017 and the realities of Brexit. First Minister Nicola Sturgeon ideally wanted to hold any second vote before the UK left the EU at the end of March 2019 – in autumn 2018 or spring 2019. But for the moment the UK Government has played hardball. Prime Minister Theresa May has declared that 'now is not the time': a sound bite that, while seemingly stretching 'now' to mean 'later', and therefore apparently uncompromising on timescale, actually leaves room for a vote post-Brexit (Hassan and Gunson, 2017). Moreover, as the game of political poker between the Scottish and UK Governments moves forward, there is a host of possible moves which makes the condition and timing of any second referendum uncertain for all involved.

Such dramatic times produce numerous challenges for the SNP. One is the extent of the party's appeal and how it positions itself in government – attempting to speak for most of the nation, while recognising the limits of its popular appeal. How can the SNP understand and reach out to non-nationalist and independence sceptical or hostile Scotland? The dynamics and timescale of a second independence referendum pose significant obstacles, as portions of the Yes and No camps embrace their certainties and engage in trench warfare.

Then there is the political effect of how to do politics after ten years in office, with all the commensurate knock-on effects: a record to defend with successes and failures, and the human cost in terms of individual politicians who have become fatigued by the pressures of both office and the continual demands of high wire politics. In the 2014 referendum, the SNP campaigned as both insurgents and incumbents: a balancing act which could be much more difficult to pull off next time.

Equally important is the human dimension in political culture and leadership. Much of what passes for political debate in modern 24/7 media is the exact opposite of any real debate. Rather, it is people talking past one another, making simple, sound bite statements. Such behaviour represents a politics of management, control and the distortion of genuine values. It happens, in part, because party managers (and media managers in particular) fear comments which depart from the official position, but also because such an approach allows them to maintain a single, coherent message, and through that control and discipline. However, all of this comes at huge cost to politics, democracy, participation and confidence in both the parties in question and the system they are part of.

The SNP have embraced this culture in their ascent to power and it has worked for them in the first decade. Party unity and a culture of being on-message have been maintained. But it has come at a significant price – just as it did for New Labour a decade previous. The SNP have gained a reputation of being control freaks and being somewhat robotic, with this unity – a large part of which is a self-denying ordinance against showing divisions in public – then used against the party by its opponents.

It is difficult, indeed almost impossible, once such a culture has become commonplace, to change it. But it must be reformed if the SNP is successfully to adapt and evolve. For while such uniformity (dubbed 'coherence') is an aid in winning power and establishing dominance in the early days of office, it provides a poor tool for reflexive government and for the choices that need to be navigated in parliament and beyond. Ten years on, the SNP needs to shift gears to a culture and leadership which allows more for ambiguity, uncertainty and doubt in certain areas, as well as more participation and creativity in others. This would acknowledge the difficulties and nuances inherent in government and independence – the absence of which, in 2014, acted as a barrier to many soft No voters making the gradual journey to Yes during the campaign.

Secondly, there is a fear inherent in the politics of control about letting go. This is a politics of the centre knowing best, and key advisers, a few trusted hands and a small number of ministers being kept in the loop and making decisions. From this there is a very conventional (indeed, old-fashioned) notion of how political change comes about, based on pulling levers and mechanistic or linear conceptions of change. It isn't surprising that the SNP leadership's presentation of independence for over a decade has been about the 'full powers' of the Parliament and getting the economic levers to be able to make informed choices. This becomes, without thinking, a narrative about the political centre of the country accruing yet more powers.

It is a by-product of such a centralising political approach that power is held in the hands of a very narrow selectorate. Thus, under SNP rule, few ministers have really prospered and left behind a legacy of legislative or wider cultural change. Instead, under both Alex Salmond and Nicola Sturgeon, ministers have mostly embraced a politics of competence – in the early years seen as a breath of fresh air after Labour domination. But, ten years on, its shortcomings are becoming more obvious, with some ministers showing a flair for such an approach (John Swinney at Finance from 2007-16, Nicola Sturgeon at Health from 2007-12) while numerous others may be seen as having illustrated its shortcomings. Ultimately, it is a self-defeating politics where decisions become made in an ever-diminishing circle, which becomes more and more out of touch with the base that gave the party power. Such a cycle never ends well. It requires constant intellectual and political effort to resist.

Third, it is important to recognise the costs that come with permanently engaged, hyperactive politics: a stance the SNP and sizeable parts of Scotland have been hooked on for the last four or five years. This results in a lack of mental space and capacity in senior politicians and activists which contributes to poor judgement. It means being less able to listen and absorb new information, which can cloud political sensitivities and the radar for fresh ideas. Studies of senior CEOs in the business world have shown that such a climate can be one of the main contributory factors in how some commercial leaders burn out or make disastrous decisions. Politics is no different, in this respect at least, and a political class and actors who have been on permanent campaigning mode for the last few years have to find a way to have some time off.

Perhaps much of this is inevitable when a party has defined the political debate for so long. It is a problem of success. But after a decade in office, it is not possible to feel the weakening of the political antennae of the SNP, and in particular its leadership? The party, even at its peak popularity in the 2015 UK general election, never won a majority of the voters, though it admittedly came close, claiming 49.97 %. That gives the SNP a huge political party dominance in the country, and a share of the popular vote which other parties can only envy. But it also means that what can broadly be characterised as 'non-nationalist Scotland' is still a majority of the nation. This has consequences for party politics, with the SNP once again being a minority administration at Holyrood and the decisions it makes being qualified in that way. But it has even bigger consequences towards the running of any second independence referendum.

It seems that the SNP leadership has still to recognise one important aspect of the wider political mood of the country after the perma-campaigning of the last few years, involving the twin caesuras of the two referendum votes and the 2015 and 2016 elections. There is a political wariness and even exhaustion across large swathes of Scotland – the second found in much SNP and Yes opinion. This is where the lack of pause and breath in the political process since 2014 affects the country, and could even be having a detrimental effect on the judgement of the SNP as to how it manages itself, its constituency and its aspirations.

The SNP *and Scotland's Civic Nationalism*

The SNP's DNA is shaped by a civic, modern, progressive nationalism – one that is very far removed from the ugly populism and little Englander nationalism articulated by UKIP and Brexit. The view put by many SNP and independence supporters is that 'our nationalism is different': benign, tolerant and inclusive, and welcoming of others including incomers to Scotland (see McCrone, 2017). One oft cited fact is that in the 2014 referendum Scottish born voters split 52.7:47.3 for independence, while voters born in England, Wales and Northern Ireland split 72.1:27.9 against independence, providing a major part of the No majority (Henderson and Mitchell, 2015). Not one prominent SNP politician drew attention to this, illustrating the strength of its inclusive, non-ethnic civic approach.

All of this is unquestionably true, but at the same time the SNP is still shaped by a nationalism that, like all ideologies, carries with it its own mobilising myths and conceits. The Irish writer Fintan O'Toole, in the weeks before the 2014 vote, offering advice from the Irish experience, commented that any nationalism operates as a 'rocket fuel that can get you out of an old order' or state, but 'burns up quickly'. Thus, it provides the momentum to establish an independent state, but offers little by way of a compass subsequently. O'Toole went on to say that:

> *What has to be broken free of us is not just the big bad Them. It is also the warm, fuzzy Us of the nationalist imagination – the Us that is nicer, holier, more caring. What a free country quickly discovers is that the better Us of its imagination is not already there, fully formed, just waiting to blossom in the sun of liberation. It has to be created and in order to create it you have to genuinely decide that you want it.*

(O'Toole, 2014)

All political philosophies have a Them and Us – even inclusive, civic Scottish nationalism. What the above, and the experience of every single country which has become independent shows, is that the post-nationalist politics of the country needs to begin the here and now, and not wait until Independence Day. This requires a politics which can do detail and scrutiny, and hold those in power to account, not giving them a free pass. Such an attitude has to involve holding the SNP to account, and being able to criticise it (from both within and without) when SNP politicians and ministers fall short. Too many SNP and independence supporters still appear to believe that blind faith and trust in public is the best way to act, as if such unquestioning loyalty produces good politics and governance, and offers comfort or security in relation to those outside the set. In the long run it does not. It stifles innovation and responsiveness, on which all creative politics depends.

Secondly, such a post-nationalist politics has to have a national project for Scotland which is about more than just the principle of independence. It cannot be, as some have suggested, a Scottish version of Brexit: populist, light on detail and centred on 'taking back control' (Macwhirter, 2017). There was the commendable aspiration towards such a project in the Scottish Government White Paper on independence, *Scotland's Future*. But even here, the social democratic sentiment on public spending and services cohabited with neo-liberal economics, cutting corporation and business taxes (Scottish Government, 2013b). This remains the broad church of the SNP's independence vision under Nicola Sturgeon, with former SNP MSP Andrew Wilson's Growth Commission considering lower business taxes post-independence to attract English and Welsh companies after Brexit. Sturgeon had moved away from lower corporation tax when coming to the leadership of the SNP and the Scottish Government, but then shied away from a 50 % top tax rate on the richest on 'pragmatic grounds' which suggest severe limits to the rhetoric of progressivism.

What is needed instead is a project for Scotland's future which moves beyond shotgun political marriages, failed economic orthodoxies and diluted social democracy. That isn't going to be easy, but to begin to map out some of this territory would at least be honest, involve acknowledging constraints and trade-offs and, in strategic places, boldness (see as an example Barrow and Small, 2016). Importantly, this 'future Scotland' could begin to take shape and root in the here and now.

A National Project for a Future Scotland

This national project has to reflect the importance of fiction and mythology in the culture of nations, politics and government. Edmund S. Morgan, writing about the rise of popular sovereignty in England at the time of the civil war, and in the US in the Wars of Independence, observed that 'fictions are necessary, because we cannot live without them... fictions enable the few to govern the many.' He went on: 'It is not only the many who are constrained by them... the governing few no less than the governed many may find themselves limited ...' Such fictions must he believed 'bear some resemblance to fact' (Morgan, 1988: 14).

Morgan believed such fictions were central to the act of successful government:

> *Government requires make believe. Make believe that the king is divine, make believe that he can do no wrong or make believe that the voice of the people is the voice of God.*

(Morgan, 1988: 13)

Addressing this requires avoiding talking about abstract and problematic concepts such as 'sovereignty', which is seldom understood or practical. Political scientist and Labour MP Harold Laski once advised that all political discussions should avoid talking about sovereignty (Laski, 1925, 44-45). Instead of invoking competing demands of sovereignty (and related to it, mandates and referendums) we could embrace the idea of what 'people' we are invoking and inventing. For underneath all such talk of sovereignties or power we are talking about who we are, the community we inhabit, and what its characteristics and boundaries are.

This entails having honesty, responsibility and an understanding of ethics. First, one-dimensional caricature does not get us very far. It plays to diminishing audiences – whether, in Scotland, it is damning and dismissing everything the SNP have done, or seeing everything they have done in positive, panglossian terms and refusing to allow criticism of anything to pass.

Take this latter sentiment. In elements of SNP and Yes sentiment there is a taking for granted that there is only permissible way of thinking. This is the mind-set of a closed tribe which doesn't allow for ambiguity and uncertainty and which doesn't understand the world beyond it. It can display, at its worst, a self-satisfaction and self-congratulation which can be the downside of over-enthusiasm and partisanship, spilling over into a zealotry (and even on occasion an intolerance of those who don't share the same views). The notion of the closed tribe has a long track record in left-wing politics, but is also inherent in such causes as self-government and independence politics (Goss, 2014). The strength of group membership and identification becomes a weakness and encourages blinkeredness. It isn't equipped for holding power to account, scrutinising detail, or the challenges of an independent Scotland, so it has to be countered by independence and SNP supporters themselves.

Second, tone, attitude and demeanour are central to politics. It isn't an accident that the SNP have been at their most effective, campaign-wise, emphasising positivity in the 2006-7 period and at points in the 2014 campaign. There is an important distinction between optimism and hope – the former being based often on unrealistic expectations, the latter being more human and organic (see Hassan, 2014: 27-28; Eagleton, 2015). This is a distinction which Yes Scotland sometimes confused in the 2014 campaign, while parts of the SNP seem to have forgotten the need for an uplifting, positive political message.

An example of this is provided by Alex Salmond, who contributed so much to the SNP victories of 2007 and 2011, as well as in 2014. He recast his political message in the first victory to notable effect. However, since the referendum defeat he has occasionally reverted back to a previous negative approach, seeming to want to dispute the result, and giving the impression that victory was stolen from him by a host of villains (the BBC and 'the Vow' for starters). This approach plays well with a small segment of committed independence opinion, which can display a bitter, even conspiratorial attitude to politics. But it isn't a mentality that is well served to looking at how independence comes up with a better offer and better politics than last time.

Third, nurturing friendly, supportive, critical comment and debate is vital to any successful politics. In this regard, former Justice Secretary, Kenny MacAskill, recently commented that the SNP Government under Nicola Sturgeon had to be wary of 'lots of talk, but less action' and said that 'warm words are inadequate'. He said of the SNP in office that 'the criticism of Labour about a plethora of consultations and reviews, is in danger of being replicated' – and we all know that story did not end well (MacAskill, 2017).

Fourth, public policy has to invoke more than a mix of pseudo-outsourcing responsibilities and talk of monies. The Growth Commission is a particularly regressive example, but Scotland has had much experience in this area, with the non-partisan Welfare Working Group being a positive one (Scottish Government, 2013a). But what none of these initiatives (Christie, Calman, even the Scottish Constitutional Convention of years ago) did was move beyond invoking to involving people directly. This when we have a powerful 'fiction' of popular sovereignty and examples all over the world of popular constitutionalism and participative and deliberative democracy – some of which are near to home such as Iceland and Ireland.

Connected to this is the micro-management of public services focusing on finance and delivery, both of which are important, but can stifle innovation if they become the sole focus. As important is the over-arching philosophy of public services, and a practice which puts people more in charge of decisions and which is willing in the centre to let go and live with the results. That requires making a culture of supporting people, allowing mistakes to happen, and not reverting to centralisation whenever there is local controversy or a media firestorm.

Fifth, where are the spaces for experimentation, learning, taking risks and making tomorrow's Scotland? There is a burgeoning debate about the role of autonomy, self-organisation and self-determination, spurred on by the crisis of the state and welfare cuts. One answer is understandably to resist Westminster's punitive policies by as much as possible, reversing or ameliorating them. The experience of the bedroom tax and disability benefit cuts are examples of this. Of course, that can sometimes transpose itself into the mundane reality of wishing to turn the clock back five or at best ten years, when we have to start from a bolder premise: namely, what kind of welfare and social security system, principles and benefits do we want to aspire to in 21st century Scotland?

A Scotland which encouraged a diverse ecology of ideas, policies and exchange could witness a richer fermenting of institutions, groups and places than we currently have. Ten years into the SNP in office there is a conspicuous absence of think tanks, research agencies and resources that are pro-independence, well funded and firmly anchored. Bodies such as *Common Weal, CommonSpace, Bella Caledonia* and numerous others all run on a mix of goodwill, activism and crowdfunding, which is not likely to be sustainable in the long run.

One task for the next stage of independence work is to engage in institution building – to make new centres of expertise, research and imagination. This isn't an optional extra, but fundamental in the short- and medium-term to how a future independence referendum will be contested, and in the longer term to the politics of independence *per se*. It has to answer a dilemma posed in this book concerning the narrow bandwidth of places and people from which current policy and ideas emerge in Scotland. There is also the need for a Scottish expression of a global conversation in an age of upheaval and disruption which, as Wolfgang Streeck has observed, involves getting ready as 'the foundations of modern society will again have to be rethought, like they were in the New Deal and after the Second World War' (Streeck, 2016: 250). An increasingly self-governing, autonomous and yet interdependent Scotland needs a plethora of interventions from all sorts of groups and professions to seriously contribute to this.

Finally, Nicola Sturgeon's SNP Government is still relatively new, with its popular mandate just a year old. It still has a window to renew, to take risks, and to break with its predecessors. It could explore ways of doing statecraft and politics that is different from what we have seen before. It could make new alliances and partnerships, host new forums, and speak, listen and reflect in a manner which made people recognise a mutual respect to relationships between government and people. It could even choose not to surround itself just with those who say what they want them to say, in that incestuous culture of co-option which defines so much of public life. A collaborative Scottish Government with a far-reaching national project would recognise the limits of its own reach, insights and wisdom, and question the inevitable cheerleaders who all administrations are surrounded by, and the safety first nature of the 'boardism' of too much institutional Scotland.

What would a Scottish politics and culture of independence look like which dared to put this approach centre stage? It would be one which was more daring, honest and human. It would admit to mistakes, on occasions not knowing all the answers, and learning from others, including political opponents. It would be, dare we say it, a political and national project, which was not only likely to be more successful in conventional terms, but would stand a greater chance of remaking the culture, attitudes and practices of our nation.

The SNP has contributed much to the public life of our nation, and has much to be proud of. But, now more than ever, we have to aspire to more than a politics of party and party loyalty. The contours and cultures of a future Scotland,

and potentially, an independent Scotland, are being made in the actions and attitudes of all of us now. That's a big responsibility.

References

Aiton, A., Burnside, R., Campbell, A., Edwards, T., Liddell, G., McIver, I. and McQuillen, A. (2016), *SPICe Briefing: Election 2016*, Edinburgh: Scottish Parliament Information Centre, accessed at: www.parliament.scot/ResearchBriefingsAndFactsheets/S5/SB_16-34_Election_2016.pdf

Bagehot (2017), 'How Brexit damaged Britain's democracy', *The Economist*, 1 April, accessed at: www.economist.com/news/britain/21719817-our-outgoing-columnist-laments-condition-british-state-how-brexit-damaged-britains

Barrow, S. and Small, M. (eds.) (2016), *Scotland 2021*, Edinburgh: Ekklesia/Bella Caledonia.

BBC (2014), 'Newsnight', *BBC Two*, 19 September.

Dale, I. (2010), *Talking Politics: Political Conversations with Iain Dale*, London: Biteback Publishing.

Devine, T. (2014), Edinburgh International Book Festival, 17 August.

Eagleton, T. (2105), *Hope without Optimism*, New Haven: Yale University Press.

Goss, S. (2014), *The Open Tribe*, London: Lawrence and Wishart.

Hassan, G. (2014), *Caledonian Dreaming: The Quest for a Different Scotland*, Edinburgh: Luath Books.

Hassan, G. (2016), *Scotland the Bold: How Our Nation Has Changed and Why There is No Going Back*, Glasgow: Freight Books.

Hassan, G. and Gunson, R. (eds.) (2017), *Scotland, the UK and Brexit: A Guide to the Future*, Edinburgh: Luath Press in association with the Institute for Public Policy Research.

Henderson, A. and Mitchell, J. (2015), 'The Scottish Question, Six Months On', Transatlantic Seminar Series, University of Edinburgh, 27 March, accessed at: http://centreonconstitutionalchange.ac.uk/sites/default/files/Scottish%20Referendum%20Study%2027%20March%202015.pdf

Herbert, S., Burnside, R., Earle, M., Liddell, G. and McIver, I. (2011), *SPICe Briefing: Election 2011*, Edinburgh: Scottish Parliament Information Centre, accessed at: http://www.parliament.scot/ResearchBriefingsAndFactsheets/S4/SB_11-29.pdf

Laski, H.J. (1925), *A Grammar of Politics*, London: George Allen and Unwin.

MacAskill, K. (2017), 'Labour's demise a lesson for Sturgeon', *Sunday Times*, 12 March, accessed at: www.thetimes.co.uk/article/labours-demise-a-lesson-for-sturgeon-ok8m7nwfj

Macwhirter, I. (2014), *Disunited Kingdom: How Westminster Won a Referendum but Lost Scotland,* Glasgow: Cargo Books.

Macwhirter, I. (2017), 'Scots have been the ragged-trousered philanthropists long enough', *Sunday Herald,* 12 February, accessed at: www.heraldscotland.com/news/15086715.Iain_Macwhirter__Scots_have_been_the_ragged_trousered_philanthropists_long_enough/

McCrone, D. (2017), *The New Sociology of Scotland*, London: Sage Publications.

Morgan, E.S. (1988), *Inventing the People: The Rise of Popular Sovereignty in England and America*, London: W.W. Norton and Company.

Nairn, T. (1977), *The Breakup of Britain: Crisis and Neo-nationalism,* London: New Left Books.

O'Toole, F. (2014), 'It is not that Scotland might become a new state but that it might become a new kind of state', *Sunday Herald,* 9 September, accessed at: www.heraldscotland.com/opinion/13178696.It_is_not_that_Scotland_might_become_a_new_state_but_that_it_might_become_a_new_kind_of_state/

Scottish Government (2013a), *The Expert Working Group on Welfare,* Edinburgh: Scottish Government, accessed at: www.gov.scot/Resource/0042/00424088.pdf

Scottish Government (2013b), *Scotland's Future: Your Guide to an Independent Scotland*, Edinburgh: Scottish Government.

Scottish Household Survey (2016), *Scotland's People: Results from the 2015 Household Survey*, Edinburgh: Scottish Government, accessed at: www.gov.scot/Publications/2016/09/7673/11

Scottish Social Attitudes Survey (2017), *Scottish Social Attitudes: Attitudes to Government and Public Engagement,* 2016, Edinburgh: Scottish Government, accessed at: www.gov.scot/Publications/2017/03/4648

SNP (2011), *Re-elect: A Scottish Government Working for Scotland,* Edinburgh: SNP.

SPICe (2017), *Scottish Parliament Factsheet: Scottish Ministers, Law Officers and Parliamentary Liaison Officers: Session 5,* Edinburgh: SPICe, accessed at: www.parliament.scot/ResearchBriefingsAndFactsheets/Factsheets/Ministers_Law_Officers_and_Parliamentary_Liaison_Officers_S5.pdf

Streeck, W. (2016), *How Will Capitalism End?,* London: Verso Books.

Torrance, D. (2009), *'We in Scotland': Thatcherism in a Cold Climate,* Edinburgh: Birlinn.

Section One: The Political and Economic Landscape

The Party and the Electorate

John Curtice

Introduction

THE FORMER SHADOW Scottish Secretary, George Robertson, famously quipped before the creation of the Scottish Parliament in 1999 that devolution would 'kill nationalism stone dead'. In practice, devolution has seemingly enabled nationalism to prosper. The SNP has been transformed from a party that was little more than a minor player at Westminster to a party that has both run Scotland's devolved government for the last ten years and which now also dominates the country's representation at Westminster. And, of course, along the way, it has had the opportunity to hold a referendum on whether Scotland should become an independent country, although that the proposition was defeated by 55 % to 45 %.

But why has devolution proven to be a golden opportunity for the SNP? What accounts for its electoral success? One possibility, of course, is that the SNP are the beneficiaries of what has been a rising tide of support for independence – those who back independence have always supported the SNP and those who support independence have become more numerous. However, there are a number of other reasons why people might support the SNP. Perhaps the party is thought more likely to provide Scotland with effective devolved government, not least by promoting Scotland's interests within the framework of the UK (Johns *et al.*, 2013). Maybe the party is simply thought to be more relevant and credible now that Scotland has its own political institutions (Curtice, 2009). If any of these reasons apply, then maybe the link between attitudes towards independence and the SNP's electoral success has not been particularly strong after all.

In this chapter we assess how far the SNP's electoral success can be accounted for by its stance on the constitutional question. Has its support rested on an ability to mobilise support for independence, or has the party in fact achieved its success by reaching out to those who do not necessarily back its constitutional vision? We address this question by analysing a unique time series of survey data on voting behaviour and political attitudes in Scotland created by the Scottish Social Attitudes (SSA) survey. Since 1999 this survey, conducted by ScotCen Social Research, has interviewed each year a representative sample of the Scottish public. When a Westminster or Holyrood election has just taken place, not only has the survey asked its respondents how they voted in that contest but also each time asked them a number of other questions about their politics. As a result, it provides us with a unique ability to track how support for the SNP has evolved since the advent of devolution.

Electoral Performance

We begin, though, by looking at the SNP's actual performance in the ballot box. One feature immediately stands out (see Table 1). First, until the 2015 UK general election, the party consistently performed better in elections to the Scottish Parliament than it did in ballots to the UK Parliament at Westminster. In the latter contests, the party was consistently only able to secure the support of around one in five voters, whereas even in the early years of the Scottish Parliament it was able to win between a quarter and a third of the vote on the constituency ballot. Even at the 2010 UK general election, by which point it had been running a minority government in Edinburgh for three years, it was still only able to win 20 % of the vote.

Table 1. SNP Performance in Westminster and Scottish Elections

Westminster Election	% SNP	Holyrood Election	% SNP
1997	22	1999	29
2001	20	2003	24
2005	18	2007	33
2010	20	2011	45
2015	50	2016	47

Figures for Holyrood Election refer to share of the constituency vote

Evidence from the SSA survey confirms that voters did indeed draw a distinction between the two kinds of election. At each Westminster election respondents to the survey were invited to say how they would have voted if a Scottish Parliament election had been taking place instead; between 1999 and 2010, support for the SNP was on average nine points higher in response to the latter question. Similarly, after each Holyrood ballot respondents were asked to state how they would have voted in a UK Parliament election. Between 1999 and 2007, the level of support registered for the SNP was on average nine points lower in this hypothetical Westminster election.

This difference in the level of support for the party in different kinds of contest is not what one would anticipate if the party's vote simply rests on the level of support for independence. Rather it is consistent with the proposition that some voters may have been inclined to think that the party was better able to use the devolved institutions to promote Scotland's interests, or that voters felt that the party was more credible in elections that concerned Scotland alone rather than the UK in general.

At the last three elections, that is, the Holyrood contests of 2011 and 2016 together with the Westminster election of 2015, the SNP have come to dominate the electoral scene, winning between 45 % and 50 % of the vote each time. Not that its performance in 2011, even though it delivered the party an overall, majority at Holyrood, gave any reason to believe that the party would be able to repeat that feat at the following UK general election. When voters were asked after the 2011 ballot how they would have voted in a UK general election, the level of support for the SNP was as much as 19 points below that registered in the actual Holyrood contest. Evidently the party's success was still peculiar to the particular context created by a Scottish Parliament election. Yet, in the event, the party's share of the vote in the 2015 UK Parliament election, held some eight months after the independence referendum, was even higher than in 2011. Moreover, when people were asked how they would have voted in a Scottish Parliament election on that occasion, the level of reported support for the SNP was only four points higher than the party actually achieved.

In short, it would seem as though the distinction between Westminster and Holyrood elections in voters' minds had been significantly eroded. Even after the most recent Holyrood election in 2016, the level of reported support for the SNP in a hypothetical contest was no more than seven points down on the vote actually registered in the ballot boxes. But why was this the case? In particular, what role did attitudes towards the constitutional question play in this apparently significant change in the pattern of SNP support?

The Constitutional Question

To investigate how the link between support for independence and people's willingness to vote for the SNP has evolved since the advent of devolution, we need a measure of support for independence that is available for all elections.

Fortunately, SSA has asked the following question on each one of the surveys it has conducted since 1999. It reads:

Which of these statements comes closest to your view?

Scotland should become independent, separate from the UK and the European Union

Scotland should become independent, separate from the UK but part of the European Union

*Scotland should remain part of the UK, with its own elected parliament which has **some** taxation powers*

*Scotland should remain part of the UK, with its own elected parliament which has **no** taxation powers*

*Scotland should remain part of the UK **without** an elected parliament*

For our purposes here, the crucial distinction is between those who choose one of the first two possible responses that indicate support for independence, and those who choose one of the remainder, each of which implies a wish to remain part of the UK, albeit perhaps while retaining a devolved parliament. By comparing the level of support for the SNP in these two groups over time, we can assess the importance of the constitutional question in determining which way people vote, and how this has evolved over time.

Table 2. SNP Support by Constitutional Preference 1999–2016

	Constitutional Preference	
% voted SNP in:	Independence	Union
1999	62	17
2001	35	9
2003	58	14
2005	33	8
2007	80	22
2010	55	12
2011	79	38
2015	85	25
2016	80	24

Source: Scottish Social Attitudes

As we might anticipate (see Table 2), support for the SNP has always been higher at any one point in time amongst those who support independence. However, that does not mean that it has always been the case that most of those who support independence have voted for the SNP. At elections for the UK Parliament at least, this has often been far from the case. In 2001 and 2005, it seems that only around one in three of those who supported independence at that time were willing to vote for the SNP, while even in 2010 the figure was only just over half. In contrast, even at the first two Scottish Parliament elections in 1999 and 2003, around three in five of those who supported independence backed the SNP, and that figure rose to four-fifths in 2007. Amongst unionists, however, support for the party in the early years of devolution was consistently on the low side, and almost as low in Westminster elections as in Holyrood ballots.

It would seem then that the relative success of the SNP at Holyrood elections rested primarily on a greater willingness amongst those who support independence to back the party in such contests. If the party was regarded as more credible in Scottish Parliament elections or better able to use the devolved institutions in Scotland's interests, such perceptions mattered more amongst supporters of independence than amongst unionists and meant that people's views on how Scotland should be governed were more likely to be reflected in devolved elections in how people voted.

However, the pattern of voting in 2011 represents something of an exception to this rule. At 79 %, the level of support for the SNP amongst supporters of independence was much the same as it had been at the previous Holyrood election in 2007. But amongst those who supported continued membership of the Union, the level of support for the SNP was close to double the level it had been at any previous election. Although the 2011 election paved the way for the 2014 independence referendum, arguably the SNP's success at winning an overall majority at that election rested on an unprecedented level of support amongst those who at that time at least did not support independence.

Indeed, the SNP have not been able to repeat that feat since. In both 2015 and 2016, support for the party amongst unionists, though not negligible, stood at just a quarter. In contrast, in both cases, four in five – or more – of those who were in favour of independence voted for the party, just as they had done in 2007 and 2011. This meant that attitudes towards how Scotland should be governed and voting for the SNP were now aligned to a much greater extent than they had ever been before at a Westminster election and matched each other as closely as they had ever done before in a Holyrood one. It would seem that one of the key legacies of the Scottish independence referendum was an electorate that was more inclined to take the constitutional question into account in deciding how to vote, and to do so irrespective of the kind of elections that is being held.

However, this was not the only legacy of the independence referendum. That ballot also instigated a rise in support for independence itself. As Table 3 shows, between 1999 and 2012 support for leaving the UK oscillated on SSA's measure at between just under a quarter and a little over a third. There was little apparent consistent trend, though all of the lowest levels of support were in fact registered between 2007 and 2012, after the SNP came to power. However, at 46%, the most recent reading, taken after the 2016 Holyrood election, is no less than twice that observed in 2012, when the first preparations for the referendum were being put in place, (and is very similar to the 44% who in the same survey said that they would vote Yes in another independence referendum).

Table 3. Constitutional Preference 1999-2016

	Constitutional Preference		
	Independence	Devolution	No Parliament
1999	27	59	10
2000	30	55	12
2001	27	59	9
2002	30	52	13
2003	26	56	13
2004	32	45	17
2005	35	44	14
2006	30	54	9
2007	24	62	9
2008	n/a	n/a	n/a
2009	28	56	8
2010	23	61	10
2011	32	58	6
2012	23	61	11
2013	29	55	9
2014	33	50	7
2015	39	49	6
2016	46	42	8

Source: Scottish Social Attitudes

So in securing the support of around four-fifths of those who supported in independence in 2015 and 2016, the SNP were mobilising a much larger group of people than they had done when they secured the support of four-fifths of independence supporters in the 2007 and 2011 Scottish Parliament elections. The party's most recent electoral success at both Holyrood and Westminster has thus rested not only on persuading most of those who back independence to vote for the party, but also on persuading more people of the merits of independence in the first place. That is certainly a far cry from what George Robertson had once anticipated.

Conclusion

In the first instance, the advent of devolution assisted the SNP by creating an environment in which voters, and particularly those sympathetic to devolution, were more likely to vote for the party (while the use of proportional representation ensured that its support was fully reflected in the number of MSPs it enjoyed). But in so doing it also created an opportunity for the SNP to secure an independence referendum that both generated an increase in support for independence and motivated supporters of independence to vote for the SNP irrespective of the kind of election taking place. As a result, the party's grip on power now looks far more secure than it did when it first grabbed the reins of power at Holyrood in 2007.

This picture raises some interesting questions about the future of Scottish democracy. If the patterns of electoral support apparently bequeathed by the independence referendum remain undisturbed, the SNP will be difficult to dislodge from power. After all, if some 80 % of the 45 % or so who support independence are now inclined to vote for the party, come what may, that provides the party with a foundation of 36 % of the vote before even a single unionist supporter votes for it. So long as the political representation of unionism remains fragmented between three different parties as at present, that would leave the SNP in a seemingly near invincible position, irrespective of its performance in office.

Moreover, the fragmentation of unionism still remains in place, despite the further progress made by the Conservatives in the 2017 election. Labour gained some ground at that election too, with the result that the party was only two points behind the Conservatives in the popular vote. Any hopes that the Conservatives might have had that they would become the unchallenged champions of unionism were not fulfilled. True, at 37% SNP support did fall considerably from the 50% that the party secured in 2015 and, indeed, the party seemed to find it rather more difficult to persuade supporters of independence to vote for the party than it had done in that previous Westminster contest. But even so, as compared with the party's longer-term track record in UK general elections its performance in 2017 was still quite remarkable.

Yet at the same time, support for independence is not sufficiently high that the party could hold a second independence referendum with any certainty of winning it. In short, the party might be insulated against the accountability that comes from the threat of losing office because of voter dissatisfaction with a government's day-to-day performance in office yet, at the same time, unable to pursue its long-term goal. Such an outcome might raise yet further questions about whether devolution is delivering what its advocates intended.

References

Curtice, J. (2009), 'At the Ballot Box', in Curtice, J. and Seyd, B. (eds.), *Has Devolution Worked?* Manchester: Manchester University Press.

Johns, R., Mitchell, J. and Carman, C. (2013), 'Constitution or competence? The SNP's re-election in 2011', *Political Studies* 61 (S1), 158-78.

The Scottish Government Under the SNP

Richard Parry

WE CAN ONLY understand the SNP's performance in charge of the Scottish Government (SG) since 2007 in the context of changes in the Whitehall system that was its progenitor. Massive staff cuts, contracting-out of functions, frequent reorganisations of ministries and rapid turnover of leaders have become hallmarks of the UK government (Institute for Government, 2017). These have made an imprint on Scottish civil service staff in reserved functions, which have fallen by 25 % since the SNP took office (Scottish Government, 2016, table 7). In contrast devolved civil service employment has been static overall, with SG core directorate numbers increasing by 25 % (table 6). Stability of form and scale in Scotland might not just be a matter of inertia but a departure from contemporary norms about cost cutting, outsourcing and reorganisation.

Nomenclature and Symbolic Power

It is sometimes hard to remember that at its foundation the devolved Scottish executive branch was purposely not called 'the Scottish Government'. In the devolved model, there was still only one entity in the UK called 'the Government', or more properly 'Her Majesty's Government'. The working title adopted in 1999, the 'Scottish Executive' was not even accurate, that term applying to the group of Scottish ministers rather than the administration they headed, but it came into use and even used the same design and typography on letterheads as that of the old Scottish Office. Although Scottish officials remain part of the Home Civil Service, they have in practice acquired the autonomy of the Northern Ireland Civil Service (the SNP's preferred model in 2007) without the need for formal detachment (Parry, 2016).

In September 2007, the SNP administration rebranded itself as 'The Scottish Government' in a sudden operation, with signs taken down from its buildings on a Saturday. For a while, Whitehall continued to use 'Scottish Executive' in its official documents before finally conceding the 'G word' legally, almost like throwing in the towel, in the Scotland Act 2012. Relationships became more like governments of equals rather than the subordinate role in traditional central-local contexts.

The Furthering of the 'Scottish Model of Government'

New systems characteristically wish to appear as innovative and non-derivative. The new Labour ministers in 1999 were caught between their party position as team players in the Blair project and their wish to do something distinctive. One model they had at their disposal was that of the Scottish Office as an integrated corporate body without multiple finance and personnel operations. There were nominal 'departments' within both the Scottish Office and Scottish Executive but they did not align completely with ministerial portfolios and did not operate like Whitehall 'silos'. Nor were there direct equivalents of the Treasury and the Cabinet Office.

This corporate tradition allowed Sir John Elvidge, Permanent Secretary from 2003 to 2010 to claim that there was a 'Scottish model of government' (2011). It differed from the UK level by smallness of scale, commonality of policy objectives, and structures that encouraged integration rather than differentiation. In Elvidge's time, this became technocratic, with depoliticised mechanisms like Community Planning at the local level and 'Scotland Performs', with performance indicators driving 'National Objectives' whose achievement was not solely or even primarily within devolved powers.

The SNP retained this technocratic thread, along with retaining Elvidge. They went beyond Labour in abolishing departments and having a small number of Cabinet Secretaries supervising ministers with distinct portfolios. Freedom from the constraints of coalition government was an important facilitator of these changes. The Deputy First Minister was a trusted No 2 (John Swinney throughout) rather than the leader of a rival party.

Ministerial Personalities and Denominations

The structure of the SG under the SNP has been relatively conservative: there are recognisable health, education, agriculture and justice ministers. An important innovation of the 1990s, to place higher education alongside industry rather than school education, was abandoned.

The building blocks are 35 directorates whose combination under Directors-General at the official level, and Cabinet Secretaries and Ministers at the political level, can be changed flexibly and without notice (details are at https://beta.gov.scot/about/how-government-is-run/civil-service/).   For   these core directorates there is no corporate entity beneath the Government itself. Seven executive agencies within the civil service (such as the Scottish Prison Service) under accountable Chief Executives continue. In addition the National Public Bodies Directory (at www.gov.scot/Topics/Government/public-bodies/ about/Bodies) lists 116 other bodies within Scottish devolved central government; their structure follows the pre-devolution institutional landscape set by the accounting rules of the UK Government.

To some extent structures will be driven by personality. Alex Salmond's first Cabinet in 2007 was tight-knit. John Swinney was at the centre in the finance portfolio. Richard Lochhead at agriculture remained very low profile throughout his nine-year tenure. Nicola Sturgeon (health), Fiona Hyslop (education) and Kenny MacAskill (justice) were given the prominent roles. Salmond's former leadership rivals, Alex Neil and Roseanna Cunningham, were outside the government initially but eventually made it to the Cabinet (as did Fergus Ewing who succeeded Lochhead). The graveyard slot was education, but the ministerial departure (Hyslop and later Mike Russell and Angela Constance) signalling a new policy course was notable in being confined to that sector.

As time went by, older devolved patterns asserted themselves – more members of the Cabinet (notably the way that in pursuit of gender balance Angela Constance and Shona Robison were included in 2014); catchier ministerial titles signifying attention to policy priorities (Rural Economy and Connectivity, Land Reform, Equalities, Fair Work etc.; only Justice has a single-word title); and a certain ministerial anonymity (the images of Keith Brown, Derek Mackay and Michael Matheson tending to morph at a level less recognisable than their predecessors).

Government-Parliament Relations and the Handling of Majority Government

The minority status of the SNP government from 2007 to 2011, and since 2016, dictated bargaining over the Budget, some avoidance of very controversial legislation, and preparedness to lose some votes in committees and the chamber. The SNP's deference to a parliamentary vote in 2007 to finance the Edinburgh tram system established their credentials as a stable minority government in which the power of executive action could be exploited. In 2016 Nicola Sturgeon embraced a minority without coalition partners almost with enthusiasm, knowing that it would require tactical concessions to the Greens to secure their votes on an independence referendum and on the maintenance of the administration for its full life. On Brexit-related issues they have further managed to split Scottish Labour and make a grand unionist coalition wildly implausible.

The result of these tactics has been to avoid Irish-style coalition politics in which the government is unstable and has to concede on policies for its survival. The fixed-term nature of the Scottish Parliament does not preclude a political turn that installs a new First Minister, but the SNP has never been in such danger. Its political project has become embedded in government.

UK *Themes Persisting: Weak Local Government and Consolidation of Public Bodies*

Modern governments tend to centraliseand assert ministerial control while blaming more distant delivery agencies. The SNP has left local government weak and short of money to fulfil its responsibilities. It was slower than England to unfreeze council tax (in 2017) and so impart some buoyancy into local revenue. It was also somewhat more purposeful in shifting NHS money into social care. 'Quango-culling' was embraced with enthusiasm under the 'simplification' strategy. The one big structural change – all-Scotland police and fire services – required some boldness in avoiding (as happened with Scottish Water) an interim consolidation of former regions before the national body was created.

On the other main UK themes – privatisation and contracting-out – the SNP has been moderate and cautious. Scottish Water remains in public ownership. Central and local government have used contracting strategically but with less ideological force than in England. New jobs have been useful as available for dispersal beyond Edinburgh.

In the organisation of government the SNP has all kinds of flexibility available to it. Its ideological and political base does not predispose it to any particular approach to the delivery of public functions. With some adroitness it funded transport investment like the new Forth crossing through conventional mechanisms. It did not attempt a further reorganisation of local government, preferring to deal with issues of excessively small units in some areas by encouraging shared services.

The Organisation of Newly-Acquired Functions and Tooling Up for Independence: the 2013-14 Work

The 1999 division between reserved and devolved responsibilities had both the coherence and the convenience of largely removing Holyrood from decisions on taxes and benefits. The biggest new devolved power was the classic 'making the trains run on time' through local control of railway infrastructure and franchising in 2005. The conjunction of ready Barnett-related money and freedom from responsibility for many high-profile policies may come to seem a golden age rather than a frustrating lack of power.

The independence project and the new powers in the Scotland Acts of 2012 and 2016 were related aspects of the SNP's occupancy of government. Somewhat controversially, the civil service machine entered into design work on an independent Scotland as set out in the content-filled *Scotland's Future* of 2013. The new Income Tax powers required decisions on delivery, resolved in a significant, underestimated endorsement of HMRC as a cross-border tax collection administration reporting to two governments.

In welfare benefits (rebranded nostalgically as 'social security') different decisions were taken. Part of the expansion in work-related training will be handled by the existing body Skills Development Scotland. It was announced on 1 March 2016 that new devolved responsibilities (mainly cash payments on grounds of disability or care needs) are to be administered by a new Scottish social security agency whose precise format remains under consultation. This reflects active thought on what a Scottish welfare system might look like, and dislike of DWP norms on work and welfare. It is a further stage of the detachment of Scotland from both UK norms and UK financial underwriting.

The Verdict: The Use of Government for Political Ends

In 2007 the SNP expected their government machine to be a unionist club orientated to London, with independence anathema. What they did not quite understand is that the civil service task as a piece of craftwork comes into its own as a facilitator of changes of government. Official thinking had not modelled an SNP minority government as a likely election outcome, but what happened had its advantages, especially single party government. The Labour-Lib Dem coalition had grown tired and the junior party fractious. Nationalism apart, the SNP was actually a model of a catch-all party, moderately favourable to both business and the welfare state. They were also receptive to technocratic approaches to government such as the national performance framework.

It is natural that other parties found it difficult to accept the loss of all the resources of government to the SNP. Labour had a legitimate line of criticism that innovation they had promoted was halted by an SNP overly deferential to entrenched interests. Any weakening in relative health and education indicators adds strength to this criticism and allows unionist parties to suggest that the pursuit of independence is at the expense of concentration on policy performance (the opposite can also be argued).

Over time, the representative nature of bureaucracy asserts itself. The SG has lost its pre-devolution antecedents faster than expected. Officials work for a machine with a strong political presence in UK terms and competent leadership. When you add up the old pros who can live with them and the young staffers who come from a similar political place, the SNP has a base in the civil service unimaginable before 2007.

The irony is that the SNP found the practices of British government all too convenient. They have run a tight ship that repels boarders. If they lack powers they ask for them, have often got them and have been free to dream of getting them all. In the process they have solidified a government apparatus – available to any successors – that has become the primary level of government in Scotland.

References

Elvidge, J. (2011), *Northern Exposure: Lessons from the First Twelve Years of Scottish Government*, London: Institute for Government.

Institute for Government (2017), *Whitehall Monitor*, London: Institute for Government.

Parry, R. (2016), 'Civil Service and Machinery of Government' in McTavish, D. (ed.), *Politics in Scotland*, London: Routledge.

Scottish Government (2016), *Public Sector Employment Web Tables*, December, Edinburgh: Scottish Government.

Why is the SNP So Pleased with the Scottish Parliament?

Paul Cairney

THE SNP HAD been in government for six years when it released its White Paper on Scottish independence. It devoted barely one page of text, in a 670-page document, to the Scottish Parliament. It praised the Parliament's competence, effectiveness, and openness, describing it as a hub for participation, setting 'an example within the UK on how a modern legislature should operate' (Scottish Government, 2013: 355). It uses the phrase Scottish Parliament frequently, but devoted *one line* to 'a government accountable to that parliament'.

This praise for Scottish political institutions contrasts with the criticism of UK politics by advocates for devolution in the 1990s. In the lead up to the referendum on Scottish devolution in 1997, the new Scottish Parliament was at the heart of debates on political reform. Elite support for devolution – articulated by political parties, local governments, and 'civil society' groups – was built on the idea of a crisis of legitimation, linked to an image of top-down Westminster politics, the concentration of government power and marginalisation of Parliament and 'civil society'. 'Old Westminster' provided a dated and ineffective form of democratic accountability (Scottish Constitutional Convention, 1995; Mitchell, 2000; Cairney and McGarvey, 2013: 11-13).

Crucially, the chance to produce major political reforms and institutional changes does not arise very often. It may only be prompted by a sense of crisis or the very infrequent opportunity, afforded by major constitutional change, to consider if bodies like the Scottish Parliament are equipped to take a greater role in Scottish politics. The SNP knew that independence offered one of those few opportunities, but sought to stress the value of continuity, even to the point of committing itself to maintain 129 MSPs (Scottish Government, 2013: 45).

What Explains Such a Shift in the Image of Political Institutions?

One *potential* answer is that the political reforms under devolution were an unparalleled success: the Scottish Parliament is a venue for the representation of many social groups, and a hub for deliberation and popular participation, it shares power with the government in a non-trivial way, its committees operate in a business-like manner and contribute to the policy agenda while scrutinising government, and plenary debates combine public enlightenment with holding the government to account.

However, while devolution had an effect in some areas – it generally produced coalition and minority governments (with the exception of 2011-16), and increased the representation of women – it had a limited impact on 'power sharing' and accountability. The Scottish system remains part of the 'Westminster family', with a traditional focus on the accountability of ministers to the public via Parliament (Cairney and Johnston, 2014), and a tendency to situate the vast majority of key resources (such as staffing) in government. The Scottish Parliament also shares with Westminster the sense that it struggles to hold the government, and wider public sector, to account. Its committees have very limited time, small clerking teams, and access to a small parliamentary research team, to help oversee a public sector with 'approximately half a million employees spending a budget of around £30 billion' (Cairney, 2015: 219-20). It remains a powerful body at the heart of accountability *on paper*, but not in practice (Cairney, 2011: 56). Indeed, there are three main signs of the surprisingly low or *diminishing* role of the Scottish Parliament in relation to the Scottish Government.

First, a significant period of SNP minority government (2007-11) showed that the Parliament generally remained peripheral to the policy process, even in such a best-case scenario when the SNP needed to cooperate with other parties to pass legislation and its budget. Early experiences of Labour-Liberal Democrat coalition government (1999-2007) had suggested that a parliamentary majority tipped the balance firmly in favour of government, prompting descriptions of the Parliament as a venue to rubber stamp government policy, with limited ability to oppose policies, little time to scrutinise legislation effectively, and few resources to set the agenda with inquiries or ambitious member or committee-driven bills (Arter, 2004). The 'legacy' reports of committees blamed the volume of government legislation for the lack of time to conduct any other business (Cairney, 2011: 45).

Yet, minority government only helped shift the balance to a small extent. From 2007, committees had more time but less inclination to conduct inquiries, and few non-executive bills addressed substantive policy issues. The government remained central to policymaking, and the Parliament continued to make minimal impact beyond a small number of areas, albeit in cases of high import: discouraging a bill on a referendum on independence, vetoing a minimum unit price on alcohol (the SNP achieved both legislative aims during majority government), and undermining council tax reform (2011: 56).

Second, the SNP signalled a further shift away from a reliance on Westminster-style democratic accountability (through periodic elections and more regular reports by ministers to the Scottish Parliament). It reinforced a Scottish Government emphasis on other forms of accountability: *institutional*, through performance management measures applied to the chief executives of public bodies, such as elected local authorities and unelected agencies and quangos; the shared 'ownership' of policy choices, such as when policymakers work with stakeholders to produce a policy that both support; and, *user based* notions of accountability, when a public body considers its added value to service users, or public bodies and users 'co-produce' and share responsibility for the outcomes. Further, the Scottish Government (2007; 2014) has maintained a *National Performance Framework* (NPF), placing new emphasis on a very broad strategic vision to be realised by actors in the public and non-governmental sectors, via mechanisms such as 'community planning partnerships' (CPPs) and 'single outcome agreements' (SOAs). These initiatives place more responsibility for policy delivery in the hands of local authorities and oblige them to develop policy in partnership with many public bodies and non-governmental stakeholders.

Without a Scottish Parliament response, these developments have the potential to further undermine its role. It already lacks the ability to gather information independently of government. While it can oblige Scottish ministers to attend meetings to provide information, it does not get enough information about what is going on locally. Scotland lacks the top-down performance management system that we associate with the UK Government, and a greater focus on long term local outcomes removes an important and regular source of information on public sector performance. Local authorities push back against calls for information, arguing that they have their own elections and mandates. More administrative devolution exacerbates this tension between elected local and national bodies and, when unelected bodies are given more powers, between democratic and institutional accountability.

For example, CPPs are not directly accountable to anyone. Instead, local authorities have their own claim for legitimacy, through their accountability to local populations via elections. They are also expected to cooperate, in a meaningful way (such as by pursuing jointly resourced projects, money and staff), with public bodies accountable directly to the Scottish Government. Local authorities work in partnership with other bodies rather than directing their activities or holding them to account. The Scottish Government may direct many of the public bodies within CPPs, but also signal a 'hands-off' approach to encourage local level partnerships. In this scenario, local authorities are responsible to their electorates for their contribution, public bodies are accountable to ministers, and stakeholders report to their members or profession. Consequently, the role of the Parliament has become unclear, and its ability to engage in meaningful scrutiny by holding ministers to account for policy delivery and outcomes (rather than a broad policy framework) is hard to find.

Third, these difficulties are already apparent under the original devolution settlement, and further constitutional changes give more powers to Scottish ministers without a proportional rise in parliamentary resources to oversee their activities. The report of the 'Smith Commission' (2014) recommended the further devolution of powers without considering properly its impact on accountability to the Scottish Parliament (Cairney, 2014). As well as devolving more powers, it encouraged the shared ownership of many policy areas (including taxation, social security spending, and energy policy) between Scottish and UK ministers without establishing how Holyrood and Westminster could coordinate ministerial oversight to make sure that ministers don't simply 'pass the buck'. Following Brexit, the Scottish Government (2016) has requested the further devolution of powers in 'Europeanised' areas such as agricultural and environmental policies (and in areas of UK responsibility, such as immigration) without proposing parliamentary reform. Further, in an independent Scotland, the SNP expected the same Scottish Parliament, which struggles to hold the government to account now, to oversee the complete range of governmental responsibilities.

In this context, a *second potential answer* is that the SNP is content to maintain its relationship with a Parliament with limited powers. This is the classic response of a political party with a realistic chance of being in minority or majority government after each Holyrood election.

The Future Relationship Between the SNP and the Scottish Government

If so, is there any realistic prospect of parliamentary reform while the SNP remains such a dominant figure in Scottish politics? The signs are not encouraging. From 2011-16, the Scottish Parliament's Presiding Officer Tricia Marwick engaged in what appeared to be a dispiriting process of minimal change in the rules and procedures of the Parliament. Marwick (2015) proposed the election of committee convenors (as in Westminster) and the introduction of a smaller number of larger committees, to give them a greater sense of independence and more capacity for scrutiny and inquiry. Yet, even these limited plans met with majority opposition. Marwick's successor as Presiding Officer, Ken Mackintosh, also initiated a review of the Parliament (the Commission on Parliamentary reform, 2016), but as an 'MOT' exercise rather than a signal of the need for major change (the author had an advisory role; this chapter contains personal views written before the Commission's report).

Consequently, it is difficult to envisage major institutional reforms in the SNP era. The most concerted period of political reform in the modern Scottish political era took place when Scottish Labour dominated Scottish politics and felt strong pressure to justify the introduction of a Scottish Parliament during a period of public scepticism about the introduction of more elected politicians, and public concern about the massive cost of the Scottish Parliament building. The SNP is more interested in constitutional change as an end in itself, and sees no reason to link this project to potentially disruptive political reforms and potentially expensive institutional change.

References

Arter, D. (2004), 'The Scottish Committees and the Goal of a "New Politics": A Verdict on the First Four Years of the Devolved Scottish Parliament', *Journal of Contemporary European Studies*, 12, 1, 71–91.

Cairney, P. (2011), *The Scottish Political System Since Devolution*, Exeter: Imprint Academic.

Cairney, P. (2015), 'Scotland's Future Political System', *Political Quarterly*, 86, 2, 217-25.

Cairney, P. and Johnston, J. (2014), 'What is the Role of the Scottish Parliament?', *Scottish Parliamentary Review*, 1, 2, 91-130.

Cairney, P. and McGarvey, N. (2013), *Scottish Politics* 2nd edn., Basingstoke: Palgrave.

Commission on Parliamentary Reform (2016), 'About Us', accessed at: https://parliamentaryreform.scot/about-us/

Marwick, T. (2015), The Scottish Parliament: an Agenda for Reform, Edinburgh: Scottish Parliament, accessed at: www.parliament.scot/POandU-KandIRO/DHI_speech_-_Final.pdf

Mitchell, J. (2000), 'New Parliament, New Politics', *Parliamentary Affairs*, 53(3): 605–21.

Scottish Constitutional Convention (1995), *Scotland's Parliament: Scotland's Right*, Edinburgh: Convention of Scottish Local Authorities.

Scottish Government (2007; 2014), *Performance*, Edinburgh: Scottish Government, accessed at: http://www.scotland.gov.uk/About/Performance

Scottish Government (2013), *Scotland's Future*, Edinburgh: Scottish Government.

Scottish Government (2016), *Scotland's Place in Europe*, Edinburgh: Scottish Government.

Smith Commission (2014), *Report of the Smith Commission for further devolution of powers to the Scottish Parliament*, Edinburgh: Smith Commission.

The SNP, the Politics of Discipline and Westminster

Kate Devlin

IN AN AGE when politicians have been accused of focussing mainly on the next day's headlines the SNP have been remarkably disciplined at doing the small things that will pay off in the long term.

On Thursday 1 December 2016, the SNP group at Westminster held a St Andrew's Day reception in the Attlee Suite of the Portcullis House building of the Palace of Westminster. SNP MPs and staffers had worked hard for weeks to source donations of Scottish produce to give to the guests. Those who attended received goody bags including a small bottle of whisky, a single Tunnock's Teacake and a stick of black pudding.

The invited guests included politicians, staff from the House of Commons, journalists and, importantly, ambassadors. Embassy staff from more than 20 nations RSVP'd, from countries as small as Malta to as big as Germany, from as close to Scotland as Italy to as far away as Japan. Represented were ambassadors, high commissioners and deputy heads of missions.

In his speech to welcome them all the SNP's Westminster leader Angus Robertson joked that since his party's stonking 2015 general election result it had had to book bigger rooms at Westminster for its events. The larger space was needed not just because the party had taken 56 of the 59 Scottish seats, on the back of a huge surge in support from voters. It was also because of the extra interest from those keen to meet and talk to the newly enlarged group.

The party was such a hit that some SNP MPs openly wondered if, as well as a St Andrew's Day do, embassy staff 'would be interested in a Burns supper next year?' The event illustrates just one of the channels over which the SNP now has greater influence as a result of capturing the vast majority of Scottish seats at Westminster.

The SNP group at Westminster have worked hard to become effective parliamentarians, mindful of their pledge to voters to 'stick up for Scotland'. But they have also been laying some of the groundwork to influence the debate in the next independence referendum in a host of different ways. This may not make as many headlines but it could well be the lasting legacy of the class of 2015.

Early Days

In the aftermath of the 2015 general election one group of professionals took a kicking – pollsters. In their final voting intentions polls, none of the major players foresaw the overall result – a tiny Conservative majority. But for months before the May 7 vote, the polls were correctly predicting that the outcome in Scotland would be an SNP landslide.

In fact, the Scottish polls were much more accurate than the forecasts of many opposition politicians. In the week before the vote one senior Labour MP predicted his party would return with 'a netball team'. When informed that included seven members, he downgraded his sports metaphor of choice to five-a-side football. In the final tally, of course, he was still out by four.

For months, however, the SNP had been preparing for the possibility that the polls were right. Angus Robertson understood that 56 MPs would mean a sea change in his party's fortunes at Westminster, even if they did not hold the balance of power in a hung Parliament. If the polls were right, the SNP would overtake the Liberal Democrats and become the third largest party in the Commons. The SNP had already leapfrogged the Lib Dems in membership numbers. Nicola Sturgeon exploited this fact, ultimately successfully, in her bid to take part in the televised leaders' debates.

After the result, Robertson hailed the election of 56 MPs as a transformational' number. He was right, in more ways than one. As the third party a whole new world would open up. The list of new opportunities was long. The SNP now had a guaranteed weekly slot at Prime Minister's Questions. The party was entitled to the chairmanship of two influential House of Commons select committees. The list goes on.

Importantly, it also included access to what is euphemistically described as the 'usual channels', the name for the way in which the Commons organises itself. The 'usual channels' oversee everything from the membership of committees to the timings of key debates. It is a club to which the SNP was now being handed the keys. But how to organise its own group to make the most of these opportunities? The vast majority of the 56 had never served as MPs before.

In preparation Robertson held one-to-one talks with every member of his newly elected team. He asked them what portfolios they were interested in and what they wanted to achieve over the next five years. The result was a team roster that would set the tone for much of what was to come. Within weeks the party had announced a 17-strong group leadership with another 32 group spokespeople. Even excluding membership of powerful Commons committees, almost all of the 56 now had a 'job'. And the SNP was not going to prevent itself from commenting on areas its opponents considered none of its business.

Dr Philippa Whitford, a qualified NHS surgeon, was appointed to cover health, a role that immediately led some Tories to cry that the NHS was devolved in Scotland. Now, voters in England would be hearing SNP voices on issues in a way that they never had before.

As the new MPs tried to hit the ground running, the seven who had previously been MPs, joking dubbed 'The Originals' by a number of their less experienced colleagues, offered help and support. But the 'newbies' also supported each other, regularly feeding back what they had learnt in group meetings.

Culture Clash: The 56 Arrive at Westminster

Within weeks of their arrival at Westminster the group was also embroiled in two rows, both of which initially grabbed much of the headlines. The first was with the veteran Labour MP Dennis Skinner. He had sat for decades in a part of the chamber known affectionately as 'rebel corner' for its huddle of cantankerous Labour MPs. Now the newly enlarged SNP group wanted to claim their own territory and Skinner's bench, separated from the rest of the now much-reduced Labour group, was in their sights.

But the SNP group moved in, taking up many of the seats around and behind him. This led to newspaper reports in which the 83-year-old Skinner complained that he was getting up at dawn every morning to be in the Commons by 8.00am to claim his seat. The campaign was quietly dropped.

The second row was over clapping. To many of the new SNP MPs, Westminster looked hideously old-fashioned in comparison to Holyrood. Within month one, Hannah Bardell, the MP for Livingston, had calculated just how much time MPs waste queuing and voting. One SNP MP complained that saying 'hear, hear' made her sound like a public schoolboy. Others were shocked that MPs could shout and bawl at each other but could not clap politely when someone made a good point.

Within weeks they were applauding in the chamber. But when the Commons Speaker, John Bercow, remonstrated with the SNP for breaking with tradition by clapping, it became clear that clapping was undermining the broader priority, to establish themselves as effective parliamentarians working for their constituents, build bridges across the House and their longer term goal of independence. This campaign also ceased.

However, the determination to work with the powers that be has not prevented a number of MPs from noting that the Speaker himself did not demur when MPs applauded his statement setting out his opposition to a state visit from American President Donald Trump.

There have been other hints of defiance. SNP MPs whistled and sang Beethoven's 'Ode to Joy', the EU anthem, the night MPs voted in favour of starting exit talks with the European Union. But mainly the group who came to 'settle up not settle down' have become good MPs. They have been praised by the Speaker for the time they spend in the chamber and their contributions to debates. They have become enthusiastic committee members.

Successes and Failures

They have also had a number of successes. Glasgow MP Alison Thewliss has led a powerful campaign against the so-called 'rape clause' plans to force women to prove their third child was the result of assault in order to receive some benefits.

John Nicolson, the party's urbane culture spokesman, a former television journalist, impressed even cynical Westminster watchers when he convinced the Commons Culture, Media and Sport Committee, dominated by pro-Unionist parties, to back the SNP's long campaign for a 'Scottish Six' programme of Scottish-led nightly news. Nicolson was the only Nationalist MP on the committee, which also contained six Tory and four Labour MPs. Ultimately the proposal was not adopted by the BBC, although the corporation did announce a new Scotland channel which will feature a 9.00pm Scottish news hour.

Alex Salmond, Stephen Gethins and others helped ensure that the Brexit referendum vote did not clash with the Holyrood elections. Their impact on high-profile votes is helped by the Conservatives tiny majority but ultimately limited by the SNP's overall size. They initially stared down a vote on so-called 'English votes for English laws', a move Scottish politicians of almost all colours argue creates two tiers of MP. But the Cameron government brought it back – only slightly watered down – and it passed by 312 to 270. The full ramifications of the change are yet to be felt and seen.

There was also controversy over the Sunday Trading Bill. The party was forced to deny Tory claims that it had flirted with backing the changes in exchange for a deal that would have, among other things, allowed a number of senior SNP figures to join the Privy Council, the small band of advisors to the Queen. Scottish shop workers stood to lose out on extra pay under the plans, leading John Hannett, from the shop workers' union USDAW, to suggest his members were mystified why the SNP went through 'such a major internal discussion in order to confirm a position they took before Christmas when nothing had changed.'

There have been failures as well. One MP made headlines for claiming for dog food on expenses. Not quite a duck house, but not exactly the 'clean break' from Westminster shenanigans that the party had pledged. Two of the new crop were forced to resign the party whip within the first few months: Natalie McGarry and Michelle Thomson. Opposition parties also accused SNP MPs of being 'robots' because of their iron discipline. But that may not last forever. One SNP MP said: 'If I believe in something I will rebel. In fact, it is probably a question of when not if.'

Early on Robertson challenged his MPs to draw up plans to speak to as many parts of British society as possible. MPs were encouraged to focus on the fields where they had expertise, from the military to pensions, from the health service to television and the arts.

This effort can be seen as a kind of 'charm offensive' – a UK-wide version of the 'de-risk' strategy before the 2014 independence referendum. Except this time directed not just at the Scottish public but those outside Scotland, many of whom might be expected, in the SNP's eyes, to make less than helpful public interventions in any second independence campaign.

And so the party's MPs have held policy roundtables with big players in the City. They have met ambassadorial teams from dozens of countries. They have talked to large and small companies, to national and international charities and to third sector organisations.

They have also been visible to the English public in a way that was unthinkable a few years earlier. They have become regular fixtures on television programmes watched by millions, from *Question Time* to *Newsnight*. The SNP's voice on day-to-day issues has been heard south of the border like never before.

The only comparison for the SNP in their experience is with that of the eleven strong Westminster group elected in October 1974. They had a high profile, made an impact because of Labour's small then non-existent majority and the focus on devolution, and produced a reaction from the other parties. The differences between then and now are as important: then they were divided and did not know so much about how to work effectively as a group, in Parliament, public and media (see Lindsay, 2009).

Post-2015 the party has tried to break down barriers within Parliament as well. They built up working relationships with politicians from other parties as they found common cause on issues. They enthusiastically joined All Party Parliamentary Groups (APPGs), unofficial groups of MPs, created to campaign on everything from accident prevention to the death penalty space exploration.

The interest was mainly to allow another avenue to campaign. But, interestingly, senior SNP sources believed membership of APPGs could have other beneficial effects for a suddenly much larger party, offering a chance for members of other parties to get to know the new SNP MPs.

The optimistic hope was that together all of these would lower opposition towards independence. At the end of the first year, one SNP MP said: 'Ed Miliband called on every Labour MP in England to campaign against independence at the last referendum. Not all of them did. But fewer will do so a second time around.' It has to be said that, inside Parliament at least, many SNP MPs report a cooling of these relationships in the wake of the Brexit referendum result, when Nicola Sturgeon said that another independence vote was back on the table.

Intriguingly, a recent study by Conservative Home found that more than one in four Conservative Party members would welcome Scottish independence. Admittedly, their reasoning might not be everything that the SNP would hope (Goodman, 2017). A total of 29 % of the Tory grassroots said that they would back independence to end 'unreasonable demands on England to provide ever greater financial and political concessions'. Still, the findings suggest that the increased presence of the SNP at Westminster and on the airwaves, on top of the 2014 vote, is having an effect, one that could even change how a future Conservative Prime Minister tackles another independence campaign.

The SNP 56 turned out to be a small interregnum in history when Theresa May called the snap UK election of 2017 – subsequently losing her majority and authority. The SNP loss of 21 seats left the party 'winning' the Scottish contest in seats and votes, but much diminished at Westminster, with 35 seats, and minus such big beasts as Angus Robertson and Alex Salmond. A new kind of tone and politics will be required from the SNP's Westminster contingent, who still make up Britain's 'third party', and who will, if they get it right, have numerous opportunities under a minority government, with two years of Brexit negotiations to make a significant impact.

References

Goodman, P. (2017), 'Scotland, independence – and our survey finding. Are Conservative Party members Just about Unionist?', *Conservative Home*, March 2nd, accessed at: www.conservativehome.com/thetorydiary/2017/03/scotland-independence-and-our-survey-finding-are-conservative-party-members-just-about-unionist.html

Lindsay, I. (2009), 'The SNP and Westminster', in Hassan, G. (ed.), *The Modern SNP: From Protest to Power*, Edinburgh: Edinburgh University Press, pp. 93-194.

The SNP and Local Government

Neil McGarvey

Introduction

THE SNP'S KEY political imperative is national in context and form. Its primary concern and focus is that the borders of the country and nation of Scotland should be congruent with that of an independent state called Scotland. Where and how local government fits into this vision of Scottish independence is of secondary concern. Local government has been a footnote in the history of the SNP. The SNP's focus and priority has tended to be on issues related to Scotland's constitution, economic performance, energy (non-nuclear and sustainable) and social justice, in that order (Maxwell, 2009). Local government is only relevant to the latter. Moreover, the contemporary history of the SNP as a political party has been one of centralisation in terms of strategy, policy and organisation. This has been accentuated since it attained office in 2007. Local government, or indeed localism, has not feature heavily in the history of the SNP. Indeed Lynch implies the party had, until 2002, not taken local government seriously (2002: 18).

This chapter, while not over-stating its importance, will point to Scottish local government as relevant to any comprehensive analysis of the SNP. It will examine briefly its role in the contemporary history of the SNP, before analysing the SNP's approach to local councils since it took over the Scottish Government in 2007.

A convincing argument could be made that traces the roots of the SNP's current dominance of Scottish politics to a decision taken in the 1980s to encourage a campaign of civil disobedience and non-payment of the poll tax. It was on this militant message of non-payment that the party won the Govan by-election in 1988, solidifying a more leftist platform and gradualist strategy in the party. It allowed it to build relations within civic society in groups such as the Scottish Trades Union Congress (STUC) and Convention of Scottish Local Authorities (COSLA). Both were amongst the broad constituency of institutions and interests providing operational support and campaigning for home rule in Scotland. A campaign the SNP joined in 1997.

After the Scottish Parliament was established in opposition 1999-2007, the SNP forged consensus with other parties on many issues relating to local government (e.g. abolition of Section 28, homelessness, electoral system reform), but remained opposed on issues such as use of public-private partnerships, housing stock transfer and council tax. Prior to 2007 the SNP campaigned for the latter's replacement with a local income tax in opposition, but the politically risky reform was quietly shelved in government.

Looking at the SNP locally, opposition, defeat and minority party status was largely the story of the SNP in local government until 2007. SNP elites tended to hold political office within the party, rather than in local government. Table 1 below outlines the performance of the SNP in local elections in Scotland since the creation of modern local councils in 1974. The SNP's rapid expansion in terms of members, branches and votes from the 1960s onwards did not spring from a local government base. It started to gain control of councils in the 1970s and 1980s in councils such as Cumbernauld, Clackmannanshire, East Kilbride, West Lothian, Perth and Kinross and Moray. But this tended to be transitory and sporadic. It struggled, until recently, to gain enough councillors to give it a local organisational base. It is only Angus Council where the SNP can point to long-standing periods of control since 1984. It should also be noted that SNP gains at the 1977 local elections were important in persuading Labour to reintroduce a second Scotland Bill after the collapse of the Scotland and Wales Bill earlier in the year.

The SNP's best performances in local elections have been the two most recent: 2007 and 2012. It was obviously significantly handicapped by the single member plurality system until the introduction of the single transferable vote method of election in 2007. At no election prior to 2007 did it achieve even one-sixth of the overall council seats available in Scotland. Its 1970s share of the vote averaged 17.5 %, in the 1980s it was 16 % and the 1990s it was 25.6 %. Breakthrough in almost all of Scotland's council chambers has proved elusive.

Table 1. SNP performance in local elections 1974-2012

Year		Vote %	Seats	Total
1974	District	12.4	62	1158
	Region	12.6	18	524
1977	District	24.2	170	1158
1978	Region	20.9	18	524

1980	District	15.5	54	1158
1982	Region	13.4	23	524
1984	District	11.7	59	1158
1986	Region	18.2	36	524
1988	District	21.3	113	1158
1990	Region	21.8	42	524
1992	District	24.3	150	1158
1994	Region	26.8	73	453
1995	Unitary	26.1	181	1222
1999	Unitary	28.9	201	1222
2003	Unitary	24.1	171	1222
2007	Unitary	29.7	363	1222
2012	Unitary	32.3	425	1223

However, since 2007 the SNP has usurped the Labour Party as Scotland's dominant party. It has the largest number of councillors across a range of local councils and was in control or in coalition in one quarter of Scotland's councils: Aberdeenshire, Angus, Edinburgh, Dundee, East Ayrshire, Midlothian, Perth and Kinross and Scottish Borders.

Local Government and the Constitutional Question

The weakness of the SNP in Scottish local government historically has perhaps led to concepts such as localism rarely featuring in party deliberation – the focus has been on the national question (see Mitchell, 2014). As has been noted previously (see McGarvey, 2002; 2006; 2009; 2011) the relationship between the Scottish Government and local government in Scotland is different in character than that between the UK Government and local government in England. The propinquity of the political actors result in more interpersonal dynamic being apparent and a more 'community' than 'network' feel to relations. Even during fraught times channels of communication in central-local government relations tend to remain open. The Scottish policymaking style is such that interpersonal relationships within intergovernmental and professional networks are utilised by both central and local government actors. Cordiality, pragmatism and community within professional, institutional policy networks underpin the central-local relationship. This factor allowed scope for the SNP, when entering government for the first time in 2007, to quickly establish a partnership with local government interests.

The SNP had between 1999 and 2007 aided by a more significant parliamentary presence that brought with it increased its professionalism and organisation, there was a 'transformation from what was essentially an amateur-activist model to an electoral-professional model' (Mitchell at al, 2011: 53). It entered office, 'intent on projecting an image of responsibility' (Mitchell, 2009: 63).

The SNP entered office with no coherent historical legacy as regards its approach in or to local government. Most SNP groups were small, out of office and lacking in coherent identity. Scottish nationalism as an ideology for governing localities is an elusive one. This provides for great flexibility and pragmatism on the part of local SNP parties. Subservience to the ultimate goal of independence have seen few keen to 'rock the boat' within the party over the past decade. Ten years of government and the ongoing expansion of SNP councillors and councils could change this. The increased numbers of councillors and potential control of more council's post-2017 is likely to add volume to local interests within the party.

To date, the 'national' party has tended to dictate the agenda as regards local government within the SNP. Since 2007, not unlike the Labour-Liberal Democrat Coalition before them, the SNP have sought to narrate a story of partnership with local government. However, the spin and communications side of government rarely projects an accurate picture of the actuality of governance. The SNP's approach to local government in the past decade is more accurately viewed, as one based around wider statecraft and national governance considerations.

The SNP Scottish Government has utilised the inherited legislative and policy framework to frame its approach to local government. It has not fundamentally changed it. Scottish local councils face the same constitutional and statutory context today as they did in 2007. Local councils in Scotland, as in the rest of the UK, remain subordinate institutions with the Scottish Parliament having devolved legislative authority. In practical terms that means the Scottish Government continues to shape the institutional, legislative and policy environment council's face.

Initially, wary of its relatively weak democratic mandate and the parliamentary arithmetic that flowed from it, the SNP reached out to local government. In the 2007-11 term of office local government was crucial to the SNP's projected image of consensus and competence in governing style. The SNP Government 2007-11 chose a governing code that avoided legislation or the imposition of 'central diktat' as a means of achieving policy aims. Instead, it sought to develop a cordial relationship with local government, as a key delivery agent for the Scottish Government. This was a key means of achieving a reputation for competence. It established, nurtured and fostered a consensual relationship with COSLA. The SNP sought to project the Scottish Government as a 'Government' rather than a devolved territorial executive body or administration. This facilitated an image of a body above the parochial politics of the self-governing locality. This has allowed it to distance itself from local government scandals in areas such as Aberdeen, Inver Clyde and West Dunbartonshire. The Scottish Government sought to project itself as being on a higher political sphere than the implementing agencies involved in 'low politics'. The party's primary objective has been to establish that the party and Scotland *could* govern itself.

In 2007 the SNP established a new 'Concordat' between the Scottish Government and COSLA on behalf of local government); enhanced policy autonomy through the introduction of single outcome agreements and new financial measures; and used its relationship with local government to effect policy change without the need for legislation. In 2007 the concordat was important, as without an automated agreement with local government, there was a danger that the SNP – local government relationship could become politicized. Freezing council tax took the local taxation issue off the agenda and allowed the SNP, in delivering a manifesto commitment, to claim a significant part of the political credit. The SNP and COSLA spoke of 'a fundamental shift in the relationship', 'mutual respect', an end to 'micro-managing' as well as, 'freeing up local authorities and their partners to get on with the job' (Scottish Government/COSLA, 2007).

The agreement temporarily halted, at least temporarily, the decline in the local government proportionate share of Scottish Government expenditure, reduced ring-fencing and allowed councils to retain efficiency savings. It symbolized a shared social democratic agenda, replacing the previous 'intra-Labour party partnership' and more importantly boosted the security and self-respect of the councils by emphasising no reorganisation would take place (Harvie, 2008).

During this period it deliberately disengaged from the centralist Gordon Brown inspired regulatory British (and 1999-2007 post devolution Scottish) norm. Although similar in style, it should be acknowledge that suggestion rather than imposition remained the operating style of the Scottish Executive from 1999 to 2007 (McGarvey and Cairney, 2008: 140). For Parry, the SNP governing style is highly technocratic and 'built upon localist and business-friendly elements' (2010: 9). Staying close to local government was a deliberate strategy. As Crawford MSP, Minister for Parliamentary Business at the time noted:

> Building support in Scottish society more widely has been at least as important as winning the Parliamentary arguments. The reputation of an administration need not depend on its Parliamentary strength.

> (Crawford, 2010)

The SNP did not seek to replicate the English system of 'detailed regulation, target setting, monitoring, inspection and direct intervention when public services go wrong' (John, 2008: 13). Indeed it deliberatively eschewed it. Lacking legislative power and taxation powers – the traditional levers of government – in office the SNP relied on leadership, cultivation of relationships, encouragement and persuasion. Indeed, contrary to expectation, one could argue the SNP impact on intergovernmental relations in that period (2007-11) was more significant internally than externally.

In its second term the SNP, now with a clear majority, was able to by-pass COSLA and establish a single, Scotland-wide, police and fire service, a policy which was strongly opposed by COSLA, and 'supported' through gritted teeth by many SNP local councillors. Relations became increasingly strained with councils between 2010 and 2016 seeing a 14.2 % reduction in Scottish Government funding with council tax remaining frozen. It has also abolished the right to buy, tinkered with council tax bandings as well as piloting free school meals. To date, SNP councillors have not raised significant voices of opposition, careful not to 'rock the boat' with SNP leadership.

However, overall despite their constitutional radicalism in terms of the governance of Scotland, the SNP record in local government would be best described as conservative incrementalism with a 'national' focus. The basic constitutional features and underpinning of local government in Scotland remain the same a decade after the SNP took office. The SNP Government, like the Labour-led Scottish Executive which preceded them, continue to use the language of social democracy, justice and fairness at both local and national level. But two decades of Labour and SNP run Scottish and local government have failed to impact in any significant way on indicators of public policy outcomes in Scotland. Scotland in 2017 remains an unequal, neo-liberal type of society with widespread inequalities in health, education, income and wealth. The SNP, like Labour before them, talk the language of social justice but there is little evidence of impact and change. Indeed there are some indicators in policy areas such as education that indicate decline rather than competence. There remains a tension in the SNP between a vision of the Scottish economy based on low taxation and enterprise and a social policy model informed by more social democratic thinking.

The SNP have talked the same language of shared services, outcomes and modernisation as New Labour did in Whitehall. Their approach to public sector reform appears Blairite, but without the additional public expenditure of the 2000s. Their approach to local service delivery is rooted in the New Labour public service reform language of rational, evidence-based policymaking especially with the promise of improved service delivery as its seductive out-come. Professional and technocratic there is little evidence of local government service improvement or enhancement (budget retrenchment has been an obvi-ous inhibiting factor). Despite the rhetorical shift to prevention, joint work-ing and policy outcomes the SNP (and, to be fair, their opponents) have often reverted to the electoral populism of focusing on crude numbers such as police and teacher numbers.

National 'Local' Government

Institutional nationalisation or centralisation (call it what you will) has been evolving over the past decade – Police Scotland, Fire Scotland, Scottish Water, local taxation, the ongoing review of Skills Scotland, Scottish Enterprise, High-lands and Islands Enterprise and the Scottish Funding Council with the sugges-tion that they will 'merge' under one board.

Year-on-year funding cuts continue to raise questions about the future and purpose of Scottish local government. The central-local financial relationship of dependence means that notions of 'partnership' between central and local government, despite all the rhetoric, remains one based around a rather unequal relationship of power, command and dependency.

Scottish local government has over the decades suffered a gradual and piece-meal erosion of its values and autonomy by Conservative, Labour and SNP led administrations. Local government's post-war purpose has tended to empha-sise local, collectivist and public service ideals in society. There has been little sign that the SNP approach of the past decade has halted their gradual erosion and replacement with more emphasis on central driven standards and declining autonomy. Indeed the evidence of the past decade suggests there could be a danger of the SNP Government in Edinburgh succumbing to similar attitudes in Westminster and Whitehall where John talks of:

> the contempt for local government by the London political elite and the Brit-ish equation of local government with bureaucratic routine, petty-fogging red-tape, corruption, small mindedness, mediocrity, embodying the limited nature of social culture outside the giant metropolis.

(2009: 19)

Bennett *et al*'s research in the early years of devolution referred to Scottish Exec-utive civil servants using a 'command model of the world' (2002: 16), similar to their counterparts in Whitehall. Despite almost two decades of devolution local government's place in the new Scottish political system remains ill-defined, as does an SNP approach to it.

Conclusion

The strategic focus of the SNP remains on national question, this inevitably leads to 'centralising tendencies' (Braiden, 2016). Scotland, like the UK as a whole, retains a system of local government that is very centralised by comparative standards. The SNP have undoubtedly played the strategic game of politics very well since 2007, re-orientating and refocusing the political debate in Scotland to one centred around the constitutional question. Even debates around the future of locally delivered public services have been re-cast around the constitution. Independence is projected to provide an opportunity to enhance the life chances, welfare and opportunities for people in local communities. However, the place of local government in this vision of a future Scotland is rarely discussed.

In the 1990s constitutional change was positively welcomed by local government. Its attraction strengthened under four consecutive Conservative administrations. An optimistic SNP scenario is that history could repeat itself. The SNP have successfully integrated its independence message with a case for an economically and socially transformed Scotland. The old unionist electioneering taunts of separatism have been flipped by the 2016 Brexit referendum vote. After the 2017 local council elections, it is not an unreasonable expectation that local government interests will once again align themselves with Scottish civic society and Scotland's dominant party in campaigning for a new constitutional solution.

An alternative more pessimistic perspective is that the weakness of the SNP in local government has meant that the independence project has had no 'Achilles heel' – there are not any 'old' SNP local administrations around to cause division or embarrass the party at national level (unlike say New Labour during the Blair project years). This could, however, change. The 2017 local elections are likely to result in the SNP takeover (as the majority or largest party) of the vast bulk of Scotland's councils. This may sow the seeds of potential internal division. It is unlikely any of the new tranche of young SNP councillors signed up to manage Scottish Government imposed retrenchment and cutbacks of local public services.

References

Bennett, M., Fairley, J. and McAteer, M. (2002), *Devolution in Scotland: The impact on local government*, YPS: York, accessed at: www.jrf.org.uk/sites/files/jrf/184263092x.pdf

Braiden, G. (2016), 'Devolution not SNP 'cuts and power grabs' tolled the bell for council powers *The Herald,* 16 December, accessed at: www.eastkilbrideconnect.co.uk/news/14970255.Gerry_Braiden__Devolution_not_SNP__cuts_and_power_grabs__tolled_the_bell_for_council_powers/

Crawford, B. (2010), 'Ten Years of Devolution', *Parliamentary Affairs,* 63(1): 89-97.

Denver, D., Mitchell, J., Pattie, C. and Bochel, H. (2000), *Scotland Decides: The Devolution Issue and the Scottish Referendum,* London: Frank Cass.

Gordon, C. (2002), 'From War of Attrition to Roller Coaster Ride: Local and Central Government in Scotland', *Public Money and Management,* 22: 6-8.

Harvie, C. (2008), 'A Year with Salmond', *Scottish Affairs* 65.

John, P. (2009), 'Why Study Urban Politics?' in Davies, J.S. and Imbroscio, D.L. (eds.), *Theories of Urban Politics,* London: Sage, 2nd edn. Lynch, P. (2002), *The History of the Scottish National Party,* Cardiff: Welsh Academic Press. Maxwell, S. (2009) 'Social Justice and the SNP' in Hassan, G. (ed.), *The Modern SNP: From Protest to Power.* Edinburgh: Edinburgh University Press. McIntosh Commission on Local Government and the Scottish Parliament (1999), *Moving Forward: Local Government and the Scottish Parliament,* Edinburgh: The Stationery Office. McGarvey, N. (2002), 'Intergovernmental Relations in Scotland Post-Devolution', *Local Government Studies,* 29(3): 29-48.

McGarvey, N. (2005), 'Local Government North and South of the Border', *Public Policy and Administration,* 20: 90-99.

McGarvey, N. (2009), 'Centre and Locality in Scottish Politics: From Bi- to Tri-partite Relations' in Jeffery, C. and Mitchell, J. (eds.), *The Scottish Parliament 1999-2009: The First Decade,* Edinburgh: Luath Press/Hansard Society.

McGarvey, N. (2011), 'Expectations, Assumptions and Realities: Scottish Local Government Post-Devolution', *British Journal of Politics and International Relations.*

McGarvey, N. and Cairney, P. (2008), *Scottish Politics,* Basingstoke: Palgrave.

Mitchell, J. (2009) 'From Breakthrough to Mainstream: The Politics of Potential and Blackmail' in Hassan, G. (ed.), *The Modern SNP: From Protest to Power,* Edinburgh: Edinburgh University Press.

Mitchell, J. (2014), *The Scottish Question,* Oxford: Oxford University Press.

Parry, R. (2010), 'Party Strategies and Devolved Public Policy: The Conservatives and the Nationalists', Political Studies Association British and Comparative Territorial Politics Conference, University of Oxford 7-9 January.

The SNP's Economic Strategy: Economic Performance in a Changing Fiscal Context

Jim and Margaret Cuthbert

THIS CHAPTER LOOKS at two distinct, but related, aspects relevant to the SNP's economic policy. The first section considers the post referendum fiscal settlement: this new arrangement means that economic policy is now operating in an unfamiliar and hostile environment. The second section examines the track record of SNP economic policy, now that the SNP has been in power for almost ten years. The combined implications of the two sections are stark. It is not just that the SNP needs to revise its economic strategy: as long as Scotland remains in the UK, the SNP should also be challenging, and seeking to redraw, the current fiscal settlement itself.

The Implications of the Fiscal Framework: Faith Alone is Not Enough

In Gerry Hassan's predecessor volume to this book we characterised SNP economic policy as it stood then as 'neo-liberalism with a heart' (Cuthbert, 2009). That is, the SNP's economic vision, as expressed in their 2007 economic strategy, favoured a low tax, low regulation, business friendly approach, and saw opportunities in globalisation, and free movement of capital and labour. But this fairly standard neo-liberal prescription was tempered by a strong emphasis on equity: and the belief that, particularly through improving access to education and training, improvements in equity and economic growth could drive each other forward in a virtuous cycle.

In the 2009 book, we criticised the SNP's strategy for, among other things, being too dependent on the flawed and discredited neo-liberal model: and recommended that their strategy should be much more resilient in the face of uncertainty. What we argue here is that since 2009 the SNP has failed to develop this resilience in its strategy, and has not sufficiently adapted to the radical changes in context that have taken place – particularly in the shape of the post-referendum fiscal settlement. This puts the SNP in grave danger of economic failure.

The most developed statement of the SNP's current economic approach is contained in the economic strategy it published in March 2015. The 2015 strategy involves basically the same approach as the 2007 version: but there have been, nevertheless, some significant changes. In particular, the pledge in the 2007 strategy that the SNP would use full tax raising powers, if it got them, 'to make Scotland the lowest taxed part of the UK' has been dropped. Another change, but more in emphasis this time, is that the latest strategy puts even more stress on the importance of tackling inequality.

The SNP's economic approach has been further elaborated, for example, in the Programme for Government issued in September 2016. This contained a number of economic proposals, some of which reflected newly acquired powers, (like the proposal to halve Air Passenger Duty by the end of the parliamentary session.) However, the steps announced in 2016 were still firmly based on the four pillars of the existing strategy – namely, investment in people and infrastructure, innovation, internationalisation, and inclusive growth.

The really significant changes since 2007, however, have been in the context within which economic policy has to operate. Important among these changes is the new fiscal settlement that now governs financial relations between Scotland and Westminster. The critical importance of this new fiscal settlement is something that has largely escaped commentators – and even, it appears, SNP policy makers.

Without going into the technical details, what the fiscal settlement implies is that, if Scotland grows its per capita tax receipts at the same rate as rUK, it will raise the same funding that it would have under the Barnett formula. If its tax receipts grow faster, it will do better. But if Scotland's tax receipts, (on devolved taxes), do not grow as fast as rUK, then Scotland will be penalised relative to what it would have received under the Barnett formula. Moreover, these penalties can be severe: if Scotland chronically underperforms, then the per capita funding the Scottish Government will have available to it will drop to about 60 % of the per capita funding on comparable services in rUK.

In effect, the fiscal settlement plunges Scotland into an economic race with rUK. If we win in that race, by growing our economy, and hence our income tax receipts, faster than rUK, then well and good, and we will benefit. But if our economy, and hence our tax receipts, lag behind, then we will suffer badly, with the further danger that we slip into a self-reinforcing cycle of decline.

Unfortunately, our chances of success in this economic race are not good. For one thing, Scotland has been pitched into this race with a limited set of economic powers. So, in effect, what we are engaged in a situation where Scotland is limited by lacking key powers. Secondly, we are starting on this race at exactly the time that the North Sea sector, which has buoyed our economy in the past, is entering into its period of secular decline. And thirdly, as the second part of this chapter shows, the evidence, difficult to interpret as it is, suggests that the Scottish economy is already underperforming – at precisely the time when the SNP's economic strategy should be starting to bear fruit.

It is relevant at this point to reflect on views expressed by a very senior Treasury official, at a seminar held during the fiscal settlement negotiations. When challenged that Scotland did not have adequate economic powers to give us a reasonable chance in the economic race that was in prospect, he disagreed. The solution, as he saw it, would be for Scotland to radically reduce the higher bands of income tax relative to rUK – and to become, effectively, a tax haven for the wealthy.

Which brings us to the position implicit in the SNP's economic strategy. Instead of reflecting on the very difficult, and different, challenges posed by the new fiscal settlement, they have instead continued with a strategy which was largely developed in an entirely different context, before the fiscal settlement was known. It is as if a general had only one strategy, which they insist on applying, whatever terrain the battle is being fought on. But if the terrain is unsuitable, either change your tactics – or change the terrain. Having blind faith in one set of tactics come-what-may is to invite disaster.

The SNP should certainly not adopt the Treasury approach of seeking to outcompete the rest of the UK by lowering taxes, particularly for high earners. This would be anathema to the majority of Scots. Which leaves the other option – of changing the terrain, rather than the tactics. In our view, a key element of the SNP's approach should be to seek to change the fiscal settlement. This is not as outlandish a suggestion as it might appear at first sight. After all, by embarking on Brexit, Westminster has fundamentally changed the bargain implicit in the post-referendum settlement, about what Scotland could expect from relations with the rest of the UK.

The Scottish government's decision to sign up to the disastrous post-referendum fiscal settlement appears to have been taken in the misplaced faith that, whatever risks and handicaps were involved, Scotland would somehow emerge triumphant. Unfortunately, (to paraphrase Edith Cavell's famous phrase), faith alone is not enough. Policy has to be informed by a realistic appraisal of changing context – not just by faith: and policy must be willing to challenge the current context if it is inappropriate, rather than simply taking it as a given.

At the high political level, the SNP's call for a second referendum is again demonstrating a welcome appetite for challenging the very basis of the UK constitutional settlement. As long as Scotland remains in the UK, the SNP has to develop a similar appetite for challenging the basis of the current fiscal settlement. These two approaches would be perfectly consistent: after all, a refusal by Westminster to re-engage constructively on the fiscal settlement would only strengthen the case for independence.

The Scottish Economy: How has the SNP *Performed?*

The aim of the SNP shown in its National Performance Framework was to create a more successful country, with opportunities for all of Scotland to flourish, through increasing sustainable economic growth.

Six areas in particular were chosen as hoped for growth areas: trade, tourism, research and development, small business growth, infrastructure, and education and training. Here, we examine where we can, what was achieved, and what state Scotland is in ten years on from the SNP forming a government. The biggest problem faced in attempting an analysis is difficulty with the data. It would be wrong to say there is a paucity of data: there is plenty of it. The problem is it is not directly relevant to judging how well the economy has done in the widest sense of helping people and businesses in Scotland to have a fulfilling, sustainable economic future.

The picture is also confused by the Scottish Government introducing the concept of its growth sectors which do not match the above original growth areas. These sectors are: Food and Drink (including agriculture and fisheries); Creative Industries (including digital); Sustainable Tourism; Energy (including renewables); Financial and Business Services; and Life Sciences. For some of these, the data is just not available.

The over-riding goal: higher sustainable economic growth with more Scots in better paid jobs.

Over the period 1998 to 2015, Scotland's Gross Domestic Product increased by 29 %, that for the UK by 38 %. (ONS). In the last four years in particular Scotland has performed less well. On an annual basis, Q2 GDP in Scotland in 2016 grew by just 0.7 %; the UK–wide figure was 2.1 %.

The table below shows annual employment and unemployment rates in Scotland compared to the UK.

Table 1. Employment and Unemployment Rates

	2008	2012	2016	2008	2012	2016
	Scotland	Scotland	Scotland	UK	UK	UK
Unemployment rate % 16 to 19 year olds	18.3	29.2	21.3	21.3	28.8	21.3
Unemployment rate 16-64	5.4	8.0	5.1	6.2	8.0	5.1
Employment rate 16-64	74.0	70.4	72.8	72.6	70.7	73.7

In all three categories, the position of Scotland relative to the UK has worsened.

It is also worrying that inequality across Scotland is very large. For example, ONS figures show Edinburgh to have a GVA per head in 2015 of £36,963: that for East Ayrshire and North Ayrshire was £15,200.

Turning to performance in the different sectors, the Scottish Government works through 33 non-departmental public bodies and six public corporations. While there will be positive returns in so doing it has allowed an aura of secrecy to creep in, together with a less comprehensive data collection and analysis system, and thus a difficulty of determining whether the needs of the Scottish public are being met in the round.

Trade: Trade is not mentioned in the Manifesto of 2007 but there has been a Government target of a 50 % increase in the nominal value of international exports over the period 2010 to 2017. The latest figures for 2008 to 2015, show total exports (excluding oil and gas) rising by 29.5 %, however, over the same period the consumer price index rose by 18.1 %, so the real increase in exports has been small. In addition, there is, and has been, a concentration on the export sale of whisky and other distilled products: 13.4 % of international exports in 2015 compared with, for example, agriculture at 0.8 % and computer/electronic exports at 4.2 %.

Tourism: VisitScotland, an NDPB, aspires to make Scotland the most economically, environmentally and socially sustainable destination in Europe. Data for this sector is extremely difficult to interpret as it includes a wide array of activity including hotels, teashops, sports facilities and visits to museums. From 2009 to 2013, the last date available, GVA from tourism rose by 25 % that compares favourably with inflation of 13.7 % over the period. Data on earnings from international inbound tourism is available for 2015 and shows a fall of 8.2 % over 2014. There is a lack of depth in surveys on tourist satisfaction. There is nothing for example, on quality of access to historic sites, the quality of paths in rural areas, cycle routes, and the availability of services such as toilets. So it is not clear that the correct evidence is being collected to enable improvements in the tourist experience to be planned and delivered.

Small business growth: There has been a rise in the number of small businesses in Scotland, a 12.5 % increase, 2008 to 2016, with those in the targeted growth sectors increasing by 26 %: but closer examination shows the number of businesses with zero employees in the growth sectors increased by 36 %: and as the percentage increase is greatest in energy, this could be due to large firms reducing their workforce and using contract labour. One of the challenges set for universities was to embed a culture of engagement between themselves and Scottish small businesses. There does not appear to be any information collated on what, if any, progress has been made on this front.

Infrastructure: Examination of large public contracts to construction companies increasingly shows very substantial and long term contracts going to multinationals. In February 2017, it was announced that three contractor teams stand to benefit from almost £200m of roads maintenance funding across Scotland over the next 12 months: all are multinationals. And even while the Scottish Government said that there would be many opportunities for small Scottish companies in building the Forth Crossing, all of the major contractors had head offices outwith Scotland – a far cry from the building of the Millau Bridge in France where most of the major contractors were French and the bridge is now owned by the French Government.

In addition, with the aim of improving public procurement, the SNP introduced the Scottish Futures Trust, an NDPB. There are two major problems. First, in letting contracts, the SFT emphasises value for money fairly narrowly defined – this is notably different from Northern Ireland where the effect of contracts on the local community and its sustainability play an important part. Second, in a major SFT initiative, there are five 'hubs', covering Scotland. Each hub consists of a number of public sector organisations and one private sector delivery partner. The term runs for a minimum 20 years. This means that the delivery partner, a private organisation, is in a key position in decision-making regarding public contracts, for a long period of time. This might work well, but there are clearly potential dangers. In a number of the hubs there is also a tier system: in Edinburgh, there are three Tier 1 contractors. Any small company wanting to be considered has to approach these contractors. This appears to be giving too much decision-making powers into the hands of a few major companies, many of which are not local. Overall, it is not likely that this environment for public procurement is one that would favour a small Scottish company trying to grow.

In summary, assessing the performance of the Scottish economy, and of the SNP's economic policy, is by no means a straightforward task. The task is complicated in particular by the fact that the sectors which the SNP has targeted for growth do not align with the ONS standard classifications: and also by the tendency for the SNP to establish various quangos as delivery partners – each of whom tends to develop their own habits of secrecy. Nevertheless, it is quite clear from the above that the Scottish economy is by no means performing well; and in important respects, (in particular in GDP growth and in diversity of trade), is lagging behind rUK. This is an important and sobering conclusion. As the other section of this chapter makes clear, under the terms of the new fiscal settlement Scotland has now been pitched into an unwelcome economic race with the rest of the UK: a race in which we are handicapped by a lack of adequate economic powers. The evidence of recent economic performance, under the SNP's economic policies, is that keeping up in this race is going to prove particularly difficult.

References

Cuthbert, J. and M. (2009), 'SNP Economic Policy: Neo-liberalism with a
    Heart', in Hassan, Gerry (ed.), *The Modern SNP: From Protest to Power*,
    Edinburgh: Edinburgh University Press, 105-19.

The Scottish Economy, the SNP and the Absence of Economic Nationalism

Douglas Fraser

FOR THE EIGHT years of a new devolved Parliament, the economy had been a problem for the Scottish National Party. Without government experience, the party was perceived as untested and therefore risky. Little of the business community was on board. And the economy was changing. Scotland had moved on from a narrative of post-industrial collapse. The long-standing gaps in growth and employment rates, when compared with the rest of the UK, were closing. Silicon Glen had declined abruptly as the century turned, but the growth of financial services and contact centres helped to absorb the electronics job losses. So the economy's relatively strong performance required a shift in SNP strategy. No longer could the party claim that Scotland was being left the poor relation.

Ten years on, that seems a distant set of challenges. The immediate ones, back then, seem now to have been easily overcome, primarily by changing the mood music. The SNP, under the second leadership of Alex Salmond, turned positive. If the economy could no longer be portrayed as being kept behind the UK by Westminster decision-making, it could be portrayed as failing to reach its potential for doing better than the UK.

From Charm Offensive to the Banking Crash

Salmond talked of an 'arc of prosperity' in which small countries, from Ireland to Iceland to Norway, were storming ahead confidently on strong growth rates. The party choreographed a series of big name endorsements during the 2007 campaign. Most notable was Sir George Mathewson, architect of what was then rampant as one of the world's biggest banks. Royal Bank of Scotland sent a signal that this small nation could be home to a global, world-beating company, just as Finland had the mighty Nokia. Significantly at the time, these endorsements were not for independence, and not all for the SNP. They were personal, for Alex Salmond. In contrast with then Labour leader and First Minister Jack

McConnell, here was a leader who could be comfortable working the nation's boardrooms.

Less high-profile, but influential in winning corporate hearts and minds, were the energetic efforts of Jim Mather and Andrew Wilson – a successful businessman and inspirational salesman, along with a smart economist. They took a PowerPoint roadshow round any business audience that would watch it. They emphasised the opportunities for cutting corporation tax, to emulate Ireland's Celtic Tiger. Not everyone in the SNP agreed with the centre right message, but this was a useful way of furthering the party cause. Promoted heavily to the media, the Mather and Wilson Roadshow was an important element in systematically removing the obstacles in voters' minds to switching to an SNP vote.

In retrospect, we know the economy was about to enter recession as the SNP took power. And the intentions of boosting the growth rate, to join the Irish Celtic Tiger, were about to be overwhelmed by the financial crisis. Scotland's two banking giants required a massive government bail-out. That threatened to knock the stuffing out of the confidence in, and of, Edinburgh's financial sector. Politically, Alex Salmond, a former RBS economist, was in an awkward position. A letter he sent to Fred Goodwin showed he had cheered on the takeover of ABN Amro and offered to help in an acquisition that turned out to be calamitous, while he had previously criticised the Labour Government for being too heavy-handed in its regulation of the banking sector (see Fraser, 2014). So he was not in a strong position to criticise the UK Government's handling of the crisis, or to offer a solution. The twin nightmares of RBS and HBOS were subjects on which he was unusually quiet.

That is while his administration put in place policies that could help support the economy through the crisis. Where it could boost infrastructure spending, it did, shifting some funds from revenue spending, and subsequently using a limited facility for bringing forward capital spend. The new Scottish Government was focussed around its objectives, and above all, with a capital P, was the Purpose of growing the economy. That was as much a message to the party as to the government machine and the electorate. Whereas his Labour predecessor had been mocked for making a priority of almost everything, Salmond wanted a focus, and it was to be on the economy.

Benchmarking Scotland

A dominant narrative for the SNP administration was the benchmarking of Scotland's performance against the UK as a whole. While ministers sought to highlight difference, through much of the downturn, Scotland was more like the

UK average than any other part of Britain, particularly and ironically the outlier that is London. When it looked better, there was credit to be taken. When it looked worse, Westminster's austerity measures got the blame. That narrative continues to run the risk of ignoring other, international benchmarks. On productivity for instance, matching Britain's performance has been a target, which was very nearly met in the figures for 2015. But by international standards, it's not much of an achievement.

Even when any administration would have felt storm-tossed by economic events far beyond its control, the priority was to have a plan, to look competent and to look busy. It helped that the economy was the subject that most absorbed the First Minister's attention. Those around him say he typically took a broad brush to policies around public services, or simply delegated. But he had a sharp focus on getting his economic policy right. The same people note that Nicola Sturgeon has the reverse approach.

Important to this was talking positively about the 're-industrialisation of Scotland', building on its potential in renewable energy. Scotland could be 'the Saudi Arabia of renewable power', including wind, tidal, wave and CCS – carbon capture and storage. There was a period when the First Minister was to be seen with corporate chiefs from around the world, making announcements of ambitious plans for manufacturing the necessary equipment. Ministers were closely involved in keeping a turbine plant in Kintyre from closing, through repeated financial crises. The plant remains open, but much of the national vision has turned to disappointment. For various reasons – including the first mover advantage enjoyed by Germany, Denmark and Spain, and to some extent due to regulatory choices made by the UK Government – there are few of these re-industrialised jobs to be found. There has been fabrication work, but not a steady pipeline of it. Turbines are almost all imported. Tidal power is making progress, but wave power has stalled, and the Scottish Government has put that technology into a sort of state-backed life support system. Grand hopes for CCS at Longannet and Peterhead foundered, as the UK Government first delayed and then abandoned its competition for £1 billion of funding.

Policy has also sought to soften the blows from plant closures. In the case of steel works in Lanarkshire in 2015, threatened by closure due to dumping of Chinese steel, Nicola Sturgeon and her ministers could take credit for a job well done. The same Indian company that took them on then went to Lochaber, not just to retain the aluminium plant at Fort William, but to set out plans for expansion of manufacturing around it. Much has been made of Orkney's base for testing marine renewables. The public spending on infrastructure – motorway upgrades, the Queensferry Crossing, the Borders railway – delivered an improbably large boost to construction sector statistics. The food and drink sector had a strong showing, and tourism handled the downturn with flexibility. Scotland retained a relatively strong rating as a destination for inward investors, helped by the decision of the incoming Tory-Lib Dem Government at Westminster to dismantle England's regional development agencies.

The Missing Agenda of Economic Nationalism

Notable episodes that worked less well start with Diageo and its Kilmarnock bottling plant. The Johnnie Walker plant employed 700. While on an investment roll to expand capacity, the distilling giant announced in 2009 that it intended to close the Ayrshire plant, and relocate to more efficient, lower-staffed bottling plants in Glasgow and Fife. Caught unawares, Alex Salmond's response was to attack Diageo, leading a public rally against the company's plans, and telling his ministers and Scottish Enterprise development agency to find a way of showing that Kilmarnock must keep bottling. It was, arguably, his most ill-judged episode as First Minister. It exposed the tensions of being both a government leader and in oppositional mode. It was a noisy protest campaign doomed to failure. And it alienated one of the country's most important inward investors. The biggest single plant closure of the downturn was Hall's of Broxburn, a meat processing plant. Again, the response of ministers was to look busy, apparently pouring effort into advising one of Europe's biggest food processing firms on how to better run its operations while remaining in West Lothian. They didn't get far with that either.

A significant shift in economic policy with the arrival of the Salmond administration was a shake-up for Scottish Enterprise. It was stripped of much of its established role, and under Jim Mather as enterprise minister, it was re-oriented to backing only the companies with high-growth potential – at first, around 2000 of them. This took it out of the political football arena, at least until 2016. Newly appointed as economy and work secretary, Keith Brown was then given the task of finding an answer to the country's sluggish rate of economic growth. He set about the enterprise agencies, a quarter century after they had been carved out of the statist era of 1960s and 1970s government intervention. The solution remains a work in progress, being delivered in phases. The first phase succeeded mainly in inviting pushback against centralisation of Highlands and Islands Enterprise and of the Scottish Funding Council (for universities and colleges) under the umbrella of one national board. One innovation within the plan is a planned agency for the south of Scotland, to mirror the efforts of HIE.

Keith Brown's new job was part of a re-shuffle that marked a significant shift in the way economic policy was handled. Whereas John Swinney had wrapped it into a wide-ranging portfolio for the previous nine years, along with control of the administration's purse strings, Nicola Sturgeon dispersed economic policy widely; along with Mr Brown's new role, separated from finance, other people at the cabinet table were handed responsibility for skills, for the rural economy and connectivity, another one covering tourism, still another for equalities, while the finance secretary handles the contentious issue of business rates. It risked a Balkanised approach to policy. But with the SNP's distinctively collegiate approach, and a strong central control from Ms Sturgeon, it has not appeared to suffer from that.

Meanwhile, the UK Government sought to have its own role in Scottish economic development. It was devising a system of City Deals, with which to incentivise the devolution of power within England. In Scotland, the same type of matching funds deal was announced for Clydeside, abruptly and mischievously bouncing Scottish ministers into having to find similar sums. This was not to enhance or incentivise devolution, but to counter it. With all seven Scottish cities to be covered by variants on the deal, it gave the Treasury and Scotland Office a locus on the ground which they had lost with devolution in 1999.

Oil and Independence

Through much of the decade, the oil and gas sector provided a bulwark against volatility and a shortage of confidence elsewhere. The price of Brent crude oil rose to relatively high levels after the financial collapse, above $110 a barrel, fuelled by emerging market growth in demand. In turn, that secured a second wind of investment for the North Sea and west of Shetland, totalling more than £40 billion over five years from 2011. But just as the rest of the economy was getting back to a more stable performance, the oil price plunged, from $115 per barrel in June 2014 to $30 in January 2016. The impact was felt more widely across the Scottish economy than many had expected. The downsides clearly outweighed the upside for fuel users in having cheaper energy. It is the best explanation for a sharp divergence in the performance of the Scottish economy from that of the UK as a whole – notably in economic output and in job creation. But economists also wonder if it can be the only explanation.

This was both an economic and a political challenge for the Scottish Government, with the depth of the plunge only becoming clear in the wake of the 2014 referendum. That campaign had 'baked' the oil revenues into the optimistic public finance forecasts deployed by the SNP, selecting the best of the boom years of the high oil price to illustrate the strength of Scotland's position relative to the UK. (Their opponents used a different set of selective statistics to demonstrate the opposite.) By 2016, oil revenues had turned negative. A partial recovery and stabilisation of the oil price, above $50, sent the message that the oil sector might be coaxed out of its slump, helped by a new regulator in Aberdeen with a mandate to require better co-operation between operators. But the chances of a tax bonanza to fund Scottish public services, to plug the deficit and to build up a Norwegian-style national wealth fund, had to be re-thought. The advice from their own advisers – not to rely on oil tax revenue, but to treat it as a windfall, and a surplus for long-term investment – is influencing the SNP's thinking as it marks ten years in office and prepares the ground for a second independence referendum. But in doing so, the absence of oil revenue has thrown up a big challenge of re-casting the economic and financial case for independence while Scotland runs a persistent, unsustainably large, non-oil, public sector deficit.

That 2014 referendum, of course, was the biggest political event in Scotland during the SNP's first ten years in power. The economic case was spelled out in detail in the white paper in November 2013, in response to pressure from critics that the SNP was failing to answer questions (Scottish Government, 2013). But having published the White Paper, it gave opponents of independence a lot of ammunition to hurl back at the Nationalist campaign. The First Minister's claim that an independent Scotland would both retain use of the pound and share in its control was flatly denied by the major parties at Westminster. There were arguments over the share-out of government debt, over co-operation with the rest of the UK in the energy market, as well as the question of whether an independent Scotland would gain quick access to Europe's single market. Only by voting to stay in the union, voters were told, could Scotland's place in Europe be secured. It hasn't worked out that way.

And one of the new strands of political thinking that has come with the rise of what might be called Brexit British or English nationalism is the case for asserting more control over foreign takeover of strategic economic assets. With the weakened pound after June 2016, foreigners found British corporate assets even more attractively priced. The issue had attracted some attention with the takeover of Cadbury – an icon of Britain's sweet tooth – and ARM Holdings, a British technology success story. In big pharma, British-based AstraZeneca was a takeover target. While contesting the Tory leadership, Theresa May talked of a more robust protection of Britain's national interests when considering such deals.

This is significant in Scotland, because of the contrast. This is the dog that has not barked. The SNP administration sells itself on fighting Scotland's corner, but has no discernible policy on protecting the country's strategic economic assets. This is not meant as criticism, but as an observation that it has come down firmly on the side of being open and encouraging to investors. It wasn't always thus. In 2006, a few months before taking office, the takeover of ScottishPower by the Spanish firm Iberdrola was strongly condemned by Alex Salmond, with an explicit expression of economic nationalism. He cited the example of the French in fending off raiding parties on its big companies. Yet his first day in office symbolised how much that changed, and how quickly. He went to Longannet power station in Fife to meet Iberdrola's chairman Ignacio Galan and to talk about carbon capture and storage. The two men, reportedly, took an instant liking to each other. Barely a word of economic nationalism has been uttered since that day.

An Assessment and Future Challenges

A review of ten years tempts the writer towards drawing conclusions, when it is clear that this is only a milestone along the road of the SNP administration. That said, what can be concluded about the story so far? One is that the initial challenge of establishing a reputation for competence and working with the business community was a quick victory. The party's opponents will tell a different story, but they struggle to match the SNP for that reputation now. Indeed, the high turnover of leadership in other parties has left them unusually short of experience with economics and finance.

The test the administration set itself of making economic growth its single, unifying Purpose, with that capital P, has not been as clear a success. That is partly because Scotland had already reached the SNP's growth target of matching the UK level, before the SNP took office. More obviously, such plans were swept aside by recession and the global financial crisis, and those best-laid plans went awry. They were replaced with the requirement to mitigate the huge risks that hung over the economy.

There was, through this, another unifying purpose, in the drive for independence. Use of devolved powers has been routinely accompanied by 'but if only we had more powers'. In parallel with government, and a calculation in almost every move, much effort was put into establishing the economic case for independence. While the drive towards a second independence referendum has absorbed energies and stifled open debate about the 2014 referendum campaign, it is hard not to conclude that the economic argument was not fit for purpose, and proved to be the most fruitful target for the attacks of the Better Together campaign. Not only did it leave a lot uncertain, and it glossed over risks: it is seen by some as having failed to address the concerns and interests of middle class, or perhaps 'aspirational' Scotland. That group includes those with a stake, and particularly those with a small stake, which they did not want to risk.

With four more years of this Parliament and no doubt hopes to hold office for much longer, the SNP can maintain its active and pragmatic approach to economic management. It has recently gained new powers over income tax, which explicitly link economic growth to the amount of funds available for public spending. That makes the economic choices harder and sharper. Economic developments have made the case for independence tougher to make. Meanwhile, other economic pressures continue, or are closing in: the productivity puzzle, expectations that inequalities can be reduced, political pressures against globalisation, the robotics challenge to employment, the decline of offshore oil, the shortage of housing, skills shortages if EU workers are excluded, and the financial questions of how to adapt public services to demographic change.

References

Fraser, I. (2014), *Shredded: Inside RBS the Bank that Broke Britain*, Edinburgh: Birlinn.

Scottish Government (2013), *Scotland's Future: Your Guide to an Independent Scotland*, Edinburgh: Scottish Government.

The Scottish Economy: Breaking with Business as Usual?

Mike Danson

Foreword

THE SLOGAN (good Gaelic word) for 2017 could be the Quaker phrase 'Speak truth to power', and challenging consensus and identifying path dependency within Scotland and Scottish institutions is a critical function of those undertaking analyses of Scotland's political economy. One role of this collection therefore is to explore the economic policies and strategies of the last decade in Scotland, and to examine whether and how they might be extended, applied and used to 'nudge' or more fundamentally shift actors and players to change attitudes and behaviours. In this contribution I suggest that since 2007 Scotland's economy progressively has come to resemble the UK as a whole. This is a notable feat given the deindustrialisation of the 1980s and 1990s followed by financial crises, and established some solid foundations for further development. However, I also argue that much more could, and increasingly can, be enacted to move industries, markets and other elements onto a higher plane of sustainable development, but that requires some fundamental economic and cultural changes at all levels.

Background

Scotland is a small open economy with a range of limited but increasing powers over some aspects of the economy. When the SNP was elected as a minority government in 2007, the UK was about to enter into a period of deep economic and financial crises. Without the macroeconomic levers and regulations available to the members of 'the Arc of Prosperity' (the countries of northern Europe), which recovered fairly quickly and strongly from the recession and fiscal problems, there was little that could be achieved independently by Scottish policies and strategies within the failing UK environment. The bailing out of the banks and financial institutions, continuing austerity packages, spiralling public and private debt imposed by successive Westminster governments have been defining the context for the Scottish economy and for strategies and interventions initiated by the Scottish Government (Cuthbert, 2013; Wilson, 2016). Nevertheless, Scotland's aggregate economic performance – measured in terms of GVA per head and unemployment, the attraction of inward investment and enterprise creation – continues to be comparable with UK and EU averages (Bell, 2016). Despite the adverse winds of change, therefore, and the reduction of activities in the North Sea oil sector in particular, this suggests a stable and well-managed economy.

Indeed, productivity in Scotland has now effectively caught up with the GB average: in manufacturing it is just above and in the rest of the economy fractionally below; significantly, only London and the South East achieve higher 'Aggregate Average Labour Productivity' (ONS, 2017, Table 1). This raises the important issue of the comparator that Scotland is judged against – using 'GB' or 'UK' both hides the gross inequalities within these 'national' economies and disguises Scotland's positive record. As all the other English regions, Wales and Northern Ireland lag behind Scotland and the regions of the south east, the unquestioning tendency to adversely compare Scotland with the 'UK' means that analysis of the deeper elements, causes and implications of uneven development are left unexplored. The poor performances of the non-core regions of the UK, Scotland apart, highlight the underlying problems of low productivity, centralisation and concentration of power which generate further inequality – the highest in the developed world – and ongoing underdevelopment. It is against this background that analyses of what more could be done or done differently in and by Scotland should be undertaken.

Ownership and Control

The economic policy discourse of the late 1970s and early 1980s was strongly influenced by discussion of who owns and manages industry (Scott and Hughes, 1975; Leonard, 2012), with appreciation especially of how external control of local and regional industries impacts on the range and level of occupations in that territory and on the capacity to (re)generate new enterprises and embed supply chains. Such considerations are recognised in the work of O'Leary (2015) in the context of Ireland where the difference between GNP and GDP is explored to demonstrate some underlying problems of relying on inward investment and of an uneven distribution of headquarters and higher functions. Similar analysis seems to be neglected closer to home.

There has been relatively little appreciation by all parties and players of this 'development of the underdevelopment' of the Scottish economy (Danson,

1991) in the last quarter of a century. Supporting and encouraging Scottish based small and medium enterprises to stay headquartered here has not been on the agenda for two decades or more. The irony that, pre-devolution, the Conservative administrations in Westminster were more sensitive to such considerations should not be lost, though their neoliberal policies of deregulation and privatisation accelerated the deindustrialisation of the Scottish economy (Davidson *et al.*, 2016; Cairns *et al.*, 2016).

If Scotland has performed relatively well in the UK context but remains unable to achieve its potential in European terms, what more could and should be done? Offering a framework for analysing this are two models of economic development.

Smart Specialisation and Triple Helix

'Smart specialisation' has come out of the Nordic countries and is an economic model where territories identify 'niche areas of competitive strength, solving major societal challenges --bringing in a demand-driven dimension, [with] innovation partnerships emphasising greater co-ordination between different societal stakeholders and aligning resources and strategies between private and public actors of different governance levels' (CEC, 2016). Scotland has many of the components of such a landscape but, whereas Norway, Denmark and Sweden for instance, have their own multinational enterprises which have maintained their operations, expanded overseas and retained higher functions within their own economies, Scotland's industrial and corporate superstructure was hollowed out over the 20th century. Although restructuring was almost complete by 2007, rebuilding a Mittelstand should have been nearer to the forefront of SNP thinking and actions (Cairns, *et al.*, 2016), therefore, with explicit requirements on the development agencies – Scottish Enterprise, Scottish Development International and Highlands and Islands Enterprise – to pursue indigenous growth.

Instead there was explicit and strong support for the entrepreneurial culture based on the two major banks with 'Scotland' in their titles – RBS and HBOS – where their respective objectives and aspirations were well furth of Scotland. An evolving realisation of the damage that these and associated financial institutions inflicted on the Scottish economy by forsaking sound Scottish banking traditions (Dow, 1997) has been captured and contrasted with the management of comparable sectors in the Nordic countries (Bone, 2016; McFarlane, 2016). Rethinking our banking and financial sector needs to be a priority, therefore (Bone, 2016; Cairns *et al.*, 2017).

The concept of the 'triple helix' of an innovation system of university-industry-government networking has been applied to promote improved competitiveness at local, regional and national levels (Danson and Todeva, 2016). With its world leading academic sector, history of effective close partnership working and delivery across government and governance institutions, Scotland should be in a position to exploit its potential in innovation, creativity and knowledge transfer. However, attempts to improve productivity, enterprise creation and innovation have been constrained by failings of local management and limited control of strategic decisions within companies due to their branch plant status (Scott and Hughes, 1975; Leonard, 2012). The lack of workplace innovation based on the initiative and empowerment of the workforce has bedevilled the Scottish and UK economies according to Keep (2014) and distinguishes our practices and class-based enterprises from those in Europe's most innovative economies: the Nordic countries and Germany (Danson and Todeva, 2016).

Addressing management, ownership and control shortcomings of Scotland's industries and promoting full utilisation of our skills' base should be prioritised going forward (Cairns *et al.*, 2016).

Ownership, Control and the Policy Landscape

This identification of how external control of the Scottish economy adversely affects productivity, supply chains, attribution of incomes and outputs frames both the terms of analysing the government's performance and of proposing alternative future strategic and policy developments. The sorts of powers required to address low productivity and incomplete supply chains are different and more extensive from those to subsidise business start-ups and attract branch plants, so future and better interventions and programmes are contingent on the sorts and range of powers required for the former to come to the Scottish Parliament and Government. Whether Brexit leads to repatriation to Scotland of control over fishing, agriculture and important social and environmental areas, as claimed by the Leave campaign (Carrell, 2016), will be important in determining support and direction for such sectors but critically also for their supply chain linkages. Devolution of further powers over employment law, a wider range of social security benefits and pensions, taxes and other key parts of the labour and training markets would enrich the infrastructure available to move the Scottish economy towards a more sustainable, inclusive and fair path and level (Fair Work Convention, 2016). An integrated policy and institutional landscape characterised by more extensive features of smart specialisation and triple (quadruple: to include the citizenry) helix economies would require such transfers of powers, and the willingness to apply them appropriately.

Institutional Capacity, Thickness and Skills

With about the highest proportion of graduates in the world, successive studies confirm Scotland does not have significant skills shortages (Brodie and Pattoni, 2017) and has economic development and training agencies recognised as world-class (Danson, 2006). However, the economy continues to suffer from poor skills utilisation as highlighted by Keep (2014) and Felstead and Greene (2013), and this in particular is where Scotland, along with the rest of the UK, lags behind its successful European neighbours (Scottish Government, 2014). Productivity would naturally be higher, and incomes and tax revenues retained in Scotland greater in consequence, if higher quality jobs were located within the Scottish branches of businesses and if more goods and services were generated here rather than imported virtually from south of the border.

The inability of Scottish employers to apply the graduate skills of over 60 thousand migrant workers from Poland and other EU enlargement countries confirms the structural problems of the economy. The need for better management and leadership is palpable and a matter of urgency if Scotland is to realise the benefits of its investment in a highly skilled and educated workforce and research in universities and laboratories. Focus on structures rather than processes has disoriented the evolution of the appropriate set of institutions and relations for Scotland's development landscape.

The threat of a post-Brexit UK characterised by deepening neoliberalism in industrial and workplace relations, dismemberment of employment and human rights, and further privatisations is diametrically opposed to the evolving political economy represented in the 'competitive and fair' Scottish Economic Strategy (Scottish Government, 2015). Repatriating these powers and controls to move the Scottish economy is essential if there are to be the sorts of fundamental changes towards the models of our globally successful neighbours. That would see the promotion of an economy with more local production, growing enterprises based here, using skills and expertise nurtured and attracted to Scotland, with workplaces thriving through innovations from the bottom up. That requires all social partners – trades unions, management, entrepreneurs, government – to be involved in an array of types of organisation: public, private, community and worker cooperatives. This inclusive and democratic approach is the foundation of the Nordic economies and offers different prospects from today's branch plant economy. Alternative forms of ownership and operations of the utilities (Cumbers et al., 2013), banks (McFarlane, 2016) and transport companies (Findlay et al., 2017) should be pursued to ensure that the excess profits of natural monopolies are shared and applied more equitably than at present under privatised models.

Public Procurement

The success of Scotland's food and drink industry, community buy-outs and financial institutions, traditionally, illustrate how sustainable and socially useful forms of enterprise can be established. Despite unfounded and ill-informed criticism, public procurement and contracting can be applied to support, guide and further such developments. Community benefit clauses and enhanced requirements around the living wage, apprenticeships, local purchasing, sub-contracting to local SMEs and other forms of creative procurement have been shown to benefit all social partners of the quadruple helix, and to generate economic multiplier and further supply chain outcomes (Christie and Danson, 2016; Findlay *et al.*, 2017). Financing public procurement and capital investment requires a new approach away from PFI/PPP, which have so damaged public finances in recent decades (Cairns *et al.*, 2017), and the commentators cited here have proposed blueprints for alternative institutions.

Taxes, Benefits and the Economy

Plans to replace the Council Tax with a more progressive form of local income tax highlighted a number of issues around the appetite for reform, willingness to pay higher taxes and the regressive nature of the existing system as a whole, but it also contributed to the debate on how to generate inclusion and greater equity in society. As Stephen Boyd argued strongly in evidence to the Finance Committee (Boyd, 2015), lower tax thresholds and higher tax rates with a reorientation towards consumer taxes characterises the Nordic economies' approach to a much more equitable society. Critically complementing these factors, the labour market offers a much superior range of opportunities at the lower and entry ends with strong trades unions ensuring jobs pay well and training is embedded. A fixation in the Scottish Parliament on imposing punitive tax rates for the highest income groups misses these factors which are potentially more important and effective in promoting and sustaining real change.

Similarly, SNP support for small businesses through low property taxes has been criticised by Boyd (2015) as inefficient while company managers are privileged in how they are treated by the UK tax and national insurance system with important implicit subsidies and advantages (Adam *et al*, 2017). These differentiated fiscal policies are part of the problem of confusing 'enterprise' and self-employment in the contracted out and 'gig economy' and have led to about 180 thousand Scottish 'entrepreneurs' being in poverty while others are needlessly subsidised (Galloway and Danson, 2106). A thorough revision of the tax, public procurement and contracting systems and programmes would move the Scottish economy towards a more effective and efficient set of measures of reward and incentive, of inclusion and equity.

Addressing both income inequality and inefficiencies in the social security system (Spicker, 2016) could be achieved through the introduction of a citizen's basic income – a concept being explored by the SNP and Green party, by Labour Councils in Fife and Glasgow, and promoted by the RSA (Royal Society of Arts) and campaign groups (CBINS, 2017). As with other elements of an economic programme designed to be inclusive and fair and to raise competitiveness, this would expand the Scottish economy through positive multiplier effects and empowerment of citizens (Danson *et al.*, 2012)

Achieving our Potential?

As in other areas of strategies and programmes, economic policy cannot be 'business as usual' or Scotland will suffer continuing mediocrity and accelerating decline within an isolated UK (Elliott and Atkinson, 2012). Independence alone will not offer a sufficient bounce and change, whether in the EU/EEA or outside; more radical understanding and plans are required to shift Scotland onto a different economic development trajectory. Integration of the aims and objectives of the range of economic policies and strategies with a more comprehensive set of controls and powers requires a better understanding of the economic relations and flows within and outwith Scotland. This demands improved understanding of the firms, markets, and other elements of the Scottish economy, rather than academic analyses crudely based on comparisons between Scotland and the UK. As argued above, promotion and support for a circular economy which boosts production and incomes locally to the benefit of the whole will repatriate activity and jobs from the City and multinationals to locally-owned and controlled enterprises – private, public and social. New and reformed institutions – financial, developmental, and democratically managed and controlled – promise a confident, inclusive and innovative economy and society, led by a government applying land value, income and wealth taxes, exploiting the natural and human resources of the nation. Within a decade we could expect to begin to reap the benefits of a different economic strategy from the neoliberalism of the past or the storms unleashed by Brexit.

References

Adam, S., Miller, H. and Pope, T. (2017), 'Tax, legal form and the gig economy', Report (R124), Institute of Fiscal Studies, London.

Bell, D. (2016), 'How closely is the economy of the UK and Scotland aligned with the EU?', *European Futures*, accessed at: www.europeanfutures.ed.ac.uk/article-3347

Bone, G. (2016), 'Banking for the Common Good: Laying the foundations of safe, sustainable, stakeholder banking in Scotland', Common Weal, accessed at: www.allofusfirst.org/library/banking-for-the-common-good-laying-the-foundations-of-safe-sustainable-stakeholder-banking-in-scotland-20161/

Boyd, S. (2015), *Finance Committee. Official Report*, Wednesday 30th September, Scottish Parliament, accessed at: www.parliament.scot/parliamentary-business/report.aspx?r=10125&mode=pdf

Brodie, C. and Pattoni, L. (2017), 'Jobs and skills in Scotland and Industries 4.0' presentation to SFC Board Meeting, *Skills Development Scotland*, accessed at: www.sfc.ac.uk/web/FILES/CNP_Councilmeeting17March2017_17032017/SDS_presentation_-_Jobs_and_Skills_in_Scotland.pdf

Cairns, I., Cumbers, A., Danson, M., Docherty, I., Kane, P., Morgan, G., McAlpine, R., McMaster, R., Sullivan, W. and Whittam, G. (2016), 'Towards an industrial policy for Scotland: A discussion of principles and approaches', *Common Weal*, accessed at: www.allofusfirst.org/library/towards-an-industrial-policy-for-scotland-a-discussion-of-principles-and-approaches-2016/

Cairns, I., Cooper, C., Watterson, A. and Wray, B. (2017), 'Building Scotland's future now. A new approach to financing public investment', *Common Weal*, accessed at: http://allofusfirst.org/tasks/render/file/?fileID=9B6146D1-ECD3-1117-25EBC91E5A2EF7E8

Carrell, S. (2016), 'Vote Leave claims Brexit would give Scotland more domestic powers', *The Guardian*, 18 May, accessed at: https://www.theguardian.com/politics/2016/may/18/vote-leave-claims-brexit-give-scotland-more-powers-eu-referendum

CBINS (2017), 'Why basic income?', Citizen's Basic Income Network Scotland, accessed at: https://cbin.scot/

CEC (Commission of the European Communities) (2016), 'Smart specialisation', accessed as https://ec.europa.eu/jrc/en/research-topic/smart-specialisation

Christie, L. and Danson, M. (2016), 'Glasgow's post-entrepreneurial approach to 2014 CWG legacy', in *New Perspectives on Research Policy and Practice in Public Entrepreneurship* (*Contemporary Issues in Entrepreneurship Research, Volume 6*), ed. J. Liddle, pp. 147-171.

Cumbers, A., Danson, M., Whittam, G., Morgan, G. and Callaghan, G. (2013), 'Repossessing the future: a common weal strategy for community and democratic ownership of Scotland's energy resources', Jimmy Reid Foundation, accessed at: http://reidfoundation.org/wp-content/uploads/2013/10/Repossessing.pdf

Cuthbert, J. (2013), 'The Mismanagement of Britain. A record of the UK's declining competitiveness – and its implications', Jimmy Reid Foundation, accessed at: www.allofusfirst.org/tasks/render/file/?fileID=8159A5A0-2A2A-40F4-90CC826176E7451D

Danson, M. (1991), 'The Scottish economy: the development of underdevelopment?', *Planning Outlook*, 34, 2, 89-95.

Danson, M., Helinska-Hughes, E. and Hughes, M. (2005), 'RDAs and benchmarking: learning from good practice when the model has broken', *Public Policy and Administration*, 20, 3, 4-22.

Danson, M., McAlpine, R., Spicker, P. and Sullivan, W. (2012), 'The case for universalism: an assessment of the evidence on the effectiveness and efficiency of the universal welfare state', *Common Weal*, accessed at: www.allofusfirst.org/library/the-case-for-universalism/

Danson, M. and Todeva, E. (2016), 'Government and Governance of Regional Triple Helix Interactions', *Industry and Higher Education*, 30, 1, pp. 13 – 26.

Davidson, N., Virdee, S., Morrison, J. and Mooney, G. (2016), 'Scotland and alternatives to neoliberalism', *Soundings*, 63, pp. 55-72.

Dow, S. (1997), 'Scottish devolution and the financial sector', in Danson, M., Hill, S. and Lloyd, G. (eds.), *Regional Governance and Economic Development*. European Research in Regional Science, 7, London: Pion, pp. 229-241.

Elliott, L. and Atkinson, D. (2012), *Going South: Why Britain will have a Third World Economy by 2014*, Basingstoke: Palgrave Macmillan.

Fair Work Convention (2016) *Fair Work Framework*, accessed at: www.fairworkconvention.scot/framework/FairWorkConventionFrameworkFull.pdf

Felstead, A. and Green, F. (2013), 'Underutilization, overqualification and skills mismatch: patterns and trends', Project Report. Skills Development Scotland. Available at: https://www.skillsdevelopmentscotland.co.uk/media/811162/underutilization__overqualification_and_skills_mismatch_patterns_and_trends.pdf

Findlay, J., Thomas, D. and Roy, G. (2017), 'Scottish ferry services' procurement, post-Brexit: challenge or opportunity?', *Fraser of Allander Economic Commentary*, 41, 1, 71-81.

Galloway, L. and Danson, M. (2016), 'In-work poverty and enterprise: self-employment and business ownership as contexts of poverty', Edinburgh: Heriot-Watt University.

Keep, E. (2014), 'Reflections on the Working Together review', blog, accessed at: www.centreonconstitutionalchange.ac.uk/blog/reflections-working-together-review

Leonard, R. (2012), 'Who owns Scotland? The realities of economic power', *Red Paper Collective*, accessed at: http://redpaper.net/2012/09/01/who-owns-scotland-the-realities-of-economic-power/

McFarlane, L. (2016), 'Blueprint for a Scottish National Investment Bank', *Common Weal*, accessed at: www.allofusfirst.org/library/blueprint-for-a-scottish-national-investment-bank-2016/

O'Leary, E. (2015), *Irish Economic Development: Serial Under-Achievement or High-Performing EU State*. London: Routledge Studies in Modern World Economy.

ONS (Office for National Statistics) (2017), 'Regional firm-level productivity analysis for the non-financial business economy: Jan 2017, accessed as www.ons.gov.uk/employmentandlabourmarket/peopleinwork/labourproductivity/articles/regionalfirmlevelproductivityanalysisforthenonfinancialbusinesseconomy/jan2017.

Scott, J. and Hughes, M. (1975), `Finance capital and the upper class' in G. Brown (ed.) *The Rod Paper on Scotland*, Edinburgh: Edinburgh University Student Publications Board.

Scottish Government (2015), *Scotland's Economic Strategy*, accessed at: https://beta.gov.scot/publications/scotlands-economic-strategy/

Scottish Government (2014), *Working Together Review: Progressive Workplace Policies in Scotland*, independent report chaired by J. Mather, accessed at: www.gov.scot/Publications/2014/08/4647

Spicker, P. (2016), 'What can the Scottish Parliament do with new social security powers?, *Common Weal*, accessed at: www.allofusfirst.org/library/what-can-the-scottish-parliament-do-with-new-social-security-powers/

Wikipedia (2017), 'List of countries by GDP (PPP) per capita' [verified and based on IMF, World Bank and CIA databases], accessed at: https://en.wikipedia.org/wiki/List_of_countries_by_GDP_(PPP)_per_capita

Wilson, D. (2016), 'The challenge of inclusive growth for the Scottish economy', IPPI Occasional Paper, University of Strathclyde, accessed at: http://strathprints.strath.ac.uk/56699/1/Wilson_IPPI_2016_the_challenge_of_inclusive_growth_for_the_scottish_economy.pdf

Section Two: A Social Justice Scotland for All?

A Fairer and More Socially Just Scotland?

Kirstein Rummery

'Social justice and fairness are the hallmarks of Scottish society.' – Donald Dewar, First Minister at the first session of the Scottish Parliament, May 1999.

'An independent Scotland could be a beacon of progressive opinion – addressing policy challenges in ways which reflect the universal values of fairness.' – Alex Salmond, First Minister, addressing Scottish Parliament, January 2012.

A Narrative of Social Justice and Fairness

SCOTLAND HAS LONG laid claim for a different national identity to the rest of the UK, and that its society is inherently based on notions of fairness, social justice, and egalitarianism. The rhetoric of social justice holds a particularly powerful sway in the way Scotland perceives its approach to social policy. The quotes above show that this perception crosses party lines and is a powerful rhetoric when making arguments for Scotland-centred social policy development: whether that is for devolution, increased policy capacity, or full independence. The political map of Scotland looks very different from the 1999 Parliament: the Labour party suffered its biggest historical electoral defeat in Scotland in 2011 (mirrored later in the general election of 2015) where it lost substantial support to the SNP. Contemporary Scottish citizens appear to politically support a party at both Holyrood and Westminster that favours maximum control over Scottish social policy to rest with the Scottish Parliament.

Prior to the 1999 devolution settlement, Scotland already had a different legal and education system incumbent since the Act of Union in 1707, with the result that criminal and education policy were already significantly different from the rest of the UK. The Scotland Act 1998 devolved to the Scottish Parliament all legislative powers not reserved to Westminster, meaning that these social policy powers were exercised by a legislature elected by, and accountable to, the Scottish electorate rather than the whole of the UK. Indeed, the Scottish Parliament has been argued to be largely a social policy making body. However, from an early stage, the Scottish Parliament opened itself up to working in co-operation with civic society and allowed relatively easy access for interest groups to policy.

This opening up of policy spaces reflects the fact that until the SNP won an overall majority in 2011, the Scottish Parliament has been ruled by coalition or minority governments. This meant that in order to push through social policies, Ministers usually had to gain cross-party consensus, and apart from the SNP which had little Westminster focus for its policy platform, the Labour, Conservative and Liberal Democrat parties in Scotland had no particular incentive to deviate substantially from the policy platform held by their Westminster counterparts. Moreover, the general population is not always fully aware of the extent of social policy power held at Holyrood versus Westminster (or at local authority level) and so electoral campaigns on specific social policy issues tend to have little effect if that policy issue is not one already associated in the public's mind with a particular political party.

This led to a certain degree of path dependency on the part of some of the main political parties, with the result that their social policies did not deviate significantly from the rest of the UK. Conversely, where there was pressure from grassroots campaigners, civic society and the third sector to develop policies that did deviate from the UK norm, a majority government is under less pressure to cater to non-political pressure because it has the power to push through social policies without working in co-operation. Nevertheless there has been some acknowledgement on the part of the Scottish Government that many of the issues Scotland faces are 'wicked issues' in social policy terms – complex, multi-faceted, and outside the scope of any one agency to tackle on its own.

Partnership and co-production are in some ways easier in the Scottish context because of scale. In tone if not in substance there are numerous spaces for different voices to be heard in the policy process, and this gives rise to some scope for policy deviation and experimentation.

A Fairer Approach to Housing?

Prior to devolution, Scotland had already begun to deviate in some substantial ways in its housing policy from the rest of the UK: for example, by continuing to invest in social housing at a time when policy priorities elsewhere were supporting owner-occupation and the development of a private rented sector. Although the 1980s Right to Buy policy extended to Scotland, favourable terms for Registered Social Landlords meant that access to social housing did not decline as significantly as in the rest of the UK and most social landlords in Scotland are small community organisations governed by residents. This means that one in four Scots currently live in social housing, and in some cities like Glasgow this rises to 40 %. Moreover in 2010 the SNP Government introduced the Housing (Scotland) Act which effectively ended the Right to Buy.

The tenant involvement in the governance of housing associations provides an accessible and legitimated route to citizen engagement in social policy development for members of the community who would otherwise be fairly inaccessible to statutory planning. So, for example, housing associations regularly send representatives to Community Safety Partnerships to plan the development of policing and other services, and are often involved in planning community care services with local authorities, particularly if they have a high number of older and disabled tenants. This is helped by the fact that unlike in the rest of the UK, both local authority and housing association tenants have a single secure tenancy under the Housing (Scotland) Act 2001, and a single regulatory framework under the Housing (Scotland) Act 2010, which provides security of tenure and monitoring of housing quality across the whole of Scotland.

In addition to an investment in social housing that is at odds with the rest of the UK, Scottish citizens also benefit from homelessness social policies which are arguably more progressive than the rest of the UK. Although the Housing (Homeless Persons) Act 1977 applied in Scotland prior to devolution, this focussed on 'priority need' – i.e. offering accommodation only to those who were considered to be vulnerable, rather than a universal provision. This had the result of making social housing the norm for low income, vulnerable households rather than for a mix of social classes. One of the first acts of the 1999 Scottish Government was the creation of a Homelessness Task Force which included representation from social landlords, the third sector and the public as well as local and national statutory bodies. It recommended the abolition of priority need with the eventual aim of providing universal access to social housing. In addition the Housing Act (Scotland) 2001 gave a legal duty to Registered Social Landlords to comply with local authority requests to house unintentionally homeless people, indicating that the Scottish Government was willing to create tensions with powerful vested interests in order to achieve social policy objectives.

Perhaps the most radical social policy development to deviate from the rest of the UK is the commitment, under the Housing (Scotland) Act 2003, to end homelessness by a specified date (2012). This has been heralded internationally as one of the most progressive housing policies in Europe and added additional obligations to the Housing (Scotland) 2001 Act to provide temporary accommodation to all homeless people waiting for permanent accommodation – including the 'intentionally' homeless. However, the target has not quite been met due in no small part to a failure to invest in building new social housing to meet demand, creating tensions between the Scottish Government, local authorities and registered social landlords.

However, this commitment to ending homelessness is not a commitment to universal access to affordable housing – and it has been asserted that unlike other universal services like the NHS and education, housing policy in Scotland has had the effect of widening inequalities between higher income owner occupiers who have an investment in a capital asset and social housing tenants who don't. Moreover, in the absence of long-term care insurance in Scotland, housing remains the primary asset that is used to contribute to the costs of social care in later life, which further exacerbates inequalities accumulated over the life course. Despite a rhetorical commitment to universal tenancy, in reality the concentration of social housing on the poorest and most vulnerable means that poverty and deprivation have a geographical concentration of disadvantage.

Over a third of households in the social rented sector are unemployed, and nearly 17 % are retired, and over two-thirds rely on housing benefit. This concentration of deprivation also leads to concentrations in social problems such as crime, drug and alcohol abuse and anti-social behaviour, making it difficult for tenants to protect their communities and creating tensions between landlords, long-term and vulnerable tenants, with racist, sectarian and disablist hate crimes particularly prevalent in deprived areas. Unlike during the 1970s and 1980s where social rented housing was the norm across different social groups, the focus on maintaining it for the most vulnerable has stigmatised and removed social cohesion. Moreover, key policy levers that could be used to address these issues, such as housing benefit, tax credits and social security, lie outside the scope of the Scottish Government to address.

The housing budget has never been a protected area like health and education, and there never has been a full-scale commitment to universal social or affordable housing from the Scottish Government. Social policies designed to achieve a mix of housing within the same community to support social cohesion have been piecemeal at best, with limited obligations on new build housing developments to provide a mix of rented and owner occupied housing. Some effort has been made to improve access to low-cost home ownership trough shared equity schemes, which are cheaper for the public purse than social housing and do provide access to capital assets for low-income groups (McKee, 2010).

However this focus in a time of economic hardship and austerity policies that, no matter how unpopular they are in Scotland do restrict significant parts of public investment, is a significant issue in social policy. The need for social housing, particularly amongst growing numbers of older, disabled and low income people, is going to grow, not decline. Moreover, older and unemployed people (including significant numbers of disabled people) are excluded from owner-occupation and the opportunity to accumulate capital assets. A social policy that is both a significant departure from the rest of the UK and focused on being fairer is, arguably, widening social divisions and inequality in Scotland.

A Fairer, More Caring Approach to Social Care

In contrast to health policy, Scotland's distinctiveness and claim to fairness in social care is based on the idea that that the foundation of social services in Scotland under the 1968 Social Work (Scotland) Act created a framework and a set of principles to drive social work to tackle disadvantage and inequality. This is often argued to demonstrate a substantial policy divergence from the rest of the UK which has seen a move towards marketisation, resource capping and new public managerialism in social work services, leaving disabled people increasingly at the mercy of service cutbacks and welfare sanctions. However, this has arguably been a difference more rhetorical than substantive. The 1968 Act gave local authorities the power to make cash payments to tackle poverty and deprivation, which was illegal in England and Wales. Nevertheless, the development of direct payments (whereby disabled people were given cash to manage their own support in lieu of directly provided care services) was a policy development that was instigated in England (where it was technically illegal and had to be done via third party trusts) and not in Scotland (where it was actively resisted, particularly by the unions).

Scottish Self Directed Support is the latest in a series of policies including the Community Care and Health (Scotland) Act 2003, which placed a duty on Local Authorities to offer Direct Payments in lieu of standard community care services. The Local Authority made the payment to the individual (or representative) to arrange the services they were assessed as needing, which for some users improved the choice and control they could exercise over their services. Scottish Local Authorities (in line with English and Welsh Local Authorities) have a duty to offer eligible people Direct Payments. From April 2005 the first nondisabled user groups became eligible: parents of disabled children and older people (aged 65 and over) who have been assessed as needing care services due to infirmity or age. Under the 2013 Act all Scottish Local Authorities would have to offer service users the option of directing their own support, which can take various forms including Direct Payments. Users will still need to undergo an assessment to see if they have needs which services could meet.

Take-up, at both institutional and individual level, has varied considerably across the UK: rates of take-up in England are more than double that of elsewhere in the UK, with some single Local Authorities (e.g. Hampshire) having more users registered than the whole of Scotland. According to Scottish Government figures rates of take-up of Direct Payments are still far higher in England than in Scotland. Some of the barriers to the take-up of Direct Payments included lack of awareness from front-line workers and managers, and the need to invest in advocacy and support organisations to help users manage their payments, as well as concerns expressed about the risks involved for vulnerable users and a resistance to the perceived 'privatisation' of social care.

A closer analysis of areas where there has been a significant uptake of Direct Payments reveals that these areas show a history of strong disability-led user organisations (and a history of quasi-legal Direct Payments, for example through third party trusts), and/or a political commitment to the development of markets in social care provision. The twin impetus of strong user demand and a policy move towards mixed markets in social care which have driven the development of Direct Payments and related schemes (such as individual budgets) appears to be less prevalent in Scotland, although according to Scottish Government figures there has been a reduction in home care directly provided by Local Authorities from 82 % in 2000 to 44 % in 2011 and Scottish users of Direct Payments report similar improved outcomes to users elsewhere in the UK.

However, institutional barriers to implementation of Direct Payments in Scotland remained embedded and difficult to tackle, including an ideological resistance to 'privatisation' in social care) and a lack of commitment from senior managers, lack of awareness and training on the part of front-line care managers, and perceived budgetary inflexibilities. In order to inform the development of Self Directed Support, the Scottish Government established three test sites to assess the impact of three interventions (bridging finance, cutting red tape and leadership and training).

These lessons had already been learned 20 years earlier in the English context, but the lessons did not transfer to the Scottish context. Nevertheless, according to Scottish Government figures uptake of Self Directed Support in the form of Direct Payments has increased in Scotland from 207 users in 2001 to 4,392 in 2011, and the total value of DPs has increased from £2.1 million in 2001 to £50.2 million in 2011. The sharpest increase nationally has been in recent years, with 29 % of DP packages ongoing in March 2011 being in place for less than a year. Under the Self-Directed Support (Scotland) Act 2012, service users still need to undergo a community care assessment to see if they have eligible needs. However, take-up of direct payments in England was reliant on user-led organisations (such as Centres for Independent Living) and user-advo-cacy organisations such as In Control supporting disabled people to run their own schemes, and offer peer mentoring and support to navigate the complexity of social care. In Scotland there are only two Centres of Independent Living, and they both rely on government funds for their core funding and are thus in a dif-ficult position to provide independent, peer-led support. There are no plans to allow user-led organisations to undertake the assessments for community care services or for self-directed support, nor for them to administer and run direct payments schemes directly themselves.

Therefore, despite a rhetoric of 'co-production', user empowerment and social justice, social work in Scotland has resisted the development of user-di-rected services until relatively recently: and under self-directed support it has retained the option of local authorities managing services on disabled people's behalf, rather than universally rolling out direct user control of resources. In spite of the apparent freedom to diverge both the norms of policy and their practice, Scottish social services have not developed in a substantially different way to the rest of the UK. Local authorities have the responsibility for providing social care services, which means that, just as in the rest of the UK, there are different service levels, eligibility and access arrangements: 32 different local authorities means 32 different sets of social care services, including variations in costs for service users.

Moreover, council tax freezes have placed constraints on local authori-ties' ability to meet the growing demand for social care services from an age-ing population. In addition, joint working between health and social care for adults has not developed in a seamless fashion, which means that disabled peo-ple have been at the mercy of gaps and overlaps in services. Scotland, probably for political rather than policy reasons, has chosen to ring-fence health spend-ing rather than redirect funding to anti-poverty and preventative programmes that would improve health inequalities, particularly amongst poorer disabled people. As outline above, self-directed support policy has facilitated the devel-opment of user-controlled services, but these do not differ substantially to systems developed in England and Wales. There is substantial marketisation, third sector and not-for-profit sector involvement in the provision of social care services in line with patterns established in the rest of the UK and adopted by Scotland.

So the argument that Scotland has not developed a better social policies for disabled people due to it not having control over the full range of spending and welfare policies is not a credible one when the lack of radical policy reform in social care policy to date is examined. The failure to apply policy lessons that lead to improved outcomes for social care users from England effectively, and the failure of Scottish civic society to develop a strong user-led movement that is willing and able to engage constructively in challenging incumbent governments to develop improved social policies means that Scotland, to date, has not shown much persuasive evidence of a more inclusive approach to social policy for disabled people.

Scotland's School Education

James McEnaney

Introduction

SCOTTISH EDUCATION HAS always been one of the main pillars of how Scotland has seen and perceived itself and, along with the law and Kirk, has asserted its difference and autonomy from the rest of the UK.

There have been numerous powerful myths and stories associated with education: from the oft-repeated line through the ages that it was 'the best in the world' to the meritocratic tales of 'the Kirriemuir career' and 'lad o'pairts', and the frequently celebrated notion of 'the democratic intellect'. These point to an education system that has championed its universalism and egalitarianism on the one hand, but also its traditional nurturing of talent and elitism.

Devolution was always going to bring change to the world of school education, a process that has not changed under the SNP. Over the last decade, however, Scottish schooling has been defined by one thing above all else: the troubled introduction of the Curriculum for Excellence (CfE).

A Case Study: The Experience of the Curriculum for Excellence

Though regularly misrepresented as an SNP policy, Curriculum for Excellence (CfE) actually emerged as the culmination of around ten years of development, starting with the 'National Debate on Education' in 2002 and continued by the work of the Curriculum Review Group (2003-2004). This new model for Scottish education replaced the previous ages 5-14 system while also incorporating both Early Years (ages 3-5) and the Senior Phase (ages 15-18), thus creating a new 3-18 syllabus. It was officially implemented in August 2010 'when the pupils who would be the first to sit the new exams in 2014 started secondary school' (Scottish Parliament Information Centre, 2013).

That the key implementation date for CfE is now calculated based on its relationship to secondary school exams, rather than the embedding of new principles and practices across schools, highlights the muddled thinking that undermined the new curriculum from the beginning. Primary schools had been working within CfE for several years by 2010, but, in a sign of the myopia that continues to restrict Scottish education (even in the midst of what was supposed to be a revolutionary, 21st century update) it was only when this process of reform could be attached to qualifications that it was regarded as being 'real'.

This represents a profound misunderstanding of what CfE is (or, perhaps more accurately, what it was *supposed* to be). CfE is in fact best understood through two aspects which are both complementary and conflicting: the ideas underpinning it (the Four Capacities and Seven Principles) and the framework for how the overall goals should be pursued (the Experiences and Outcomes).

The Four Capacities describe the type of person we want a student to become – *confident individuals, successful learners, responsible citizens* and *effective contributors* – as distinct from a list of things we expect them to know. A series of attributes and capabilities are collected under each of the capacities, outlining the sort of behaviour that we seek to foster as young people develop.

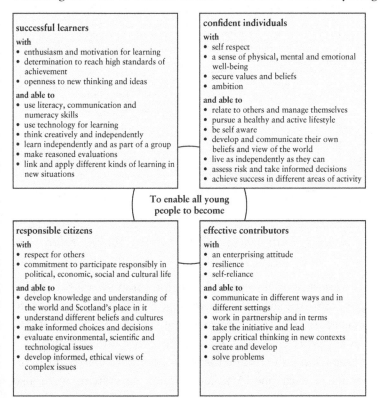

successful learners

with
- enthusiasm and motivation for learning
- determination to reach high standards of achievement
- openness to new thinking and ideas

and able to
- use literacy, communication and numeracy skills
- use technology for learning
- think creatively and independently
- learn independently and as part of a group
- make reasoned evaluations
- link and apply different kinds of learning in new situations

confident individuals

with
- self respect
- a sense of physical, mental and emotional well-being
- secure values and beliefs
- ambition

and able to
- relate to others and manage themselves
- pursue a healthy and active lifestyle
- be self aware
- develop and communicate their own beliefs and view of the world
- live as independently as they can
- assess risk and take informed decisions
- achieve success in different areas of activity

To enable all young people to become

responsible citizens

with
- respect for others
- commitment to participate responsibly in political, economic, social and cultural life

and able to
- develop knowledge and understanding of the world and Scotland's place in it
- understand different beliefs and cultures
- make informed choices and decisions
- evaluate environmental, scientific and technological issues
- develop informed, ethical views of complex issues

effective contributors

with
- an enterprising attitude
- resilience
- self-reliance

and able to
- communicate in different ways and in different settings
- work in partnership and in terms
- take the initiative and lead
- apply critical thinking in new contexts
- create and develop
- solve problems

The Four Capacities. Source: The Curriculum Review Group, 2004

The Four Capacities are complemented by the 'Principles for Curriculum Design', which frame young people's learning within the categories of challenge and enjoyment, breadth, progression, depth, personalisation and choice, coherence, and relevance. Though this aspect of Scottish education has received much criticism for its perceived imprecision, the idea of founding a school curriculum on these sorts of 'key competencies' is in fact part of 'a wider global trend, evident in many modern national curricula' (Priestley and Minty, 2013).

In contrast to those overarching concepts, the Experiences and Outcomes – which were developed separately – are essentially an attempt to map a child's education up to the end of S3 through a progressive series of 'I can…' statements. These were grouped within broad curricular areas, though some – literacy, numeracy and health and well-being – are regarded as the 'responsibility of all'.

This maintained the general approach of the discarded 5-14 curriculum but with guidelines that, paradoxically, were both less specific (in terms of the learning 'outcomes' that should be achieved) and more prescriptive (by outlining the sort of pupil 'experience' that would be seen) (Priestley and Minty, 2013).

Writing (continued)				
	Early	First	Second	Third	Fourth
Organising and using Information – considering texts to help create short and extended texts for different purposes		I am learning to use my notes and other types of writing to help me understand information and ideas, explore problems, generate and develop ideas or create new text. LIT 1-25a	I can use my notes and other types of writing to help me understand information and ideas, explore problems make decisions, generate and develop ideas or create new text. I recognise the need to acknowledge my sources and can do this appropriately. LIT 2-25a	I can use notes and other types of writing to generate and develop ideas, retain and recall information, explore problems, make decisions, generate and develop ideas or create original text. I recognise when it is appropriate to quote from sources and when I should put points into my own words. I can acknowledge my sources appropriately. LIT 3-25a	I can use notes and other types of writing to generate and develop ideas, retain and recall information, explore problems, make decisions, or create original text. I can make appropriate and responsible use of sources and acknowledge these appropriately. LIT 4-25a
	within real and imaginary situations. I share experiences and feelings, ideas and information in a way that communicates my message. LIT 0-26a	By considering the type of text I am creating, I can select ideas and relevant information, organise these in a logical sequence and use words which will be interesting and/or useful for others. LIT 1-26a	By considering the type of text I am creating, I can select ideas and relevant information, organise these in an appropriate way for my purpose and use suitable vocabulary for my audience. LIT 2-26a	By considering the type of text I am creating, I can independently select ideas and relevant information for different purpose, and organise essential information or ideas and any supporting details in a logical order. I can use suitable vocabulary to communicate effectively with my audience. LIT 3-26a/LIT 4-26a	

One of six pages of 'writing' Experiences and Outcomes. Source: Education. gov.scot

Though the Es & Os were supposed to provide a helpful framework for pupils' learning they quickly became the shackles of a stifling, 'box-ticking' approach to schooling, with teachers forced to spend more and more time proving that students had engaged in an 'experience' and achieved a corresponding 'outcome'. Teachers spent time 'unpacking' the Es and Os in an attempt to clarify the actual, specific requirements of each one. A range of auditing systems were also developed to allow teachers to 'evidence' their engagement with each of the Es & Os relevant to their specific role.

In contrast to the original, noble ambitions, many came to see CfE as little more than the absurd bureaucracy that grew up around it. This problem could be addressed through the simplification of CfE documentation and, arguably, the abolition of the Experiences and Outcomes (Priestley, 2016) – unfortunately there seems little prospect of real progress in this area.

As previously noted, the introduction of Curriculum for Excellence also resulted in new secondary school qualifications – Standard Grade and Intermediate qualifications were replaced by new Nationals and major changes were made to the Higher and Advanced Higher specifications. The process of aligning Senior Phase qualifications with CfE principles and standards was only completed in 2016 – when Advanced Higher courses were finally migrated to the new system – but is already being revised through significant adjustments to internal and national assessment arrangements for the National 5, Higher and Advanced Higher as courses.

Changes brought about by CfE have, therefore, been hugely complex, with the inter-connected pressures and problems not well represented in national discourse. Criticism of CfE is often reductive or politically motivated – and often both.

What has never been properly understood by politicians, bureaucrats, the media or the broader public is that the entire ethos of Curriculum for Excellence makes far greater demands of teachers than the system it replaced. Where they had previously administered centrally-produced assessments, this new approach allowed, and expected, teachers to create whole suites of ongoing assessment material, much of it embedded into the day-to-day learning taking place in their classes. Classroom teachers were to do more than simply *deliver* a curriculum, they were also to *design* it. This point was reinforced by the production of a series of 'Building the Curriculum' documents which, over 316 pages, provided 'advice, guidance and policy for different aspects of Curriculum for Excellence' (Education.gov.scot, n.d.).

The entire project was hugely ambitious and hinged on two principles: that teachers are experts who should be trusted to operate as the skilled professionals that they are, and that they would be given sufficient time, space and support to do their jobs properly. Instead, recent years have seen an increasing emphasis on accountability measures (and the inescapable bureaucracy that comes with them) that were adopted at least partly in response to significant failures in both the design and introduction of CfE. This process resulted in the nation's teachers facing unsustainable workload pressures which, combined with the social and professional implications of a decade of austerity policies, have inevitably impacted upon their ability to provide the sort of education that they want to deliver for our children.

Early recommendations such as a de-cluttered primary curriculum and a restructuring of the first years of secondary have never been delivered (The Curriculum Review Group, 2004). Teachers have never had the freedom promised to them, nor the time and resources to make a system like CfE work. Although Scottish schooling has spent the last decade dominated by CfE, the truth is that it has never truly been realised – instead we have been 'trying to shoehorn an exciting new curriculum into a set of structures unable or unwilling to accept it' (Pieper, 2017).

Fifteen years on from 'the National Debate on Education', and seven years on from the point at which it was allegedly implemented, there are in fact two versions of CfE: the one that was promised and the one that we have ended up with.

Education in Hard Times

All of these issues have been exacerbated by one key problem: there are now around 4000 fewer teachers in Scottish schools than there were when the SNP came to power (dropping from 55100 in 2007 to 50970 now). To place that number in its proper context, it is the equivalent of the total teaching staff in Argyll and Bute, Clackmannanshire, Na h-Eileanan Siar, Inverclyde, Moray, Orkney and Shetland combined. In fact, the only council area to employ more teachers than the total number lost since 2007 is, unsurprisingly, Glasgow; even population centres like North Lanarkshire, Fife and Edinburgh fall several hundred short (Scottish Government, 2016). In addition to the loss of teaching staff, schools have also had to contend with a 10 % drop in support staff between 2010 and 2015 (Seith, 2016).

Though it is true that pound for pound, quality of teaching is of greater importance, than quantity of teachers, there is no question that our school system is struggling to cope with staggering cuts to staffing levels, which are a factor not just in larger class sizes, but also in the need for multi-level teaching, an increased administrative burden on teachers, reduced access to Continuing Professional Development (CPD) activities, inadequate support for pupils with Additional Support Needs, and a lack of cover when teachers are absent,.

Add to this the associated social consequences of austerity economics, which have done huge damage to the lives of thousands of young people, and the result is frustrated teachers desperate to do the very best for their students, angry at seeing that dedication and professionalism taken advantage of.

The replacement of the thousands of lost teachers and associated support staff should therefore be made a priority over the coming years. Though a subsequent reduction in class sizes would be welcome, the government should also give serious consideration to a reduction in teachers' class contact time. Though this often seems counter-intuitive to those outside education – who instinctively think that 'teachers should be teaching' – it is worth remembering that Scottish teachers spend more time in front of their classes than almost any other OECD country (OECD, 2016). Giving teachers more time to prepare material, mark students' work, engage with research, collaborate with colleagues not only improves the quality of education being delivered, it also makes teaching a more attractive profession.

The government should also abandon plans to reintroduce a system of national standardised testing, which was announced in 2015 by Nicola Sturgeon in response to apparently falling standards and political pressure from both the Conservatives and Labour. The First Minister continues to claim that such a system, recently tendered to the same company which previously ran the international PISA tests, is vital to help close the 'attainment gap' between rich and poor pupils, but little – if any – evidence has been provided to support this assertion.

The Scottish Government has been forced to defend the lack of written advice (which amounted to just four unsolicited emails and a series of un-minuted meetings) and rising costs (up 50 % and now standing at around £3 million per year) associated with the standardised testing plans, and has also faced criticism over the now-inevitable return of school league tables. The day after they were announced, the proposals were branded as 'at best a disappointment and at worst a retrograde step which will simply serve to worsen the problem' (Boyd, 2015). In his first speech to the EIS conference as Education Secretary, John Swinney was loudly heckled when he insisted that standardised testing is needed. Nationwide testing of children as young as four years old is nonetheless due to be introduced from August 2017.

Swinney – appointed Education Secretary in May 2016 – has also engaged in a wide-ranging review of the way in which school education is organised in Scotland. The plans – which involve removing education powers from councils and transferring them either to schools themselves or to new, as yet undefined, 'education regions' – have been widely criticised. As yet the government has entirely failed to make the case for its proposals but as with standardised testing (and other areas of government policy) the SNP remains determined to push through this unnecessary and distracting policy change.

Genuine (and worthwhile) educational reform – as opposed to stasis and the status quo or imposition by misguided ministerial diktat – is possible, but only if politicians can learn to accept that change should not be driven either by their prejudices or their political needs. Short-term thinking and the ongoing weaponisation of schooling by Scotland's political parties does a terrible disservice to our young people, many of whom are already struggling through a system which, in so many ways, still advantages the most affluent at the expense of the most vulnerable. Change for the sake of change – or for the sake of headlines – will do nothing to address this.

That said, if the government is truly interested in a major structural reform of Scottish education, then there is one standout candidate: the establishment of a state-funded, universal kindergarten system for children from the ages of three to six or seven, and a corresponding focus on the critical importance Early Years learning. In recent years a new campaign for such a change – Upstart Scotland – has attracted both interest and support. Not only would this genuinely radical reform bring Scotland's school starting-age into line with the vast majority of countries around the world, it just might allow us to do the very thing we have been trying to do for the last decade: begin the process of delivering a truly excellent 3-18 curriculum.

References

Brian, B. (2015), 'Programme for Government: Analysis from Education Perspective', *CommonSpace*, available at: www.commonspace.scot/articles/2323/programme-for-government-analysis-from-education-perspective

Curriculum Review Group (2004), *A Curriculum for Excellence*, Edinburgh: Scottish Executive.

Education.gov.scot (n.d.), 'Building the Curriculum', available at: www.education.gov.scot/scottish-education-system/policy-for-scottish-education/policy-drivers/cfe-(building-from-the-statement-appendix-incl-btc1-5)/Building the Curriculum

Education.gov.scot (n.d.), 'Experiences and outcomes', available at: https://education.gov.scot/scottish-education-system/policy-for-scottish-education/policy-drivers/cfe-(building-from-the-statement-appendix-incl-btc1-5)/Experiences and outcomes

OECD, (2016), *Education at a Glance 2016: OECD Indicators*, Paris: OECD Publishing, available at: http://www.oecd-ilibrary.org/docserver/download/961604 1e.pdf?expires=1490691787&id=id&accname=guest&checksum=88F73177F91CB8EE608056FC7B7232A2

Pieper, K. (2017), 'Clever(ish) Lands', *Just Trying to be Better Than Yesterday*, available at: https://justtryingtobebetter.wordpress.com/2017/03/21/cleverish-lands/

Priestley, M. (2016), 'CfE post-OECD: Time for a simplified curriculum', *Holyrood.com,* available at: https://www.holyrood.com/articles/comment/cfe-post-oecd-time-simplified-curriculum

Priestley, M. and Minty, S. (2013), 'Curriculum for Excellence: 'A brilliant idea, but...', *Scottish Educational Review*, 45(1), pp. 39-52, available at: www.scotedreview.org.uk/media/scottish-educational-review/articles/355.pdf

Scottish Government (2016), *Summary statistics for schools in Scotland*, Edinburgh: Scottish Government.

Scottish Parliament Information Centre (SPICe) (2013), *SPICe Briefing: Curriculum for Excellence*, Edinburgh: Scottish Parliament.

Seith, E. (2016), 'Teacher workload to rise as support staff axed', *Times Educational Supplement Scotland*, available at: www.tes.com/news/school-news/breaking-news/teacher-workload-rise-support-staff-axed

Upstart Scotland (n.d.). *Upstart Scotland*, available at: www.upstart.scot/

The Early Years Agenda

Suzanne Zeedyk

THE LAST TEN years have been significant not only for the SNP in Scotland, but for the field of early years. This decade has seen considerable attention given by scientists and policymakers to the need for young children to have high quality experiences of care, learning and play. Scotland has joined in that international discussion but policies are still failing to take sufficient account of the scientific evidence now available. In this chapter, I will briefly summarise the evidence on the importance of the early years and then evaluate two relevant policy areas introduced by the SNP.

The Science

Human brains develop more quickly during the first three years of life than they ever will again. The experiences that children have during these formative years have a biological impact, shaping brains and bodies in ways that hold lifelong consequences. Scientists have had a growing understanding of these developmental processes for the last several decades, but it is only during the past ten years that this knowledge has begun to make real headway in affecting policies and practice related to children. International organisations that have been particularly effective in disseminating this information include Zero to Three, Harvard Centre on the Developing Child, The Heckman Equation, and ACEs Too High.

There are at least two key insights to emerge from this work that have major implications for governmental policy and funding decisions. First, James Heckman's economic analyses show that the best financial returns are yielded by investing in services targeted at the first five years of life (Heckman, 2013). Rates of return are as high as 13 %, depending on which variables are assessed over which time periods: educational achievement, juvenile imprisonment, mental health, job performance, etc. That is, for every £1 invested during the early years, up to £13 is saved later on. However, various analyses (e.g. Scottish Government, 2010; WAVE Trust, 2013) suggest that public spending patterns have not accommodated this information. As with many other countries, Scotland still invests more of its education budget in the later years than in the early years of childhood. This means that Scotland continues to direct its finances toward coping with social problems, rather than preventing them.

A second major insight concerns the vital importance of relationships for young children. Born with immature brains and physiology, babies are dependent on familiar, consistent relationships in order to feel safe. Theories relating to attachment, self-regulation and emotional trauma explain this developmental process. When infants do not feel safe, they develop in a way that orients their physiology toward anxiety. This has massive impacts across the whole of their life, affecting mental health, physical health, the ability to learn, the ability to manage behaviour, and the ability to sustain fulfilling relationships. This is why it is so crucial that policy makers and practitioners fully grasp that relationships have a *biological* impact on children's development. It pushes us to take seriously unsettling observations, such as those by research scientist Darcia Narvaez (2014), who argues that 'nearly all daycare settings provide inadequate care for babies', and physician Gabor Mate (2010), who contends that 'emotional nurturance is disrupted by Western society'.

This summary of early years science, even in its brevity, leaves us well placed to reflect on policy directions established by the SNP Government. I will focus on two areas that have received considerable public attention: childcare and play.

It is worth emphasising these are but two of many SNP policy areas that fall within an early years remit, including midwifery, health visiting and the novel 'Early Years Collaborative'. Tellingly, such examples fall under the remit of health, and are thus funded through health budgets, rather than early years budgets. Such divisions are part of what restrains Scottish society in successfully tackling many of the societal challenges we face. A better understanding of early child development would enable us to think beyond the restrictions that stem from what are, ultimately, mere budgetary structures. To better serve families and children, we don't always need more money. What we need is to change the way we think.

Childcare Policy

One of the most preeminent policy directions being undertaken by the SNP Government, after ten years in power, is an expansion of government-funded childcare. At the SNP Conference in 2014, First Minister Nicola Sturgeon pledged a 'childcare revolution', describing childcare as 'one of our biggest infrastructure projects for the next Parliament' (BBC News, 2014). Terms like 'revolution' and 'infrastructure' signal a clear vision. By 2020, the Scottish Government will be funding 30 hours of childcare per week for all 3- and 4-year-olds, as well as 2-year-olds classed as 'vulnerable'. This allocation of 1140 hours per child per year constitutes an increase from the earlier allocation of 600 hours.

The relevance of information on attachment and brain development for the childcare sector is palpable. Childcare operates during the most critical period of human development, laying down physiological foundations that an individual will draw on for the rest of their life. If childcare is not of a sufficiently high quality, then it undermines healthy development and damages children's potential. Let me stress that last statement by repeating it: poor quality childcare damages children.

It takes courage and curiosity to contemplate the idea that government funded childcare could damage children. Yet this is not a radical claim to make. Young children have a biological need for emotional safety, and that can only be fulfilled by providing care that is grounded in familiar, stable relationships. We need to pay attention to the way that relationships in childcare settings become strained by high staff-child ratios, too much time spent recording evidence, erratic staff rotas, underpaid staff, and inattentive drop off and pick up routines. Although some children may cope with poorer quality childcare, it does not allow them to thrive. Young children must have emotionally attuned environments to thrive. Scotland, like all societies, wants its children to thrive, as articulated by Nicola Sturgeon in her 2014 SNP Conference speech, when she said she wanted comprehensive childcare that would 'give our young people the best start in life and a bridge to a better future' (BBC News, 2014).

That leaves us asking whether the SNP's childcare policies are sufficiently grounded in attachment theory and human biology. Arguably, they are not. Although relevant information and terminology is used in key policy documents, such as *Building the Ambition* (Education Scotland, 2016) and *Pre-birth to Three* (Education Scotland, 2016), the early years workforce is not yet sufficiently steeped in an understanding of child development. Childcare qualifications do not require robust training in attachment or self-regulation. Inspection criteria for settings do not require evidence of relation-led practice. Use of the term 'emotional trauma' is as yet rare within policy documents.

It is essential that these gaps are addressed if Scotland is to have the childcare provision it desires. As the expansion in government-funded hours rolls out, a greater number of children are likely to be enrolled in childcare, for longer periods of the day. If childcare is less than high quality, then it means government policy will have a damaging effect on an even larger proportion of our children. This impact can occur without anyone intending it or even being aware of it: policymakers, practitioners and parents included. In the coming years, Scotland will benefit from or suffer the consequences of the quality of provision that is implemented in 2020.

That leaves us with one final point to consider. Many commentators worry that the expansion of government-funded childcare is motivated by a wish to move parents into the workforce, rather than a wish to serve children's needs. For example, critics have queried why funding is being put only into professional childcare, instead of also making funding available for parents who wish to stay home with young children (Carnochan, 2015). Others such as the Scottish Childminding Association), Common Weal and the group Fair Funding For Our Kids have highlighted inequities across local authorities in terms of the types of government-funded childcare available to families. Even without realising it, these critics are challenging the neo-liberal values that lie at the heart of contemporary Anglo-America culture in which all human beings – parents, non-parents, children – are evaluated in terms of their value to the present or future economy (Jarvis, 2017). It is indeed possible that, rather than creating a childcare system that gives children the best start in life, the SNP are, unintentionally or otherwise, creating a childcare system that feeds the neo-liberal values currently undermining British society.

Play Policies

A second area of activity that reflects the Scottish Government's engagement with the early years agenda is their support for play. Initiatives funded include Play Talk Read, Go2Play, Play Scotland and the Play Strategy for Scotland.

Play is a vehicle for many aspects of development, a key one being the attachment system. When children are feeling safe, they are able to move further away from the adults who serve as their safe base, both physically and mentally. This risk-taking is fundamental to play. A child's ability to take risks – to move beyond the bounds of safety – is founded in being able to trust in the dependability of key adults in their life. Risk-taking remains central to all psychological growth throughout life: learning new skills, being creative, making relationships, leaving home, taking a new job. When we make the link between play, risk-taking and the attachment system, we comprehend that play shapes a child's physiology. Children's play is not frivolous; it is essential to their development.

However, Scottish culture arguably views play as frivolous. 'Learning', conceived as an academic activity, has more cultural value than 'play'. This can be seen in the now popular phrase 'learning through play', while the phrase 'playing for play's sake' sits at odds within Scottish culture. The title of the 'Play Talk Read Programme' also conveys this bias. If it were called the 'Play Talk Laugh Programme', it probably would not gain funding from the Scottish

Government or support from Scots voters, because it does not seem serious enough. The Bookbug programme, which does emphasise play and music and laughter between parents and children, is funded through the Scottish Book Trust – although probably not because of the laughter Bookbug generates, but because of the perceived path to literacy. In 21st century Scotland we feel relaxed with the idea that children's play offers a path to academic learning, but we do not yet recognise play and learning as equivalent. Play remains subservient to higher goals in our thinking.

Ironically, in drawing a boundary between play and learning, we end up undermining children's academic progress. A good example of this unintentional damage is the SNP Government's response to the Upstart Campaign. Launched in 2016, Upstart's vision is to alter traditional educational structures by introducing a kindergarten stage (Palmer, 2016). Rather than starting formal schooling at the age of 4-5 years, as is the case currently, Upstart argues that Scottish children should begin formal schooling at the age of seven. Until then, a play-based curriculum should be implemented, allowing children two to three more years of the kind of creative play that would support their physiological, physical, mental and emotional development.

The Upstart Campaign's arguments are correct. Their case is based in a wealth of evidence relating to children's development and to the strong academic achievements in countries such as Finland where children do begin formal schooling at age seven (Palmer, 2016). Yet, Upstart's efforts have, as yet, failed to influence the SNP Government's discussions about Scotland's struggling academic outcomes. This is surprising, given that the Government has explicitly staked its reputation on substantial improvement of educational outcomes (Financial Times, 2016). The Scottish Attainment Challenge, introduced in 2015 to reduce the attainment gap common in deprived areas (Marcus, 2016), does not appear to be based in an understanding of attachment, self-regulation or stress. The problem is that, unless efforts to close the attainment gap are based in an understanding of physiological development, then academic attainment policies can never be effective.

Throughout its time in government, the SNP Government has promoted laudable initiatives such as GIRFEC (Getting It Right For Every Child) and Curriculum for All. More recently, it has endorsed the catchphrases 'Best place in the world to grow up' and 'Best place in the world to learn'. Yet these policies are still not grounded in contemporary knowledge of child development. It would be possible to change this situation rapidly, because we have the knowledge and the specialists in Scotland to help us achieve widespread understanding. What it takes to make this shift is the curiosity and the will.

Future Opportunities

The early years agenda offers a message of hope, because it generates solutions to a wide range of societal challenges. Why then has it proven so challenging to implement the insights from the science? Perhaps it is because the early years agenda isn't just about our children. It is about our very humanity. The discoveries we are making about the human brain reveal the critical importance of relationships to our health and happiness. It is ideas about how we should relate to one another that lie at the heart of all human cultures. Perhaps we have found it so hard putting the science into practice because it makes us take such a close look at who we are and how we interact.

If we have the courage to look closely at who we are *now*, then we have a better chance of becoming the kind of country we *aspire* to be. The SNP Government was elected on a platform of equality and inclusiveness, and their message has been persuasive enough to keep them in power for a decade. Our population is only five million in number, and our young Parliament does not feel remote to its citizens. If Scotland cannot achieve the kind of reforms that evidence tells us will benefit our children's health and happiness, then what hope do larger countries have for reform? Scotland can be a beacon to the world in its early years policy. All it takes is the courage and the will.

References

BBC News (2014), 'SNP Conference: Sturgeon pledges child 'revolution', *BBC News Website*, 15 November 2014, accessed at: www.bbc.com/news/uk-scotland-scotland-politics-30068370

Carnochan, J. (2015), Quoted in: 'Paying mums and dads to look after their kids', *Daily Record*, 17 May 2015, accessed at: www.dailyrecord.co.uk/news/scottish-news/paying-mums-dads-look-after-5710576

Education Scotland (2016), *Building the Ambition: National Practice Guidance on Early Learning and Childcare,* accessed at: www.education.gov.scot/improvement/Pages/elc1buildingtheambition.aspx

Education Scotland (2016), *Pre-Birth to Three: Positive Outcomes for Scotland's Children and Families,* www.education.gov.scot/improvement/elc2prebirthtothree

Financial Times (2016), 'SNP focuses on education in reshuffle', *Financial Times,* 18 May 2016, via www.ft.com

Heckman, J. (2013), *Giving Kids A Fair Chance: A Strategy That Works,* Massachusetts Institute of Technology Publications.

Jarvis, P. (2017), 'All parents need our full support', *Early Years Educator*, April, 18 (12), 8.

Marcus, G. (2016), 'Closing the Attainment Gap: What can schools do?', *Spice Briefing* 16/68, accessed at: www.parliament.scot/ResearchBriefingsAndFactsheets

Mate, G. (2010), *In the Realm of Hungry Ghosts: Close Encounters with Addiction,* Knopf Publishers.

Narvaez, D. (2014), *Neurobiology and the Development of Human Morality: Evolution, Culture and Wisdom,* W. W. Norton & Co.

Palmer, S. (2016), *Upstart: The Case for Raising the School Starting Age and Providing What the Under-Sevens Really Need,* Floris Books.

Scottish Government (2010), *The Financial Impact of Early Years Interventions in Scotland,* accessed at: www.gov.scot/Topics/Research/by-topic/children-and-young-people/EarlyYears

WAVE Trust (2013), *The Economics of Early Years Investment,* WAVE Trust Publications, www.wavetrust.org/sites/default/files/reports/economics-appendix-from-age-of-opportunity_0.pdf

Higher Education: The Story So Far

Lucy Hunter Blackburn

THE HEADLINE STORY of higher education during the SNP's first decade in government has been one of growth. The entry rate of 18 year olds into university has risen, with the figures from the most disadvantaged areas growing fastest (UCAS, 2016). The total number of Scots applying and accepted into university is also up, even though the number of 18 years olds in the population has fallen (UCAS, 2016; UCAS, 2017). Scottish universities have increased their recruitment from the EU and the rest of the UK (UCAS, 2016). Total spending on student support via the Student Support Agency Scotland is up, in absolute terms and per head (SAAS, 2016). A Scottish Government press release on higher education without the phrase 'highest ever' or 'record number' has become a rarity. Meantime, the average final student debt reported for Scottish students remains lower than for the other UK nations (Denholm, 2016).

While this is a record the Scottish Government may feel very comfortable defending, critics can make some awkward points. The rate of increase in acceptances and in application and entry rates to university at 18, including among the most disadvantaged, has been at least as high in England (UCAS, 2016; UCAS, 2017), despite the substantial policy divergence. What is really at work here: local decisions or wider socio-economic trends? Despite rising entry rates, it is also the case that more school leavers are being turned down, because the supply of places funded by the Scottish Government has not risen as fast as demand. As a result, the 'acceptance rate' for 18 years olds fell sharply after 2009 and has yet to recover (a pattern not seen across the UK as a whole) (UCAS, 2016).

Applicants from other UK nations, whose places are no longer capped, are now more likely than Scots to receive an offer from a Scottish university, reversing the long-standing position which obtained up to the start of this decade (UCAS, 2016). Increased spending on student support has been achieved by a sharp rise in the use of student loans for living costs, accompanied by a substantial reduction in the use of targeted non-repayable student grants (Hunter Blackburn, 2016a). Free tuition does account for some of Scotland's lower average final debt, but so do the larger numbers here on shorter HNC/D courses, and the full effects of recent grant cuts have not yet worked their way through into the published figures (Hunter Blackburn, 2016a). Until England abolished national maintenance grants in 2016, Scotland was the only part of the UK where the poorest students took out a disproportionately large share of all student borrowing each year (Hunter Blackburn, 2016a).

Further, the budget of the Scottish Funding Council for universities has not kept up with all this expansion: at £1.014 billion, revenue funding for universities in 2017-18 will be almost £90 million lower in real terms than it was in 2007-08, and capital spending at £46 million is around half what it was a decade before, again in real terms (Scottish Executive, 2006; Scottish Government, 2016). This overlooks that universities are now able to earn extra income by charging higher fees to students from the rest of the UK: no official figure exists for the value of this, but it is likely to be approaching the amount needed to make up the real-term fall in revenue funding, compared to 2007-08. However, this still suggests that funding per student has fallen, before taking into account any cross-subsidy from overseas students. The decline dates largely from after 2014-15. Up to then, settlements were more generous, with government ministers prioritising meeting universities' concerns about a funding gap with England over other areas of spending, not least colleges, whose funding settlements were tougher.

The SNP and Free Tuition

The ideological centrepiece of the SNP's first ten years in government has been free tuition. On entering office, one of its first acts was to abolish the previous government's 'graduate endowment', relying on help (now long since unacknowledged) from the Liberal Democrats. There was, however, a period around 2010 when the commitment to free tuition briefly appeared to become more negotiable. NUS Scotland started to talk about the potential use of some student contribution to increase the total money available. A government consultation paper sought comments on the possibility, while repeating the government's opposition (Hunter Blackburn, 2016b). The commitment was only fully re-charged after the UK Government announced its plans to raise fees south of the border to £9,000. It was in response to this that Alex Salmond famously promised in the run-up to the 2011 Holyrood elections that 'the rocks will melt with the sun' before he would allow fees to be charged.

Even when whole-hearted, the commitment to free tuition has contained contradictions. In contrast to Scandinavia, it has only included part-timers at lower incomes, and excluded post-graduates. UK-domiciled border-crossers in either direction are exposed to the full force of the English system. The decision to allow Scottish universities to charge students from the rest of the UK some sort of fee had a logical basis in containing a cross-border flood. However, the decision to go straight to the new English level, rather than experiment with what was needed to control numbers, seemed to be done as much with an eye to potential extra income (Raffe, 2016) as managing flows. Scotland uniquely in the UK currently has no legal maximum fee, although Ministers have a reserve power to set one.

The contradiction within the government's attitude to fees, which were deemed an intolerable distortion of the spirit of higher education for Scottish and EU undergraduates, but an essential element of university finances from everyone else, has become clearer with time. Questioned by the Parliament's Public Audit Committee in February 2017, John Swinney repeatedly emphasised universities' income generating powers, of which fees are a substantial part, when defending a tight financial settlement for the coming year (Scottish Parliament, 2017). The Scottish Government has been keen to promote Scotland as a destination for international students, especially as Westminster's attitudes have become more inward. It's not just about the money, money, money. But it would be disingenuous for anyone to underplay how important that is. The tension between the desire to recruit more international students outside the free tuition policy and the strong pitch against a 'marketised' system was nowhere more apparent than in the White Paper on Scottish independence (Riddell, 2016a).

Some positions have shifted over time. After June 2016, the defence of the position of EU students became a central Scottish Government policy. But in 2011, considerable political and administrative energy was spent trying (unsuccessfully) to persuade the European Commission to allow some sort of charge to be applied to EU students coming to Scotland (BBC News, 2011). In 2007, the SNP's successful electoral strategy included a high-profile campaign targeted on students to 'Dump the Debt', promising to abolish outstanding debt and replacing loans with grants: any criticism of the realism of this was vigorously rebutted (Hunter Blackburn, 2016b). By 2017, total annual lending to students had more than doubled, no pre-existing debt had been abolished, and means-tested maintenance grants had become a nugatory element of the system (SAAS, 2016).

Conservative-led governments at Westminster have occasionally ridden to the SNP's rescue. The wobble on free tuition around 2010 appears to have been a response in part to emerging evidence that the move to a £3,000 fee, backed by a loan, in England in 2006 was proving to be reasonably successful in increasing available resources, without clear evidence of having disrupted applications (see for example Crawford and Dearden, 2010). It was when the new coalition government announced its plan for a rise to £9,000, filling the front pages in Scotland as well as England, that free tuition once again became a totem around which the Scottish Government could define itself. Similarly, in 2015 as the Scottish Government was coming under increased pressure over its decision to cut grants in 2013, the new Conservative administration in London announced it would abolish them altogether. With evident relief, the Scottish Government took up a new defensive line that at least Scotland still had some grant. Comparisons with other devolved UK nations which had managed not to cut them at all were not welcome.

Widening Access

Having entered government apparently sincerely (but wrongly) believing that free tuition was a panacea policy for improved access, the government took time to develop a distinctive widening access agenda. It was as late as 2013 before a specific intervention, targeted additional places for disadvantaged students, had a clear observable effect (Hunter Blackburn *et al*, 2016). Discovering an enthusiasm for the role of colleges in higher education, a feature of the Scottish system long pre-dating 2007, also took time. Including college HE has long given Scotland a clear edge in participation rates over the rest of the UK, with movement from colleges to university ('articulation') substantially supplementing direct university entry at 18. At the administrative level, initiatives to promote articulation had never gone away. They got a boost in 2013, with some extra places reserved for these students. But the political rhetoric took a while to catch up. As late as 2015, the Widening Access Commission was charged specifically with looking exclusively at access to *university* (COWA, 2016). Only as attention was drawn to Scotland's lower levels of entry into university at 18 compared to the rest of the UK (Hunter Blackburn *et al*, 2016) did the college route once again became central to the political narrative about access.

With the government apparently determined not to expand the system further, shifting attention away from universities moreover suited a broader developing narrative. In February 2017, a bullish John Swinney told the Parliament, 'there will clearly be competition for places, as we do not operate a system on the basis that everyone who wants to go to university can go to university' (Scottish Parliament, 2017). Pressed, he maintained this line, even when asked specifically about those unable to go university despite having good enough results. The firm defence of rationing marked a subtle but significant development.

A lost narrative over the decade has been that of lifelong learning. Early in government, the SNP extracted higher and further education from the Enterprise Department, where these functions had spent the last several years, and put them back with Education. It was a symbolic move, firmly locating colleges and universities as an extension of the school system. Somewhere along the way, lifelong learning went missing as a government priority. This attitude was best exemplified in the language used to justify the removal from further education colleges of courses not leading to recognised qualifications, largely used by women returners and other older entrants, sweepingly dismissed as not being 'substantive'. An irony of the focus on younger students is that if free tuition as a policy can be claimed to have had any distinctive positive effect, based on inter-country comparisons, that claim seems to be strongest for older (lower-income) part-time university students, where numbers have declined less than in England, in particular.

There is not space here for proper attention to research, where there was development of, but not a major break with, earlier policy. Considerable similarity with the rest of the UK persisted, although after the 2014 REF, funding began to be somewhat less concentrated on 'research-intensive' institutions (Riddell, 2016b). On governance, the Scottish Government has legislated in response to domestic concerns rather than in reaction to the rest of the UK, but it is too early judge how far this has made university governance more transparent and democratic, the stated intention, and how far more gloomy predictions of a deadening effect on institutional autonomy may be fulfilled (Riddell, 2016c). More generally, a more centralising, hands-on approach by government, and a diminishing place for the Scottish Funding Council, was an emerging theme over the decade (Raffe, 2016).

The SNP entered government with two higher education policies, in essence. One, free tuition, it has stuck to firmly, showing only a brief moment of hesitation: but this has not proved to be the hoped-for policy-to-end-all-policies, and embraces more contradictions than are often acknowledged. The other, the end of student debt, has been quietly reversed. A much more complicated agenda for higher education has emerged in the past few years, of governance legislation, access commissions, and now a student support review. There is now 'no room for complacency' on access; robust defence of the 2013 student funding reform as 'best in the UK' is giving way to more nuanced acceptance of possible short-comings.

The period ahead is likely to see some breaks with the past. The generous approach to university funding taken up to 2014 has not proved to be sustainable and, after a period of unusually warm relations, Scottish universities are reverting to a more challenging tone with government. The political interest in universities meeting difficult new targets for widening access will be high, with all that implies. There is emerging evidence that the Scottish public is more open-minded than the political rhetoric suggests about whether to continue with free tuition in its present form (Allardyce and Boothman, 2017). As time passes the pressure the policy places on the availability of funding for better grants, more places, or the Scottish budget more generally, has become increasingly apparent. Yet the maintenance of the policy of free tuition, with all its implications, remains the defining legacy of the SNP's first decade in charge of Scotland's higher education system, and the party shows no sign, yet, of planning to retire it from its central role.

References

Allardyce, J. and Boothman, J. (2017), 'End free care and tuition, urge Scots', *Sunday Times*, 12 February. Available at: www.thetimes.co.uk/article/end-free-care-and-tuition-urge-scots-7q32dj6pg

BBC News (2011),' EU students could be charged to study in Scotland', 16 March. Available at: www.bbc.co.uk/news/uk-scotland-scotland-politics-12758097

Crawford, C. and Dearden, L. (2010), *The Impact of the 2006-07 HE Finance Reforms on HE Participation*, BIS Research Paper number 12, London: Department for Business, Innovation and Skills.

COWA (2016), *A Blueprint For Fairness: The Final Report of the Commission on Widening Access*. Available at: www.gov.scot/Resource/0049/00496619.pdf

Denholm, A. (2016), 'Scottish student debt on the rise but still lowest in UK', *The Herald*, 17 June. Available at: www.heraldscotland.com/news/14562911.Scottish_student_debt_rising__but_still_lowest_in_UK/

Hunter Blackburn, L. (2016a), 'Equity in student finance: Cross-UK comparisons, Special Edition: Widening Access to Higher Education in Scotland', *Scottish Educational Review*, 48(1), 30-47.

Hunter Blackburn, L. (2016b), 'Student Funding in the UK: Post-devolution Scotland in a UK context', in Riddell, S., Weedon, E. and Minty, S. (eds.), *Higher Education in Scotland and the UK*, Edinburgh: Edinburgh University Press.

Hunter Blackburn, L., Kadar-Sata, G., Riddell, S. and Weedon, E. (2016), *Access in Scotland*, The Sutton Trust, 2016. Available at: www.suttontrust.com/wp-content/uploads/2016/05/Access-in-Scotland_May2016.pdf

Raffe, D. (2016), 'Higher Education Governance and Institutional Autonomy in the Post-devolution UK', in Riddell, S., Weedon, E. and Minty, S. (eds.), *Higher Education in Scotland and the UK*, Edinburgh: Edinburgh University Press.

Riddell, S. (2016a), 'Devolution and Higher Education Policy: Negotiating UK and International Boundaries', in Riddell, S., Weedon, E. and Minty, S. (eds.), *Higher Education in Scotland and the UK*, Edinburgh: Edinburgh University Press.

Riddell, S. (2016b), 'Research Policy in Scotland and the Rest of the UK', in Riddell, S.; Weedon, E. and Minty, S. (eds.), *Higher Education in Scotland and the UK,* Edinburgh: Edinburgh University Press.

Riddell, S. (2016c), 'Scottish Higher Education and Devolution', in Riddell, S.; Weedon, E. and Minty, S. (eds.), *Higher Education in Scotland and the UK*, Edinburgh: Edinburgh University Press.

SAAS (2016), *Higher Education Student Support in Scotland 2015-16*. Available at www.saas.gov.uk/_forms/statistics_1516.pdf

Scottish Executive (2006), *Scottish Executive Draft Budget 2007-08*. Available at: www.gov.scot/Publications/2006/09/05131713/0.

Scottish Government (2016), *Scotland's Budget: Draft Budget 2017-18*. Available at: http://www.gov.scot/Publications/2016/12/6610.

Scottish Parliament (2017), *Official Report of the Public Audit and Post-Legislative Scrutiny Committee*, 2 February 2017. Available at: www.parliament.scot/parliamentarybusiness/report.aspx?r=10776.

UCAS (2016), *End of Cycle Report 2016*. Available at: www.ucas.com/corporate/data-and-analysis/ucas-undergraduate-releases/ucas-undergraduate-analysis-reports/ucas-undergraduate-end-cycle-reports

UCAS (2017), 'UK application rates by the January 2017 deadline'. Available at: www.ucas.com/corporate/data-and-analysis/ucas-undergraduate-releases/ucas-undergraduate-analysis-reports/ucas-undergraduate-analysis-reports

A Public Health Politics That is a People's Health

Tony Robertson, Sara Marsden and Anuj Kapilashrami

Introduction

IT IS FUNDAMENTALLY unjust that systematic inequalities in Scotland today mean that some people live healthier, longer lives than many others. This is not just a concern for those most unfairly impacted: while declining deaths from alcohol, heart disease, most cancers and respiratory disease are encouraging, Scotland's population as a whole remains, in European terms, comparatively ill (McCartney *et al*, 2012; Whyte and Ajetunmobi, 2012). In the last few years there have also been worrying increases in inequalities in mental health (driven by poorer outcomes for the most deprived groups) while narrowing inequalities in overweight/obesity have been driven by increases in obesity amongst the most deprived groups (Taulbut *et al.*, 2016) Therefore, it is clear that people in Scotland face some long-standing challenges to their health, as well as emerging threats.

There are gross inequalities in the distribution of factors that promote and protect positive health and wellbeing. These inequalities disproportionately burden people experiencing multiple deprivations and marginalities, for example, black and minority ethnic groups, refugees, asylum seeking and undocumented migrants and young people affected by austerity policies. A recent assessment of the UK Government's progress with economic, social and cultural rights confirmed that determinants of poor mental health and access to comprehensive services are unequally distributed in society. For example, certain ethnic groups in the UK are likely to have higher rates of diagnosis and admission, and are also at higher risk of detention in mental health facilities. These groups are also more likely to have poorer treatment outcomes and to disengage from services than are their white Scottish counterparts (Clarke *et al.*, 2015).

Much of our health is influenced by these wider 'social determinants of health', that is, 'the conditions in which people are born, grow, live, work and age. These circumstances are shaped by the distribution of money, power and resources at global, national and local levels. The social determinants of health are mostly responsible for health inequities (inequalities) – the unfair and avoidable differences in health status seen within and between countries' (World Health Organisation, 2016). These determinants go beyond health-care services to include 'upstream' social, economic, political, environmental and notably, commercial determinants, which can be defined as the 'strategies and approaches used by the private sector to promote products and choices that are detrimental to health' (Kickbusch et al., 2016).

While these commercial determinants can benefit health (e.g. through selling healthier products such as fruit and vegetables), big business tends to favour unhealthier choices such as tobacco, alcohol, and processed foods high in salt, fat, and sugar. This is not only apparent in Scotland; it is a global trend (Stuckler et al., 2012; Moodie et al., 2013; Monteiro et al., 2013). So much so, that the production and unregulated marketing of these unhealthy foods, have been described as shaping and 'manufacturing epidemics' (Stuckler et al., 2012). As well as marketing, companies can promote their products and brands (and maintain their profits) through lobbying, corporate social responsibility deals and their extensive supply chains (Kickbusch et al., 2016). The challenge for public health is therefore how to tackle these commercial powers in the battle for people's health.

Policy Changes

To make the most significant change in the health of populations, we must tackle the 'upstream' causes of health and health inequalities i.e. the political and economic factors in our societies that determine health at the local, national and global level. In terms of commercial determinants of health, potential policy levers include stricter regulation and universal or group-specific consumption bans (e.g. age restrictions for the sale of tobacco or alcohol products); pricing mechanisms to increase costs (e.g. sugar tax or minimum unit pricing for alcohol/MUP); advertising and marketing bans (e.g. plain packs or bans on junk food adverts to children); restrictions in sales (e.g. licensing hours or limiting sales to specific outlets or locations); or restrictions on the contents of products (e.g. additives or colourings) (Frank et al., 2015)there are few published comparisons of how the UK's devolved jurisdictions 'stack up', in terms of implementing SDoH-based policies and programmes, to improve health equity over the life-course. Based on recent SDoH publications, seven key societal-level investments are suggested, across the life-course, for increasing health equity by socioeconomic position (SEP. So, we ask here, what has the Scottish Government been able to achieve in this area, and what effect has it had on population health and health inequalities?

Alcohol

Scottish legislation in recent years has imposed limits on price-based alcohol promotions in licensed premises and the positioning of products in off-sales establishments (September 2009); limited off-sales promotions (October 2011); and attempted to introduce minimum unit pricing (MUP) of alcohol since 2009. However, although Holyrood passed MUP legislation in 2012 (setting the minimum unit price at 50p per unit alcohol), implementation has been stalled by several legal battles led by the whisky industry. The public health evidence for the introduction, though, is strong and suggests it would be an effective tool for reducing alcohol-related health inequalities and improving the health of the population (Holmes *et al.*, 2014; Booth *et al.*, 2008).

Evidence specific to each policy intervention is difficult to ascertain, but between 1996 and 2007, alcohol related hospital admissions for those under 75 were seven times higher in the most deprived areas compared to the least deprived (Scottish Government, 2017) However, between 2007 and 2015, the absolute gap between these groups had reduced to a difference of five times as many admissions. Relative inequalities (the ratio between the least and most deprived) have seen little change since 2008 however, with around 1.7 times as many admissions in the most deprived group. Therefore, the need to drive forward tougher legislation, such as MUP, over the next decade and beyond, is clear.

Tobacco

Since 2013, the Scottish Government has pushed for Scotland to be tobacco-free (defined as having less than 5 % of the population smoking) by 2034. Societal shifts in attitudes to smoking have helped make this a more realistic policy goal, and we have seen smoking legislation implemented consistently since 2006. These restrictions on the availability of tobacco products have included: a ban on smoking in enclosed public spaces (2006); raising the legal age to purchase tobacco to 18 years (2007); banning tobacco products from vending machines (2013); and a tobacco display ban in large (2013) and small retail stores (2015). Since May 2016, cigarettes and hand-rolling tobacco have been required to be sold in standardised (plain) packaging, although a grace period of 12 months continues until May 2017 where previous stock (without plain packaging) must be phased out. In addition, the Scottish Government has also imposed a ban on selling smaller packs of rolling tobacco or cigarettes with fewer than 20 per pack for this same deadline. A complete ban on all menthol cigarettes is also expected by 2020.

Previous research suggests that these anti-smoking policies have the potential to influence change in smoking habits and health. Data from the Scottish Health Surveys, a large, nationally representative sample of the population, has shown that cigarette consumption has declined in the country, particularly since the late 1990s (Scottish Goovernment, 2016). In 2015, adult smoking prevalence in this survey was estimated at 26 % and 24 % for men and women respectively. When we want to best assess the evidence for health change as a result of a given policy, we can utilise 'natural experiments'. This is where two similar populations (or regions, countries etc.) experience different policies such as, for example, the indoor smoking ban between Scotland (established in March 2006) and England (established in July 2007). In research published in 2008, it was found that the number of admissions for acute coronary syndrome (a range of disorders including heart attacks and unstable angina) decreased by 17 % in Scotland following the smoking ban, while only decreasing by 4 % in England over the same time period. It is notable that around two thirds of the decrease in hospital admissions involved non-smokers who were now being exposed to much lower levels of second-hand smoke (Pell *et al.*, 2008).

In terms of changes in smoking over recent years, recent evidence (again from the Scottish Health Survey) shows that smoking prevalence has declined by approximately 6 % between 2003 and 2013. However, the patterns by most and least deprived 20 % of the population show that relative indices of inequality (the ratio between these groups) have increased over this time-period, with more deprived groups 2.6 times as likely to smoke than their more affluent counterparts in 2003, but 3.7 times more likely by 2013 (Frank *et al.*, 2015)More recent data from the 2014 and 2015 surveys suggest this picture is starting to improve, but still inequalities remain greater than was the case in 2003 (now at just over three times higher smoking rates than in more deprived groups).

Unhealthy Food

In comparison to progress on alcohol and tobacco, regulatory and legislative action in relation to unhealthy food products has been much more limited. This may be partly due to the devolution settlement, with the Scottish Government more limited in its powers in relation to the most effective levers in this area, for example in relation to taxation of goods. There are also clearly greater difficulties in defining what unhealthy food ingredients and products are. For example, a meal of burger and chips could be deemed unhealthy, but equally, it may still contain important nutrients and healthier salads and vegetables as part of the meal. However, growing levels of obesity in Scotland and beyond are now being observed. Again using data from the Scottish Health Survey, we can see that obesity levels (a body mass index of 30 or over) for adults (16+) are currently at 28 % and 30 % for men and women, respectively. This is an increase in 6 % and 4 %, for men and women respectively, since 2003 (Scottish Government, 2016). If this sample is truly representative of the population, this would mean approximately 1.29 million adult Scots are currently obese (compared to approximately 1.07 million in 2003).

Despite these concerning trends, policy in this arena has fallen short of a strong interventionist approach to food marketing and diet, relying predominantly on voluntary measures. The focus has largely been limited to the marketing of unhealthy foods to children, although with 15 % of Scots children in 2015 estimated to be obese, this is an important target demographic (Scottish Government, 2016). In 2007/08, a UK-wide ban on advertising foods high in fat, sugar or salt during children's television programmes was introduced and monitored by Ofcom.

Around this time, legislation was introduced in Scotland to limit the availability of unhealthy foods in schools' vending machines and cafeterias, including bans of sugar-sweetened drinks, and limiting deep-fried foods to a maximum of three servings in any one week (Scottish Government, 2008) However, since children of this age can generally leave school at lunchtime to buy food elsewhere, such steps have limited potential to improve diets (Frank *et al.*, 2015) The UK Government has proposed a sugar tax on sugar-sweetened drinks to begin in April 2018, a measure shown to reduce consumption in Mexico by 12 % in the two years following the introduction of a similar tax, with reductions also higher in more deprived groups (thereby reducing the inequality in consumption)(Colchero *et al.*, 2016).

Conclusion

One contribution to the above has been the creation of the People's Health Movement (PHM) – an evolving network of campaigns committed to social justice and fairness. This arose from discontent with emerging global orders, growing inequities and the failure to meet the promises of the 1978 Alma-Ata international primary health conference, including the goal of achieving health for all by the year 2000. The Scottish arm of the movement, together with its allies, launched the Scottish People's Health Manifesto in 2016 making a strong commentary on the health threats and priorities for health in Scotland (Kapilashrami *et al.*, 2015). Developed and agreed upon by participatory dialogue between hundreds of individuals, organisations and community groups from across the country, the PHM manifesto was conceived as a way to spark debate, discussion and action to mitigate and ultimately prevent the harm caused by these wide-ranging threats.

The Scottish Government has taken active steps to tackle some commercial determinants of health, and despite corporate resistance, at least made some progress on tobacco control, with health indicators showing improvement. However, more determined effort is needed, in particular to tackle inequalities in health which remain stubbornly high. While some of the economic, welfare and tax levers needed to tackle inequalities remain with Westminster, more should and can be done, including driving forward policies such as MUP for alcohol sales, shaping a more progressive income tax system and pushing commercial determinants of health higher up the agenda.

The political momentum generated by post-Brexit talks and the prospect of another independence referendum in Scotland offers a unique opportunity to demonstrate strong public health leadership and for political parties to agree on a progressive health policy that tackles the above commercial determinants, while simultaneously addressing poverty and health inequalities arising at the intersections of income, gender, and ethnicity, among others. Such a response should embrace and build upon core demands and priorities outlined in the Scottish PHM manifesto that include health and care services, but go far beyond this including, for example, tackling poverty and inequalities, ensuring health is a core component in all policies, and putting democratic debate and accountability higher up on the agenda.

References

Booth, A. *et al.* (2008), *Independent review of the effects of alcohol pricing and promotion*, Sheffield: University of Sheffield.

Clarke, K. *et al.* (2015), 'The Right To Health in the UK', in *Implementation of the International Covenant on Economic, Social and Cultural Rights in the United Kingdom of Great Britain and Northern Ireland: Parallel Report: Submission to the Committee on Economic, Social and Cultural Rights.* London: Just Fair, accessed at: http://media.wix.com/ugd/8a2436_4b339b-81cc104497a9d9626522c7f796.pdf

Colchero, M.A. *et al.* (2016), 'Beverage purchases from stores in Mexico under the excise tax on sugar sweetened beverages: observational study', *British Medical Journal*, 352, accessed at: www.bmj.com/content/352/bmj.h6704. abstract

Frank, J. *et al.* (2015), 'Seven Key Investments for Health Equity across the Lifecourse: Scotland versus the rest of the UK', *Social Science and Medicine*, accessed at: www.sciencedirect.com/science/article/pii/S027795361530023X

Holmes, J. *et al.* (2014), 'Effects of minimum unit pricing for alcohol on different income and socioeconomic groups: A modelling study', *The Lancet*, 383(9929), pp.1655–1664.

Kapilashrami, A. *et al.* (2015), 'Social movements and public health advocacy in action: the UK people's health movement', *Public Health*, e.fdv085.

Kickbusch, I., Allen, L. and Franz, C. (2016), 'The commercial determinants of health', *The Lancet Global Health*, 4(12), pp. 895–896.

McCartney, G. *et al.* (2012), 'Has Scotland always been the 'sick man' of Europe? An observational study from 1855 to 2006', *Eur J Public Health*, 22(6), pp. 756–760, accessed at: www.ncbi.nlm.nih.gov/pubmed/22021374

Monteiro, C.A. *et al.* (2013), 'Ultra-processed products are becoming dominant in the global food system', *Obesity Reviews*, 14(S2), pp. 21–28.

Moodie, R. *et al.* (2013), 'Profits and pandemics: Prevention of harmful effects of tobacco, alcohol, and ultra-processed food and drink industries', *The Lancet*, 381(9867), pp. 670–679.

Pell, J.P. *et al.* (2008), 'Smoke-free Legislation and Hospitalizations for Acute Coronary Syndrome', *New England Journal of Medicine*, 359(5), pp. 482–491, accessed at: www.nejm.org/doi/abs/10.1056/NEJMsa0706740

Scottish Government (2008), *Healthy Eating in Schools: A Guide to Implementing the Nutritional Requirements for Food and Drink in Schools (Scotland) Regulations*, Edinburgh: Scottish Government.

Scottish Government (2016), *The Scottish Health Survey 2015 edition*, Edinburgh: Scottish Government.

Scottish Government (2017), *Long-term monitoring of health inequalities: March 2017 Report*, Edinburgh: Scottish Government.

Stuckler, D. *et al.* (2012), 'Manufacturing epidemics: The role of global producers in increased consumption of unhealthy commodities including processed foods, alcohol, and tobacco', *PLoS Medicine*, 9(6), p. 10.

Taulbut, M. *et al.* (2016), *'Pulling in different directions? The impact of economic recovery and continued changes to social security on health and health inequalities in Scotland'*, Edinburgh: NHS Health Scotland.

Whyte, B. and Ajetunmobi, T. (2012), *Still the 'sick man of Europe'?*, Glasgow: Glasgow Centre for Population Health, accessed at: www.gcph.co.uk/assets/0000/3606/Scottish_Mortality_in_a_European_Context_2012_VII_FINAL_bw.pdf

World Health Organisation (2016), *Social determinants of health*, accessed at: www.who.int/social_determinants/sdh_definition/en/

Baby Boxes: A Case Study of One Policy Idea

Dani Garavelli

EVEN THE TIMING of the launch of the baby box pilots was symbolic: 1 January, the day newspaper photographers traditionally lay siege to labour wards in the hopes of snapping the first baby born after the Bells. A New Year; a fresh start; a shot of hope.

At Clackmannanshire Community Healthcare Centre, First Minister Nicola Sturgeon stood surrounded by midwives, mums-to-be, new mums and – centre stage – the box itself: a safe sleeping space, decorated with puffins and filled with clothing, nappies and accessories; and, of course, the Scots poem, 'Welcome Wee One', by Makar Jackie Kay.

The message sent out by the boxes – to be given to each new baby, regardless of its parents' income – is unambiguous: 'In Scotland, every child is cherished by the state.' The policy suggests a level playing field and fits with the Scottish Government's top priority: the eradication of social inequality.

New-borns, social justice and heart-warming photo opportunities. In all this, what's not to like? And yet, the baby boxes do have their decriers. Some of the most vocal see the inclusion of the Scots poem as evidence they are Trojan horses, smuggling Nationalist propaganda into unsuspecting households. A more enduring criticism is that they are just a gimmick; an eye-catching policy plucked from another country's health system.

'This is classic SNP', says one former Scottish Government special adviser. 'There's great intent behind it, but it rapidly becomes iconic. They say: 'X is good at childcare, and X does this, so if we do this, we will be good at childcare', where you'd hope it would be part of a wider system or approach.'

The Baby Box and the Strengths and Weaknesses of Policy-making

There is a great deal about the baby boxes – and the public response to them – that is emblematic of the strengths and limitations of SNP policy-making, and the current state of Scottish political discourse.

On the plus-side the idea is well-motivated and fits with the theory that, if we are to help break the cycle of poverty, it is important to intervene in children's lives as early as possible. But – like free prescriptions and university tuition fees – it raises questions about universal provision: who does it benefit most? And how can it be done without raising taxes?

Some critics would prefer to see resources targeted towards society's most vulnerable. Others dislike the faint whiff of moral superiority around the policy, and the gap between the symbolism – that every baby is born equal – and the reality – that some babies go home to nice detached houses and others go home to squalor.

Not for the first time, the SNP's zeal to see a pledge enacted means some aspects of delivery seem poorly thought -through. One only has to look at the time set aside for evaluation – just three months, when some of the contents of the boxes cannot be used until six months – to wonder how seriously the Scottish Government is taking the exercise.

The polarised nature of the response is also par for the course in post-indyref Scotland. The Yes voters who accuse sceptics of being apathetic about infant mortality; the No voters who say 'no-one will put their baby in a box' (despite clear evidence that people do) create a heightened atmosphere in which people take up their default positions, and there is little space for genuine concerns to be aired or pitfalls to be identified and avoided.

This is – in part – was what led to the arguments over the Named Person Provision ending up at the Supreme Court. You might hope both sides would have learned a lesson and work constructively to ensure the rhetoric is less overblown this time round.

The baby box phenomenon now sweeping Europe and parts of the US began in Finland in the 1938. There, after each new birth, mothers are offered the choice between the box or a maternity grant. More than two thirds choose the box because it is worth more and because receiving it has become regarded as a rite of passage, uniting mothers across generations and the social spectrum.

The possibility of bringing the baby boxes to Scotland has been on the SNP's radar for at least eight years. A flurry of positive newspaper stories and aggressive lobbying by the Baby Box Company – a rapidly growing US firm – plus a change in First Minister, from Alex Salmond to Nicola Sturgeon, may be responsible for its inclusion in the SNP's 2016 manifesto. As I write, two pilots are underway – one in Clackmannanshire and one in Orkney – with a national roll-out planned for the summer.

That the baby boxes played a part in bringing down Finland's infant mortality rate (from 65 per 1,000 live births in 1935 to below two per 1,000 in 2015) is indisputable. But they did so, not in isolation, but by connecting parents to a pioneering maternity and early years service.

In Scotland, the box has been sold on the idea we will be able to replicate that success story, but the context is very different. Infant mortality is already relatively low (3.7 per 1,000 births – with around 40 deaths a year from Sudden Infant Death Syndrome or SIDS). There is research linking SIDS to co-sleeping, but touting the baby boxes as a solution may be creating a hostage to fortune.

Of course, the baby boxes are not 'only' about reducing infant mortality; they are also aimed at improving the life chances of the country's most disadvantaged children. But – as with the Named Person Provision – the SNP struggled to effectively communicate its thinking to the public, allowing the initial debate to become dominated by a discussion of SIDS at the expense of other potential benefits.

Some sceptics also worry the SNP regards the baby boxes as an end in themselves rather than as a catalyst for an ongoing conversation. In 2009, former Senior Director for Skills at Scottish Enterprise and early years advocate Alan Sinclair included baby boxes in a list of potential policies he sent to Sturgeon, then health secretary, along with Nurse Family Partnerships for single teenage mums, and mother and baby well-being clinics. Significantly, his proposal tied the receipt of a baby box to regular attendance at ante-natal classes.

'In the Finnish system, there are rights and responsibilities: if you don't come to the classes, you might not get the box', Sinclair says. 'This is important because it is an opportunity to forge links with women you might otherwise not connect with.'

'The box itself has a novelty value. But the substantive bit is how you use it to capitalise on 'the golden moment' – the point in a pregnancy where women are desperate to make a change in their lives.'

It would be unfair to suggest the baby box is not part of a bigger SNP vision. In the past ten years, the party has invested heavily in maternity and early years services. The baby box policy fits with Getting It Right For Every Child (GIRFEC), its flagship programme aimed at improving outcomes for children and young people, its Best Start grants, to be given to low income families, and Ready Steady Baby, its pre and post-natal information guide.

But – when it comes to implementation – the SNP does seem to have missed opportunities to engage. In England, several hospital trusts are running baby box pilots in conjunction with the Baby Box Company, which supplies them for free (in the hopes of landing a contract in the future). To receive a box, parents must sign up to the Baby Box University, an online educational resource created by the local NHS Trust.

The Scottish Government decided to self-finance its pilots at a cost of £100,000. There are valid arguments for not involving a commercial company, but one of the reasons for its reticence appears to have been its determination not to attach conditions to the boxes. All mothers in Scotland will have to do to receive one is to register at the time of the 20-week scan. Nor – due to the logistics of storing them – will the boxes be handed out by a midwife or health visitor who could use the encounter to build a relationship. Instead they will be couriered directly to people's homes.

Mark McDonald, Minister for childcare and early years, says the boxes will contain sign-posting to websites on issues such as breast-feeding and general well-being. 'In relation to post-natal contact with services, we are already ahead of our 80 % target, but there is more to be done', he says. 'We have commissioned Ipsos Mori to undertake some qualitative research round the pilots and we will continue to monitor how the boxes are being received, how they are supporting interaction with services.' The contract for the national roll-out is being limited to two years to allow for the policy to be developed or refined further down the line.

A more fundamental objection is that giving the boxes to all babies – regardless of need – wastes money that could be spent on front-line services or targeted towards society's most disadvantaged. The arguments in favour of universalism are well-rehearsed. Giving to all reduces stigma, creates a sense of social solidarity and makes middle class people more willing to pay their taxes.

'I take the view that universalism is important to create a cohesive society', says McDonald. 'Children don't choose the circumstances they are born into. The baby box is given to all at the very start of their lives so it's a leveller.'

'However, the policy also ties in with other approaches such as the Best Start grants, which are focused on those in most need. It's about ensuring you develop that cohesive society through a universal offering, but that you also have targeted support that fits around it.'

The estimated £7 million a year price tag is a tiny fraction of the Scottish Government's £33 billion budget. Even so, it is hard to make the case for handing free baby clothes to the well-off when money is scarce; even harder when newspapers are reporting crises in labour wards and neo-natal units.

Some critics believe many of the goods the boxes contain could be obtained for free from companies promoting their brands (as they do through Bounty packs) and that -like free tuition fees – the baby boxes create the illusion that something is being done for the poor, while benefiting the middle classes.

There is also the question of how giveaways should be paid for. 'I am all in favour of universal provision but it has to be underpinned by progressive taxation', says former Scottish Labour leader Johann Lamont. 'If you refuse to raise money from other places, then what's it coming at the expense of? Maybe it's at the expense of organisations that work closely with vulnerable families. Maybe it's at the expense of a midwife or health visitor.'

There's the rub. Public services have to be funded. Yet, repeatedly, the SNP co-opts some aspect of the 'Nordic model', without the Nordic taxes, because – as the backlash and subsequent U-turn over the rise in business rates demonstrated – raising taxes is always a minefield.

As author Dominic Hinde has pointed out the SNP has traditionally preferred stimulus through lowering taxes and has been reluctant to heavily tax middle class earners. 'A top tax rate of 45% and retention of a council tax are the opposite of the progressive taxation on which the Nordic model was historically built', he wrote in *The Scotsman* (Hinde, 2016). The decision not to follow England in raising the tax threshold from £43,430 to £45,000 was not a shift in direction, but a concession won by the Green Party as the minority SNP Government struggled to get its budget through.

'The SNP cannot develop wider reforms without bumping up against big ideological/budget issues', says the former special adviser. 'It can't consider wholesale reform because it's too politically risky, but piecemeal reform with a limited budget is never going to achieve that much.'

When it comes to the baby boxes, the SNP's heart is in the right place. Its commitment to improving early years has been consistent and impressive. But the fear is that unless it acts more radically, it will be confined to tinkering round the edges of social deprivation; that the boxes' message – 'every baby is born equal' – will never have the chance to develop from a sincerely-expressed aspiration into a statement of fact.

References

Hinde, D. (2016), 'Would the SNP's Nordic model work?', *The Scotsman*, 18 April, accessed at: www.scotsman.com/news/dominic-hinde-would-the-snp-s-nordic-model-work-1-4103712

Scotland the Just? The SNP, Crime and Justice

Sarah Armstrong and Mary Munro

PERHAPS NOTHING REVEALS the contradictions in Scottish culture, politics and identity than the nation's approach to criminal justice. Scotland the fair; Scotland the harsh. Scotland the forward-looking, outward-facing European. Scotland the tradition-bound and locally focused champion. Having a home-grown youth justice model – the Children's Hearing System – that has been claimed as one of the most welfarist approaches in the world contrasts with also having one of the lowest ages (a mere eight years old) of criminal responsibility. These competing impulses in the Scottish psyche are an intangible part of the justice brief, shaping policy and reflecting back a certain tension in Scottish attitudes about crime and punishment.

Ten years of SNP rule furnish plenty more examples from the Justice Secretary's in-tray, and a range of factors further influences how these are managed. First, there are direct and indirect pressures created by unexpected events (the terrorist attack at Glasgow airport, the fatal illness of the Lockerbie prisoner Abdelbaset al-Megrahi; global recession in 2008 and Brexit in 2016); second, the need to respond to changing political priorities (for example, 'booze and blades' culture, drugs, bigotry, serious organised crime); third, the drive towards systemic reforms of structures and processes (addressing Scotland's high prison populations and re-offending levels, responding to offending by women, the governance of the police, the place of victims in the justice process, law reform). The nature of the responses to such issues will be derived variously from perceptions of political expediency, moral world view or principles, the capacity of the civil service to make things happen, and not least the personal style and approach of the incumbent.

On this last point, for seven of the SNP's first ten years in power justice was headed up by the same person, Cabinet Secretary Kenny MacAskill (2007-2014, still the longest serving Justice Secretary in Scotland since devolution), and the decisions taken during his tenure dominate this brief discussion of criminal justice under the SNP. More recently, Michael Matheson (appointed to lead justice in 2014 by Nicola Sturgeon) has taken up the reins, making some important

decisions that might be set in the context of the government's increasing emphasis on social justice and reduction of inequality in Scottish society.

Scotland and Criminal Justice

Has the SNP changed direction of Scotland's approach to criminal justice? The
justice elements of the SNP 2007 manifesto were not substantially different in
rhetoric or programme intention from Labour's insofar as both promoted community sentences as way to reduce the prison population. There was, however,
from the outset, a more substantial difference in style and less deference to tabloid headlines under MacAskill, in contrast to a tendency to respond instantly
and talk up crime and justice issues in crisis terms under Labour (for a wider
discussion see Mooney et al., 2014).

MacAskill made good on SNP promises to oppose privatisation of public
services by deciding not to seek commercial tenders for a replacement prison at
HMP Low Moss (though the SNP came in too late to stop HMP Addiewell being
built and operated under PFI/PPP). Nonetheless, in common with elsewhere,
there continues to be extensive commercial presence in the provision of penal
services, including electronic monitoring and prisoner transport.

Prisons have long been treated in Scotland, as elsewhere, as a measure of
the justice system's health. Hence the country's persistently heavy use of imprisonment compared to other parts of Europe has long been a niggle for policy
makers, and a justification for the red-tops to claim, spuriously, that Scottish
wrongdoers are just more numerous and more hardened than in other places.

MacAskill tackled the prison issue head on by appointing Henry McLeish,
his friend and former First Minister in the Labour-Liberal Democrat coalition, to
lead a Scottish Prisons Commission. The enquiry published its report *Scotland's
Choice* in 2008, making far-reaching and still influential recommendations
including that the Scottish prison population should be downsized substantially
– gesturing towards the practices of Scotland's Nordic neighbours, and reflecting the SNP's wider admiration of Scandinavia on policy generally. Its call for the
enhancement of constructive justice policies was later, in part, reflected in legislation (Community Justice and Licensing (2010) Act) restructuring community
sentences as community payback orders, legislating for a Scottish Sentencing
Council and introducing the controversial presumption against short sentences.

Nevertheless, no administration has yet managed to make much of a dent in
the prison population, which remains persistently high. Added to this – despite the
fall in crime rates in Scotland, across the rest of the UK and internationally – both
the chances of being convicted and of being victimised continue to be skewed in
terms of indices of poverty (see McAra, McVie et al., 2015).

Voter analysis suggests that attitudes to crime policy (including knife crime and community sentences) were not a significant factor in predicting SNP support in the 2011 Holyrood election, compared with matters such as the overall competence of the minority administration. Labour and Tory strategists had attempted to talk up an antisocial behaviour agenda and 'tougher' penalties for knife crime rather atavistically it seems now, misreading the extent to which such matters were then preying on the public mind.

A Change of Course?

Perversely it was in the months immediately before and after the landslide 2011 result that the wider SNP leadership took a particular interest in justice affairs, and not to good effect. This was provoked by two matters. First, high-profile examples of sectarian bigotry, especially in its connections with football, resulted in an uncharacteristically hasty introduction of emergency legislation – the Offensive Behaviour at Football and Threatening Communications (Scotland) Act 2012 – early in the new session. A messy and stop-start process of reviewing and debating the Bill did not augur well for the quality of the legislation that followed. Second, this stushie coincided with the 'discovery' of the criminal jurisdiction of the UK Supreme Court over Scotland arising from a high-profile homicide case (Fraser v HMA). The SNP administration chose to take this as a violation of the independent traditions of Scots law.

The vehemence of the response to this decision by both MacAskill and Salmond was striking, albeit foreshadowed by earlier similar reactions to the decision of Cadder V HMA 2010, in which the distinctive Scottish evidential standard of corroboration was found to fall short of human rights standards. Unique Scottish justice practices in addition to corroboration, like the 'not proven' verdict and the large size (15 people) and simple majority decision of juries have since come under review and triggered intense debate, hinting again at the tension between fervent loyalty to a Scots law tradition and a desire to modernise and take guidance from international standards.

Following the landslide SNP victory in the 2011 election, the scene was set for more radical and far-reaching reforms than had been feasible prior to the political shift (for a more detailed review see Croall *et al*, 2015). Chief among these was the reform of the police and the formation of the new national Police Scotland in 2013 (see chapter by John Carnochan). The SNP administration endured accusations of excessive centralisation both in the practice of policing and its oversight.

By contrast, if there is a continuum from centralisation to localisation, it may be argued that reforms to community justice in this period are towards the latter rather than then former. As a result of a 'harrowing' Prisons Inspectorate report into conditions at Scotland's only penal establishment for women, HMP Cornton Vale in 2011, MacAskill appointed former Lord Advocate Elish Angiolini to chair a commission to identify better outcomes for women offenders. The 'Angiolini report' (Commission for Women Offenders, 2012) may have potential for a more profound influence on penal culture in Scotland than any previous intervention. Echoing prior reform efforts focusing on women, it recommended the closure of HMP/YOI Cornton Vale. This recommendation was adopted but justice watchers were disappointed when the closure of one prison was succeeded by Scottish Prison Service plans for a brand new women's institution, HMP Inverclyde in Greenock. The new Justice Secretary, Michael Matheson, refused to sign off plans for the new establishment in early 2015 in a move that was both supported and encouraged by MacAskill, and has opened up the possibility of a more radical discussion on the role of custody for women, and perhaps ultimately for men too.

Other consequences of Angiolini have been the establishment of the new national body Community Justice Scotland (to launch in April 2017) to 'provide leadership for the sector' (Scottish Government, 2016). Criminal justice social work continues to be a function of local authorities. However, the Community Justice Authorities, set up in 2005 as a vehicle for local control, have been abolished and their functions transferred to the existing Community Planning Partnerships. It remains to be seen if the aim of 'community empowerment' in relation to crime and justice suggested by this approach can actually be achieved.

Dealing with young people in conflict with the law has been a primary territory of contradictory impulses. The low age of criminal responsibility, as noted at the outset, has long been an embarrassment for many in Scotland and legislation will now raise this from eight to (the still low, many would argue) twelve. The practice of stop and search by the police is another example. Edinburgh researcher Kath Murray discovered that many young people as young as 11, and disproportionately those living in deprived areas, were being stopped and searched by police on a regular basis. Scots might have been shaken to learn that in the land of the 'Kilbrandon' ethos that gave rise to the Children's Hearing System, police in some parts of Scotland were rousting young people at rates many times higher than in New York or London.

MacAskill's defence of the use of stop and search, as well as support for expanding the carrying of guns by police, led many to feel this was inconsistent with his earlier reformer's approach to the justice brief, and these policy stances perhaps exemplify the tension between Scotland's progressivism and conservatism, and between populism and central government control. While there are now proposals for a statutory basis to regulate stop and search, in 2016 Matheson announced an expansion in the numbers and roles of armed police to surprisingly little public reaction.

This space has been too small to mention, let alone discuss meaningfully, all areas of criminal justice. Gender-based violence, for example. has long been a concern in Scotland, and the SNP, like prior administrations, has legislated actively in this area, with laws now targeting revenge porn, stalking and coercive control. This might be treated, if it has not yet been explicit, as part of a wider agenda around hate crime and the legislative quest for equality.

Sexual offences (where rising recorded rates bucks the trend of generally falling crime levels) also are driving a huge amount of activity in police, prosecution and court workloads, as well as being reflected in the composition of imprisoned populations; consequences of this are still unclear. Young people in conflict with the law continues to be a locus of intense reform, and most recently the holistic philosophy of a 'Whole Systems Approach' drives the contemporary diversionary agenda for young people, though whether this can be given credit for a recent sharp drop in the number of imprisoned young people in Scotland is open to question, as England has seen a similar fall in numbers with a very different approach to youth justice.

Finally, Brexit looms over most areas of Scottish, as well as UK, policy. Aside from technical matters of disentangling from Europe, the key issues for justice are likely to be around human rights (especially if the UK Government acts on plans to withdraw from the ECHR and produce its own 'British Bill of Rights') and law enforcement. While the SNP Government strongly supports the intention of Prime Minister Theresa May to maintain membership in Europol and to preserve a European Arrest Warrant, it has been less vocal in raising concerns about human rights post-Brexit. With the UK's recently passed legislation (UK Investigatory powers Act 2016) granting unprecedented powers to gather personal information of citizens, it may be in this area that we need the most boldness. Scotland the Just? This remains to be seen.

References

Commission for Women Offenders (2012), *Final Report*, accessed at: www.scotland.gov.uk/About/Review/commissiononwomenoffenders/finalreport-2012

Croall, H., Mooney, G. and Munro, M. (eds.) (2015), *Crime, Justice and Society in Scotland*. London: Routledge.

McAra, L. and McVie, S. (eds.) (2015), 'Poverty, Inequality and Justice', *Scottish Justice Matters* 3:3.

Mooney, G., Croall, H., Munro, M. and Scott, G. (2014), 'Scottish criminal justice: Devolution, divergence and distinctiveness', *Criminology and Criminal Justice* 1-20.

Scottish Government (2016), *National Strategy for Community Justice*.

An Era of Compassionate Justice? Assessing a Decade of SNP Governance

Lesley McAra

Introduction

THIS CHAPTER WILL offer a critical assessment of criminal justice policy across the decade in which the SNP has been in power in Scotland (as a minority [2007-11], majority [2011-16] and once again minority administration [from 2016 onwards]).

As I aim to demonstrate, the SNP Government has embraced a criminal justice agenda predicated initially on a compassionate approach to matters of crime and punishment, that has matured into an evidence-based set of practices which have had positive impacts on conviction and (more recently) imprisonment rates. However, the changes wrought by the three SNP administrations have not been without controversy (particularly the fall-out from the changes made to the institutional architecture of justice) and their longevity dependent on the strength of political will in the face of populist pressures.

The chapter begins with a short overview of key developments in criminal justice policy, locating the SNP's agenda within its broader historical context. This is followed by an assessment of the impact and likely success of policy transformation. The chapter concludes with some reflections on the futures of criminal justice and its contribution to polity building and governance in these uncertain times.

Overview of Key Transformations

The SNP years have seen major transformations in criminal justice policy, with a more progressive agenda developed (particularly in the first phase of SNP governance) around a narrative of compassionate justice. Such transformations are arguably indicative of a number of stochastic features of 'statecraft' (meaning exhibiting a pattern of behaviour but one which is not always substantively predictable) which have also been reflected in the other devolved nations within the UK as they have sought to establish their right to rule namely: *differentiation* from the past; construction of new or revised institutional *architecture*; selection and nurturing of new *audiences* (groups to whom policy 'speaks'); and introducing greater *complexity* into policy discourse (see McAra, 2017: 946).

The Legacies of the New Labour/Liberal Democratic Coalition Years

An irony of the immediate post-devolution settlement (1999 onwards), was that criminal justice discarded some of its distinctively Scottish identity and became heavily politicised, with the problems of youth crime, in particular, forming a centre-point of governance (McAra, 2016). Prior to devolution criminal justice policy could be characterised for the most part as welfarist in orientation, set in train by the Social Work (Scotland) Act 1968, which transferred the functions of the former probation service to social work and enabled the children's hearing system. Post devolution the Labour-Liberal Democrat coalition Governments began to look south of the border for policy inspiration, and to promulgate a more populist narrative around crime and its control. In the search for legitimacy governments often use the fight against crime as a means of asserting their right to rule (Hall, 1979): and in the early post devolution years such imperatives drove a criminal justice agenda that was harsher in rhetoric and more complex in terms of institutional ethos (imbued variously with the tropes of risk management, just deserts, managerialism, restoration and invoking new audiences including failing parents, persistent offenders, and communities).

Accompanying these changes, the coalition administrations constructed over 100 new institutions to deal with aspects of criminal justice. Many of which had overlapping competencies, and set a series of stringent (and mostly unscientific) targets. The most notorious of which was the target set for the 10 % reduction in the number of young persistent offenders from a baseline of 1201. Academics (who pre-devolution had formed an integral part of extant policy networks) were largely left out in the cold (McAra, 2011; 2016; 2017). Consequently in 2007, the SNP inherited a criminal justice landscape that was overburdened with targets, one in which young people had been steadily demonised, and one in which research evidence was largely absent.

The snp Years: A New Agenda

Following the precepts of statecraft, the new snp administration enjoined an entirely different, more progressive narrative about criminal justice, and drew much more heavily on research to develop the evidence-base. A watershed moment came with the decision in 2009 to release on compassionate grounds Mr Abdelbaset Ali Mohamed Al-Megrahi, the man convicted of the Lockerbie bombing. The then Cabinet Secretary for Justice, defending his decision, stated:

> In Scotland, we are a people who pride ourselves on our humanity. It is viewed as a defining characteristic of Scotland and the Scottish people. The perpetration of an atrocity and outrage cannot and should not be a basis for losing sight of who we are, the values we seek to uphold, and the faith and beliefs by which we seek to live.

(www.scotland.gov.uk/Topics/Justice/law/lockerbie)

Over the period of snp rule, and building on the Cabinet Secretary's statement, criminal justice has been explicitly tied to a set of national outcomes aimed at the production of a flourishing society. As part of this, efforts have been made to reduce the number of short-term sentences of imprisonment and revise the custodial estate for women (with plans for a number of small scale community houses). The Prison service has reformulated its core ethos as one of rehabilitation (with the ambition of transforming Polmont Young Offenders Institution into a 'learning environment, see HMIP, 2016). In addition there has been a renewed emphasis on restorative and reparative principles, through the instigation of community payback orders (implemented via the Criminal Justice and Licensing [Scotland] Act 2010) and more recently the introduction of a Sentencing Council for Scotland (operational from 2015) to promote greater consistency in sentencing.

Additionally there has been greater emphasis on diversion and minimum necessary intervention in youth justice with the implementation of the Whole System Approach (from 2011) (see Scottish Government, 2015). The latter aims to provide a model of interagency working (akin to the Christie Commission imperatives [Christie, 2011]), which takes a holistic view of how young people are processed across and through youth justice, with the aim of keeping as many young people out of formal measures where possible, and supporting early years intervention. Consideration is now being given to extending the Whole System Approach not only to women who come into conflict with the law, but to all adult offenders (via the new Justice Strategy for Scotland to be published later this year).

In keeping with the SNP's more progressive and compassionate approach, the minimum age of criminal prosecution in the courts has also been raised to age 12 and, at the time of writing, serious consideration is being given to raising the age of criminal responsibility (currently aged eight) in line with this. Again in accordance with stochastic dynamic described above, the SNP has made substantial changes to the architecture of justice, with greater centralisation of services including: the creation of a single national police force 'Police Scotland' (in 2013), the national children's panel in the wake of the Children's Hearing (Scotland) Act 2011, and Community Justice Scotland (which will formally launch in April 2017, replacing the 8 community justice authorities across Scotland with one national body and devolving their day to day responsibilities for offender management to the 32 local authorities).

Impact and Assessment

What then has been the impact of these changes? In terms of *system activity*, first of all, the SNP era has been defined by major reductions in crime as measured by a range of official statistics. As show in figures 1 and 2 below, offence referrals to the Reporter (mostly for children between the ages of 8 to 15) and conviction rates for those aged over 16 have reduced by some 80 % (since 2007/08). There also been a recent reduction in imprisonment rates (of some 8 %, see figure 3). While this is a relatively small reduction (and it remains to be seen whether it can be sustained over the longer term), it is, nonetheless, very welcome, after many decades in which the Scottish prison population has risen inexorably. Importantly the aggregate reconviction rates of offenders caught up in the criminal justice system (which were relatively stable over the new labour/liberal democratic coalition years – running at around 32 % per annum), have reduced in the period since the SNP took office (by around 13 %) and the average number reconvictions per offender has gone down by around 15 %.

Deeper interrogation of the reconviction data also provides some evidence of the success of the SNP's Whole System Approach to youth offending, as contrasted with the earlier Labour-Lib Dem Government's more punitive approach (which now appears to have had a longer term stigmatising effects on those coming into conflict with the law). For example, reconvictions rates for young people under the age of 21 have reduced over the SNP years by around 16 % in contrast to slight increases (around 4 %) in reconviction for older offenders between 31 and 40 (those who would have been teenagers during the early post-devolution years) (see McAra and McVie, 2015a for a review of the research evidence).

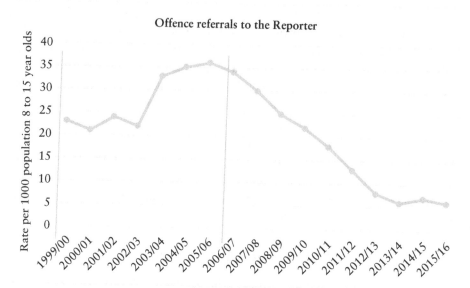

Figure 1 Offence Referrals to the Children's Reporter
(Source: Scottish Children's Reporter Administration statistics and population data from the National Records of Scotland)

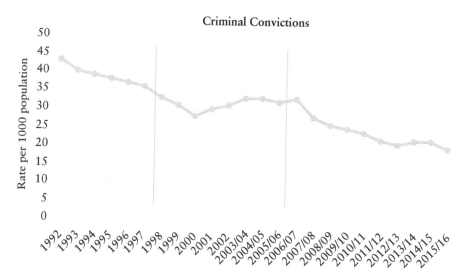

Figure 2 Criminal convictions in Scottish Courts
(Source: www.gov.scot/Topics/Statistics/Browse/Crime-Justice/
PubCriminalProceedings)

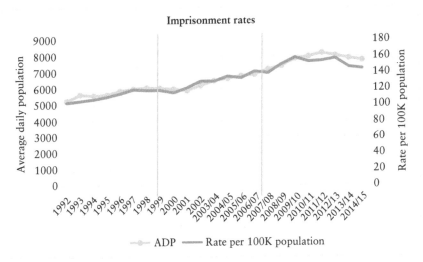

Figure 3 Rates of imprisonment in Scotland
(Source: http://www.gov.scot/Topics/Statistics/Browse/Crime-Justice/TrendPris)

The changes in system activity just described have also been accompanied by major reductions in police recorded crime and crime victimisation. Some caution is required in interpreting these statistics, as the downward trend in police recorded crime certainly predates the SNP years (as shown in figure 4). While the Scottish Crime and Justice Survey does suggest that victimisation has dropped over the past ten years, in contrast to the Labour-Lib Dem Government years (see figure 5), it should be noted that the methodology of the surveys has been altered over time and caution is therefore required in the interpretation of longer-term trends.

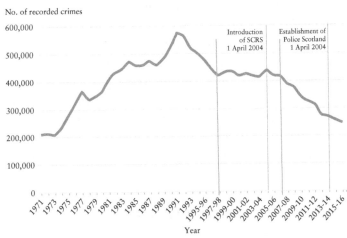

Figure 4 Police Recorded Crime Rates (SCRS=Scottish Crime Recording Standard)
(Source: http://www.gov.scot/Topics/Statistics/Browse/Crime-Justice/
PubRecordedCrime)

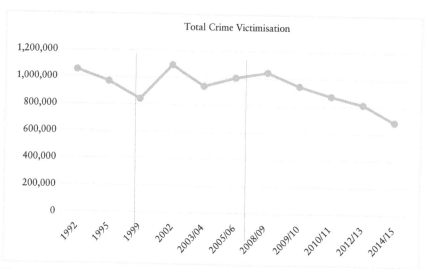

Figure 5 Crime victimisation in Scotland
(Source: http://www.gov.scot/Topics/Statistics/Browse/Crime-Justice/
crime-and-justice-survey/publications)

Architectural Change

While official statistics are suggestive of the positive impacts of policy, some of the institutional transformations led by the SNP Government have been somewhat less successful – most especially the construction of the single national police force. On implementation, immediate concerns arose over what has been termed the 'Strathclydification' of policing (see Henry and Fyfe, 2015 for further discussion) as the new Chief Constable rolled out policing practices and targets that he had honed in Strathclyde. The policing of sex work was a particular source of anxiety as locally developed initiatives (including protection zones, the licencing of saunas) were disbanded and a zero tolerance approach adopted. The arming of police was also a source of controversy as were stop and search practices (particularly so called 'consensual' stops of children under the age of 12). Indeed, research by Kath Murray (2015) has highlighted the massive increase in stops following the instigation of Police Scotland and the ways in which these have impacted differentially on young people from the most deprived communities.

What Works in Reducing Offending?

As noted earlier, the decade of SNP governance has been marked by a greater willingness on the part of politicians to listen and act on evidence provided by the academy. In youth justice the Edinburgh Study of Youth Transitions and

Crime (co-directed by the author of this chapter with Susan McVie) has provided the evidence base for the more diversionary elements of the policy frame.
Sarah Armstrong and Fergus McNeill played a key role in the Prison's Commission work (2008) which paved the way for transformations in community
punishment and prisons policy. Similarly Fergus McNeill's work on desistence
has caught the attention of the current Cabinet Secretary for Justice and has
been integrated into prison regimes (see Liebling *et al.*, 2017).

However a strong finding of the Edinburgh Study is that poverty forms the
backdrop to the lives of the young people who become involved in the most
serious and persistent offending and is one of the strongest predictors of imprisonment in the adult years (McAra and McVie, 2015b). While Scotland has
experienced a reduction in recorded crime there is a growing body of evidence
which suggests that such reductions are greatest in the most affluent areas, with
concentrations of crime victimisation remaining stable within the most deprived
communities (Bates, 2015). Moreover wider social and cultural transformations
may have rendered young people less available for policing – with the growth
in internet use transforming the location of youth transgressions (see McAra
and McVie, forthcoming). Taken together these findings would suggest that for
longer term effectiveness governments need to find more radical solutions to the
problems of poverty and find ways of promoting the well-being of young people
who are vulnerable to victimisation on-line.

Concluding Reflections

The progressive and compassionate approach to matters of justice that has characterised the SNP's first ten years of office, is somewhat fragile. History reminds
us that political agendas can be undermined as a consequence of unforeseen
events, and politicians rarely take the longer-term view. Many of the new policies
introduced by the Scottish Government are slow-burn – especially those which
are focused on early and effective intervention which may require more than
15 years to be demonstrably successful. There is evidence in Scotland that SNP
Ministers do continue to play to populist pressures where this is perceived to have
political traction. A recent example has been the decision by the Cabinet Secretary
for Justice to transform early release arrangements for long-term prisoners, in the
face of robust research evidence highlighting its likely damaging consequences.

We live in uncertain and turbulent times, with constitutional issues domi-
nating political debate. A core part of that debate should be how to create and
sustain a society in which all sectors of the community can flourish. While the
SNP Government has promoted an ethos in criminal justice which links closely to
the research evidence on what works, it needs to resist the stochastic dynamics

of statecraft which result in governments continually remaking and refreshing their policy agendas. Fundamentally strength of character is needed to deliver and sustain compassionate justice over the longer term.

References

Bates, E. (2015), 'Does Place Matter?, in *Scottish Justice Matters*, 3 (3): 9-10.

Christie, C. (2011), *Christie Commission on the Future Delivery of Public Services*, Edinburgh: Scottish Government.

Henry, A. and Fyfe, N. (2015), 'Broadening and Deepening the Debate about Police Reform in Scotland', in *Scottish Justice Matters*, 3 (2): 21.

Liebling, A., McNeill, F. and Schmidt, B. (2017), Criminological Engagements, in Liebling, A., Maruna, S. and McAra, L. (eds.), *The Oxford Handbook of Criminology*, 6th edition, Oxford: Oxford University Press.

McAra, L. (2011), 'The Impact of Multi-level Governance on Crime Control and Punishment' in Crawford, A. (eds.), *International and Comparative Criminal Justice and Urban Governance*, Cambridge: Cambridge University Press.

McAra, L. (2016), 'Can Criminologists Change the World? Critical Reflections on the Politics, Performance and Effects of Criminal Justice', *British Journal of Criminology*, https://academic. oup.com/bjc/article-abstract/doi/10.1093/bjc/azw015/2623920/ Can-Criminologists-Change-the-World-Critical

McAra, L. (2017), 'Youth Justice', in Liebling, A., Maruna, S. and McAra, L. (eds.), *The Oxford Handbook of Criminology*, 6th edition, Oxford: Oxford University Press

McAra, L. and McVie, S. (2015a), 'The Case for Diversion and Minimum Necessary Intervention', in Goldson, B. and Muncie, J. (eds.), *Youth Crime and Justice*, 2nd Edition. Sage.

McAra, L. and McVie, S. (2015b), 'The Reproduction of Poverty', *Scottish Justice Matters*, 3 (3): 5-6.

McAra, L. and McVie, S. (forthcoming), 'Trajectories in Crime and Justice: Remaking the Case for Diversion', in Goldson, B. (ed.), *Cross-national Comparisons of Youth Justice*.

Murray, K. (2015), 'Policing, Prevention and the Rise of Stop and Search in Scotland', *Scottish Justice Matters*, 3(2): 5–6.

Scottish Government (2015), *Preventing Offending: Getting it Right for Children and Young People*, www.gov.scot/Publications/2015/06/2244

Law and Order: Politically Astute and/or Smart on Crime?

John Carnochan

LAW AND ORDER is the usual mainstay of any political campaign and 'Being Tough on Crime' is a timeless political mantra that has cross party utility. Many, politicians included, believe that creating a new law or rigidly enforcing existing laws is the answer to some of our most persistent and corrosive societal problems. Firstly, make the behaviour or practice that is causing concern illegal, then have the police enforce the new legislative solution. Ensure we punish the offenders and all will be well, problem solved, electorate content and job done.

Seldom do politicians state an intent or even an aspiration to be *Smart on Crime*. It is as if being smart by understanding the cause(s) and responding in a thoughtful way that might prevent reoffending or indeed reoccurrence is beyond the brief or remit, it's certainly not beyond the intellect.

In 2007 Scotland got a new Government when the SNP came to power. Some believe their victory was as much about not wanting more of the same as a fervent desire for independence. Whatever the reasons, there was a raising of expectations that governing would be done differently. A hope of aspiring towards a common good defined and framed by Scotland's national identity and a common good. If this meant being radical then there appeared to be an appetite for that too.

There was an expectation that SNP would be different they would develop policy founded on evidence and research and not just long held beliefs that more of the same would do. They would do what was required to make things better and in relation to Law and Order they would be 'Smart on Crime'.

The new Government seemed to recognise the necessity to focus whole systems collaboratively on issues identified locally, delivering solutions locally and involving local communities in the process. There were hopes that this Government might be bold enough to deliver the long-term prevention policies that would extend beyond the next 10 years, certainly beyond the political electoral cycle.

It started well with the establishment of the Early Years Task force, recognising the importance of early years to later life behaviours and trying to bring about collaborative practice through whole system thinking.

There was and still is a commitment to tackle the damaging and pervasive effects of alcohol and the introduction of Minimum Unit Pricing is a prevention policy well founded in evidence.

At this time in Scotland the levels of violent crime particularly knife crime, was high and receiving wide media attention. There was a groundswell of support for the Government to get tough on knife crime, this included the introduction of mandatory sentencing for anyone found in possession of a knife. Opposition political parties continued to support this proposition despite the lack of evidence that such a policy would have any significant or lasting impact on the problem. The new SNP Government stood strong against this suggested response.

This early promise appeared to falter in 2012 with the introduction of The Offensive Behaviour at Football and Threatening Communications Act (Scotland) 2012. This new legislation is an example of the belief that we could arrest our way out of the deep-seated cultural stain of sectarianism. The Act has been a failure by any measure and has succeeded only in distancing the police from a large section of the Scottish population.

There were other decisions made and polices enacted that relied less on evidence and more on populism or self-interest, the provision of an extra 1,000 police officers and ring fencing that number is an example. The figure of 1,000 has no foundation in evidence and was not arrived at through any process of modelling or logic, it was and remains a random figure perhaps selected simply because it is a memorable number and an eye-catching electoral headline.

There is an almost universal acknowledgment that there have been significant and radical changes in the challenges police officers face every day. The emergence of technology and cybercrime, hate crime, child abuse, anti-terrorism, human trafficking, domestic abuse, the list is endless. Arbitrarily increasing the number of police officers is not a smart way to deal with the challenges.

The Christie Commission reported in 2011, it found the impact of failure demand on individual public services was having a significant negative consequence. The Commission recommended among other things that: 'Public services are built around people and communities, their needs, aspirations, capacities and skills and work to build up their autonomy and resilience.'

Many believed there was a need to review the purpose and role of policing in a 21st century Scotland. An inclusive review that would involve communities and individuals, not only professional agencies this. This would, after all, be in keeping with the ethos of whole system change and community empowerment.

Instead of a review the Government created The Police Service of Scotland (PSoS), a single body serving all of Scotland. The creation of PSoS in 2013 could perhaps be viewed as a radical and brave reshaping of a major public service. It was heralded as a way of improving standards of policing throughout Scotland by taking advantage of economies of scale and the adoption of best practices. It was in reality more about saving resources than changing policing. Prior to the creation of the single service the eight Scottish Chief Constables found it extremely difficult to agree on many matters. There was from each at various times a real sense of 'we are different here'. It seemed there were too many Princes in the kingdom and a single force would be more effectively and efficiently managed and controlled.

Public funds should always be spent wisely, not just in times of austerity. The largest single cost in the police was people and therefore to save money there needs to be fewer people employed. The addition of the extra 1,000 officers and the ring fencing of that number meant the largest number of job losses came from the non-warranted police staff and their functions were now being carried out by police officers. Local police offices were closed at a time when there was a raised expectation of community involvement in local decision-making.

The early days of Police Scotland were very much about centralised command and control. Local planning and delivery of services is possible within the current structure but requires empowering local police officers to act locally and in collaboration with local communities and other service providers.

If the reason for change is to save money then that is how all decisions will be framed and money will be saved and services compromised. If the reason for change is to provide a service that is fit for 21st century purpose then that will produce a more effective and efficient public service. The former is about cost the latter is about service.

The governance arrangements of the eight Forces involved Police Committees made up of elected councillors overseeing the running of *their* local police force, including the recruitment of the Chief Constable. The Chief Constable of Police Scotland is appointed by the Justice Secretary. The local boards could not interfere in any operational matters but they could ensure any local policing plans and priorities were considered in a broader context that was locally relevant.

The new Governance arrangements for Police Scotland involve the creation of The Scottish Police Authority. They have a Chair and board members who applied for the part time role. The role of the SPA is to oversee the running of Police Scotland and to hold the Chief Constable to account for the forces performance. Disappointingly, there seems to be very little real connection to local accountability or local involvement.

The most striking example of this absence of local connection and account-ability was the introduction of stop search measures as a response to knife crime, violence and alcohol abuse. Stop Search is a legitimate and effective policing tactic. However, the effectiveness of the tactic was measured by Police Scotland using a crude performance framework. It was applied relentlessly and univer-sally throughout Scotland, no accommodation for local context was permitted. The tactic was so abused that an independent panel was eventually established by Scottish Government to review the practice. This resulted in changes to the practice particularly relating to consensual search and the searching of children.

There is no doubt that in the early days of the SNP Government there was an obvious desire to be smart on crime, to do the right thing no matter if it was populist or not. This desire now appears to be tempered more with a need to be politically astute rather than being *Smart on Crime*.

Section Three: 'We are the People'? Publics, Democracy and Citizenship

A Decade in the Life of Scotland's Public Services

Martin Sime

Introduction: Scotland as a Village?

IT WAS REPORTED at the time of his appointment that Sir Peter Housden, recently retired head of the civil service in Scotland and Permanent Secretary to the Scottish Government, only took the job because he was excited by the prospect of getting all public service leaders into the same room. He had great plans to drive change from the top.

Until then the ambitions and practice of the Scottish Leaders Forum (SLF) had been modest – a bit of corporate drum-banging, some leadership development and a platform for those climbing the ladder. Alas the SLF never managed to move up the gears as Sir Peter intended. Its recent history can be seen as a microcosm of wider plans to reform public services – a story of much good intent and fine rhetoric floundering on the absence of any workable strategy to achieve change.

Looking back over the decade of SNP Government, it is remarkable to note how little has actually changed. Of course, we now have new buildings, some different procedures, and some different faces at the top. More theoretically, the description of the overriding ethos and values of public service have been modernised – using a finely tuned public sector instinct for adopting new language, it is now normal to talk about co-production, asset-based approaches and the like.

However, the trick is to change the words and the conversation, but to leave the actual practice barely touched. Ultimately, there has been little reform of public service over the decade. It is worth questioning the value of a change in ethos, if it only extends to dialogue about services, rather than practical application.

Change has been thwarted by a combination of strong vested interests, most powerfully the professional associations and public sector unions, and a risk averse culture of doing things as they have always been done. On top of this a pervasive patrician sense that public servants are best placed to know what is good for us remains largely intact to this day.

To be fair, such a simple critique is bound to fray on the diversity of purpose within the family of public service. Social care assessments and water purification have little in common; monument preservation and heart surgery likewise. A good case can be made that successful co-production techniques have helped us sort our rubbish, but the management of European funds has become ever more centralised and dictatorial. The picture of co-production, broadening perspectives and stakeholder leverage is therefore patchy at best.

To the cognoscenti this diversity is corralled into planning and strategy arenas where coherence can be found in performance frameworks and community planning partnerships. Most of this common infrastructure, which still soaks up an enormous amount of time and energy, can best be described as ' just about managing'. Translating the fine rhetoric of reform has been problematic. Shared values remain quite thin on the ground while the paying of lip service to a 'new' ethos is a necessary, if not always a useful, characteristic of successful public service leadership

The Culture of More

News and current affairs programmes offer daily examples of the ever more sophisticated ways in which various interests ratchet up demand for more for our public services. More money, more staff, more services and new buildings dominate the discourse and thus it becomes the Chancellor/Scottish Government that prevents us from meeting the many needs we see in our communities. Such claims are often backed up with surveys (often of vested interests), exaggerated claims about the potential impact investment (or failure to invest) would have, all cheered on by an ever expanding inspection industry with a few academics or business leaders joining the chorus.

There are at least two fundamental problems with this cacophony wanting more. Firstly, there is often an untested assumption that more inputs will deliver better outcomes. Do more police and more prisons make us safer? Do more doctors and hospitals make us healthier? Such fundamental questions are seldom raised because they would involve standing up to the noise. And the SNP's approach has been largely pragmatic rather than confrontational – more money was eventually found for Colleges a few years back; a recent and highly orchestrated howl from local government delivered extra cash, and so on. It is perhaps inevitable that minority government encourages such compromises.

Where the clamour for more hits the real world is around limitations on the size of the public purse. In truth our public service funding is rather precariously dependent on the state of the UK economy, UK fiscal policy, the continuation of the Barnett formula, the price of oil and so on. We don't have any sovereign wealth funds to smooth over economic turbulence, we have yet to confront the full cost of no redundancy and final salary pension commitments made to teachers, police and nurses or even to begin to insulate other public services from demand-led costs such as social care and medicines which are bound to rise with our changing demography. We are living hand to mouth and the emphasis remains on fire-fighting and managing, rather than fundamental systematic change.

Ambitions for Change

It was clear at the outset of the decade that the new minority SNP Government understood the need to reform public services, not least to draw a line under the previous regime but also to develop a more inclusive approach to governance. On a political level they needed to cement some new alliances, most notably with trade unions and the third sector. They also needed a strategy to manage relationships with a potentially hostile local government who were required to deliver many of those services. Adopting a big tent approach had its merits but also ruled out any of the more fundamental changes which any of these social partners might object to.

This consensus ambition eventually led to the creation of the Christie Commission, where trade union and third sector interests were well represented alongside the public sector (Christie, 2011). The task was simply to set out an agenda for the reform of our public services; to make the case for change.

The report itself was both radical and practical. It made the case for reform in such a clear way that it won many plaudits and was widely, almost universally, welcomed. Above all it had a lasting impact on the way in which we talk about our public services, catalysing the aforementioned change in guiding rhetoric. The Christie Commission highlighted the case for change based on costs and demography and it highlighted the crucial role that self-help and community development trusts and housing associations could play. Another achievement was introducing prevention and early intervention as key priorities, that are still in play today.

Why Christie Failed

'Failure' is perhaps too harsh a word for a Commission that captured the imagination and proved to have an enduring influence on how we understand and debate the need for public service reform. Perhaps it is more accurate to say that

Christie's ambitions have not yet been realised. Ministers continue to reiterate their commitment to the principles of Christie in policy, action plans and the overall rhetoric of the current administration.

It seems that everyone involved underestimated the complexity of the task of reforming the public sector and public services. For a start, Christie recognised that the two were not the same thing. Yet there has never been a plan to create a parity of esteem between third and public sector provision or the conditions and job security of their workforces. That fault line is even more in evidence today.

More fundamentally, what Christie and those charged with its delivery lacked was any kind of narrative about *how* to reform public services. Of course there are other questions to what those services should be, how they are organised, the role of users and the public, and whether, for some, they should remain universally free. But even with its strong emphasis on prevention and an unchallenged case for reform, there was no common understand or even open discussion about how to go about effecting change.

And the system, as all good bureaucracies do, soon found ways to absorb and claim ownership of the reform agenda while actually doing their best to thwart its intent. Professional protectionism has been a constant, if silent, theme of the last ten years.

To begin with, enthusiasm was high and the launch of a series of Change Funds, eventually amounting to over £500 million of public expenditure, suggested a serious intent to overcome a practical barrier to change – still running the old while establishing the new. Most of this money was directed into the interface between health and care where the preventative investment case was especially strong. But much of it was sucked into health service improvement and many of the new community initiatives which received short-term support simply closed when the Change Fund money ran out. The Change Fund strategy ended up changing not very much.

Public Sector Musical Chairs

It was perhaps inevitable that institutional change would become the default agenda when front line service reform proved elusive. Christie argued that there was a strong need for closer collaboration in the public sector, particularly around shared services and joint planning but a focus on structural reform was not likely to lead to the kind of service changes which were required. It is, Christie argued, how people experience public services that matters most.

In any case, structural reform accelerated into the vacuum created by the failure to deliver front line change. It started modestly enough with consolidation of police and fire services (ending such things as eight different police uniforms and almost hands-free governance). Colleges were next, at least in part to beef-up the role of a new skills agency, itself the merger of some other public service functions. The integration of health and care followed swiftly on, a huge project described caustically as 14 public bodies coming together with 32 public bodies to create 31 new public bodies. Despite the absence of any public debate about the business case, or merely even cost/benefit analysis, such reorganisations continue. Most recently with the establishment of Historic Environment Scotland and highly controversial plans to oversee enterprise, further and higher education and skills quangos with a new 'super' Board. This review has also led to ten work streams being established, tasked with improving performance and governance – with energy obviously being diverted from the delivery of services.

It would seem that the public sector is never happier than when they are charged with reorganising themselves but the energy which is needed and the attention which is required have no doubt diverted attention from any reform of the services themselves.

Elephants in the Room

It suits all of the principal actors – the SNP Government, local authorities, professional associations, trade unions and the third sector – not to consider the role of the private sector in public services, at least in a strategic sense. True, profit making companies are central to the delivery of capital projects, in the provision of residential and domiciliary care, in the fast growing Agencies providing staff for health and education and so on. Procurement and commissioning processes can't usually exclude private companies so they are much in evidence lobbying for their commercial interests in areas such as digital.

But they are marginal to the rest of it. Local government, unlike the third sector, is immune from competitive tendering under some nebulous concept of 'best value'. Pre-school nursery care in Scotland appears to be somewhat shambolic with expensive private provision unable to integrate with awkwardly timed local government 'education' services. Public subsidy of public services delivered by the public sector is the dominant model. While the prison estate, the water industry and much else have reached their own compromises, the vested interests have no incentive, or indeed desire, to disturb the status quo.

The absence of any serious debate about how funding for public services can be made sustainable illustrates a similar theme: some things are best left unexplored. I'm not sure how many politicians understand the commitments made to final salary pension schemes for public sector workers because if they did they would recoil at the scale of the commitment that they have placed on future generations. Likewise the escalating share of the Scottish budget which is being consumed by Private Finance Initiatives (PFI)/Public Private Partnership (PPP) capital, interest and revenue payments. Both of the above will narrow options for the rest of the budget, now and over the next few decades, undermining the prospects for reform.

On the other hand, as a society, we do tend to sweat the smaller stuff. Challenges to the cost and benefit of universally free medicine and travel for the over 60s are often raised. Tuition fees remain a hot potato, but living costs while in further and higher education barely gets a mention. The ever escalating cost of free personal care is yet another elephant in the room. Only in a political culture which is unwilling to confront its holy cows would ever dream of launching Buurtzog community nursing pilots which ignored the central feature of its success in Holland. It is an insurance based healthcare system where people get to choose who provides the service.

Looking Ahead

Public debates about the ethos and values of public services are thin on the ground. Beyond Audit Scotland and the odd academic, there is a lack of independent and authoritative commentary that grapples with the real issues inhibiting reform or in defence of what we have. Almost everyone in the system is aligned to the task of protecting their own interests. After a decade of SNP Government, there is better understanding around the scale of the problem facing public services, but we are not much further forward in knowing how to confront it. Big tent politics, and a cycle of what feels like annual elections and referendums simply adds to the inertia.

It seems likely then that any attempts to disrupt this cosy club way of doing things will have to come from elsewhere. There are a few strands and initiatives which, if widely adopted do have the potential to disrupt the status quo. Two relatively new developments in health and care illustrate this potential and perhaps give some reason to be more hopeful.

Firstly, rights-based approaches have an honourable tradition in mobilising support for the interests of citizens around the world. They are a potentially powerful tool for change and can be used to establish and protect entitlements, to challenge powerful and vested interests, including government, in the courts, or to legitimise behaviours of citizens. The application of such rights-based approaches to our public services is best explained by example.

While lobbying to seek improvements to the lives of people with dementia, Alzheimer's Scotland was able to persuade the Scottish Government to take a rights-based approach to post-diagnostic support. People are now entitled to a named support worker and a care plan with health and local government required to provide it. This puts the individual at the heart of the public service they are receiving and represents a positive change, with professionals on tap, rather than on top.

The second, related example is about putting people who have social care needs in charge of the budget and services they need. A self-directed support law was passed by the Scottish Parliament in 2013. Given the scale of the potential disruption to local government and other provision it is perhaps no surprise that take up has been slow. However, self-directed support could be a game changer given the expectation that many would seek more informal and personal support, involving friends, neighbours and family instead of what are often seen as anonymous care workers.

There is further potential in the application of the self-directed principle that was first advocated by Harry Burns, the former Chief Medical Officer. He argued that the idea of putting the service user in charge is central to their progress – self-management makes a fundamental difference to well-being and life chances. Applying this insight to other public service arenas could a game changer. Citizens would make demands of the system rather than being told what they need. Public services would be reformed accordingly.

To its credit, the Scottish Government is grappling with these ideas and their possibilities, but the challenge remains to tackle the vested interests who find ways to resist and delay. Judging by how difficult they are finding it to reform the way education is delivered, success isn't just around the corner.

Which brings us back to the central issue. The prevailing ethos of Scotland's public services remains a rather patronising idea that the state knows best. The culture of municipalism, while borne out of an honourable ambition to protect citizens from the twin evils of rapacious companies and Tory Governments, is fraying at the edges but still holds sway. During a recent debate about who runs education, The *Convention of Scottish Local Authorities (COSLA)* issued a press statement with the revealing claim that 'local government is best placed to meet all the needs of every child'. The recent farrago about named person legislation included the hiring of an extra 500 public sector workers. Despite knowing perfectly well what keeps people away from reoffending, our prisons are full of those very same people because the money is spent on the system rather than ways to reduce dependence on it.

In summary, while the SNP have been successful in managing public services they have largely failed in their efforts to change them. At least their new responsibilities for welfare are being set out based on some laudable principles but their interaction with the rest of the public service ecosystem is bound to be problematic. We have yet to work out how change to the old ways can be delivered. Whatever political scenario emerges for the future, that task seems urgent.

References

Christie, C. (2011), *Christie Commission on the Future Delivery of Public Services*, Edinburgh: Scottish Government.

Where Does Policy Come From in Scotland?

Ben Wray

POLICY OCCUPIES AN awkward position in politics, mediating uneasily between ideas and legislation, between principle and pragmatism. It is not as important to elections as identity and narratives, and not as significant to governing as leadership and power – but no one wins elections or governs well without effective policy. Analysis of policy in Scotland – how it is made, who makes it and in who's interest – should give us a good insight into how power really operates after ten years of SNP Government.

There is no full proof-map of power and policy in Scottish politics that can be conclusively drawn. That's because influence in policy terms is not an exact science: even if Nicola Sturgeon were to write this chapter as honestly as she can, could she really be sure of the organisations and individuals that have had a bearing on the policies she proposes? Some influence might have a sub-conscious effect: while civil servants aim to develop policy based on the weight of objective evidence, there is no doubt that newspaper headlines and campaigns have an impact. Plus they must balance evidence with manifesto commitments. A complex brew goes into what Oliver Escobar has called 'the black box' of governance and policy making.

Nonetheless, through analysing key individuals and institutions and their networks of influence, as well as looking at case studies of policy development in recent years, we can start to sketch an outline of power and policy in Scottish politics.

In doing so, this chapter argues that the evidence points to a narrow and self-referential group of policy influencers in Scotland – a group that could accurately be described as a governing class with corporate power having significant influence. Policy developed in this way is quite often lacking in rigour, is not especially innovative and almost always serves the needs of elite socio-economic and insider groups. This is reflected in an examination of policy change at Holyrood over the past decade. If Scotland is to genuinely change, it will be necessary for this policy environment to change also.

Understanding Policy

The policy process has no real start. There is no formal point in which the governing institutions of Scotland declare 'here we begin policy'. It moves in waves under the pressure of four dynamics: developing a manifesto for an upcoming election; upholding manifesto commitments after an election; in response to significant political changes; and in preparation for pending major set-piece political events, such as the Scottish Budget.

The central relationship here is the one between Ministers (most importantly the First Minister) and civil servants, with pressure being applied in both directions depending on the nature of the challenge. Think of it as a gauge running from 'political' on one side to 'technical' on the other: when the pointer is at the political side of the gauge the pressure goes from minister to civil servant, demanding rapid policy development to deal with the problem or rise to the opportunity. The more the pointer goes towards the technical side the more the pressure goes the other way, with civil servants outlining the objective realities and what they see as the range of prudent options. Conflict arises when the political and the technical collide.

Once a course has been set, it will then be up to the civil service to develop a process for moving towards a policy outline to a final policy proposal that can be proposed for legislative consent. This will typically involve private and public input, including asking academics and industry experts for advice, organising 'stakeholder forums', public consultations, and so forth.

Within these parameters, a range of influencers input into the thinking of ministers and the civil service. These can be split between governmental and non-governmental. Governmental organisations include the First Minister's office, the Cabinet, government departments, government agencies, government/governing party appointed advisors/commissions, parliamentary committees and local authorities.

The lines of communication and control are different depending on the leadership style, but the Scottish Government under Nicola Sturgeon's leadership is widely known to be of the close-knit top-down style, closer to Tony Blair's 'sofa government' than Theresa May's 'cabinet government'.

Key non-governmental influencers include:

- Corporations
- Think-tanks
- Professional lobbyists
- Media
- Political parties
- Third sector organisations

- Professionals associations/trade unions
- Academics

Although this is a diverse group with very different resources available to them, they are what could be categorised as organised opinion: they have vested interests and, usually, money to facilitate getting their message across in defence of those interests. They influence government through formal and informal channels. Formally, they are generally the people that civil servants go to for due diligence, and will always respond to open calls for written evidence and so forth. Informally, they use the media, personal contacts and social forums to exert policy influence. A Jimmy Reid Foundation study in 2013 showed 67 % of people who gave evidence to parliamentary committee's earned over £34k, of which two-thirds were from a professional organisation, a lobbying firm or held a business interest (Reicher, 2013).

Key individual influencers at the highest level cut across many of these organisations, including a history of moving between governmental and non-governmental jobs. This fluid and dynamic elite level influence has been called 'flex networks' by Janine Wedel, an anthropologist who has analysed the policy environment in Eastern Europe post-Soviet Union. Wedel argues that flex network individuals are defined by:

> ... manoeuvring between government and private roles plus their skill at both relaxing the government's rules of accountability and businesses' codes of competition and at conflating state and private interests. The essence of these groups is that the same collection of people interacts in multiple roles, both inside and outside government, and keeps resurfacing in different incarnations and configurations to achieve their goals over time.

Andrew Wilson, head of lobbying firm Charlotte Street Partners, would be an important but typical example of a flex network individual. Wilson began his career as a civil servant, moving to be a researcher and economist for SNP HQ. He then went to RBS to be a business economist, before being elected to the Scottish Parliament in 1999.

Wilson served as a shadow minister for finance, economy, transport and lifelong learning, before going back to RBS in 2003 as deputy chief economist then head of communications during the financial crisis. He then entered the world of lobbying through WPP, one of the three big global marketing and communications firms, before setting up Charlotte Street Partners (CSP) in 2014, a lobbying firm described by a report by Spinwatch, Unlock Democracy and the Electoral Reform Society as being one of 'the best connected – and most discrete' (Spinwatch et al, 2015: 6). Staff include Kevin Pringle, top 'spin doctor' in the SNP until the summer of 2015. CSP operates in strict secrecy on behalf of its clients, but is known to have lobbied on behalf of the fracking sector in Scotland, including through a dinner set-up with Nicola Sturgeon and 50 top Scottish business figures.

Wilson's story is especially significant because of his most recent appointment by Sturgeon as chair of the SNP's Growth Commission, a new body set-up in September 2016 to renew economic policy for independence. With the First Minister's announcement of her desire for a second referendum between autumn 2018 and spring 2019, all eyes are now on a commission (of which not one trade unionist is among its members) led by the head of a secretive lobbying firm for the answers on currency, borders, trade and other areas that will define a major part of the case for Scottish independence.

Understanding the prominence of flex network individuals like Wilson is important in grasping how policy is shaped in the neoliberal era, where the lines between government and business have become increasingly blurred. Beyond the obvious fact that policy forged in this way is likely to produce outcomes that reflects that socio-economic groups material interests, the lack of critical engagement that comes from a narrow group of elite influencers means policy is likely to be complacent, assuming that their perspective is shared universally without backing this up empirically.

Furthermore, the same voices from the same people who have been in and around circles of power for years can breed a sterile culture where innovation from outside the bubble is feared. Politicians know that if they back the powerful and it goes wrong, the powerful will help them to minimise the impact. If they go against the powerful then they will have to stand or fall by themselves. Much of Scottish Government domestic policy in recent years is reflective of a fearful and uninspired elite policy environment.

One pertinent example of this would be the Scottish Government's plans to cut Air Passenger Duty (APD), recently devolved under the Scotland Act 2016 and set for introduction in May 2018. The plan, to cut the tax by at first 50 % then later entirely, has been consistently backed by the Scottish Government in the 2014 white paper on independence and since then across two public consultations. Despite this, at no time have they been able to provide any evidence for why they support a policy which would cut Scottish Government revenue by £137.5 million beyond two reports both commissioned by the airport/aviation industry lobby. Finance Minister Derek MacKay had to admit as much at a Scottish Parliament Finance Committee hearing in March 2017, where he was told to go and get some independent evidence for the APD cut by the committee chair SNP MSP Bruce Crawford.

The economic premise of the APD cut is that the shortfall in direct revenue will be recovered in indirect revenue from increased economic activity. But the two reports from York Aviation (on behalf of Edinburgh Airport) and Price-WaterhouseCoopers (on behalf of a host of aviation firms) that advocate this position failed to analyse the negative impact on the Scottish economy from a fall in domestic tourism due to increasing numbers of Scottish tourists flying abroad, which according to a Common Weal report (still the only independent report published on the subject) would, at minimum, cancel out all gains from increased airport activity (Dalzell, 2016).

The government processes in developing this policy are instructive: a 'stake-holder forum' was set-up consisting entirely of aviation and airport companies, with a lone environmental representative, who complained that everyone else in the room 'was very much on the same page'. In written submissions to the Scottish Government's Air Departure Bill consultation, aviation firms packed it out with multiple submissions all saying the same thing, to give the appearance of public responses being weighted towards supporting the tax cut.

Another example is the Scottish Government's approach to education reform, most prominently plans to introduce national standardised testing for P1, P4, P7 and S3 as part of its national improvement framework to address the attainment gap between children from poor and wealthy backgrounds. Sturgeon has said the purpose is not to bring back league tables but has admitted there may be no way of stopping the media from using the data in this way, and it's not clear at all how more testing tackles inequality in attainment.

Other areas that fall into a similar category of fearful and uninspired are maintaining the council tax with only slight tweaks despite a Scottish Government commission which concluded that the tax, introduced by the Tories in 1993, 'cannot go on' and was in need of 'substantial reform'. College mergers have drastically reduced the ability of those in-work to go to college part-time, and an Audit Scotland report has found no evidence that the re-structuring has brought more efficiency or led to improvements.

Mergers and re-structuring's has generally been a go-to position of government policy over the past decade, an approach which has the clear benefit of looking like change but often appearing to be without genuine purpose. The constituency that always gains from re-structuring's are IT firms that get a whole new set of proprietary software to create and elite individuals who get lucrative positions on new fancy boards. One notorious example of this is the Glasgow Colleges Regional Board (GCRB) that was set-up to oversee Glasgow's three new 'super-colleges' but, after a year in existence costing 14 times it's equivalent in Lanarkshire and with £400,000 'top-sliced' off the college budget to fund its own operations, the GCRB was still not ready to take on its role of managing the colleges. This led to the Scottish Funding Council stepping back in to takeover, and the GCRB's chair, former First Minister Henry McLeish, resigning. All of this has the hallmarks of policy designed with not enough purpose and too much lobbying influence.

The Hold of 'Insider Policy Scotland' and Democratising and Opening Up Policy

The picture painted above of how the SNP in office have made key policy pronouncements is part of a wider canvas of how policy, ideas and public spending choices have happened over the course of devolution, which is itself, part of a historic set of trends evident over the course of post-war Scotland.

A number of factors have reinforced this. One is a small Scottish policy community with few alternative sources of ideas and thinking which have the capacity and resources to challenge conventional thinking. Another is a capacity of Scottish Government and public bodies to engage in a closed circle set of discussions which passes for engagement, but which is in effect government and public bodies talking to themselves in an exercise in self-reinforcement of existing views. Neither of these have been substantially changed by the experience of devolution, despite initial expectations to the contrary.

Another contributory factor has been the institutional propensity of policy makers and decision makers to make policy by consensus. This has meant continually setting up working groups, advisory boards and panels, and commissions, which government knows prior to their activities what it wants to get out of them. Sometimes this is justification and buy-in to a policy, sometimes it is merely a fig leaf of activity, pretending something is being done, when often the status quo is being strengthened. This world of insider policy Scotland is one certain key group such as business membership organisations (CBI, SCDI) and professional bodies know how to work, having the staff, resources, expertise and critically, contacts. But for any groups sitting outside this and with few resources, the experience can be a depressing and demoralising one. There is little evidence that the substance of this has changed under the SNP, compared to under the previous Labour-Lib Dem administration.

How can we change this? This chapter has so far avoided mentioning the general public deliberately because they are by far the least directly active influencers on government policy between elections. Yes, they are polled for their opinions and they are asked questions in focus groups, but this is so that messages can be devised and narratives developed to convince them of already designed policy. The actual policy development process has already been conquered by the elite flex networks, and citizens are just tested for the best way of pitching it to them.

This is what has to change. There are three aspects to changing this: citizen-led democracy, decentralisation and redistribution: all of which aid opening up and being able to make the policy process more transparent.

It is not just enough to have effective checks and balances on legislation. We need new processes for the development of policy in the first place which are more diverse and more representative of society at large. One way to do this would be to set-up national policy academies across the range of policy areas, where civil servants work alongside academics, industry specialists, trade unionists, citizens and others to deliberate and democratically co-produce policy. This would break down the culture of civil servants always seeking convenient voices and path of least resistance policy approaches and open them up to new, more accountable, ways of thinking and working.

Public consultation should not be an exercise in getting people to ratify government's pre-determined plan. As far as possible it should start early in the policy development process and help frame what question is asked, which should mean the solution to the question is much more open to changed thinking. Those involved in public consultation should as far as possible have input into the process all the way through to legislation and perhaps even to assessing progress after implementation: the point is to get past tokenism and get citizens genuinely involved in policy formation.

Power needs to be pushed downwards in Scotland to get more diversity and innovation in policy-making. Like most governments, in power the SNP has been a centralising force, reducing local authority control while increasing its own at Holyrood. The answer isn't to pass power back to regional authorities that are themselves distant from citizens, but instead to establish a new layer of genuinely local democracy based on the actual communities that people live in. This could get thousands of people across Scotland into the policy process whose ideas, energy and – most importantly – rootedness in communities that experience the front-line of the effect of government policy are gold dust that is currently not being made use of.

Finally, economics can't be artificially separated from politics – the further inequality deepens, the more democracy is undermined and plutocracy advances. While Donald Trump's government of billionaires is a stark illustration of this, it is not necessary to look any further than Westminster to see plutocracy at work: Gordon Brown, Tony Blair, Alistair Darling, Peter Mandelson, William Hague, Mervyn King and George Osborne – some of the biggest names in British politics over the past decade – are all now working on behalf of banks. The latter of these figures – our former Chancellor – is now also, remarkably, the editor of London's most read newspaper, the Evening Standard. The revolving door between corporate, media and political power is no less of a threat to Scotland, independent or not.

For this reason, the redistribution of power and wealth is a prerequisite for long-term policy change, which if it is to happen will require abandoning the deeply ingrained assumptions of neoliberal economics that is still so influential across the political and policy class in Scotland.

References

Dalzell, C. (2016), APD *Cut: A flighty economic case: A Response to the Consultation on Air Passenger Duty*, Biggar: Common Weal, accessed at: http://allofusfirst.org/tasks/render/file/?fileID=3D5BC022-9AB9-1037-DE7D2CD46BFAECCA

Reicher, S. (2013), *Not By the People: The Launch of the Commission on Fair Access to Political Influence*, Biggar: Jimmy Reid Foundation.

Spinwatch, Unlock Democracy and Electoral Reform Society Scotland (2015), *Holyrood Exposed: A Guide to Lobbying in Scotland*, Edinburgh: Spinwatch.

Wedel, J. (2004), 'Flex Power: A Capital Way To Gain Clout, Inside and Out', *Washington Post*, 12th January.

'We, the People Who Live Here': Citizenship and the SNP

Andrew Tickell

ON 18 JUNE 2015, once our parliamentarians had shuffled through Westminster's crumbling lobbies and the tellers had finished counted heads, the House of Commons voted by 71 votes to 514 not to extend the Brexit referendum franchise to the estimated 2.2 million EU citizens then resident in the UK.

The seventy-one MPs who backed the amendment were a motley crew. SDLP and Plaid Cymru MPs joined a smattering of Liberal Democrats with nothing to lose, and stubborn old warhorses from the Labour benches like Paul Flynn and Dennis Skinner, to try to enfranchise the Polish, German and Spanish citizens whose lives were put in the balance by the poll.

The overwhelming majority, however, came from the 56 SNP MPs returned to the Commons by the General Election of 2015. It was a telling parliamentary moment, and perhaps a decisive one. When the votes were tallied the following summer, the Leave campaign's margin of victory was just 1,269,501 votes. But beyond the tempting counterfactuals, the Commons vote and the debate which accompanied it represented a fundamental clash of citizenship discourses, revealing just how far the modern SNP's conception of citizenship has departed from orthodox British ideas of who is and ought to be inside and outside the political community.

The Conservative MP for Tonbridge and Malling, Tom Tugendhat, argued the SNP amendment rested on a fundamental confusion about the nature of citizenship. The SNP, he argued, were 'seeking to change the social contract between citizens who have specifically not chosen to be British and citizens who are British' by proposing to allow Greek and Swedish residents of this country to contribute to determining the future basis of the UK's relationship with the European Union. 'In changing that contract', he suggested, the SNP 'would bounce people who have not made that choice into a relationship with the state that they do not wish to have' (Tugendhat, 2015). From the despatch box, the Foreign Secretary denounced the SNP amendment in even more emphatic terms, arguing that 'the European referendum is about delivering a pledge to the British people to consult them about the future of their country. It would be a travesty to seek to include EU nationals whose interests might be very different from those of the British people' (Hammond, 2015).

Eighty-eight % of MPs agreed with Philip Hammond. The amendment fell. Minutes later, so too did a second proposal to allow sixteen and seventeen year olds across these islands to participate in the Brexit referendum. Again, SNP MPs deployed the language of civic inclusion. Again, by a slimmer margin, Westminster rebuffed the idea.

In Edinburgh, by contrast, a dramatically different common sense of citizenship prevailed when devolved parliamentarians were deciding who ought to have a say in Scotland's constitutional future. The SNP Government opted to use the local government franchise, extending the independence referendum franchise not only to British residents, but also to all European nationals on the local government roll. This prompted nary a peep of dissent across the Parliament. While there were testy exchanges between MSPs on extending the franchise to sixteen and seventeen-year-olds, and excluding prisoners from the voting roll, not a single dissenting voice was raised in Holyrood about the idea that European citizens habitually resident in Scotland could and should contribute to the independence poll (Tickell, 2015). The key parliamentary committee pronounced itself 'content that the Bill delivers an appropriate franchise for the referendum' (Scottish Parliament, 2013: 28).

Hammond's 'travesty' was Holyrood's bland cross-party consensus – perhaps reflecting the distinctive mandates which MPs and MSPs have been elected on since the advent of devolution. Most European citizens form no part of the parliamentary electors of Runnymede and Weybridge who will decide Philip Hammond's fate at the next Westminster election, while the Europeans of Glasgow Southside will help decide whether Nicola Sturgeon retains her seat. Such things undoubtedly focus the political mind – but it would be a mistake to analyse the two Parliaments' diverging political practice only through the lens of cynical political self-interest. Holyrood's more expansive franchise has arguably had unforeseen secondary effects on cross-party perceptions of where the boundaries of the political community ought to be drawn, whether in terms of young people, or resident Europeans. Amendments to the Scotland Act allowed Holyrood to extend the franchise to sixteen and seventeen year olds on a permanent basis (Scottish Elections (Reduction of Voting Age) Act 2015). As the 18 June 2015 dramatically illustrated, the common sense of citizenship seems radically to have diverged across the United Kingdom.

The SNP have now been – to some extent, unconsciously – vociferously responsible for championing this divergence. In government in Holyrood, and in opposition in Westminster, the party has developed a coherent, sustained, and attractive conception of Scottish citizenship, emphasising 'we the people', but 'we the people who live here', in the language of the independence White Paper (Scottish Government, 2013: i). This expansive, residential conception of citizenship has become dominant in the SNP's mature thinking – though it arguably has deeper roots in the party's intellectual traditions and political practice.

You still find odd stray threads of harder, older SNP citizenship discourses. In the SNP's 1997 manifesto, Margaret Ewing married cosmopolitanism with critique, thundering that with independence, 'citizens of Scotland, *wherever they have come from*, will be full participants in a 21st century democracy, not subjects of an outmoded and decaying eighteenth century state' (Ewing, 1997: 10). It is difficult to imagine such trenchant language being used today in the soft-focus, glossy, productions emanating from party HQ – but you can still pick out the golden thread of 'we the people who live here', years on.

Who Shall Be Citizens?

Neil MacCormick, legal philosopher, SNP MEP, and Regius Professor of Public Law and the Law of Nature and Nations at the University of Edinburgh, was a central figure in the development and promotion of this now dominant political perspective. 'Who shall be citizens?' he asked, at the turn of the millennium. Professor MacCormick's answer? 'All persons principally resident in Scotland and all those born in Scotland, with no restriction on dual citizenship; a free right to renounce citizenship, with no less or residential rights in the case of renounced citizenship; absolute prohibition on any loss of citizenship otherwise than by fully voluntary renunciation' (MacCormick, 2000). The SNP Government's independence White Paper honoured MacCormick's intellectual legacy, committing the new state to an 'inclusive approach to citizenship' (Scottish Government, 2013: 254). Ensuring that British citizens 'habitually resident' in Scotland on independence will automatically be considered Scottish citizens as would 'Scottish-born British citizens currently living outside of Scotland. Other people will be able to register or apply for Scottish citizenship on independence based on clear criteria' (Scottish Government, 2013: 16 – 17).

You could also hear MacCormick's ghost on the 18 June 2015, as SNP MPs wrangled across the Commons in the interests of EU citizens with baffled Tory parliamentarians. Discounting allusions to 'Scottish blood', invoked by one Conservative member, Edinburgh East MP Tommy Sheppard emphasised that 'I have none whatsoever in mine. I am a member of the Scottish National Party and I represent my constituents because I have chosen to make my life in Scotland.' 'It is not a question of identity or genetics', he told the Commons, 'it is a question of residence. The thing I am most proud of in the Scottish referendum is that that was the principle we applied. We said that if people choose to come and live in this country, make their future here, contribute to the country and be part of it, they have an equal say with anyone else in the future of their country' (Sheppard, 2015). Sheppard's themes were echoed by several of his colleagues.

North East Fife's Stephen Gethins suggested 'Scotland is a mongrel nation, which counts many peoples as Scots. We want to see them as an integral part of our country. What better way to say that they are an integral part of our country than by giving them the vote and putting them in a position to decide?' depicting the franchise as a way of demonstrating 'open, inclusive and democratic country' (Gethins, 2015). Alex Salmond invoked the example of Christian Allard – a French national, who represented North East Scotland in Holyrood between 2011 and 2016. 'Why on earth should he be denied a vote?' Salmond demanded of the Treasury benches, contrasting the UK Parliament's approach with Holyrood's. 'We allowed European citizens to vote in the Scottish referendum because our view of nationality has a civic basis', he argued:

> *Unlike Conservative Members, with their narrow-minded nationalism and narrow view of people's interests, we take a broad view of the matter. We believe in civic nationalism – we believe that if someone engages in a country, lives in a country, works in a country and pays tax in a country, they are entitled to vote on the future of the country.*
>
> (Salmond, 2015)

As Mitchell, Bennie and Johns note, 'conceptions of identity are not the same as conceptions of citizenship, though these are often conflated. Citizenship concerns the relationship between the individual and the state: rights; duties; and responsibilities. It also involves membership and a state can define membership, as citizenship, either relatively inclusively or exclusively. Though conceptually distinct, we would expect the definition of national identity to be closely related to notions of citizenship' (Mitchell, Bennie and Johns, 2012: 109). This conflation is profoundly true of the modern SNP rhetoric in this field.

But the conception of citizenship articulated by Sheppard, Gethins and Salmond is not a flash in the pan, nor can it be understood as a calculated effort to secure electoral advantage. 20 years earlier, at the party's 1995 Perth Conference, Mr Salmond's keynote address underscored identical themes of plurality and polyphony:

> *No minority should be asked to give up their culture or badges of identity to be fully accepted as Scots. There will be no cricket tests in a free Scotland. We see diversity as a strength and not a weakness of Scotland and out ambition is to*

see the cause of Scotland argued with English, French, Irish, Indian, Pakistani, Chinese and every other accent in the rich tapestry of what we should be proud to call, in the words of Willie McIlvanney, 'the mongrel nation' of Scotland.

(Salmond, 1995)

Indeed, reappraising the evidence of 2014, cynics could see the cosmopolitan citizenship and democratic participation Mr Salmond lionised as a declaration against his own political interests. Examining voting behaviour by key demographics, the Scottish Referendum Study identified that while a small majority of Scottish born voters supported independence (52.7 %), only 27.9 % of voters born in the rest of the United Kingdom, and 42.9 % outside the UK, backing the Yes campaign in September 2014 (Henderson and Mitchell, 2015). To their credit, the SNP have made nothing politically of this finding, doubling down on the old cosmopolitan formulation that to live and work here is to become a meaningful part of the political community.

But not all is sweetness and light. Fear of tabloid reaction ensured that prisoners remain unenfranchised, despite empty rhetoric about Scotland being a progressive beacon of human rights and accommodating citizenship. With characteristic overstatement and hypocrisy, the former SNP Cabinet Secretary for Justice described this loss of nerve as both 'shameful' and 'the wrong thing' done 'for the right reasons' (MacAskill, 2015). Penetrating beyond the cosmopolitan bromides, the SNP has also never undertaken programmatic thinking about its immigration priorities, mostly reacting to, and sometimes reacting against, the policies or particular decisions of the UK Government of the day, piling in behind sympathetic cases while keeping conveniently mum on what a Scottish Home Office might look like.

The 2013 White Paper was conspicuously silent about what 'clear criteria' an SNP-led Scottish Government might apply to its would-be citizens. In focussing on the status of those who already live in Scotland, the SNP have been able almost entirely to neglect the debateable lands of how citizenship or leave to remain is acquired, by whom, and the spectrum of approaches to immigration and nationality which an independent Scotland might adopt. The devolution settlement has helped foster this evasiveness. 'Immigration and nationality' is a reserved matter over which Holyrood enjoys no legislative competence (Scotland Act 1998, Schedule 5, B2). Until 2015, the SNP's Westminster representation was a poorly-resourced skeleton crew. The serious-minded analysis of a significant number of reserved matters in the party has suffered as a consequence.

The party's 2015 manifesto embodies the SNP's slipperiness when faced with more complex trade-offs and choices. The 2015 platform advocated an 'immigration policy that works for Scotland', without specifying what 'working' might mean in this context. The platform reiterates the now familiar cosmopolitan outlook, while fudging more substantive – and more controversial questions – emphasising on the one hand that 'diversity is one of Scotland's great strengths' and 'those who have come to Scotland from other countries make a significant contribution to our economy and our society' while stressing that 'effective immigration controls are important' and supporting 'sensible immigration policies that meet our economic needs' (SNP, 2015: 9). The 2010 platform was similar, arguing 'for Scotland to take responsibility for immigration so that we can develop a system here at home that more closely meets our needs. An 'earned citizenship' system, similar to those in Canada or Australia, would allow Scotland to attract high-skill immigrants who can add to the strength of our economy and help deliver growing prosperity for the whole nation' (SNP, 2010: 19).

As the 2013 White Paper observed, 'Deciding who is a citizen is a defining characteristic of an independent state and future Scottish Governments will have the power to determine rules on citizenship and nationality' (Scottish Government, 2013: 271). Ten years into an SNP administration, and perhaps approaching a second referendum on our constitutional future, the party's more fundamental analysis of these issues remains curiously unclear. 'We the people who live here' is a nice phrase and a fine principle, which the party's parliamentarians has invoked to defend honourable and sometimes unpopular causes – but it can only be the beginning, and not the end, of our understanding of the meaning of citizenship and the brass tack choices with which an independent state will have to contend.

References

Gethins, S. (2015), House of Commons Hansard, 18 June, Column 558 – 559.

Hammond, P. (2015), House of Commons Hansard, 9 June, Column 1053.

Henderson, A. (2007), *Hierarchies of Belonging: National Identity and Political Culture in Scotland and Quebec*, London: McGill-Queen's Press.

MacAskill, K. (2015), 'We can't fight for Human Rights Act and not back prisoners voting', *The National*, 27 May.

MacCormick, N. (2000), quoted in Mitchell, J, Bennie, L and Johns, R. (2012), *The Scottish National Party: Transition to Power*, Oxford: Oxford University Press, 109.

Mitchell, J, Bennie, L and Johns, R. (2012), *The Scottish National Party: Transition to Power*, Oxford: Oxford University Press.

Salmond, A. (1995), Speech to Perth Scottish National Party Conference, quoted in Henderson, A. (2007), *Hierarchies of Belonging: National*

Identity and Political Culture in Scotland and Quebec, London: McGill-Queen's Press.

Salmond, A. (2015), *House of Commons Hansard*, 9 June, Column 1072.

Scotland Act 1998.

Scottish Elections (Reduction of Voting Age) Act 2015.

Scottish Government (2013), *Scotland's Future: Your Guide to An Independent Scotland*, Edinburgh: Scottish Government.

Scottish National Party (1997), *Yes We Can Win the Best for Scotland: Westminster Election Manifesto 1997*.

Scottish National Party (2010), *Elect a Local Champion: Westminster Election Manifesto 2010*.

Scottish National Party (2015), Stronger for Scotland: Westminster Election Manifesto 2015.

Scottish Parliament, Referendum (Scotland) Bill Committee (2013*), Stage 1 Report on the Scottish Independence Referendum (Frachise Bill),* 7 May.

Sheppard, T. (2015), *House of Commons Hansard*, 18 June, Column 537.

Tickell, A. (2015), 'Prisoner Voting Gambits: Disappointment all round in Chester, McGeogh and Moohan', *Edinburgh Law Review*, Vol 18, 289–295.

Tugendhat, T. (2015), *House of Commons Hansard*, 18 June, Column 541.

Constitutional Monarchy: Kingship or Republic for 21st Century Scotland?

William Henderson

Introduction

'CONFERENCE SUPPORTS THE long-held principle that the sovereignty of Scotland lies with the people of Scotland', acknowledged the 63rd Annual National Conference of the SNP, at Rothesay. Those were the words at the start of resolution number 14 on the 1997 SNP Conference Agenda. The resolution text went on to declare that 'the people should have the right... to choose the Head of their newly independent State' and finally 'resolved that within the term of office of the first independent Parliament of Scotland a referendum will be held on the question of whether or not to retain the Monarch as Head of State for Scotland.'

An amendment that would have mandated the SNP to campaign in that referendum for an elected Head of State was defeated. However, the resolution itself passed and thus the SNP became committed to holding a referendum on the issue. That referendum, however, was to take place in a context of the SNP winning a majority of Scottish constituencies in the House of Commons, negotiating with Her Majesty's Government about the independence process.

Two decades ago the SNP mandated itself to hold that referendum on the monarchy within the first term of an independent Scottish Parliament. That parliament did not exist, and it still does not. Devolution at that point had not taken place and the successful devolution referendum had only just been held a fortnight before the SNP Conference in Rothesay. How then did the SNP move from this position just two weeks after the vote for a devolved legislature to the position set out in the independence referendum White Paper in 2014?

A Referendum Policy, but not a Referendum on Independence

Despite the debate at the 1997 SNP Annual Conference on a referendum and whether to be expressly republican in that plebiscite, one of the notable issues that the SNP has had to contend with for decades has been a relative consistency of support for the monarch in Scotland. Scottish attitudes to monarchy over the post-war period have shown continued affection, but declining deference, mirroring wider social trends. As historian Richard Finlay has observed much of this respect was in spite, not because of, the way the royal family functioned, with large elements of their public behaviour and associated rituals in Scotland barely changed from the height of Victoria: 'Balmoralism, Highland Games and tartanry still characterised much of the royal family's image north of the border, almost to the point of caricature' (Finlay, 2005: 34).

The SNP membership itself is one such place where scepticism of the institution of monarchy can be found. In 2009 a major academic study supported by the Economic and Social Research Council, and facilitated by SNP Headquarters, was conducted of the SNP membership. The results are enlightening from a perspective of the personal views of the membership (as it then stood, prior to the post-independence referendum increase in membership). When asked to agree or disagree with the statement that 'The monarchy has no place in a modern democracy' the results from SNP members were that 57 % of SNP members concurred with the statement (35 % strongly agreeing, and 22 % agreeing), while only 20 % of members objected to the statement (6 % strongly disagreeing, and 14 % disagreeing).23 % of respondents were in neither camp (Mitchell, Bennie and Johns, 2012). How then has the more recent policy position managed to survive?

Part of this is down to the SNP historically having never been a republican organisation, although the party clearly has many republicans within it. The student and youth wings, the Federation of Student Nationalists and Young Scots for Independence, have at times been particularly vocal in pursuing opposition to a hereditary Head of State. As well as the youth and student wings though there have been other sporadic attempts to change this policy platform within the SNP, including that of the short lived '79 Group, whose newsletter was headed 'For a Scottish Socialist Republic', and openly pursued three goals of independence, socialism, and republicanism.

However, one needs to only look at the historical response generally of Scottish Nationalists to matters like the Royal Titles Act 1953 (Mitchell, 1968; McHarg and Mullen, 2006) to gain an understanding of the more established position. This campaign and related litigation focused not upon the existence of the institution of monarchy itself but instead on the numeral the monarch should use – Queen Elizabeth I or II? (Mitchell, Bennie and Johns, 2012).

The Move Towards Current Party Policy

That mainstream position in Nationalist thinking was one that was departed from in 1997 at the Rothesay conference. There has though been a notable shift again though in this area of policy over the years. The 1997 UK general election manifesto, immediately preceding the Rothesay conference, had stated that 'the SNP propose the reform of the Monarchy, which while allowing the Queen and her successors to remain Head of State would ensure that their duties and payments were clearly and openly understood. In the absence of the Queen from Scotland the elected Chancellor (Speaker) of the Scottish Parliament will act as Head of State.' Already by that point the SNP was speaking about 'reform' to the system, but with continuity of the hereditary system. The response of the SNP in 1997, prior to Rothesay, to mention of The Queen had been 'defensive, insisting that it wanted to end the Union of Parliaments, not the Union of Crowns' (Mitchell, Bennie and Johns, 2012). That is a position that can be recognised today, including from the 2014 Scottish Government White Paper.

In 2003 the Scottish Parliament manifesto stated: 'With Independence, the Queen and her successors will remain as Head of State of Scotland, as defined within the written Constitution, subject to the democratic consent of the people in a referendum.' Here there is no mention at all of the timescale contained within resolution number 14 passed at Rothesay. The language more broadly is interesting as it does not say that a referendum will be held on 'whether to retain the Monarch as Head of State for Scotland.' The manifesto text is flexible enough to even allow argument that a referendum on the issue is simply the right of the people of Scotland, or that the referendum is about the written Constitution.

The 2010 manifesto for the UK Parliament declared that the party 'has long campaigned for fair votes and the removal of anachronisms like the unelected House of Lords, and we will continue to press for the abolition of the Act of Settlement.' Unlike the UK unelected upper house, the unelected Head of State received no mention. The emphasis in this respect was placed upon removing the anti-Catholic discriminatory provisions on hereditary succession.

In the 1990s the SNP developed a strong platform on the Act of Settlement, with Mike Russell, Chief Executive and later MSP, at the forefront of developments calling for change (Lynch, 2002; Johns and Mitchell, 2016). This issue though was only partly dealt with by the UK Parliament in passing the Succession to the Crown Act 2013, which also addressed the endemic sex discrimination that existed in the system.

When the SNP entered the devolved administration at Holyrood in May 2007 a shift took place. It was noticeable to many, but not all, and has required a period of adjustment for this to bed down over the last decade. Then, the SNP conference on 27 October 2007 endorsed a document entitled 'National Conversation White Paper, Choosing Scotland's Future'. Within paragraph 3.25 of that Scottish Government publication was set out the following:

> On independence, Her Majesty The Queen would remain Head of State in Scotland. The current parliamentary and political Union of Great Britain and Northern Ireland would become a monarchical and social Union – United Kingdoms rather than a United Kingdom – maintaining a relationship first forged in 1603 by the Union of the Crowns.

With that change it formally removed any reference to the holding of a referendum on the subject. However, that is not the end to the story as the SNP strongly expresses belief in the sovereignty of the people of Scotland. Although it is not expressly set out in policy, if there was clear demand by the people for a referendum on the issue in an independent Scotland, who would say no? And what form of monarchy is envisioned?

Shaping a 'Modern Law of Kingship'?

George Buchanan's historic work, *De Iure Regni apud Scots Dialogus*, has been mentioned as being part of the ideological basis on which Scotland and the monarch could base relations in a modern state of independent Scotland (Harvie, 2007). Alex Salmond for many years as First Minister spoke about a concept of 'the community of the realm of Scotland', which stems in part from the notion of popular sovereignty espoused by Buchanan calling for monarchs to be accountable to the people (Mason and Smith, 2004; 2006).

Buchanan had in fact gone as far as stating that he wanted 'the people, who have granted him [the monarch] authority over themselves, to be allowed to dictate to him the extent of his authority, and... require him to exercise as a king only such right the people have granted over him.' In the context of the SNP proposals for constitutional monarchy this role would appear to include the formal openings of the independent Scottish Parliament, if the monarch is available, and that would be about the sum of it. Whichever model for Head of State an independent Scotland ends up with it would be fairly safe to say that 'the distinction between the republican and monarchical model would be to restrict very sharply the real power of the president or monarch' (Himsworth and O'Neill, 2009).

This approach is not a far cry from arguments for actual republican reforms that have been made over recent years including that 'all of the Crown's prerogative powers... be abolished and, where necessary, replaced with legislation', stopping just short of calls for 'the Crown and the queen to be removed from the constitution' entirely (Gray and Tomkins, 2005). For how long then with such a constitutionally restricted role for the monarchy after independence will the position of the Head of State be based on the hereditary principle?

The SNP has understandably taken a line of least resistance, although one that looks overly cautious at times as what is not expressly stated, but is clearly implied and should be obvious to anyone with even a rudimentary understanding of sovereignty is that with statehood for Scotland comes the opportunity for the people of Scotland to shape their own destiny, literally like never before.

What would exist is the ultimate set of rights and obligations that it is possible to exercise on the international plane and within the domestic arena the opportunity, or the right, to continue with the current system of government or to change that for something else. What is missed in all of this is the immense array of options that independence places in the hands of the ordinary people of Scotland for shaping the country they wish to live in. It is the central principle of independence that allows the choice to the people of Scotland to continue with the current system (unlikely), to reform and create a modern constitutional monarchy, or move to a republic.

However, on this point of the options for independent Scotland's Head of State the positioning of the SNP sits largely where Scotland as a whole does, at present. Where the modern SNP membership, post-2014 increase, sits on the issue is unknown as we only have the 2009 survey responses to go by. The issue seems to not be discussed at all and there would appear to be no appetite to change that.

As the late Stephen Maxwell noted, the subject of the monarchy in the SNP attracts a range of perspectives but ultimately 'the need to draft and agree a Scottish constitution would itself be an opportunity for a major public debate about the future of Scottish democracy' (Maxwell, 2012). By that point it would be up to the people of Scotland to determine the shape of government for our country.

Given current feeling and polling there would be no reason to expect that would be anything other than a constitutional monarchy, likely on a model similar to that put forward by the SNP. However, constitutions are subject to change and the sovereignty of the people, much referred to by the SNP, would mean that system could change depending on the form of future debates. There are countless examples of where the constitutional development of a country has been shaped by the historic and political situation in which peoples find themselves at given points in time (Ashton and Finch, 2000). Scotland would find itself as no exception in this respect.

References

Ashton, C. and Finch, V. (2000), *Constitutional Law in Scotland*, Edinburgh: W. Green.

Finlay, R. (2005), 'Scotland and the Monarchy in the Twentieth Century', in Miller, William L. (ed.), *Anglo-Scottish Relations from 1900 to Devolution*, Oxford: Oxford University Press.

Gray, A. and Tomkins, A. (2005), *How We Should Rule Ourselves*, Edinburgh: Canongate.

Harvie, C. (2007), 'Common Ground', *The Guardian*, 24 August, accessed at: www.theguardian.com/commentisfree/2007/aug/24/commonground

Himsworth, C.M.G. and O'Neill C.M. (2009), *Scotland's Constitution Law and Practice*, Edinburgh: Bloomsbury Professional 2nd edn.

Johns, R. and Mitchell, J. (2016), *Takeover: Explaining the Extraordinary Rise of the SNP*, London: Biteback Publishing.

Lynch, P. (2002), *The History of the Scottish National Party*, Cardiff: Welsh Academic Press.

Mason, R.A. and Smith, M.S. (2004), *A Dialogue on the Law of Kingship among the Scots: A Critical Edition and Translation of George Buchanan's De Iure Regni apud Scotos Dialogus*, Aldershot: Ashgate Publishing.

Mason, R.A. and Smith, M.S. (2006), *George Buchanan's Law of Kingship*, Edinburgh: The Saltire Society.

Maxwell, S. (2012), *Arguing for Independence*, Edinburgh: Luath Press.

McHarg, A. and Mullen, T. (2006), *Public Law in Scotland*, Edinburgh: Avizandum.

Mitchell, J., Bennie, L., and Johns, R. (2012), *The Scottish National Party: Transition to Power*, Oxford: Oxford University Press.

Mitchell, J.D.B. (1968), *Constitutional Law*, Edinburgh: W. Green 2nd edn.

Scottish Government (2014), *Scotland's Future: Your Guide to An Independent Scotland*, Edinburgh: Scottish Government.

Scottish National Party (1997), *The 63rd Annual National Conference of the Scottish National Party*, Edinburgh: Scottish National Party.

Gender, Power and Women: Movement and Government Politics

Lesley Orr

2007: *After Labour*

FOLLOWING THE 2007 Holyrood election, the SNP formed its first minority government. Just twelve of the forty-seven SNP MSPs (25.5 % – a dramatic fall from 42.7 % in 1999) and only two of the party's 15 newly elected list constituency MSPs were women. Unlike the Scottish Labour Party, with gender parity of representation, the SNP had rejected the use of any equality measures and its female candidates were less likely than men to be standing in safe or winnable seats (Mackay and Kenny, 2009).

The 2007 manifesto said next to nothing about gender equality, and made no pledges specifically to improve women's lives. Despite its reputation as a 'macho' party, supported disproportionately by older, male and rural voters, the SNP's election campaign made no special efforts to attract women's votes. Notwithstanding the handful of talented and high profile women within its ranks, the parliamentary party which took up the reins of government was indubitably male and pale, reflecting the inordinate over-representation of white men in political and public life. As the established Labour-dominated political order was rudely interrupted by the election of the first SNP administration in Scottish history, many in the women's sector, campaigning for better policy and legislation, or delivering vital services, pondered – with mingled curiosity and apprehension – what this would mean for their work to tackle violence against women (VAW) and broader gender injustice.

For all their limitations, there had been important achievements in the early post-devolution years of Labour-led administrations. Among the first intake of MSPs in 1999 were a significant number of Labour women who were veterans of community activism, trade unionism and local council Women's Committees; some had a history of involvement in organisations such as Women's Aid and

Rape Crisis. As experienced feminist activists with a structural analysis of gender inequality they made a distinctive impact on the style and agenda of the new Parliament. Strategic VAW policy, rooted in partnership with the women's sector, became an important arena for newly devolved powers to test and demonstrate distinctively Scottish ways of working in key social policy areas. And gender analysis was vital, framing the impact of VAW on women's health, poverty, education, housing and the criminal justice system, as cause and consequence of women's inequality.

Although these developments were strengthened by cross-party support, and several individual SNP members showed great personal commitment, collectively the party lacked the hinterland and grounding in the Scottish Women's Movement (revitalised during the 1990s campaigns, constitutional debates and 50:50 Campaign from which female SNP members had largely been absent) which facilitated close relationships and networking across the Scottish Executive, trade unions and third sector. What were the prospects for women under the new Scottish Government? The portents did not seem particularly auspicious.

A Significant Shift: The Indyref Campaign as Catalyst

In 2017 the SNP government is led by First Minister Nicola Sturgeon. One of the 50 most powerful women in the world (Forbes List), she is a high profile feminist who uses every opportunity to articulate her commitment to gender equality, and her vision of a Scotland where glass ceilings are 'smashed to smithereens'; a country in which there are no limits on women's ambitions, and where girls can aspire to be whatever they choose. Since the 2016 election she leads a parliamentary group that includes 27 women (42.9 %). For the first time, the SNP used All Women Shortlists (AWS) in seats where the party is expected to win, but women were also placed in favourable list positions – topping half of the party's regional lists. Eight of the nine SNP women selected under AWS were elected – and 13 of the 17 new SNP MSPs elected to Holyrood for the first time in 2016 are women. Sturgeon's Cabinet, comprising five women and five men, intentionally models and promotes gender equity in governance as a positive symbol of her global leadership. Tasmina Ahmed-Sheikh is the National Women's and Equalities Officer, a role which also operates at branch level.

The advent of Sturgeon as party leader and First Minister has undoubtedly marked a major step change in the SNP's commitment to gender equality, but perhaps the real catalyst was the independence referendum campaign, which opened up new spaces of possibility for women's engagement and politicisation. Across Scotland, free from the straitjacket of old style party politics, women found creative ways to discuss the issues and to imagine what kind of country they wanted to live in. Engender, the Scottish Women's Convention and other organisations worked hard to identify and highlight diverse women's concerns, rooted in the particularities of their everyday lives. As female votes were targeted, a potent story emerged, shaped by and for women who scorned the preposterous #PatronisingLady advert (which seems to suggest women were less able to make up their minds), while regarding Scottish independence not as an end in itself, but as the best hope for creating a country 'that embraces the politics of dignity, justice, and care, in which all participate, animated by the spirit of equality and liberation' (Orr et al, 2014).

This was not some idealistic vision of an independent Scotland as a feminist nirvana, but a call rooted in evidence-based assessment of the dire impacts of Westminster policy. UK Government austerity measures and so-called welfare reforms were sharply accentuating the feminisation of poverty, resulting in a grotesque (and ongoing) transfer of resources out of the hands of women– who are disproportionately affected by poverty, low pay, precarious employment, care responsibilities, disabilities, discrimination and abuse. The referendum debate galvanised discussion about which constitutional arrangements would offer the best hope of transforming politics as if women counted. Here was a challenge to the SNP – not only as a devolved administration but in its prospectus for independence: was it bold enough to act on its own rhetoric, by creating a framework of gender equality governance, resting on economic policy and budgeting which values the citizenship of care, for coherent and strategic action across departments? Would it enshrine political commitment at the highest levels, with ministerial accountability and strong compliance mechanisms? Would it commit to material improvements in women's lives across key areas: politics and power, social security, employment and the labour market, education and training, media and culture, violence against women and women's rights? Would it tackle the deeply embedded economic structures and social norms which shape men's as well as women's lives?

The emergence of Women for Independence: Independence for Women (WFI) was a remarkable game changer. With lively local groups, innovative methods and a national campaigning profile, it created a pathway into political awakening and activism for hundreds of women, and an enduring legacy. Following a landmark gathering three weeks after the referendum, WFI was constituted for the continuing task of fighting for a fairer Scotland, as members shared their testimonies, their anger, their hopes, their ideas and their determination to carry on the struggle. WFI has facilitated the participation and confidence of many talented women, a large proportion of whom (+90 %) voted for the SNP, which 25 % subsequently joined (25 %). The party's changing membership profile bears this out: from 64 % male and 36 % female before the referendum to 55 % – 45 % in the post-2014 surge of new members (Johns and Mitchell, 2016). Recent recruits, especially from WFI, tend to more progressive and left-ward outlooks.

Nevertheless, old attitudes and cultures die hard, and at branch level attempts to address discrimination or casual misogyny are reportedly often met with apathy and resistance. As a current member of the WFI National Council says 'feminism and Scottish independence are linked, because it's about the politics of self-determination at personal, inter-relational and national levels.' Several have been elected as MPs and MSPs, leading high profile campaigns on women's issues (e.g. Alison Thewliss MP against the 'rape clause', Gillian Martin MSP for free period protection) and appointed to key Scottish Government positions (Jeane Freeman MSP, Social Security Minister). Many more are SNP candidates in the 2017 local council elections, supported by WFI which has been proactive in encouraging members to stand, recognising that women and their families disproportionately rely on local government services and jobs, and the challenge is to ensure effective practical responses. The growing influence of women in SNP politics has been evident in recent motions and debates at party conferences.

What Has Changed?

It is clear that in significant ways, this has been a decade of change in the presentation and ethos of the party in relation to women. The First Minister's own political compass has always pointed towards tackling poverty and gender injustice. Her oft-repeated claim that equality for women is at the heart of the SNP's vision for a fairer Scotland seems to indicate a real paradigm shift since 2007. But in what ways has the nation changed for the women who live here? Beyond the rhetoric, what is the substance of that vision, and where is the evidence of policy and action to justify the First Minister's claims of progress?

In 2007 the incoming SNP administration sought to prove their capacity and competence in relation to 'women's issues'. Their political strategy was to reassure existing organisations and initiatives of continued support and even increased funding. Partnership working with academic and third sector feminist expertise – especially in the context of a minority government – was validated. Key agendas and infrastructures for policy development were maintained, for example 'Close the Gap' (an STUC-based partnership project on women's pay and participation in the labour market) and the explicitly gendered Scottish approach to addressing VAW (which diverged significantly from the rest of the UK, and has been widely recognised as pioneering). 'Equally Safe' (2014) is the current iteration of this flagship approach. Women's organisations were able to build new relationships with some unexpectedly strong allies in government.

An immediate change was the sense that the SNP did not have to placate or defer to Westminster, and that the party in government at Holyrood was no junior partner, waiting for instructions from the big boys in London.

There was scope for new ideas and potential for bold thinking – particularly in economic policy. Since 1999 the Scottish Women's Budget Group had made the case for gender analysis that recognises the links between structural inequality and economic disadvantage as a precondition for effective policy. From 2007, the 'shift in political emphasis and character of government created new opportunities to reframe the discourse on gender budgeting as central to economic policy.' Feminist economist Ailsa McKay's appointment to the Parliament's Equal Opportunities Committee as Special Adviser on the Budget sharpened the focus on the implications of budget decisions for women's economic status, and equality as a driver for growth. Both Salmond and Swinney paid tribute to her influence on Scottish social and economic policy, and her untimely death in 2014 was widely mourned. (Campbell and Gillespie, 2016)

Over the decade, these early auguries have borne some good fruit, and since 2014 actions have certainly gathered pace. The SNP Government has listened to women and prioritised accessible, affordable childcare as one of the most important ways to improve their lives. The recent introduction of baby boxes is one of a range of initiatives to support women through maternity and post-natal years. At national level the Equality Fund has been sustained, three year rolling funding for organisations such as Women's Aid meets a long called-for demand, and new domestic abuse legislation is keeping pace with important developments in understanding the impact of coercive control as a course of conduct. Following effective lobbying by WFI, Cornton Vale prison will close and the government's approach to female offenders is changing. New powers will enable legislation to ensure a 50:50 balance on public sector boards by 2020. A range of measures to mitigate the impact of UK welfare reform has been introduced. 'Securing Women's Futures' – a report by a coalition of women's and equality organisations – called for the Scottish government to seize the opportunity to design a social security system which will increase women's equality and rights. The report's recommendations were emphatically echoed in the responses to public consultation, and the Minister has recently committed to measures, including split payments of Universal Credit, which demonstrate willingness to take on the UK Government.

Mind the Gap, Still

These and other initiatives are welcome, demonstrating genuine commitment and strong leadership. But is the SNP truly 'Bold for Change', as it claimed on International Women's Day 2017? The consensus among SNP women, WFI activists and equality experts interviewed for this article is that there remains a gap between rhetoric and reality; between top-level pledges, and awareness and implementation at point of delivery, whether that is local or national. Existing strategies (e.g. 'Equally Safe') levers and mechanisms (e.g. General Equality Duty, gender impact assessment and gender budgeting) require much stronger acceptance, data availability and enforcement to translate good intentions into outcomes. Poverty, precarity, poor health, violence, isolation, constraints on safety and space for action – these remain underlying systemic problems affecting far too many women's lives. Additional barriers and discrimination make life particularly challenging for BME, disabled, LBT, refugee and asylum seeking women. Engender's recently published report, 'Sex and Power in Scotland 2017', demonstrates the stark realities of women's unequal access to power, decision-making and participation throughout all areas of public life, and the consequences:

> *Women are the majority of unpaid carers, lone parents, recipients of social security, low-paid workers, and survivors of domestic abuse and sexual violence in Scotland. The drivers of this systemic gender inequality and women's experiences of public life must inform policymaking, cultural production and corporate agendas, or else these systems will continue to entrench inequality between women and men.*

(Engender, 2017: 4)

So what do women in Scotland want? The SNP must pay heed to its critical friends, including WFI, which conducted a major listening exercise prior to the 2016 election. They want long term and more adventurous approaches to care and wellbeing; they need flexible and accessible childcare; more power, participation and budgeting in and for the communities where people actually live. They challenge public sector bodies to take gender impact assessment seriously, because they know from harsh experience why it matters. They see the links between radical land reform, responsive health services, affordable and locally produced food. They call for a progressive justice system that protects the rights of women and children rather than punishing them for the poverty, abuse and ill-health they suffer.

'Inclusive growth', defined as 'growth that combines increased prosperity with greater equity; that creates opportunities for all and distributes the dividends of increased prosperity fairly' is, since 2015, enshrined in Scotland's Economic Strategy. But this remains a work in progress. Since 2007, the SNP in government and as a movement has been enriched and enlivened because women's voices and experiences are telling alternative stories about citizenship and community. But there is no room for complacency. This requires the mainstreaming of gender, of using laws, policies, services, and budgets to distribute power, income and resources more equitably, recasting social security as lifetime investment in wellbeing, and reframing care, not as a 'women's issue', but as core to economic development and sustainability. All this would place gender analysis at the centre of government policy and budgeting, demonstrating real boldness for transformative change.

References

Campbell, J. and Gillespie, M. (eds.) (2016), *Feminist Economics and Public Policy*, London: Taylor and Francis.

Engender (2016), *Sex and Power in Scotland 2017*, Edinburgh: Engender, accessed at: www.engender.org.uk/content/publications/SEX-AND-POW-ER-IN-SCOTLAND-2017.pdf

Mackay, F. and Kenny, M. (2009), 'Women's Political Representation and the SNP: Gendered Paradoxes and Puzzles', in Hassan, G. (ed.), *The Modern SNP: From Protest to Power*, Edinburgh: Edinburgh University Press, 42-54.

Johns, R. and Mitchell, J. (2016), *Takeover: Explaining the Extraordinary Rise of the SNP*, London: Biteback Publishing.

Orr, L., Scott, M. and Whiting, N. (2014), 'An Open Letter to the Women of Scotland', Facebook, 21 August, accessed at: www.facebook.com/women4independence/photos/a.432863023417704.88144.420267048010635/722694114434592/?-type=1&theater

LGBTI Scotland: A Story of Progress

David Jamieson and Jen Stout

IN THE LATTER part of the 20th century, Scotland lagged behind much of the UK, as well as many other northern and western European countries, in adapting to the emergence of the LGBTI community, its social movements and demands for equality. Scotland's less progressive status in this regard can be seen in the failure to follow England and Wales in decriminalising sex between men aged 21 and over in 1967. This remained the case until 1980; in Northern Ireland this was the case until 1982.

The traditional picture of a Scottish society held back by religious conservatism and a heightened culture of machismo has, by 2017, largely or wholly given way. A report in 2015 deemed Scotland the best country for LGBTI equality in Europe (ILGA-Europe, 2015), a title it maintained into 2016. Politicians, including Scottish Labour leader Kezia Dugdale, celebrated the 'gayest Parliament in the world'. After the 2016 Scottish elections, the Parliament's three largest opposition parties were all led by members of the LGBTI community: Ruth Davidson (Scottish Conservatives), Kezia Dugdale (Scottish Labour) and Patrick Harvie (Scottish Greens). But how far do these changes really go, and what portion of the advances can be claimed by the SNP after ten years in power?

Searching for clues as to the SNP's ideological coherence, many naturally turn to the big questions of taxation, economic strategy, and its attitude to redistribution. But we wish to argue that the issue of LGBTI rights – often unhelpfully ghettoised as a facet of 'identity politics' – works well as a barometer of the party's struggle between political ends and pragmatism.

The Early Scottish Parliaments

The SNP took charge in 2007 of a Parliament that had already witnessed fast-paced progress on LGB (not, at this stage, transgender) rights. One of the first, and boldest, acts taken by the initial Labour-Liberal coalition was to repeal the controversial Section 28, which was Clause 2a in Scotland, subsequently added to the Local Government Act 1986.

The implicit message of this clause, which banned the 'promotion' of homosexuality in schools, and indeed the tone of the heated debate around it, is almost unimaginable in Scotland today. In the months leading up to the vote by MSPs, giant billboards with images of 'doe-eyed infants' urged citizens to support 'the protection of children' (Cameron, 2015). This messaging fed into established, bigoted superstitions about homosexuality's inherent danger to children and to society as a whole.

While SNP leadership at the time backed the repeal, the role of one man – Stagecoach millionaire Brian Souter – highlighted starkly the contradictions of the party. Souter was then, and for many years remained, a major SNP donor, praised by Salmond for his 'entrepreneurial' skills. He also saw fit to bankroll the 'Keep the Clause' campaign, which promoted the idea of a moral majority standing against an out-of-touch Scottish Executive. It brought together the most right-wing of Scotland's religious leaders, from the Catholic Cardinal to evangelical Protestants, and had the backing of major newspapers; most notably the *Daily Record*. Against this coalition, the Scottish Fight the Clause Campaign lobbied for repeal of Section 28/Clause 2a.

It was not the last time this arrangement of forces would meet, nor, as we shall see, the last time the SNP would be embarrassed by a high-profile supporter over LGBTI rights. In a significant victory for grassroots pressure and political will, on 21 June 2000, MSPs voted 99 to 17 to repeal the clause; Westminster followed suit three years later.

Civil rights and anti-discrimination milestones followed, both in Westminster and Holyrood: this was an expected part of New Labour's agenda, but also a result of EU directives and court rulings which were 'domesticated' into UK and Scots law. Civil partnerships were supported by the Executive in 2003 and became law a year later at Westminster; 2006 saw a successful campaign by rights groups in Scotland to allow same-sex couples to adopt.

For all the advances to follow from the momentum created by the Section 28 victory, the Scottish Parliament also became a scene of retrenchment. Early scandals, including the ever-inflating costs of the Parliament building itself, led Jack McConnell's Labour to become more politically passive. Whatever the ambitions of early New Labour, Scottish Labour remained a model of patronage politics, cautious to maintain its close relationship with the leadership of the Catholic Church.

Nonetheless, as the SNP years approached, momentum and good morale remained with equality campaigners. The human rights discourse during these years was a great help for activists pursuing legislative change on issues such as the age of consent, adoption, and military service (Kollman and Waites, 2011);

by the 2000s the focus was also on discrimination in employment and the market place. Responses to this included sexual orientation equality law covering employment in 2003, and goods and services in 2007.

The Equality Act 2010, one of the last pieces of legislation Labour achieved before Conservative rule resumed, consolidated this progress. Crucially, this act recognised gender reassignment as a protected characteristic – alongside age, disability, race, religion, sex and others – thus marking a milestone for transgender rights, though problems with accessing gender identity recognition remain.

The SNP's First Term: 2007-2011

The designation of the SNP, especially after 1990, as a centre-left, socially liberal party has, in the Scottish context, no necessary bearing on the party's approach to LGBTI rights. As the coalitions of the early Scottish Parliaments show – as well as Scottish Labour's longer record – the 'small c' conservatism of Scotland's political class dictates that parties balance progressive political action against the values (perceived or otherwise) of various Scottish constituencies.

Early in the SNP's first majority Government, the party was caught indulging in this model of patronage politics – behaviour that alarmed many hoping for advances on LGBTI rights.

In 2009, then Scottish Education Minister Fiona Hyslop was found to have been lobbying Whitehall in an attempt to garner exemption for Catholic adoption agencies from UK equality legislation that would see them have to work with LGBTI couples seeking adoption.

When this attempt failed, Hyslop met with a Scottish Catholic adoption agency, St Margaret's Children and Family Care Society, to discuss the re-wording of their constitution, to help them successfully exploit a loophole in law, then giving some religious organisations the right to cater only to heterosexual persons (Hutcheon and Gordon, 2009).

Despite this, groups such as the Equality Network continued to have a good working relationship with the SNP. During the party's first year in power, the Scottish Government became the first in Europe to fund a transgender rights project – the Scottish Trans Alliance.

Interestingly, it was a private member's bill in 2009 that saw progress on tackling discrimination. Green MSP Patrick Harvie's proposal to widen the definition of hate crime to include offences against LGBT and disabled people gained cross-party support, and when implemented in 2010 brought Scotland into line with the rest of the UK. Another long-overdue reform came in 2009 with the Sexual Offences (Scotland) Act, which removed the terms 'gross indecency' and 'sodomy', historically used to prosecute gay men, from the statutes.

A Step Change: 2011-2015

Though nowhere near as high profile as the infamous Section 28/Clause 2a battle, the SNP's backing of marriage equality again saw the LGBTI movement pitched against the forces of social conservatism.

The Scotland for Marriage campaign, organised by an array of reactionary religious groups including the Care and the Christian Institute as well as small schismatic churches such as the United Free Church and the Christian Brethren, spearheaded the opposition. The hierarchy of the Catholic Church in Scotland appealed to its parishioners, and messages of opposition made their way to the Scottish Government in the tens of thousands. In another embarrassment for the SNP, former leader Gordon Wilson signed the campaign's petition.

The Equal Marriage campaign, an alliance of activists headed-up by the Equality Network, responded with their own petition, submitting evidence to the consultation process. The campaign culminated with a march of over a thousand people in Edinburgh; on 4 February 2014 MSPs voted 105 to 18 in favour of equal marriage.

By the time of the first marriage between two men in December 2014, a more far-reaching reality was in view. The open confrontation between the two camps had tested the limits of organised reaction. Support for equal marriage was, according to the Social Attitudes Survey, by then at 68 % – up from 41 % in 2002 (ScotCen Social Research, 2014).

Growing Pressure: 2015-2017

The most important development on the LGBTI front since the 2014 referendum has been the emergence of the demand for 'inclusive education'. The Time for Inclusive Education (Tie) campaign was formed by two activists, Jordan Daly and Liam Stevenson, who met organising pro-independence events. Afterwards they turned their dynamic efforts to the cause of reducing the epidemic of homophobic bullying and isolation of LGBTI students in Scottish schools, which sees more than one in four attempt suicide in their time at school.

The campaign has mustered substantial 'civic society' support, including trade unions, celebrities and many teachers and students. Tie's demands are centred on legislating for the provision of education about the spectrum of sexualities and sexual and gender identities. They dominated the 2016 LGBTI Scottish elections hustings, which saw numerous party leaders, including First Minister Nicola Sturgeon, pledge support. Action, however, has been frustratingly slow.

The SNP has historically been a party that has drawn support from, and had roots in, traditional and even conservative Scotland, with support from

Protestant communities along with a strong base in the semi-rural northeast. The project of the party since the beginning of Salmond's leadership has been to break into the working class, urban and more Irish Catholic population in the Clyde basin – an area where labourism enjoyed a strong grip until the seismic 2014 referendum campaign and its aftermath. If there is hesitation around assenting to demands such as those forwarded by the Tie campaign, they must come in part from a fear of disturbing this constituency.

It must be stressed that self-identifying Catholics have mostly supported advances in legal equality in recent years. In 2014, 60 % of Catholics supported marriage equality, 59 % of Church of Scotland respondents and 58 % of other Christians. Interestingly, 81 % of non-religious people supported it, but a mere 33 % of regular church attendees.

The distinction must be made, and no doubt already exists in the minds of Scottish Government ministers, between the leadership of the Catholic Church and its congregation. Though the Catholic Bishops Conference has in the past been able to mount effective, focused campaigns, today it has never before been so distanced from its own flock.

However, the peculiarities of the Scottish education system have frustrated Tie campaigners – as when their petition was thrown out of Parliament in January 2016 on the basis that the school curriculum is not statutory. Faith schools could prove another institutional complication, as it may well be the case that the Scottish Government doesn't want to be seen in a pitched battle with Catholic schools.

But ultimately the issue will be decided by the balance of forces for and against inclusive education, and the forces on Tie's side are very substantial. 67 MSPs, a majority in Holyrood, now back Tie, many of them from the SNP – a fairly rare example of rank-breaking in the disciplined party.

Future Prospects

The homophobia of Section 28/Clause 2a cast a long shadow. Calling for inclusive education and teacher training in 2016, Stonewall Scotland said that a full three quarters of primary school teachers weren't sure whether mentioning non-heterosexual relationships in schools was still banned. Among secondary school teachers, it was nearly half.

This chilling effect means that the next battles for LGBTI rights in Scotland may, just as in the 1980s and 1990s, be in large part about schools and education. Equally, issues around trans rights and gender recognition, never far from headlines and policy agendas worldwide, could provoke the biggest backlash. In response to Nicola Sturgeon's 2016 pledge to prioritise legal reform of gender recognition – permitting self-recognition and a third, non-binary option, as called for by the Scottish Trans / Equality Network's Equal Recognition campaign – the Free Kirk predicted 'confusion and brokenness among our children'.

To the extent that the SNP can continue, with its customary caution, to carry the LGBTI equality agenda forward, it will be prompted by a growing eco-system of radicalising elements of LGBTI movements. Just as Scotland's largest Pride event in Glasgow heads in a more political direction, being led in 2016 by the Tie campaign, Scotland has joined many other countries in holding more radical Free Pride events, celebrating the movement's history of anti-systemic, and anti-capitalist, action. The movement has benefited from the growth of social media and other new platforms with which to organise and share information.

These forces may prove vital with the rise of the new nationalist and radically conservative and homophobic right around the world. Young activists in movements like Tie know fine well that Scotland is not genetically immune to the rise of reactionary movements. But building on a history of struggle, the actions of a small, socially progressive nation like Scotland will have implications far beyond its borders.

References

Cameron, R. (2015), 'Scotland once led the way on gay rights. What's gone wrong?', *The Guardian*, 22 July.

Gordon, T. and Hutcheon, P. (2009), 'SNP and Catholic Church's secret plan to sidestep legislation and gay adoptions', *Sunday Herald*, 31 May.

IGLA Report (2015), 'Annual Review of the Human Rights Situation of Lesbian, Gay, Bisexual, Trans and Intersex People in Europe', available online at: http://www.ilga-europe.org/sites/default/files/Attachments/01_full_annual_review_updated.pdf

Kollman, K. and Waites, M. (2011), 'United Kingdom: changing political opportunity structures, policy success and continuing challenges for lesbian, gay and bisexual movements', in: Tremblay, M., Paternotte, D. and Johnson, C. (eds.), *The Lesbian and Gay Movement and the State: Comparative Insights into a Transformed Relationship*, Ashgate: Farnham, 181-196.

ScotCen Social Research (2014), 'Attitudes to same-sex marriage in Scotland', available at: www.scotcen.org.uk/media/563091/141216_ssa-_same-sex-marriage-brief.pdf

Power to Which People: The Few or the Many?

Lesley Riddoch

IN RECENT MONTHS it has been the tensions and competing claims around London, Brussels and Edinburgh which have been making headlines in newspapers far and wide about Scotland. But the issue of who has power and who exercises it with or on behalf of whom is not just about major capitals and urban centres – or certainly ought not to be.

Travelling all across Scotland from Glasgow to Inverurie and from Inverness to Portsoy, I have heard similar complaints about creeping centralisation in Scotland. It is a concern that takes different guises in different places, and prompts scrutiny of how the Scottish Government, led by the SNP in minority and majority formations for the past ten years, has handled these issues in the past, and what its stance might be moving forward.

Part of what is at stake in the centralisation-decentralisation debate is illustrated in matters of procurement which have a real impact at all levels of society. For example, at the Senscot social enterprise conference in Edinburgh in 2016, there was disquiet over a delay to the Scottish Government's ten-year plan on procurement and social enterprise. Not for profit, locally-run businesses – like the Hollywood A-listers favoured Social Bite café – have been squeezed out of government and council contracts which are too big for small firms to tackle.

The reality is, and has been, that the most successful contract-clinchers tend to be big multi-nationals because they look like safe bets. As one speaker at the Senscot event wryly noted: 'no-one ever got fired for hiring IBM.' This remains the case, even though some big firms win their deals on the back of zero-hour contracts and sub-Scottish Living Wage pay rates.

Senscot members have long encouraged the Scottish Government to break down large contracts, but instead they are being urged to scale up and form consortia to match the large commercial firms against whom they must compete. The government has also sent out indications that it wants to broaden the definition of 'social enterprise', prompting concerns that conventional firms with decent corporate responsibility statements may soon qualify. One participant commented: 'We'll be up against Trump social enterprises next.' So why relax this definition? No-one really knows. A concern to look friendly to private companies and investors seems to be part of the picture. But on whose and what terms and to what ends? That issue should surely be at the heart of the debate.

Highland Troubles

Meanwhile, the disparate forces of the great and good across the Highlands were united in fury back in November 2016 over rumours that local control of Highlands and Islands Enterprise (HIE) would be axed. A government review recommended a new single board to co-ordinate the work of HIE, Scottish Enterprise, Skills Development Scotland and the Scottish Funding Council and former Deputy First Minister (now Education Secretary) John Swinney confirmed that the Scottish Government backed the plan.

Ministers were undoubtedly taken aback by the outraged response to what was seen by many as the latest pruning exercise from the centre, and this story no doubt has further twists and turns connected with it. For the moment, the Scottish Government seems to have put such plans on pause, forced to by losing a vote in the Scottish Parliament, and wider opposition in the Highlands and across Scotland (Taylor, 2017).

But this begs the question, surely the anger and opposition could have been foreseen? The Highlands is a fiercely independent-minded area with strong memories of the Highlands and Islands Development Board (HIE's successful and popular forerunner), which was established in 1965 to tackle rural unemployment and depopulation.

Since then there has been a presumption for Highland opt-outs from Scotland-wide structures. It is also an area reeling from the UK government's recent boundary review which proposes a single Highland constituency the same size as Northern Ireland – all in the name of 'fairness' and 'uniformity'. So it is no wonder any further erosion of local control is going to be viewed as the last straw by many Highlanders, illustrating the differences in perspective, agenda and needs between the Central Belt and other parts of Scotland. Holyrood administrations and their Scottish Office predecessors have been seen as lacking in sensitivity and awareness on this front for many years, despite occasional diplomatic forays and rhetorical flourishes.

Power to the Centre: The Story of 'Devolution' So Far

It seems though that the Scottish Government has been merging and pruning so many operations in a low-key and relatively uncontested way, that no lively opposition was expected.

First came the removal of police, fire and rescue services from local control. Then came the merger of colleges amid predictions that smaller campuses would end up closing. Then it was mooted that Fife College closures in Kirkcaldy and Glenrothes would be likely as a new super-campus is constructed in Dunfermline. Next came the creation of fourteen health and social care partnerships with their attendant bureaucracies. Audit Scotland has said, however, that this has not yet produced any shift in spending from hospitals into community settings.

Then came the high profile plan to top-slice council tax and hand cash directly to head-teachers. Doubtless the first dreadful set of test results from primary schools in East Lothian helped explain why the Scottish Government wanted and wants more cash on the frontline fast. You can understand that. But again, who is controlling what here? Then came Nicola Sturgeon's November 2016 SNP conference speech offering the equivalent of childcare vouchers to parents. Recent planned or discussed changes also include shifting road maintenance from councils to Transport Scotland, bin collection moving from councils to individual towns and placing a requirement on councils to share other services.

Critics of over-large bureaucracies may be jumping for joy at this kind of news, but this isn't the oft-promised bonfire of the quangos. Education, police, health and social care are the most important public services and councils are part of our democratic system. If there is something quango-like or quasi-governmental about councils it is because they are currently too big and remote and are crying out for reform – a point COSLA has hammered home when the councils' umbrella body recently reconvened its Commission on Strengthening Local Democracy to push again for a new structure of at least 100 small town and island councils (see COSLA, 2014).

Now cynics will of course suggest (and some did) that 100 councils means 100 directors of education earning £150,000 and all the add-ons that go with that. But it really doesn't have to be that way. Across Europe, bureaucracies are smaller and more modest than those in Scotland, and while some services are shared by neighbouring councils, the town and island-sized local democracies which underpin them are never compromised.

Who Speaks for Decentralisation?

Yet no political party bar the Scottish Green Party currently backs the creation of more, truly local councils and wider democracy. So the existence of over-paid council executives in distant, elegantly-fitted council buildings will doubtless be used as justification for bypassing local democracy altogether and creating a myriad of random and casual arrangements with community groups instead. What's wrong with that you may ask? Isn't community control precisely what critics like myself have long been advocating? Isn't a flexible network of diverse local deals better than rigid, risk-averse council bureaucracy?

It is quite possible that this mongrel nation will successfully manage a mongrel pattern of local control with development trusts, housing associations, councils, community councils, social enterprises and tenants groups all 'co-producing' services as the late Campbell Christie recommended in his commission on public services. But there are big snags with a mixter-maxter approach. There is too little debate about this anywhere near governing circles. The concerns about where this direction of travel are leading and the opportunities that could arise from looking at different patterns of service, and at the strengthening and genuine spreading of local democracy, are not discussed as they should be.

We need to be clear. As the late Canon Kenton Wright pointed out, power devolved is power retained. In bypassing democratic structures, and making direct deals with local players, a small group of players in the Scottish Government is set to control even more aspects of everyday life. This has to be questioned, and alternatives posed. Unsupported community groups quickly burn out; bypassing 'local' councils leaves that problematic dimension unchanged; and the competitive 'deal' approach – borrowed from English Tories – means smaller, poorer and less vocal communities get left behind.

There is no democracy in Europe without a tier of genuinely local, representative democracy yet that's where Scotland seems to be heading thanks to a systematic process never explicitly listed in any SNP manifesto. The Scottish Government is merging, amalgamating and enlarging while active citizens are doing the opposite – trying to wrest more local control, autonomy, power and cash from central control. Surely we need honest and open debate before this ad hoc process of centralisation goes much further? And also to start discussing what the terms devolution and greater democracy actually mean in the Scotland of the early 21st century?

References

COSLA (2014), *Commission on Strengthening Local Democracy*, Edinburgh: COSLA, accessed at: http://www.localdemocracy.info/news/final-report/
Taylor, R. (2017), 'Mixed response to Scottish government U-turn on HIE', Shetland Times, 31 March, accessed at: http://www.shetlandtimes. co.uk/2017/03/31/mixed-response-scottish-government-u-turn-hie

How Deep is Our Democracy?

Katie Gallogy-Swan

WE ARE FACING a global democratic crisis. Trump, Brexit, the concurrent rise of far-right parties across Europe, and indeed, our own indyref, are all symptoms of a growing anti-politics and anti-establishment consensus. These are the desperate death rattles of a political system at breaking point; riddled with the internal rot of colonialism, inherited corruption, and systemic inequality. And then there's Scotland. In Scotland, the SNP can rely on the strongest trust in political leadership in Europe. Indeed, in an international context of anti-immigrant rhetoric, sabre-rattling, and fake news, Scotland's democracy appears to be one of few beacons offering hope amid the chaos.

But high levels of trust alone are no reason to applaud the SNP and smugly announce the democratic job done – indeed, such political complacency continues to have cataclysmic consequences. A closer look at the state of democracy in Scotland reveals major chasms that have the potential to quickly flood with the fear and fascism currently threatening other European social democracies. This chapter will focus on some examples of these democratic issues, and propose opportunities to innovate for a radically democratic future Scotland.

The Power of Deeper Democracy

Democracy is ultimately about equalising power. The argument has long been won that it is more than a vote at the ballot box: while voting forms a significant part of releasing power, it can only succeed if people believe it has *real* influence. For example, though Holyrood, European, and Scottish council elections are all proportional or semi-proportional and thus fairly representative of people's voting intentions, turnout for these elections continues to be unacceptably low. The reasons for this poor engagement are myriad, traced back to widespread alienation and increasing inequality in Scotland over recent years – if people feel like they have no power and no influence when they vote, they have little reason to invest in the system (see Scottish Government, 2017). This reveals the necessarily holistic nature of protecting and strengthening democracy: a project which must acknowledge diverse factors such as poverty, internet access, health and wellbeing, and urban planning to facilitate a deeper democratic culture.

In a deeper democratic society, each citizen not only understands the political decisions that are being made on their behalf, but has the mechanisms and access to influence these decisions. More than decision-making, this vision of deep democracy is fundamentally about the good life: a life free from insecurity, anxiety, and fear, and defined by empowerment. This means that there are many vital parts to a democratic toolkit that cannot be overlooked, for example equality, political education, independent media and scrutiny, support for communities to participate and organise equally, opportunities and invitations to influence, and pathways into representation – particularly for underrepresented and marginalised populations. A toolkit such as this ensures citizens have the best possible opportunity to engage fruitfully with the democratic process, leading to high levels of trust that their voice matters. In each of these indicators, Scotland's democratic muscle is far from healthy (Electoral Reform Society Scotland, 2013).

Fake Democracy and the Limits of Participation

One reason for this democratic weakness is a particularly British culture of leadership: top down, centralised, and fearful of releasing true power to communities. This clashes with the SNP's message of accessibility and familiarity, and the increasing popularity of deliberative practices. The result is a hollow appeal to engagement: Scots are encouraged to get involved, but are rarely afforded a substantial opportunity to influence, or to understand how their actions impact decision-making.

This is particularly glaring in the SNP's attempts to perform participation. Consultation – a method of accruing political legitimacy by inviting public opinion – has been deployed consistently by the SNP. However more often than not, their seemingly innocuous attempts at participation at best obscure political decisions, and at worst present barriers and disenfranchise citizens further.

For example, the Land Reform Bill of 2015 invited consultation responses, however, the survey was 45 questions and ten pages long. These questions ranged from invitations to redefine legal terms to inquiries into deer management. For an issue that affects every person in Scotland, this opportunity to influence and educate was an abject failure. Even if we ignore for a moment that the consultation for a major piece of legislation was only available online in a downloadable word document, the questions themselves were a technocratic nightmare and didn't connect to the gravity and potential impact a Land Reform Bill could have on people's lives. Presenting bureaucratic barriers like this further alienates people from the political process, encouraging a paternal democratic culture which leaves communities frustrated, deskilled, and disaffected. Politics as an 'insider's' and 'expert's' job is reified, and vitally, the real expert potential of local people is lost.

Another example of performed participation is the SNP National Survey launched in September 2016, hailed to be 'Scotland's biggest ever political listening exercise', which aimed to engage two million people in questions about Brexit, independence, and Scotland's constitutional future (Brooks, 2016). By December, the project was quietly wrapped up, and no figures or details were released of the findings. With no clear plan of what would happen to the data, how it would be interpreted, and what it may influence, the investment in what amounted to an online survey and a lot of printed paper and mail-outs, smacked of the bromidic 'inclusion' and 'engagement' that has come to pepper SNP legislation and strategy documents. This hoovers up the valuable time and energy of engaged citizens who *do* want to participate and influence, increasing cynicism and delegitimising the political process.

Why is this dangerous? Every fake opportunity to influence hollows out trust in Scottish democracy, leaving it liable to collapse. People are not stupid: they can sense that the 'listening exercise' and many other consultations are lip service, with no real pathways to power. And this is why they fail – not because people do not want to engage; the most dangerous myth in building democratic capacity. What is at stake here is more than just the *quality* of the engagement, but the democratic culture of Scotland: we can have a flourishing democracy of debate and action, strengthening collective capacity and understanding; or we can have a cavernous void of black-box policy-making.

The Indyref and After

In 2014, in the run up to the referendum on Scottish independence, we got a taste of what a vibrant democracy might look like. People across Scotland began to be public organisers, debaters, agitators, and role models. That such a monumental decision on the constitutional future of Scotland was launched so firmly into the mainstream, manifesting in a variety of opportunities to learn, act, and shape, meant we saw the most engaged electorate in Scotland's history.

How did this happen? It certainly wasn't thanks to the centralised Yes Scotland campaign or Better Together, but because people acted on their own behalf. The grassroots effort was the lifeblood of the campaign, reaching hitherto forgotten communities, exposing unchallenged Scottish issues, and daring to act without invitation. Reclaiming this rhetorical ground from 'establishment' politicians meant more people were a part of the public debate than ever before. Indeed, in her first speech as First Minister, Nicola Sturgeon commented on this new era of Scottish democracy:

> *All of us, regardless of party, have been inspired and, indeed, challenged by the flourishing of democracy that we have witnessed during and since the referendum. Democratic politics in Scotland has never been more alive.*

(Sturgeon, 2014)

So where is this energy now? After the referendum decision, this collective raised consciousness could not simply 'go back in its box'. Within days, the SNP's membership had skyrocketed to record numbers, and the Scottish Greens also witnessed an influx of new members. While some recently-founded local activist groups began to reframe their priorities, the vast bulk of those with the stamina to stay involved were funnelled into Scotland's political party system. This does not of course mean the end of debate and organising, and indeed there have been inspiring moments of intraparty activism. However, being a member of an establishment political party means that previously untethered activists are now faced with a choice between party loyalty and their own political independence. The reality is that post-indyref, newly educated and energised by the prospect of a better society, Scots were faced with a democratic system with no space for them, so defaulted to the party line.

More worrying than the stifling effect party membership can have on a healthy democratic culture is the legislative decisions since indyref. The Community Empowerment Bill for example, though a nod in the right direction, is shakily being implemented with little resource and widespread criticism from civil servants and community organisers alike. Participatory budgeting – another incredible opportunity to release power to communities, has instead seen community groups scrap it out over pocket change. The media landscape continues to struggle in Scotland, with little prospect for new journalists and unprecedented job cuts across the sector. And the Lobbying Bill, which with bravery could have legislated truly world-leading transparency into our Parliament, was a missed opportunity. Key pieces of democratic policy have fallen far short of expectations, posing the question: are these policies intended for real change, or to placate the 'challenge' posed to parties by Scotland's 'flourishing' democracy?

At this point many people might claim that we are doing a lot better than other democracies, and that these projects at least show that the political will to release power exists. However, this argument ignores our recent history and the current democratic crises sweeping the world. Rhetoric on democracy, transparency, engagement, and participation will become but a cipher for corruption if the emancipatory capacity of these words are not respected. The hard work of developing a deeper democratic culture will not be won overnight, but will be crippled far quicker by theatrical overtures to 'accessibility'. To truly lead us into a democratic future, the SNP must be courageous now, and push against a political legacy that teaches them to fear the collective power of the electorate.

The Missing Voices of Local Democracy

This opportunity for bravery will come sooner rather than later, as the upcoming Local Democracy Bill is being prepared. With the least democratic local government in Europe, the 'silent crisis' of our local councils needs action now. A few indicators reveal a snapshot of the problem. In Scotland, the average population size of a council is 163,200, compared to the EU average of 5,630. The average area covered by a council in Scotland is 2,461 km, compared to a 601 km average in the UK, and 49 km in Europe. There is one councillor for every 4,270 people in Scotland, whereas in England, it is one to 2,860, and in Finland, one to 500 (Bort *et al*, 2012). This lack of representation is a democratic failure for which every establishment party in Holyrood bears responsibility.

If we refocus from this big picture to the specifics of how communities and neighbourhoods sustain themselves, a complex, messy reality of 'making do' comes to the fore. It is one where in our most vulnerable communities there is a daily struggle to counter powerful yet detached forces: over-stretched local government, a housing crisis, unacceptable poverty and destitution, immigration and asylum, and a populist, xenophobic press. If any community stands out in this respect, it is Govanhill in Glasgow – ignored by national media until Nicola Sturgeon became First Minister. Subsequently the right wing press discovered urban inner city Glasgow as a way to discredit her – as it sits in her constituency, Glasgow Southside. *Scottish Daily Express* and *Scottish Daily Mail* front covers such as 'Govanhell' and 'A damning portrait of Dickensian squalor in Sturgeon's own seat' are not about a sudden conversion to compassion and caring about poverty, but are instead exploitations of poverty with the sole aim of embarrassing the SNP.

Yet, the undoubted community vibrancy in the area, mixed with the anger, fury and resentment of others, has little way of making a wider impact or resolution, thanks to the political centralisation at national and local level. Those pushing for real change are often stopped in their tracks with bureaucratic hoops to jump through, run out of stamina before the next election, or simply feel helpless before the scale of the local challenges. Yet expertise, ideas, and solutions are there at this very local level – we just have no way of extracting, mobilising, and promoting these ambassadors and leaders to effect sustainable change. 'You are at the vanguard of something', Philip Tartaglia, Catholic

Archbishop of Glasgow, said of Govanhill (Ross, 2016). There are many equivalents to Govanhill across Scotland and such areas are test beds for how we get Scotland right: supporting community self-organisation, listening to the challenges facing society's disenfranchised, and seeking conflict resolution.

Faced with austerity and constitutional chaos, the SNP are limited. But there are innumerable exciting, innovative, and truly radical options to explore to revitalise our local democracy. Only fear and the crippling culture of institutional bureaucracy will hold them back. With the Local Democracy Bill, the SNP could create a democratic pathway for communities and citizens to reap the rewards of the Community Empowerment Bill and Participatory Budgeting. Or, they could elaborate on their record as an establishment party with little time for deeper democracy, leaving the door open for continued alienation, rising resentment, and community disintegration.

Scotland's Second Democratic Revolution?

When Nicola Sturgeon became First Minister, she pledged to lead 'an outward looking Government... more open and accessible to Scotland's people than ever before' (BBC, 2014). This vision can and must be realised. With the democratic research landscape replete with exciting innovations, solutions, and methodologies, there is no excuse for placeholder 'engagement'. More than this, the SNP must commit to tackling the deeper inequality which has increased under their leadership, and which impacts on citizen and community capacity to act, organise, and exercise the democratic muscle. For this we require ambition and vision.

With so much to improve, the opportunities are endless. Maybe it is a Citizen's Assembly, acting as a second chamber in Parliament. It could be mini-publics at different tiers of decision-making, involving citizen juries in policy. Digital democratic tools can be explored, and more effort can connect democratic research with policy makers. Citizenship education and injecting democracy into our schools would skill future generations to be democratic actors from the start of their lives, rather than unlearning institutional constraints as adults. They could develop deeper and more regular opportunities for more people to influence policy, and support independent media and journalism to scrutinise the political process. They could seek democracy in more public bodies such as Creative Scotland and Scottish Enterprise, which are supposed to represent a section of society. They could protect and encourage industrial democracy, and expose private lobbying from big financial interests. Maybe we will finally get round to the desperately needed restructure of our local democracy, bringing it into modernity with the collective exhale of democracy experts and local people across Scotland. We have no lack in ideas. What we need to know, is beyond independence, what is the SNP's democratic vision for Scotland? How do they plan to enact it? And can we all be equal partners in creating and growing it?

References

BBC (2014), 'Sturgeon vows to be 'most accessible' first minister ever', *BBC News*, 7 November, accessed at: www.bbc.co.uk/news/uk-scotland-scotland-politics-29942740

Bort, E., McAlpine, R. and Morgan, G. (2012), *The Silent Crisis: Failure and Revival in Local Democracy in Scotland*, Biggar: Jimmy Reid Foundation, accessed at: http://reidfoundation.org/wp-content/uploads/2012/04/Silent-CrisisCover.jpg

Brooks, L. (2016), 'Nicola Sturgeon launches 'biggest listening exercise in SNP history'', *The Guardian*, 2 September, accessed at: https://www.theguardian.com/politics/2016/sep/02/nicola-sturgeon-snp-listening-exercise-europe-brexit-scottish-independence

Electoral Reform Society Scotland (2013), *Democracy Max: An Inquiry into the Future of Scottish Democracy*, Edinburgh: Electoral Reform Society.

Ross, P. (2016), 'Govanhill Raisers', *Sunday Times*, 29 May, accessed at: www.thetimes.co.uk/edition/scotland/govanhill-raisers-k9gc89xlk

Scottish Government (2017), *Poverty and Income Inequality in Scotland 2015-16*, Edinburgh: Scottish Government.

Sturgeon, N. (2014), 'First Minister's Acceptance Speech', *Scottish Parliament*, 19 November, accessed at: https://news.gov.scot/speeches-and-briefings/first-minister-acceptance-speech

Taking the Temperature: Scotland's Environment after Black Gold

Sarah Beattie-Smith

Introduction

'IT'S SCOTLAND'S OIL'. That one phrase defined the SNP throughout the 1970s while the party built an argument for Scottish independence on the basis of the nation's wealth, and on the black gold beneath the North Sea. It is a slogan which has stuck with the SNP in the decades since, and which has branded them as the party of oil and gas. So how did a party so wedded to fossil fuels become a Government which passed world-leading climate change legislation and embraced renewables?

This chapter explores the SNP's environmental record over their first ten years in Government and assesses the party's green credentials. Starting in 2007, it looks at the relative importance of environmental policy in the SNP's election campaigns and at what the party did (and did not do) in Government.

The Trouble with Oil

In 2007, the SNP's manifesto pitched a vision of a 'Greener Scotland' where nuclear power was phased out in favour of renewables. Fossil fuels like oil, gas and coal barely got a mention, except to say that the SNP wanted to devolve power over oil and gas to Scotland and to 'invest our oil wealth in a fund for future generations' (SNP, 2007:7). This positioning of the oil and gas industry purely as a source of wealth creation and jobs rather than as a major producer of climate changing emissions continued in the SNP's narrative on the industry over the next decade.

This simplification also served to distinguish the SNP-led Scottish Government from successive Governments in Westminster. As the colour of the UK Government changed over the decade from New Labour to the Conservative and Liberal Democrat coalition to a Conservative majority, support for renewable energy and particularly for onshore wind generation waned. At the same time, public subsidy and UK Government support for nuclear power increased.

The opposing views of the Scottish and UK Governments on nuclear and renewables provided a helpful narrative for both Governments. While the UK Government positioned itself as a responsible, grown up leader with nuclear power while rejecting unreliable' wind power, the Scottish Government flashed green credentials and rejected 'unsafe' nuclear power.

However, these narratives ignore the fact that both the SNP Government in Scotland and successive Governments in Westminster provided significant subsidies and tax breaks for the oil and gas industry throughout this period. Indeed, as pro-independence campaigner Gordon MacIntyre-Kemp pointed out, 'in the 24 countries where Shell extracts oil and gas, all except the UK made Shell pay taxes. While the UK gave Shell £80 million in tax rebates, Shell paid Norway £2.7 billion. So, Norway generated 62 times more tax from one company than Westminster generated from the entire UK industry last year' (MacIntyre-Kemp, 2017).

Such tax breaks for oil and gas companies are regularly called for by SNP representatives. In 2016, Aberdeen's Kevin Stewart MSP called on UK Chancellor George Osborne to take action: We want to ensure the North Sea basin has a future to secure jobs – we want to maximise extraction... We want to see George Osborne get his hands in his pooch and repay Aberdeen and the North Sea oil and gas industry for all the money we have given to the Treasury over the last 40 years' (McKiernan, 2016).

Once again, the old trope of 'it's Scotland's oil' reared its head. While the SNP repeatedly called on the UK Government to 'repay' Scotland for the tax revenues gained from oil extraction off Scotland's coast, successive Westminster Governments could claim that any tax breaks for oil and gas were effectively a subsidy to Scotland, unable to support itself.

However, while the two governments argued over whether tax breaks for the oil industry were subsidy or repayment, the very fact that the industry received such Government support was at odds with climate science.

The 2009 Climate Change Act

One of the pledges in the SNP's 2007 manifesto was to establish a cross party and non-party group of stakeholders to produce a piece of landmark legislation to limit climate changing emissions. The resulting 2009 Climate Change Act established legal targets for the amount by which emissions were to reduce over time, against a baseline of 1990 levels. This world-leading Act set a target of a 42 % reduction in emissions by 2020 and an 80 % reduction by 2050. It was praised around the world, with the Chair of the Intergovernmental Panel on Climate Change calling it 'a matter of pride' for the Scottish Government (Pachauri, 2013).

But the Act initially caused problems for the SNP Government, as the start of annual emissions reduction targets was pushed back to the next administration, after which the targets were repeatedly missed. Critics suggested that the SNP had simply passed a new law without changing any of its other programmes or activities (Friends of the Earth, 2010). For example, plans for a new Forth Road Bridge, motorway extensions and bypasses all signalled the party's support for motorists and fossil fuelled cars above their ambition to extend public transport or support active travel and electric vehicles and thus reduce emissions.

In the face of this criticism, and as the SNP headed for majority government in 2011, they began to place much greater importance on proving their environmental credentials. Where the 2007 manifesto included half a page on suggested measures to make Scotland greener (such as the questionable ideas of the use of bio-fuels and hydrogen for road vehicles), the 2011 manifesto contained four times as much information and significantly stronger environmental policy. New policy pledges included action on biodiversity and the marine environment; support for renewable heat and a move towards a zero waste Scotland; and significantly expanded detail on the SNP's support for renewable energy (SNP, 2011).

2011 and the Road to the Referendum

The 2011 manifesto set out a bold vision for a greener Scotland. It reflected many of the asks of the environmental NGOs, such as ambitious targets for waste reduction, continuation of the Climate Challenge Fund (originally a Scottish Green Party idea) and a recognition of the need for a managed transition away from oil and gas and towards much greater investment in renewable energy. While big ideas like green procurement and access to environmental justice did not catch on as many had hoped, the signal from the SNP was a positive one.

The 2011 election also marked an important moment for the SNP. They had gained the first majority Government in the Scottish Parliament's history and were now free to push ahead with whatever priorities they chose without needing the support of other parties. This was both a blessing and a curse. The party could command a majority and pass legislation which had been blocked in the previous parliament, but it was no longer able to blame other parties for a lack of progress. All eyes were now on the SNP to deliver.

Of course, this new majority also paved the way for a referendum on Scottish independence. As the attention of the Scottish Government turned to the production of a White Paper on independence and to securing a Yes vote in

2014, policy decisions were increasingly framed in terms of whether they would increase public support for the SNP Government and for independence.

More difficult policies were often set to one side in favour of inspiring long-term ambitions or short-term populist ideas. For example, the idea of introducing minimum standards of energy efficiency in private housing was mooted as early as 2012 as a way of cutting emissions and tackling fuel poverty. However, despite numerous working groups and discussions on the idea, consultation on a watered-down version targeted only at privately let homes was only conducted in early 2017 – a full five years later.

Several years of missed emissions reduction targets and a lack of momentum behind relatively straightforward policies and programmes on issues like energy efficiency led to critics questioning the SNP's commitment to environmental policies.

Yes to a Greener Scotland

In 2012, the SNP led the launch of the Yes campaign for Scottish independence. On stage with First Minister Alex Salmond was Patrick Harvie MSP, co-convener of the Scottish Green Party. The Greens had long been in favour of independence and many Greens saw independence as a way to take stronger action on the environment and climate change at a time when the UK Government appeared to be moving backwards.

The inclusion of the Greens in the official Yes movement and the creation of a parallel 'Green Yes' campaign created a space to discuss the alternative routes that an independent Scotland could take with regard to the environment. Increasingly, debate turned to Scotland's natural wind, wave and tidal resources as well as oil and gas. Within this debate, one policy area became iconic.

In the United States and Australia, the process of hydraulic fracturing or 'fracking' was being employed by the oil and gas industry as a way of extracting natural gas from between layers of rock and sediment. Other similar unconventional gas extraction techniques such as underground coal gasification were also developing apace, attracting questions in Scotland of whether such practices could or should be employed here. The sheer volume of gas extracted in the US was pushing down prices for fossil fuels and making the country less dependent on foreign oil – both attractive prospects for a UK Government keen to untangle itself from wars in parts of the world rich in oil, and for a Scottish Government keen to prove that it could provide affordable energy and energy security in an independent Scotland.

However, the evidence emerging from the US and Australia showed serious negative consequences to such practices. Contamination of water and land by the chemicals used in fracking, seismic events and the significant additional climate changing emissions produced by these practices all sounded loud warning bells for many in Scotland.

At a grassroots level, the Yes campaign took on fracking as a symbol of what the UK Government wanted to introduce and what could only be avoided by voting Yes. Greens, socialists and many ordinary members in the SNP put pressure on the SNP Government to reject fracking and all forms of unconventional gas. Yet the official Yes campaign and the SNP Government – often very closely intertwined – were nervous about rejecting a form of technology which some said could cut costs while securing Scotland's energy independence at a time when many middle class voters were nervous about the potential costs and insecurities associated with independence.

By the time 18 September 2014 came around, the SNP Government had still not taken a firm stance on fracking and unconventional gas. It would not be until the following year when Energy Minister Fergus Ewing announced a moratorium. At the time of writing, the question has still not been put to rest in Scotland. A Scottish Parliament vote in 2016 to ban fracking saw the SNP abstain and little has changed since then.

Conclusions

Over a decade in power, the SNP has presided over a changing nation. Today, Scotland regularly produces more energy from wind than it requires to power the whole nation. Tens of thousands of people are employed in low carbon industries and communities across the country own, share or benefit from community-owned and shared renewable energy generation. These are significant successes which owe much to the SNP's leadership.

However, there exists a continuing tension within the party. A tension between embracing this sustainable future and the transition away from oil and gas which must come with it; and the old dream of capturing Scotland's black gold, taming it and using it to create a wealthier, fairer nation for future generations to enjoy. If Scotland is to become that new nation, the SNP must fully embrace sustainability and give up the dream of Scotland's oil.

References

Friends of the Earth Scotland (2010), 'Scottish Government sets emissions targets as people's climate summit convenes', 21 April, accessed at: www.foe-scotland.org.uk/news210410

MacIntyre-Kemp, G. (2017), 'Why is Norway still getting much more tax from oil?',

Business for Scotland, 24 March, accessed at: www.businessforscotland.com/norway-still-getting-much-tax-oil/

McKiernan, J. (2016), 'Aberdeen MSP demands oil tax breaks', *Aberdeen Evening Express,* 14 March, accessed at: https://www.eveningexpress.co.uk/fp/news/local/msp-demands-oil-tax-breaks/

Pachauri, R.K. (2013), Letter to the Minister for Environment and Climate Change, 21 February.

SNP (2007), *It's Time: Manifesto 2007*, Edinburgh: SNP.

SNP (2011), *Re-elect: A Scottish Government Working for Scotland*, Edinburgh: SNP.

Section Four: The Politics of Place and Belonging

Scotland's Public Sphere: From Unspace to Diverse Assembly?

Gerry Hassan

SCOTLAND'S PUBLIC SPHERE – its character, parameters and different ecologies – is vitally important. Yet explicit or implicit discussions concerning its nature and qualities are rare to non-existent (exceptions include Hassan, 2014b; Silver, 2015).

Even more problematically debate about many of the key institutions in the public sphere take place without clearly being contextualised in the wider historical, socio-economic and political framework. This chapter attempts to offer an initial overview of this terrain, to position it within the context of the SNP's record in office and to review why this matters to the future independence debate and future of Scotland.

The public sphere first came to attention in the work of the sociologist Jürgen Habermas and can be viewed as the space where non-state actors discuss politics (Habermas, 1991). It is the arena where the public become active, engaged citizens: in short, where they constitute and act as a 'public' and one distinctive from civil society: a term more widely used which focuses on associations of all sorts – political, civic, non-political.

Examples include debates on the BBC and broadcasting, the mainstream media and press, and wider environment of politics, policy and ideas. There is, for example, significant popular dissatisfaction with many of the institutions in public life and the public sphere. This book has separate chapters on broadcasting and the print media, so the exploration below will relate to how such areas are relevant to the public sphere.

Take the BBC. It has been the subject of sustained criticism and comment – both during and after the indyref. This has included books such as 'London Calling: How the BBC Stole the Independence Referendum' (Ponsonby, 2015), numerous other analyses, comment pieces, and even protest marches on BBC Scotland headquarters at Pacific Quay, Glasgow. Alex Salmond and other prominent SNP politicians have led their voices to this campaign. Numerous surveys show this dissatisfaction chimes with a large part of the public – with in one recent study 36% of Scots believing that the BBC was biased against Scottish independence (*The Herald*, 2017).

Then there is the mainstream press and its role in the indyref and after. This is rightly characterised by much pro-independence opinion as being overwhelming anti-independence and hence, not representative of Scottish public opinion. However, this is often done in a way which presents a caricatured, homogenised press which is far from the complex realities.

Scotland's pro-unionist press is regularly presented as at war with modern Scotland. An oft-cited fact stated is that of 37 major national titles only one supported independence in the referendum – the *Sunday Herald*. Then there are the roles of others – from the *Daily Record* and 'the Vow', to the *Daily Telegraph* and the fabricated 'Nikileaks' story of Nicola Sturgeon and the French Consul General in the midst of the 2015 UK general election. Beyond this there has been the rising hysteria of the *Daily Mail* and *Daily Express* Scottish editions –simultaneously denouncing, with every fibre, Scottish nationalism, while giving unapologetic expression to British nationalism.

Why is 'the Public' Often Missing from Scotland's Public Sphere?

What is commonly missing from many perspectives is not just the tendency to stress problems and shortcomings in such bodies, or to come from an über-partisan independence perspective. That is understandable. It is where most of the energy in political life has come from in recent years. More seriously, they tend to ignore a wider landscape, the backstory which has produced such a situation and the human element and contributions in the media.

First, there is a tendency to caricature such organisations. The BBC and STV did not have a good referendum. Even more than that they have not had a good record in covering Scottish politics post-devolution. Indeed, in a strange paradox seldom explored, both main broadcasters covered Scottish politics with more wit, verve and imagination pre-devolution than they have subsequently. They took more risks pre-1999; they gave space to voices for change. It wasn't perfect, but it was stellar compared to what came after.

The Scottish Parliament in the realm of broadcasting ushered in a world of seeing politics as about the Parliament and politicians, not the wider social conversations and settings. Hence, politics on BBC and STV was presented as a minority interest appeal seen at its worst in BBC's *Newsnight Scotland* (1999-2014) where a professional political class spoke to itself in what at times seemed a secret insider language. Both channels in the run-up to the Parliament explicitly axed programmes which drew on wider social currents – what are called mediated access programmes – where the public played an active part in discussions such as *Scotland 500* and *Scottish Women*. Post-devolution one study observed 'audience access programming had largely disappeared from the television schedules north of the border' (McNair *et al.*, 2005: 49).

Why this failure post-devolution has happened – and why we have not witnessed a panoply of different programmes and genres – comes down to a number of factors. There has been an absence of Scottish leadership, a failure to shape change at key moments (the BBC and 'the Scottish Six' in 1997-98, both BBC and STV in the indyref), lack of resources and a failure to successfully advocate for greater resources, editorial limitations, lack of imagination, and an unwillingness to take risks.

Second, the mainstream press has numerous different shades. Only one newspaper supported independence in 2014 but numerous other papers have distanced themselves from unconditional unionism. Thus, The *Scottish Sun* has supported the SNP since 2011, while the *Daily Record* (despite 'the Vow') and *Sunday Mail* have moved from slavish Labour loyalty to a more questioning stance. And *The Herald* has inched slowly and hesitantly towards independence.

Blind fury misses the constraints and pressures on papers, from declining, aging readerships, squeezes on advertising and budgets, and the diminished standing and status of papers in society. *The Herald* found in the indyref that whenever Iain Macwhirter or the late Iain Bell wrote a pro-independence piece, the paper received piles of negative letters and comments. This was because of the demographics of much of the paper's readership – older and in large part, anti-independence.

Third, much of the anger and comment on the BBC and media misses that all organisations are, when it comes down to it, made up of human beings and cultures. Therefore, how a body such as the BBC ended up with its unsatisfactory coverage is the sum of many influences. The line just wasn't 'imposed' from on high – whether from Glasgow or London.

Journalistic staff pushed and argued and were often over-ruled or just ignored by senior management. In the BBC Scotland offices, then Director Ken MacQuarrie and Head of News and Current Affairs John Boothman, both of who have since left their posts (the former going on to be Head of Regions and Nations for the BBC at UK level), have to take a big share of responsibility. Critically important is that BBC Scotland is not accountable to Scottish audiences in any meaningful way, and its senior management report to London – distorting the entire culture of the BBC here. Then there are the decisions and worldview of BBC senior personnel in London and their disdain and dismissal of Scotland and

Scottish politics, and in places, incomprehension (and indeed at times hostility) towards the indyref.

Fourth, equally important as present day cultures are influences of cultural histories and collective memories of such institutions. All the organisations mentioned began their lives in certain social positions of privilege with corporate missions and mandates. The BBC had a Reithian purpose – elitist, benign, to educate and inform the masses of their place in the great civilising project that was Britain. It was a project both of incorporation and Empire: confident that the British ruling classes knew what was best for the little people of the world at home and abroad.

In Scotland, the BBC attempted to assert a more Scottish identity with the establishment of the Broadcasting Council for Scotland in 1953 chaired by Lord Clydesmuir representing bourgeois, respectable opinion to the great unwashed. When BBC Scotland took the moniker in 1968 it literally involved changing the window display. Legend has it that the newly appointed controller Alasdair Milne on taking office on New Year's Day 1968, and with little to do in a near-empty office, changed the signage of the BBC headquarters in Glasgow to 'BBC Scotland'. No greater autonomy was won: a position which continues to this day.

The Scotsman and *The Herald* both have their origins as pillars of the conservative and liberal unionist establishments, and only really began to break from that explicitly in the late 1960s and early 1970s. This was as society was dramatically changing: the economy shifting from manufacturing and being male dominated, the hold of religion loosening, while authority and power became more contingent, and the press, along with the rest of institutional Scotland, tried to follow.

These papers at the time believed they were telling truth to power. Magnus Linklater (editor of *The Scotsman* 1988-94 and *The Times* Scottish edition 2007-12) reflected on Arnold Kemp (editor of *The Herald* 1981-94 and deputy editor of *The Scotsman* 1972-81) that: 'He would often repeat the observation that it was the journalist's job 'to reveal to the powerless that which the powerful would rather keep secret" (Kemp, 2012: 4). But this is mostly, if not entirely, mythology. The evidence of the time points in the opposite direction.

Until the late 1960s both papers were inexplicably interwoven with the legal, education and assorted professional elites of the West and East of Scotland who provided readers, resources and copy. It was only as the first devolution debate emerged from the late 1960s and 1970s that both papers shifted from their previously uncritical unionist position. Indeed, the two papers, along with a large segment of society shifted from their groupthink from one perspective to another: pro-devolution in the 1970s, and part of the anti-Thatcherite and home rule consensus of the 1980s.

From this it can be gathered that many of the institutions of public life which have been meant to hold authority to account and scrutinise power, have traditionally done nothing of the sort. Instead, they had close, intimate relationships with power and elites. Thus, it isn't an accident that in BBC, STV and most of the mainstream media, there has been, with honourable individual exceptions, little investigative journalism.

Recent examples of misbehaviour in public life show this is still the case. There was the lack of scrutiny of the Royal Bank of Scotland under Fred Goodwin's leadership before the crash; the liquidation of Rangers FC and the role of 'succulent lamb journalism'; and the controversies of the Catholic Church in Scotland and their numerous sexual, abuse and ethical scandals (with an exemplary exception of Catherine Deveney who when she was at *The Observer* single-handedly first broke this story). In all of these cases, Scottish institutions choose to be kowtowed and coerced by a mixture of cowardice and consent into buying into Alpha Male, macho leadership and their allure, charisma and rhetoric. Would that we could be sure such examples wouldn't happen today?

Fifth, the dominant Scotland in much of the above has been a very narrow frame of the nation. It has been based on the Central Belt, fixated on Glasgow and Edinburgh (a mere 20 % of the population in 2016), phenomenally male, middle class and white. This had three important Gs: geography, generation and gender, which gave rise to a set of elite narratives which loved to wax lyrically about how progressive and inclusive they were, and never noted the missing voices.

The above perspectives were challenged by the democratic explosion of the indyref, but since there has been retrenchment. One of the ways this occurs is the pronounced lack of interest in public life of relational space: i.e.: who is in and out of any conversation or decision. Thus, 'the missing Scotland' which emerged in the indyref was about more than voting participation, and rectified by more than voting (Hassan, 2014a; Sullivan, 2014). Since September 2014, the complacent assumption in too many places has been that the one-off event of 84.6% voting has addressed this exclusion. That is how the politics and cultures of marginalisation and shutting out voices continually have an easier time and strangely, parts of left-wing and nationalist Scotland have often bought into this.

All of the above has to be located in the wider terrain of Scottish public life with its historical dominance of institutions, authority and elites in a managed, internally manipulated system of consent and dissent. It is to this last area that I want to turn and explore further.

Scottish Autonomy, the Public Sphere and Unspace

Scotland, as everyone knows, never went away. That basic point matters through all post-union history to this day. It was never conquered, assimilated or abolished – unlike Ireland or Wales. Scotland's partial autonomy post-1707 over the course of the 18th and 19th centuries and well into the 20th century rested on 'the holy trinity' of law, education and the Kirk – an institutionally dominated identity and public sphere for all the talk of 'the democratic intellect' and lay church.

This has contributed to the unspace of much of public life and the grip of conservatism, punitive elites and conformity throughout large parts of our history. Unspace is the management of privileged voices, actors and opinions, the continual gatekeeping of this, and the marginalisation and stigmatisation of dissent and non-conformist views (Hassan, 2014b; 2016). All nations have such cultures, and small sized nations particularly, but what has made Scotland different has been the absence of a democratic culture through most of our history: our managed autonomy sitting side by side our managed society.

Within elite opinion there were powerful exceptions to this such as the ideas of the Scottish Enlightenment of Ricardo, Hume and Adam Smith, but there was a chasm of difference between the culture of these men and how the majority of the people of Scotland lived (see Barr, 2008). Large areas of public life well into post-war Scotland were shaped by the sounds of silence – about religious discrimination, corruption and cronyism in public life, the closed nature of elites and more.

Unspace has been aided by radical, left-wing and nationalist perspectives wanting to buy into the notion of Scotland as a diverse, disputatious assembly. The reasons for this are complex, suffice to say that sequentially at their peak, Liberals, Labour and SNP have all found it in their self-interest to reinforce such a mythology. But that is more effect, than cause.

A huge influence on Scotland's unspace has been our relationship with the rest of the UK. Scotland has operated in the union by asserting – particularly as the state has grown since the 1920s and 1930s – as a corporate Scottish lobby – which has advocated and represented national interests in Whitehall and Westminster. To do this effectively, it had to represent as unified and national a voice as possible, and so the success of this lobby – under successive Secretaries of States such as Walter Elliot, Tom Johnston and Willie Ross pre-devolution – has been related to how effectively they could claim to speak for Scotland. It wasn't an accident that Johnston was called 'the King of Scotland' by Winston Churchill or Ross 'the hammer of the Nats'.

This twin track process of Scotland acting as an interest group and lobbying force in the union, and its effects within Scottish society have encouraged and aided unspace and pressures for conformity. Damagingly, this hasn't yet been reversed by the Scottish Parliament, with Scotland still seeing itself as operating by winning monies, powers and favours out of London, while centralisation continues apace north of the border. Would, if Scotland, became independent, with one part of the chain broken, we be able to challenge the other part?

The Scottish public sphere is undoubtedly influenced by the shadow and overhang of what can only be described as the London public sphere – made up as it is of UK media, decision makers, think tanks and corporate business based in the UK capital. This has a distinct take on the UK and is increasingly focused on a view of 'global Britain' that while supposedly outward looking is increasingly narrow and Londoncentric. It doesn't have the interest or inclination in reflecting or understanding the rest of the UK. A good example of this in the media came from the BBC's coverage of the post-Brexit vote. In its main after-the-event analysis with Laura Kuenssberg over the course of one hour not one mention was given to Scotland, Wales and Northern Ireland despite the territorial and constitutional dynamics of the vote. Instead, the entire focus was on London as the UK and a vague thing called 'the North' (meaning North of England) which was never defined.

Ten years into SNP Government and coming up for nearly two decades into devolution, Scotland is a society rich in paradoxes. We have just lived through three years of the democratic uprising and spirit of the indyref: an event unprecedented in our history and which we are still feeling the impact of. The self-organised, self-determining zeitgeist of DIY Scotland beyond the SNP and official Yes Scotland isn't one which could be sustained at the same level over the longer term. Hence, post-indyref there has been a return to business as usual in large parts of public life. In the media, BBC and STV have resumed reporting on Scottish politics as a specialist minority interest and as if relevant to people from a far off distant world.

Similarly, the absence of a range of diverse bodies and institutions in public life such as the emergence of non-SNP independence supporting think tanks and research agencies has come at a cost (leaving aside the contribution of the pro-independence think-do tank hybrid Common Weal). It has meant that too much debate is dominated by party voices, an absence of facts, and little policy. Such a situation reduces many discussions to assertion and counter-assertion, and a politics of faith – either in the merits of independence or the maintenance of the union.

All of this leaves a large void where there should be more detail, policies and plans: not least on what independence might look like and the choices involved. In many respects, this suits the SNP leadership, as currently most policy initiatives spring from them, but thus isn't a healthy state of affairs, and is one which independent or not, favours the forces of power and the status quo in domestic public life.

Culture Eats Strategy

Such absences can be seen across Scottish Government policy and particularly in broadcasting and cultural policy. The SNP have done little on broadcasting since the Broadcasting Commission of 2007-8 created a cross-party consensus for a dedicated digital public service TV channel. Ten years later, BBC Director General Tony Hall committed to a new BBC Scotland TV channel with £30 million of additional monies and 80 new journalistic staff broadcasting from late 2018: a significant breakthrough after two decades of stalling on a 'Scottish Six' (*BBC*, 2017).

This still begs big questions – with BBC Scotland no further forward in autonomy, challenges of content and commissioning, and issues of wider cultural development and innovation in broadcasting and nationally. Significant in this is STV's decision to broadcast an integrated Scottish, UK and international news programme weekdays at 7pm ('the Scottish Seven') on the new STV2 channel. If successful, in audience, commercial and news terms, this could have a wider impact on the media and political environment in Scotland (STV, 2016).

Culture ministers have come and gone over ten years, but made little strategic impact, with the current holder of the post, Fiona Hyslop's major achievement being the lack of deep cuts to the Creative Scotland budget. Considering the arts and cultural community's role in the indyref and importance in how Scotland sees and promotes itself, such inherent conservatism, caution and lack of imagination in this arena is galling. Where is the ambition and daring on culture? On broadcasting, in film, in infrastructure, and in breaking away from the discredited New Labour idea of creative industries which the SNP still cling too.

The future dynamics of the public sphere are pivotal to how the SNP evolve in office, the outcome of the independence debate and the kind of Scotland which emerges. The indyref saw an upsurge of activism and energy – one which cannot be permanently sustained, but which also points to a long-term weakening of established authority. The spaces, places and gaps which this revealed can be seen as an opportunity. Yet, with traditional media in retreat, how do we encourage and reinforce pluralism, dissenting voices and innovation? How do we aid a Scotland which refuses to confine itself to a single story, and which never embraces the notion of a 'settled will' of the Scottish people? The story has to continually go on and never have an ending or final destination.

A fundamental in this is recognising the limits not just of the SNP, but nationalism per se, even a benign, progressive force such as Scottish nationalism and the urgent need to think now in pre-independence times about the contours of a self-governing, self-determining post-nationalist Scotland. In an age where social democracy across the West has proven an insufficient barrier against corporate crony capitalism what values and principles should be our moral compass? Merely rejecting what we don't like – Thatcherism and New Labour –isn't going to be enough of a future guide.

We have to ask questions about how we hold institutions, power and authority to account. How do we prevent in a small country which is often (like Westminster) compared to a village – future abuses such as RBS, Rangers FC and the Catholic Church? And when they do happen we need to be able to learn and adapt, seeing the dangers of charismatic styles of leadership, bloviators and institutions which shield themselves from the light of scrutiny. Equally important is daring to think about culture in a way beyond the safety first, minimalist approach which has characterised the Scottish Government – with the SNP seemingly content not to rock the boat, while buying into a New Labour and essentially neo-liberal idea of culture in the form of the creative classes. And some of the silences from independence opinion and the arts and culture community on this, exasperates the problem: of conformity, incorporation and becoming quasi-insiders for little real gain.

None of this is an add-on or luxury to the SNP or independence project. Instead, it is as critical as the economic prospectus to our future prospects. The Scottish trait and grip in places of conformity, groupthink and not asking difficult questions is one of our biggest obstacles to being a thriving independent nation. It matters in the short-term, as floating No voters decide which way to swing, but even more it matters in the longer-term: for how we hold the future Fred Goodwins, David Murrays and Keith O'Briens to account, and the kind of society and nation we aspire to be.

The SNP have told a decent story of Scotland for most of the last ten years. They have shifted perceptions and aspirations. But now isn't a time to fall back on past laurels and plaudits. A nation has to keep reinventing and reimagining itself. We need to start thinking and acting as if we are an independent nation, encouraging what I have called an 'independence of the Scottish mind', but at the same time, recognising that merely blindly defending the SNP against its accusers while understandable, isn't a substitute for serious politics and a serious culture.

References

Barr, J. (2008), *The Stranger Within: On the Idea of an Educated Public*, Rotterdam: Sense Publishers.

BBC (2017), 'New TV channel for BBC in Scotland', *BBC Scotland News*, 22 February, accessed at: http://www.bbc.co.uk/news/uk-scotland-39042666

Devlin, K. (2017), 'Poll: One in three Scots think BBC biased against independence', *The Herald*, 11 February, accessed at: www.heraldscotland.com/news/15085861. Poll__One_in_three_Scots_think_BBC_biased_against_independence/

Habermas, J. (1991), *The Structural Transformation of the Public Sphere: An Inquiry into a Category of Bourgeois Society*, Cambridge, Mass: MIT Press.

Hassan, G. (2014a), *Caledonian Dreaming: The Quest for a Different Scotland*, Edinburgh: Luath Press.

Hassan, G. (2014b), *Independence of the Scottish Mind: Elite Narratives, Public Spaces and the Making of a Modern Nation*, London: Palgrave Macmillan.

Hassan, G. (2016), *Scotland the Bold: How Our Nation Has Changed and Why There is No Going Back*, Glasgow: Freight Books.

Kemp, J. (ed.) (2012), *Confusion to Our Enemies: Selected Journalism of Arnold Kemp (1939-2002)*, Glasgow: Neil Wilson Publishing.

McNair, B., Hibbert, T. and Schlesinger, P. (2005), *Mediated Access: Broadcasting and Democratic Participation in the Age of Mediated Politics*, Luton: University of Luton Press.

Ponsonby, G.A. (2015), *London Calling: How the BBC Stole the Independence Referendum*, n.p.: NNS Media Ltd.

Silver, C. (2015), *Demanding Democracy: The Case for a Scottish Media*, Edinburgh: Word Power Books.

STV (2016), 'STV to launch integrated Scottish and international news show', *STV News*, 21 September, accessed at: https://stv.tv/news/scotland/1367651-stv-to-launch-integrated-scottish-and-international-news-show/

Sullivan, W. (2014), *The Missing Scotland: Why over a million Scots choose not to vote and what it means for our democracy*, Edinburgh: Luath Press.

Means and Ends: Progressive Nationalism and Neopolitical Practices

Ken Neil

EVEN IF BY now the observation is pat, it is nonetheless significant: indyref 2014 generated a refreshed and reinvigorated engagement of the people of Scotland and many others with political topics of concern and with the very apparatus and operation of democratic politics in the UK. Unquestionably, too, some of that engagement, both for 'yes' and for 'no', was, to say the least, unedifying and better left as private thought than actualised as public acts, whether textual, oral, or physical. Up to and beyond indyref 2014 too many protagonists believed any political public act was vindicated by nothing more than the two-stage tactic of making the act public, having first labelled it political.

A Festival of Democracy? Understanding Indyref1

Bluntly, then, indyref surfaced, from all quarters, unwelcome, thuggish tribalism. 'Patly', however, indyref surfaced, from all quarters, a heightened sense that political engagement through public discourse is important, rewarding and even constructive. While reflecting on parallel episodes of enmity and intellectual erasure all-too-visible amid the 2016 EU Referendum, the journalist David Torrance mused on the dichotomy: 'there are two dominant accounts of the independence referendum, one in which it was uniformly awful and another in which it was a 'festival of democracy. Both are caricatures and the truth, as ever, lies somewhere in between' (Torrance, 2016).

While registering necessarily the negative dimensions of partisan politics, especially when played out in front of a nationalist backdrop, and while welcoming Torrance's moderation, this brief offering is positioned all the same on a point somewhere 'in between' but closer to the festival than Torrance would journey. Indyref was indeed in many ways remarkable in its reach and effect. Public participation in political discourse was commonplace and legible and understood to be of the people: those to be affected by the political decision-making were to have their stake in the shaping of that decision-making over and above and as well as, for some, the marking of a cross. People of all types all over Scotland and beyond were concerned with the prospect of independence and its practical meanings, as far as they could be discerned, and also, importantly here, with the very idea of democratic engagement itself.

Several commentators have considered and commended these positive dimensions. Gerry Hassan, most recently in his book *Scotland The Bold* (Hassan, 2016), has noted the positive dimensions of the widespread political engagement around indyref and a constructive corollary to boot. Observing the burgeoning of new forms of democracy and participation Hassan makes the key point of extension that there was also a burgeoning of the mind-set amid and because of these new forms that participation in political discourse did not require elite pedigree nor permission from an elite. New forms saw new participants; new participants saw new forms: both together see new ideas and impetuses.

In this book and in *Scotland the Bold*, Hassan deploys 'unspace' as the term to describe the site and character of the nemesis of these new forms; the ubiquitous, the normative, the characterless and the lumpen non-progressive. Unspace 'can be found everywhere in the world'. It is the site and character, 'the power and mandate of institutional speak'. It is a force that 'rewards certain modes of acting, talking and exchange, and disavows, marginalises and ignores other forms'. It has a 'narrow range of permissible behaviours and frowns on spontaneity, frivolity, and informality' (Hassan, 2016: 181).

New forms are challenges to the established patterns of unspace, and offer loose 'messy or fuzzy spaces' by contrast to the rigid channels and behaviours of unspace. Instead of the 'institutionally-focused subjects and agendas' of unspace, fuzzy space propagates 'subjects and agendas that are value orientated'. Whereas discussions in unspace are filled with 'jargon and buzzwords', discussions in fuzzy space 'mirror everyday conversations'. As for the upshots of discussions in both spaces, unspace predetermines them and ensures that they are 'controlled by the power players' with 'very low or no ownership of outcomes and actions', and, fuzzy space ensures 'outcomes demand further engagement of participants' and encourages 'more collaboration and action' (Hassan, 2016: 183).

Yes Scotland was keen, and with confidence, to see the Yes campaign as more a movement than a campaign, less unspace, perhaps, than the Better Together enterprise. There was indeed during indyref a sense of there being a fuzzy festival of Yes activities, a momentum altogether different from conventional campaigns, and much more constructively fuzzy than the 'national conversation' of 2007.

New forms of democracy and political engagement arose by force of passion for the movement and were deployed deliberately to engage and persuade a population by practical demonstration that these new forms might yet have more support and impact within an independent Scotland. New state; new political practices. In a virtuous circle disruptive to the aged unspace, ran the logic of the movement, new forms of democratic participation played a significant role in attempting to bring about the national political context in which these new tactics would go beyond being new and would become characteristic of national self-governance.

Now, as Hassan would caution too, we must be vigilant about the actual quotient of difference, critique and novelty resident in fuzzy responses to unspace, for absorption is too ready an eventuality. This precariousness is exemplified by the 'echo chamber' criticism levelled at much pro-yes sentiment. That Hassan can see this snare is evident in his observation that pluralism must be a watchword, and, moreover, 'dissent... and the evolution of counter-stories have to be encouraged' (Hassan, 2016: 184). It would indeed be delusional to award unconditional plaudits to new forms of political practices that might replace one form of, albeit formal, enclosed affirmative unspace with another, albeit informal, enclosed affirmative unspace, and Torrance would no doubt concur.

A second *caveat en passant* is to point out that constructive and meaningful embarkations into fuzzy territory do not mean that the values, agendas, buzzwords and bozos of unspace are changing into the bargain.

But with caveats now fielded, for this author at least the positive dimensions remain: an anti-unspace festival of engagement was indeed widely experienced by way of indyref and the constructive dimensions of that engagement should not be historicised as belonging only to the advent of referendum. The alternatives-to-unspace significance of indyref has much relevance *now* for the conduct of contemporary politics in Scotland and the development of the public sphere. This is the crux of this brief offering. The point might be thrown into relief by observing that the movement and momentum of indyref up to and beyond the 2012 Edinburgh Agreement can be contextualised by international currents in political engagement in the second decade of the 21st century.

Publics on the Move

In the spring of 2011, for one example of reforming intent manifest in European public sphere, the Real Democracy Now movement saw thousands of engaged protesters encamp in Madrid's Puerta del Sol square and precipitate a 'horizontal' movement of engagement across some sixty public squares in Spain, later described as the 15M movement. The acute causation of widespread dismay with the positions expressed by unspace political parties during regional elections of 2011 was supplanted by a movement of hope that turned its attention to new forms of constructive, fuzzy political engagement.

Political scientist Isabell Lorey explains that the 15M movement was as much about the new formations of collaborative action and participation generated by the communities gathered in the squares as it was about direct dissent in the face of austerity. To underline the point, Lorey cites political activist and researcher Marta Malo who captured the new engagedness in saying '[i]t is not a matter of taking the street anymore, it's a matter of making the square' (Lorey, 2013: 79). Energised by youth, but open and inclusive, the square as site became the ground from which grew new attitudes and participatory practices, means to better ends for the assembled hopeful, and *ends in themselves* inasmuch as the practices inspired an inclusive citizenry to take a stake in the formation of new occasions for the public sphere towards new beginnings for their nation.

In an earlier exploration of Scotland's public sphere, civic spaces and unspace tendencies, Hassan has suggested that devolution and the establishment of the Scottish Parliament has in some sense created an 'undemocracy', a condition involving the 'appearance, institutional arrangements and partial discourse of democratic politics and practice, while the reality is very different' (Hassan, 2014: 65). If so, this condition must be understood, of course, in the wider contemporaneous context of managed societies and the bureaucratisation of lived relations. Even so, for Hassan, Scotland's public sphere risks being straightjacketed by unspace predilections and a decline in actual participation in civic debate and the public sphere, if not particular to Scotland, then salient in her recent democratic electoral history, save indyref.

The SNP ten years on, and nearly three years past indyref, has a proven track record in organised governance, but to what extent has the Government valued, harnessed, implemented, iterated and celebrated the new forms of political engagement that gave the Yes movement its grassroots credentials and situated it in an international tendency seeking alternatives to the intransigent political polarities faulted by Torrance and to the unspace exclusions highlighted by Hassan. And these are neopolitical practices to be used not as props in a spectacular theatre for a definitive end, but as distinctive and daily characteristics of and a means by which a progressive Scottish Nationalism might seek to pragmatically empower and enrich the citizens of Scotland from wheresoever they hail in all their difference.

The indyref in 2014 was undoubtedly a catalyst for myriad political events, practices, engagements, discussions and conclusions, the like of which, perhaps, Scotland has never seen before. Many constituents of the 'missing Scotland' absent from 2010 Westminster elections, then for the Scottish Parliament in 2011 (Hassan, 2014) felt energy and agency during indyref. High-octane referendum versions of these engagements are, of course, impossible to sustain and *making the square* is to be understood, largely, figuratively. What is more, maybe the fun and the force of the festival are to be lost if assimilated into the political everyday.

On the other hand, across the next ten years, in marking out and deploying new political *modus operandi* as practices that might find fuller formation in an inclusive self-determining state, in addition to existing *end* propositions about Scotland's Future, something more of the value of public *means* in the here and now – and for then – might usefully be added.

At time of writing, in March 2017, Scotland's First Minister has announced formally the manifesto intention to host a second referendum on independence – indyref2. Modestly, all of the above pertains still. A closing remark might offer some caution, whatever one thinks about the timing of indyref2 and the most appropriate way of voting.

If this small contribution is an appeal for further adoption of modes of progressive neopolitical practices fostered by indyref1 in order to make them manifest at the heart of the way in which Scotland's Government engages with its people in political self-determination, then let's hope that the necessary theatre of indyref2 doesn't retard or eclipse those manifestations, fledgling as some of them are. The topical concern of Scotland's electorate is about *ends* once again over the coming months, but it should also be about differentiating convivial and formal *means*; as *means* can, surely, assist the *ends* and sustain them beyond that moment.

References

Lorey, I. (2013), 'On Democracy and Occupation', in Gielen, Pascal (ed.), *Institutional Attitudes: Instituting Art in a Flat World*, Amsterdam: Valiz.

Hassan, G. (2014), *Independence of the Scottish Mind: Elite Narratives, Public Spaces and the Making of a Modern Nation*, London: Palgrave Macmillan.

Hassan, G. (2016), *Scotland The Bold: How Our Nation Has Changed and Why There is No Going Back*, Glasgow: Freight Books.

Torrance, D. (2016), 'Selective memory syndrome and the politics of hate', *The Herald*, 20 June.

Alternative Scotlands: New Spaces and Practices and Overcoming 'Unspace'

Vérène Nicolas

Introduction

DEMOCRACY AS WE understand the term is not exactly in good health across the developed world. We are seeing signs of anger, mistrust and powerlessness in most countries – much, if not most of it, understandable.

A view shared by many in contemporary Scotland is that here we are different: we criticise and are discontented by the inadequacies of Westminster, but on the whole, we are comfortable with our own domestic arrangements and trajectory as a nation. However, the evidence doesn't seem to support this.

Gerry Hassan argues that the last 10 years of SNP Government have not made a dent in the culture and practices of 'unspace,' 'undemocracy' and 'unpolitics' in Scottish public life (Hassan, 2014, 2016). This ties up with concerns about the state of democracy (COSLA, 2014) and the impact of the 'marginalisation of dissent and non-conformist voices' on our capacity to address Scotland's major challenges. Therefore, where can we turn for fresh ideas, hope and creativity for Scotland's democratic future?

The concept of 'fuzzy, messy space' catches the imagination. It evokes images and values that many of us long to find in a world where many of our human interactions and workplaces feel stressful and constrained.

The opposite of unspace is fuzzy, messy, unofficial space. It is shaped by diversity in people attending; there are few barriers to access and involvement; there is relatively open conversation, and people can articulate challenging or unfinished thoughts. There is a distinct sense that people can make mistakes and speak from personal and individual perspectives, and that overall the 'feel' is completely different: one more relaxed and tolerant allowing for fun, play, humour and irreverence.

(Hassan, 2014: 66).

Beyond 'Unspace'

This short chapter attempts to open an inquiry through the lens of a handful of projects, all based in Glasgow: Friends of Kelvingrove Park, the Scottish Assemblies for Tackling Poverty, Bridges out of the Poverty Glasgow, Govanhill Baths, Pollokshields Playhouse, the Galgael Trust and the Children's Wood and North Kelvin Meadow. They were chosen because of their qualities of openness and inclusion, and a sense that something fresh, countercultural and dynamic is happening around them. All but one of those projects were interviewed as part of this research.

This chapter highlights some key characteristics of these spaces, why they are important to a healthy democratic process, and what practices make them so attractive. The question of how those qualities and practices may infuse vibrancy, pluralism and critical thinking within the 'unspace' of Scottish public life is also explored.

A key characteristic of all the studied projects is their capacity to attract a wide range of people – thanks to a wide range of activities and a non-judgmental, open and relaxed space. These projects provide a natural habitat for people of all backgrounds, age and race to interact, work or play together, and get to know each other. This is often mediated by those spaces welcoming children and young people and/or offering cultural, crafts or sports activities that nurture learning, wellbeing and community. For the more politicised spaces, this is achieved by creating a space where people experiencing poverty have a voice, a sense of companionship and access to service deliverers and policy makers.

In this sense, the concept of 'fuzzy spaces' seems to complement that of 'third spaces' defined by Oldenburg (1989) and other theorists of urban planning. They are public environments such as cafes, pubs, public libraries, parks, local businesses, community centres and churches that play an anchor role in communities and foster a wide range of human interactions. What distinguishes the projects that took part in this study from 'third spaces' may be in their origin and values: most got established as a result of or were the focus of a grassroots-led campaign to save a public asset (e.g. Pollok Park for Galgael, Govanhill Baths, North Kelvin Meadow and Kelvingrove Bandstand for Friends of Kelvingrove Park). They developed into a cultural, organised space as a strategy to demonstrate the need for such an asset to remain public and inclusive.

Many of the alternative values embodied by the founding group during their campaign are now embedded in the project's culture. They include a can-do culture, 'acting as if we own the place', social innovation ('Dynamic Self-Governance'), holding public bodies to account, celebrating diversity and caring for the most marginalised.

It is interesting to note that in the case of the Pollok Park campaign (and maybe other projects too), people seemed to be attracted to the fuzzy space itself (as distinct to its political dimension), because it felt more interesting, inclusive and generative of a sense of personal agency.

Though several of those projects said they don't intently take part in shaping public debate, by virtue of creating an opportunity to live 'in the company of strangers', they arguably help develop and exercise what US activist and educator Parker Palmer calls 'democratic habits of the heart': a range of qualities and skills that citizens need to mobilise to have influence in the democratic process. Palmer's five habits are: 'We must understand that we are all in it together'; 'We must develop an appreciation of the value of 'otherness'; 'We must cultivate the ability to hold tension in life-giving ways'; 'We must generate a sense of personal voice and agency'; and 'We must strengthen our capacity to generate community'.

All the projects involved in this study play a role in nurturing these habits, albeit in various degrees of conscious intention, depth and attention to process. Nonetheless, 'fuzzy spaces' could potentially play a key role in creating a genuine democratic culture in Scotland, including by strengthening people's ability to hold institutions and power to account. In my opinion, this would require wider recognition of this role as well as support to consciously develop intention and capacity in this sphere.

It's worth highlighting some practices already used in the studied spaces: free classes, skilfully facilitated learning journeys in community, multi stake-holders conversations over several years, outdoor activities for children and young people, access to culture and heritage, decision-making circles or assemblies, 'conflict kitchens', un-programmed weekly gatherings (including food) and of course cooking, planting, growing, creating beauty, singing, story telling and playing. A key characteristic of 'fuzziness' identified in this research is that it is a space where people engage as individuals – as distinct to being in a role – and therefore, as one person shared, 'we reveal our common humanity to each other, build trust and tap into our resourcefulness to face challenges together.'

A key question emerging is what would be required for the qualities and practices embedded in 'fuzzy' spaces to infuse 'unspace' and help shape a more inclusive and vibrant public life in Scotland. Already, most of the studied projects were interacting with and being challenged by the rigidity, inertia and 'business as usual' nature of institutionalised space (including within their own organisation). Some of them could also foresee threats to their 'fuzziness' resulting from the emergence of a more formalised and regulated space to ensure sustainability. Projects of a more political nature are actively engaging with key institutions of public life as part of their mission. They are therefore confronted with the challenge of engaging with professionals shaped by 'unspace', while actively trying to challenge unhelpful assumptions, ask deeper questions, invite 'non-knowing' and 'contradictions', and find ways to hold tensions creatively so that those in roles feel willing to drop their mask.

This short contribution doesn't do justice to the richness and depth of inquiry that emerged from this limited research. My sense is that all people who took part in conversations were affirmed by the idea that their project may have qualities associated with 'fuzzy, messy spaces'. It may have helped clarify why they feel passionate about what has been created. Could this be specifically about what happens in people when they feel invited to expand into fuzzy space: a space in which you don't always have to be careful that you're right; a space where you can play creatively with ideas; a space where ignorance will not be held against you because it is accepted that everybody is on a learning curve?

References:

COSLA (2014), *Effective Democracy, a Report of the Commission on Local Democracy*.

Hassan, G. (2014), *Independence of the Scottish Mind: Elite Narratives, Public Spaces and the Making of a Modern Nation*, London: Palgrave Macmillan.

Hassan, G. (2016), *Scotland the Bold: How Our Nation Has Changed and Why There is No Going Back*, Glasgow: Freight Books.

Oldenburg, Ray (1989). *The Great Good Place: Cafes, Coffee Shops, Community Centers, Beauty Parlors, General Stores, Bars, Hangouts, and How They Get You Through the Day*. New York: Paragon House.

Palmer, P. (2011), *Healing the Heart of Democracy: the Courage to Create a Politics Worthy of the Human Spirit*, San Francisco: Jossey-Bass.

Glasgow: The Challenges Facing Scotland's First City

Sue Laughlin

I dream of a city of bread and festivals where those who don't have the bread aren't excluded from the carnival. I dream of a city in which action grows out of knowledge and understanding... where social justice is more prized than a balanced budget; where I have a right to my surroundings, and so do all my fellow citizens; where we don't exist for the city but are seduced by it, where only after consultation with local folks could decisions be made about neighbourhoods... where no one flaunts their authority and no one is without authority... I want a city where the community values and rewards those who are different.

(Sandercock, 2003)

THE SNP GOVERNMENT sees Scottish cities as being instrumental in the delivery of a modern Scotland. It has placed them at the heart of its commitment to social justice through the effective delivery of its economic strategy and in creating inclusive growth (Scottish Government, 2016).

Laudably, inclusive growth is expected to deliver prosperity with greater equity, to create opportunities for all and to ensure that the dividends of this greater prosperity are distributed fairly. On the evidence so far, the last 10 years have not however been a success as inequality has widened.

Glasgow is Scotland's largest city and as such might be expected to play a central role in the Government's ambitions for the country. Any consideration of progress made in Glasgow has to be considered against the strategic backdrop of the Scottish Cities Strategy but has also to take into account the inevitable tensions that exist between two powerful seats of government led by different political parties. Perhaps unsurprisingly, Glasgow City Council appears to have cleaved more to Core Cities, a self styled group of the second largest cities in the UK behind London and all Labour controlled. By becoming part of the global Resilient Cities movement it has also made a claim to be viewed in an international context.

Glasgow as an Economic, Cultural and Sporting Centre

Indeed, by placing itself as an economically important city within the UK context rather than primarily emphasising its role in Scotland, Glasgow has been attempting to position itself as outward facing and world-class, capable of withstanding future shocks and stresses. A certain kind of city has been emerging and recent strategic and economic plans for Glasgow boast about its ambition and its success. Much is made of internationally competitive sectors, world-class universities 'that drive innovation and support commercialisation and economic impact' (Glasgow City Council, 2016a).

Its cultural venues and sporting events are similarly presented as noteworthy – the 2014 Commonwealth Games are considered to have been a success both in themselves and in helping to regenerate a previously disadvantaged area of the city. Glasgow has become a desirable tourist destination and has recently been voted as the world's friendliest city by readers of the Rough Guide. It presents itself as hopeful, able to build on strong economic foundations that have weathered the economic downturn. Its latest branding, 'People Make Glasgow', dominates the city and ostensibly places the population at the heart of the decisions that are made about its current and future wellbeing. Pride is often expressed on the welcome that has been given to asylum seekers and refugees, its ethnic mix a further sign of its attractiveness to incomers.

Inequality and the City

Yet, Glasgow is conflicted. Despite the apparent successes, it has had no choice but to acknowledge in its political statements that it remains a city of inequality, that the succession of measures that have been put in place to tackle poverty and hopefully enrich and empower disadvantage communities have not had the impact that were intended (Glasgow City Council, 2016b). Glasgow's overall record of poor health, its profound health inequalities and its tag, the 'sick man of Europe', although clichéd, still resonate. Casual observation of the city centre, with its empty shops and homeless people sheltering in their doorways are also a reminder that policy decisions taken with good intentions can have negative as well as positive consequences.

Where explanations exist for the enduring nature of poverty and health inequalities, a reading of its many strategies for improvement shows that a discourse has been created that portrays addressing these factors as largely external to control by Glasgow politicians. Indeed, the Glasgow City Council portrays itself as beneficent but buffeted by the decisions of Scottish and UK Governments on the one hand – unfair financial settlements imposed by the SNP on a Labour controlled Council and the austerity measures and welfare reform imposed by the Tories – and a population that is perceived to be resistant to change on the other. A revealing quote from Glasgow's Economic Strategy highlights a tendency to pathologise certain sections of the population rather than to consider what structural deficits exist which might account for the problems it is describing:

> Economic inactivity is decreasing, but far too many of our citizens are unable to take part in the labour market. Glasgow had the third largest inactive working age population in Scotland in 2015. This is challenging enough, but 77.7% of those individuals do not want a job.
>
> (Glasgow City Council, 2016a)

That there are financial pressures on public services in Glasgow is undeniable and the difficulties that it poses for decision-making in the public sector when there are so many competing demands are enormous. The changing demography especially as the population lives longer has created a requirement to think differently about the nature and extent of health and social care. Workers in that sector report the need to operate simultaneously in a state of crisis management and to plan creatively in a new environment of integration where the resources to bring together two different cultures are not available. The pressure to maintain other public services that benefit poorer communities such as libraries, sports and leisure facilities constitutes a reality that should not be downplayed.

The Scottish Government has undoubtedly paid insufficient attention to Glasgow's place as the hub of Scotland's economy and how this might best be supported. Its freeze on Council tax has had a differentially negative impact on Glasgow, adding to the burden of inequality. But some problems are of Glasgow's making alone. A tendency to blame others for the dilemmas it is experiencing appears to have precluded fresh political thinking and an unwillingness to embrace alternative voices. Despite rhetorical commitment to improved engagement with local communities and some evidence of serious city-wide conversations (Glasgow City Council, 2016) this has been undermined by centralising power through cabinet style political decision making. Democratic accountability of many services has been further diluted by removing them from direct Council control. Arms Length Organisations (ALEOs) have been seen to be the answer to attracting the capital required to fund Glasgow's aspirations while remaining within the orbit of the Council's strategic direction. Critics maintain that they take public assets out of public services, fragment services and often end up costing more money than they save. At least one ALEO in Glasgow is now being brought back under direct Council management because of its perceived failures in providing the required quality of service delivery.

Recent research carried out to explain the Glasgow Effect, the term coined to describe the excess mortality in Glasgow as compared with the similar cities of Liverpool and Manchester, is instructive. It makes a compelling case about the ways in which policy mistakes produce major repercussions contrary to the stated intentions (Walsh *et al*, 2016). While focussing on political and economic decisions taken prior to the SNP being the party of Government it nevertheless provides a number of lessons which have implications for recent and extant policy.

The explanatory model for the excess mortality in Glasgow argues that a city already experiencing high historical levels of disadvantage was made more vulnerable from the 1960s onwards by both national and local government planning in a way that was absent or less marked in the comparator cities. Scottish government was implicated by its regional policy of locating new types of industry and a socially selected sample of the population to New Towns and away from a city that was considered to be declining. These areas became the beneficiaries of subsequent further investment despite awareness that the change in Glasgow's demography and the lack of investment was creating negative socioeconomic consequences.

The type of urban change that was taking place within the city then exacerbated this decline further. Construction of poor quality housing estates and limited budgets for housing repairs together with the prioritisation of commercialisation and gentrification in anticipation of producing greater wealth for the city likely had a compound effect on an already vulnerable population. In the face of these profound economic and social changes, local, community based initiatives targeting health behaviours were always destined to fail.

The Limits of Official Glasgow Responses

The questions that need to be asked in the face of these findings relate to the future impact of the last 10 years of policy making and of the current planning for the future. One might also ask about the extent to which such evidence has become the source of political reflection and whether it has or is likely to lead to a change of course in the city's direction of travel. In its quest for world-class status, has the city sowed the seeds of a new health emergency? The evidence from a sizeable literature on the characteristics of cities with similar aspirations is probably yes. This can be illustrated by considering two policies with the avowed intention of tackling inequality, Glasgow's City Deal and Thriving Places.

The advent of City Deal brings national and local government back into closer alignment. For the Glasgow City Region it comprises an £1.14billion injection into local infrastructure to support the delivery of an economic strategy that purports to be about inclusive growth. As such it is a metaphor for national endeavour. A language of fairness and a commitment to tackling poverty and disadvantage dominates the strategy.

The City Deal is seen as the means, its funds used to drive and support certain types of employment sectors that will create the wealth for dispersal across the city. These are sectors perceived as having high value and fostering innovation such as creative industries, financial services and digital technology, sectors which create only small numbers of elite jobs. Investment will be made in creating desirable spaces in which these industries can flourish, that public money is required to facilitate private development. Although some money is being made available for new housing projects, these are likely to end up bought or rented by young professionals who can take best advantage of the new developments.

By contrast, Thriving Places is an initiative for those communities that have been left behind. City Deal is not for them, they have to make better use of existing assets and resources achieved by more effective working across organisational partners. None of the nine areas identified as requiring a targeted method for tackling child poverty and unemployment feature as being the direct beneficiaries of City Deal. The ambitions are limited, the residents have not been invited to shape the future for the city.

> *The tea dances have been one of the Project's biggest successes. Running since December 2015, more than 1000 people have joined in and many of them are now regulars .... Becoming a real inter-generational and multi-cultural community event, pupils from St Mungo's Academy serve tea and cakes and even join in the dancing and each week they see more refugees and people from asylum seeking communities come to see what goes on at a tea dance and watch footage of old Glasgow.*

(Glasgow City Council, 2016d)

Tellingly, the economic strategy references the explanatory model about the Glasgow Effect but concludes that another Health Commission is required to tackle poor health rather than that gentrification and commercialisation pushes disadvantaged communities and individuals further to the margins. That tea dances are considered to be progress for some communities but already wealthy companies need more public investment is the route to further inequality.

What happens to Glasgow matters to Glaswegians and it also matters to Scotland. Whether a more congenial partnership between the Government and the Glasgow City Council would have created a different type of city is moot. Recent public advocacy of the City Deal by the leader of the SNP in Glasgow would suggest not. What is however clear is that if Glasgow is to become a more just city and contribute significantly to a more just Scotland, a serious look at what such a city looks like is overdue.

> *The right to the city is far more than the individual liberty to access resources: it is a right to change ourselves by changing the city. It is moreover, a common rather than an individual right since this transformation inevitably depends on the exercise of collective power to reshape the processes of urbanisation.*
>
> (Harvey, 2008)

References

Glasgow City Council (2016a), *Glasgow Economic Strategy*, 2016-23, GCC.

Glasgow City Council (2016b), *Strategic Plan Refresh*, GCC.

Glasgow City Council (2016c), *Our Resilient Glasgow*, A City Strategy, GCC.

Glasgow City Council (2016d), 'North East communities reaping the benefits of a Thriving Places approach', GCC *News Archive*, accessed at: www.glasgow.gov.uk/index.aspx?articleid=19217_

Harvey, D. (2008), 'The Right to the City', *New Left Review*, 53.

Sandercock, L. (2003), *Cosmopolis II: Mongrel Cities in the 21st Century*, London: Continuum.

Walsh, D., McCartney, G., Collins, C., Taulbut, M. and Batty, G. D. (2016), *History, politics and vulnerability: explaining excess mortality in Scotland and Glasgow*, Glasgow: Glasgow Centre for Population Health.

The Story of Land Reform: From the Margins to Centre Stage?

Alison Elliot

PROGRESS ON LAND reform is a measure of the success of the Scottish Parliament. Under Westminster, reform of Scotland's property law was too complex and too demanding of parliamentary time to be given adequate scrutiny. One of the attractions of devolution was that now attention could properly be given to this, and other, neglected areas of legislation.

Things were so bad that Scotland still had feudal tenure at the start of the 21st century. A major priority for the first post-devolution executive was to abolish feudal tenure and introduce measures of land reform and reform of agricultural tenancies. Several other pieces of legislation that change 'the arrangements governing the possession and use of land in Scotland in the public interest' (the definition of land reform in the report of the Land Reform Review Group (LRRG)) have been introduced in the eighteen years of the Scottish Parliament (the LRRG identified 38 of the 205 Acts passed by the Parliament up to 2013 as containing some land reform provision) (Land Reform Review Group, 2014).

In the Land Reform Scotland Act of 2016, a Scottish Land Commission was established to ensure that legislation on issues to do with land was kept up to date and the debate about its reform continued to be prominent. In addition, the Government is now required to publish a Statement of Land Rights and Responsibilities every five years to give democratic underpinning and a strategic coherence to the direction of reform in this area.

Land Reform has emerged from the shadows of legislative neglect to be prominent in the policy world of the future. How has the landscape changed in this period and what impact has the SNP Government had on its progress?

Community Ownership

Scottish land reform is distinctive in the importance given to community ownership as a tool of reform. The 2003 Act built on the models of ownership that had emerged in Assynt and Eigg whereby ownership did not simply transfer from one individual to another but became part of the wider development of the whole community. In a sense, this was an indirect reflection of the feudal mind-set, whereby ownership of land was tied to conditionalities between the feudal superior and local community. However inappropriate these condition-alities had been, the idea that the land created a bond between its owner and those who lived on it was strong. If the owner of the land was not enabling the local community to flourish, then it made sense for the community to take over ownership and attend to its own development. The 'Community Right to Buy' was the much trumpeted innovation in the 2003 legislation.

It was innovative, but it was also cautious. Only in the case of crofting com-munities was it actually a right to buy; for others it was a right of pre-emption, whereby the community could intervene when the land came on the market and have first bite at the sale. The price to be paid for this privilege was a difficult process of deadlines, governance requirements and pernickety detail that was daunting to all but the most committed communities. The drafters were anxious because, in abolishing feudal tenure, they had cleared the way for an absolute understanding of land ownership that opened up the possibility of challenge under the European Convention on Human Rights. Community ownership shouldn't be made too easy.

Expanding the Rights Agenda

Land reform has rights scattered through it. The right of an owner to the peace-ful enjoyment of his possessions is enshrined in the ECHR and is frequently seen as a trump card held by land owners who want to resist 'interference' in how they exercise that right. However, ECHR allows for people to be deprived of their possessions in the public interest and it notes that the state does have the right 'to control the use of property in accordance with the general interest'. Howev-er, the introduction of the community right to buy, or the walker's right to have access to the countryside expanded the kinds of rights that were at stake in this area. There is now also greater awareness of the Covenant on Social, Economic and Cultural Rights and the role of land in ensuring basic human rights to shel-ter and food. So the rights narrative around land reform has expanded.

Manifesto Commitments

The 2007 manifesto for the SNP did not focus on land reform nor particularly on community development. However, in 2011, a Community Empowerment and Renewal Bill was promised as well as a review of Land Reform and a new Scottish Land Fund.

It can be argued that the Scottish Government saw land reform as an element in community empowerment. The Land Reform Review Group was established in the autumn of 2012 (Scottish Government, 2012). The preamble to its remit emphasised how 'the expansion of community ownership [have] contributed positively to a more successful Scotland by assisting in the reduction of barriers to sustainable development, by strengthening communities and by giving them a greater stake in their future'. The remit asked the group to identify how land reform will 'assist with the acquisition and management of land (and also land assets) by communities, to make stronger, more resilient and independent communities which have an even greater stake in their development'.

The Review operated in two phases and, although it began by emphasising the community dimension of the topic, it ended by offering a comprehensive view of land reform, which included land registration, succession law, housing, taxation, and issues to do with salmon fishing and deer culling as well as tidying up archaic provisions that required attention. It spent a lot of time considering publicly owned land, such as land or assets owned by local authorities, the Forestry Commission, or the Crown Estate, as well as privately owned land.

The Review made 64 recommendations. Apart from four, which related to tax provisions and business rates, the Government undertook to address all of them, although not all of them made it into the 2016 Act. At the same time, a review of agricultural holdings had been undertaken and the following Land Reform Scotland Act of 2016 incorporated recommendations from each review. The Scottish Land Commission includes a Tenant Farming Commissioner as well as a commissioner with expertise in urban issues, picking up on concerns expressed both by the LRRG and by the Community Empowerment Act of 2015.

Shifting the Focus

The detail of the recommendations in the LRRG report ranged widely. However, underlying most of them was the proposal that the arbiter of decisions about the ownership and use of land should be the public interest. This should be determined by the democratically elected representatives of the day, so allowing for different political or philosophical perspectives on property ownership to emerge. The proposal that there should be a Statement of Land Rights and Responsibilities produced by each government also provided space for these issues to be decided openly. For some people, this is a radical and disturbing proposal, because it challenges the idea that the bedrock of social and economic policy should be individual property rights. However, it is widely accepted as being reasonable and is consistent with other legal developments.

Party Politics

It is fair to say that, during the course of the Review, the only issue on which parties differed was that the Conservative Party drew a red line under the possibility of a transaction going through in the face of an unwilling seller. By the time of the passage of the bill through Parliament differences between Labour and SNP in particular were evident, as well as the SNP being challenged at its 2015 conference to be more radical in the bill's provisions. In general, the differences appeared to relate to a dimension that ran within parties rather than between them and the Labour Party adopted the role of 'holding the Government's feet to the fire'.

Covering the Country: Urban and Rural

It had been argued since the start of the post-devolution interest in the topic that land reform should apply to our cities as well as the countryside. Land is needed for shelter and for operating businesses whether the surroundings are rural or urban, and many of the same examples of bad behaviour can be demonstrated in an urban as in a rural setting. People buy land as an investment, without any intention of looking after it, and derelict and neglected property blights our cities as well as our countryside. As long as land reform relates only to rural issues, the majority of the electorate can treat it as a romantic notion that does not apply to them.

Without calling it land reform, the 2011 Government began to address these issues through their Community Empowerment Bill, looking at questions of the acquisition of community assets, protection of Common Good land and considering the possibility of introducing an urban community right to buy.

The LRRG took this further, addressing the question of how planners could overcome the barriers to acquiring land necessary for developments when they were blocked by 'passive' owners – many taking no active interest in their land other than to watch it grow in value. They proposed introducing a Compulsory Sale Order, which would allow communities to sell, possibly at auction, land which is an eyesore or otherwise inhibiting more sympathetic development. They recommended that the Government consider the feasibility of a majority land assembly measure that would remove the capacity of one owner to block a development that was advocated by surrounding owners, and they encouraged consideration of setting up Urban Partnership Zones to address the problems following from fragmentation or multiple ownership of land.

None of the urban recommendations made it into the 2016 Act, although they are being considered by Government and the presence of an urban land specialist on the Land Commission should ensure that these issues do not disappear.

Culture and Legislation

There is a narrative about land reform that is deeply embedded in Scottish literature, drama and ballads and which reflects a history in which land ownership has been a cause of division and has revealed a cavalier attitude to justice. As long as people read 'Sunset Song' or books by Neil Gunn or poems by Iain Crichton Smith, they will meet the unjust land owner and the oppressed tenants. While historical injustices should not be forgotten, it doesn't necessarily serve the interests of the country today when the debate is shaped by them.

Mind you, people still struggle to get access to the land they want to satisfy their ambitions and to implement their initiatives. Further legislation may open up land based opportunities to allow the land to work for 'the many, not just the few', as it has done for communities that benefit from the local assets or stretches of land which they now own.

But the dynamic between legislation and culture is an important one in this area and one must not underestimate the value of changing the culture as well. Frequently, one comes across examples where the provisions of the Land Reform Act have not been used, but the fact of its being there has brought people round the table to work out a satisfactory deal. The Protocol for Negotiated Sales, developed jointly by Community Land Scotland and by Scottish Land and Estates, is a good example of how progress can be made outwith the legislative process, once such a rapprochement is culturally possible.

There is still passion around land reform but, as the subject is normalised, it can take on a more constructive nature. Addressing the new challenges of urban land reform can help in shifting that focus. A recent conference was shown a photograph of buildings left derelict in the North East of Glasgow for decades. 'What does that say to the child who looks out on that each morning?' asked the MP for the area. 'It says, 'You don't matter''. There are challenges a-plenty for the new Scottish Land Commission to address as the subject enters a new phase.

References

Land Reform Review Group Final Report (2014), *The Land of Scotland and the Common Good*, Edinburgh: Scottish Government.

Scottish Government (2012), 'Land Reform Review: Remit', www.gov.scot/About/Review/land-reform/Remit

Section Five: Cultures of Imagination

The SNP and the Press

Peter Geoghegan

THE SNP'S ELECTORAL success has coincided with a period of historic decline in the nation's press. In May 2007, as the first SNP administration was entering Holyrood, *The Scotsman* sold 63,240 copies. By early 2017, the paper's official daily circulation was below 20,000, with well-placed sources admitting that some days the number of paid-for sales were in four figures.

Correlation, of course, does not equal causation. The Scottish press's travails reflect systemic problems that have affected the newspaper industry across the UK, and internationally. These difficulties predate the SNP's slenderest of electoral victories – at over 60,000, *The Scotsman's* sales in May 2007 look extremely healthy in a contemporary light but actually represented a 7.5 % year-on-year fall.

Sales figures, however, do not tell the full story of the Scottish press during a decade of nationalists in power at Holyrood (Geoghegan, 2015). Senior SNP figures have differed in their approach to the press – and the relationship between journalists and the party has fluctuated, too – but in general there has been a marked wariness between Scottish nationalism and the Fourth Estate. As a former SNP press officer put it: 'within the party and within the membership there is often a suspicion of the media.'

Increasingly, and as the Scottish media retrenches, this suspicion manifests itself in attempts to bypass the press altogether, to speak directly to SNP supporters through social media and other proprietary channels.

But back in 2007, the SNP, with just single seat margin over the opposition Labour party, had little choice but to engage with Scotland's press. This shift began back in the early 1990s. With Chris McLean as the party's press officer, the SNP began to receive a more favourable hearing, at least in some quarters of the Scottish press. The Scottish edition of *The Sun* backed the SNP in the 1992 general election, even proclaiming its support for independence with the memorable headline: 'Rise Now And Be A Nation Again.'

Nevertheless, in the years before devolution, the relationship between the press and the SNP often fluctuated quite wildly. At election time the party often battled for television coverage and a hearing on the national stage. McLean later remarked that the party found more understanding of the Scottish situation among international media than the London press (Smith, 1994). Arguably the most significant factor in a sustained uptick in relations between the press and the SNP was Alex Salmond's decision to coax Kevin Pringle from the private sector into a special advisor role. Pringle, who has been involved with the SNP since university, was previously the party's director of communications and he quickly set about forging a different working different relationship between the SNP and the nation's press.

'Kevin (Pringle) is probably one of the best operators of his generation, certainly the best in Scotland', said a veteran political correspondent who had spent more than two decades covering the SNP for the broadsheet press. 'He saw his job as non tribal, which a lot of SNP press officers didn't.'

In 2015, Pringle left a role as SNP strategic communications director – a post he took up three years earlier – and joined Charlotte Street partners, a lobby firm set up by former SNP MSP Andrew Wilson and Malcolm Robertson, son of Labour former NATO general secretary George Roberson. By then, relations between the press and the SNP had deteriorated, particularly in the wake of the 2011 Holyrood victory and the build-up to the 2014 independence referendum.

Many journalists complain that the SNP administration became increasingly guarded after 2011. Effectively three tiers of press interface have been simultaneously in play: the SNP press office, the Scottish Government itself and ministers' special advisors, or Spads. The SNP press office, complained one journalist, became a 'parallel news organisation putting out party propaganda' that is picked up and reproduced largely on social media rather in traditional press outlets. Pringle's successors were often seen as more partisan, too.

Where Labour in government was often leaky and riven by splits, the SNP – bound by the teleological goal of independence – has, by and large, been regimentally on message. Over the past decade, Scottish Government press and special advisors have become less autonomous. Where policy announcements were once regularly made to the media at St Andrew's House, now they are press released and briefed after. After 2011 'the message became much more centralised', says one senior journalist. 'The Yes Scotland campaign, the SNP press office became more centralised. It was very difficult to unpick sometimes who was reasonable for policy decisions.'

At the same time the capacity of the Scottish press itself has seriously shrunk. Scotland used to boast one of the highest concentrations of newspaper readers in the world. The *Sunday Post* sold 1.7 million copies every week in a country whose population was barely three times that. The glory days of Scottish journalism are long gone. When the Scottish Affairs Committee at Westminster discussed 'the crisis in the Scottish press industry' in 2009, *The Herald* was selling just under 60,000 copies a day; now that figure is less than 35,000. The newspaper industry globally is struggling against falling advertising revenue and the migration of readers on line. But the problem is particularly pronounced in Scotland where the two major indigenous 'quality' titles *The Herald* and *The Scotsman* are owned by local newspaper conglomerates, Newsquest and Johnston Press respectively, while having to compete against London titles who can offer far more extensive UK-wide and international content.

A former *Scotsman* journalist says both Newsquest and Johnston Press failed to innovate. 'The underlying truth is that the managers at Newsquest or Johnston Press do not care, or even seem to know, what quality journalism is or what it takes to deliver. In another life the men who run these companies would be selling baked beans or floor mops door-to-door. Neither company embraced the Internet. They saw it as a threat, rather than an opportunity', he says.

When Newsquest, the UK subdivision of the American local publishing giant Gannett, paid £216 million for *The Herald* and its stable-mates, *The Sunday Herald* and the tabloid *Evening Times*, *The Sunday Herald's* journalists alone occupied almost an entire floor in the group's offices; 13 years later, there are less than staff assigned solely to the Sunday paper. In the last financial year profits at *The Herald* rose by more than a quarter, to £11.6 million. Turnover was flat; all the gains were made by cutting more than £2 million from costs, mostly staff. Newsquest did cause a splash when, seeing a gap in the market, it launched a pro-independence daily, *The National* – at the SNP Party Conference in November 2014. The National pledged to treat the SNP with healthy scepticism, but such promises soon fell by the wayside as, cash strapped and wary of alienating core readership, the paper quickly fell into reprinting SNP press releases. The SNP, meanwhile, gave the National very limited access as the readership was already secured politically. Dedicating every front page to an eye-catching visual left the paper too often spinning stories to fit political agendas. Readers soon drifted away. The paper's first edition sold out, but sales are now less than 10,000 a day. Newsquest's promises of investment were never met – at the time of writing, the overwhelming majority of a skeleton staff are on freelance day contracts without any entitlements.

The situation on the east coast is, if anything, worse. 'This is a great business and these are great newspapers,' a Johnston Press executive told a room full of *Scotsman* journalists in December 2005 just after the local media group had purchased the paper and its sister title, *Scotland on Sunday*, for £160 million, almost double the price paid by the Barclay brothers ten years earlier. Almost immediately the successful Scotsman.com development team was broken up and the website relocated three hundred miles south to Peterborough; advertising was outsourced to a London agency with little local expertise. The biggest change was staffing: in 2005, the *Scotsman* had more than five hundred journalists and production staff, according to accounts filed at Companies House. Now barely a fifth of that figure produce a paper largely stripped of original features and reporting. Its Brussels bureau and international stringers have long since been axed.

In 2014, *The Scotsman* left its purpose-built £20 million sandstone and glass offices in the shadow of the Scottish Parliament as part of another round of cost-cutting. Rockstar North, creators of Grand Theft Auto, took over the lease. Curiously, penny-pinching at Johnston Press has not extended to the boardroom; in 2014, its chief executive, Ashley Highfield, was paid £1.65 million. Ever more desperate attempts are being made to find new revenue streams: one scheme, Friends of the Scotsman, encourages organisations to take out subscriptions in exchange for editorial content – advertorials. Last year, an internal email to Johnston Press staff classified *Scotland on Sunday* as a 'sub core' title, fuelling rumours that it might be sold, or closed. Both the Scotsman and the Herald now comfortably outsold by D.C. Thomson's regional titles, *The Dundee Courier* and the Aberdeen-based *Press and Journal*. The once robust Scottish tabloid market is struggling too: sales of the *Daily Record* plummeted by 63.5 % between 1992 and 2011 (it currently sells around 200,000 copies).

The Golden Age that Wasn't and the Coming of Devolution

The golden age of the Scottish press is often romanticised. Many titles were unadventurous, taking the loyalty of their readers for granted, and unwilling to criticise shibboleths of Scottish society: the Labour Party; the Old Firm, particularly the blue half. But after the 1979 devolution referendum, the press took on the role of national champion. Both *The Herald* and *The Scotsman* published their own proposals for a devolved assembly years before the 1997 referendum, but they weren't concerned only with Scotland: they covered British and international news, and saw themselves as competing with the London nationals.

Rather than further invigorating Scotland's media, devolution, when it finally arrived, seemed to bring with it a less ambitious Scottish press, and less interest on the part of the London papers in what was going on in the country (Silver, 2015). The independence referendum also brought out increasing tensions between the SNP and the Scottish press. Nationalists were often angered by the overtly political stances taken by some titles: the 18 September 2014 edition of *The Times* came with a wraparound red, white and blue cover featuring a quote from 'Auld Lang Syne' on the reverse and a brief history of the Union on the inside pages. *The Telegraph*'s Scotland editor, Alan Cochrane, appeared to confirm many nationalists' view of the press when, in his post-referendum memoir, he wrote about spiking an unflattering column about Alistair Darling, head of Better Together: 'It's not really good journalism but what the hell does journalism matter? This is much more important' (Cochrane, 2014: 245). Indeed, only one newspaper, *The Sunday Herald*, backed a 'Yes' vote.

Nationalist fury at editorial positions, however, often betrayed a fundamental misunderstanding of the history – and financial model – of the Scottish press. Where titles such as *The Guardian* and *The Telegraph* appealed to demographics, Scottish papers have been historically city-based. Having expanded nationwide, particularly in the 1990s and early 2000s, the papers retrenched to their regions after the financial crisis: Scotsman in Edinburgh, Herald in Glasgow, and the DC Thomson titles in Aberdeen and Dundee. None could afford to take a pronounced position on an issue as divisive as independence. 'One of the key things the SNP and yes movement hasn't accepted is that the indigenous Scottish media is not like the UK/London media in the way it is structured', says Severin Carrell, the Guardian's Scotland editor. 'It is much more difficult to take an ideological position that reflects one social group when your market is regional not demographic. What that means is it looks like you have an entire industry that is hostile to independence but what you have its an industry with very different structures.'

The SNP's relationship with the Scottish press has also been a function of the party's leadership. Alex Salmond courted the press, at the same time as he actively barred some journalists from the press conference in which he announced his intention to step down the day after the referendum. Salmond also had extensive contacts with Rupert Murdoch when the newspaper magnate was attempting a controversial takeover of BSkyB. The move fell through amid angry reaction to revelations of phone hacking by News International journalists.

Where Salmond was seen as a constant source of 'good copy', many in the press gallery see Nicola Sturgeon as a far more aloof figure. 'At least Salmond would talk', says one Holyrood lobby journalist. 'Sturgeon is the exact opposite. She blocks and bars journalists. She and Salmond are very different people in that regard.' At the same time, SNP press officers have increasingly sought to engage directly with supporters on Facebook and other social media platforms, bypassing the press altogether.

With Scotland set for years of constitutional tumult, the role of the press will come under ever-greater scrutiny. As newspaper staff have been cut back – and the limits of access journalism have become all too apparent nationally and internationally – the press is even less equipped for the demands of a second referendum set against the complexities of Brexit's three-dimensional chess. Few in the SNP hierarchy will be concerned that many nationalists prefer the new pro-independence websites that sprang up during and after the referendum. But a lively blogosphere is not a replacement for a national press. As Iain Macwhirter wrote in 2014 'Scotland has a national political system, but is in danger of losing a national media' (Macwhirter, 2014). If anything the danger is even graver, and more pressing.

References

Cochrane, A. (2014), *Alex Salmond: My Part in His Downfall: The Cochrane Diaries*, London: Biteback Publishing.

Geoghegan, P. (2015), *The People's Referendum: Why Scotland Will Never Be the Same Again*, Edinburgh: Luath Press.

Macwhirter, I. (2014), *Democracy in the Dark: The Decline of the Scottish Press and How to Keep the Lights on.*

Silver, C. (2015), *Demanding Democracy: The Case for a Scottish Media*, Edinburgh: Word Power Books.

Smith, M. (1994), *Paper Lions: The Scottish Press and National Identity*, Edinburgh, Polygon.

The SNP and Broadcasting

Christopher Silver

ON 5 MAY 1980 the doyen of modern Welsh nationalism, Gwynfor Evans, announced that he would go on hunger strike unless the UK government reversed its decision to scrap plans for a Welsh language television station. Alongside the Plaid Cymru President's threat, Welsh nationalists undertook a campaign of direct action consisting of non-payment of TV licences, sit-ins at television studios, and the sabotage of television transmitters (Turner 2013: 82).

The promise of a Welsh station was a key concession that Plaid had managed to gain from both Labour and Tory politicians following a decade-long lobbying effort during the 1970s. For Evans, Home Secretary William Whitelaw's U-turn on his party's commitment to the channel represented nothing less than a 'direct challenge to the existence of the Welsh nation' (Hansard, 2016). Cabinet minutes released in 2010 revealed that the possible martyrdom of Evans was pivotal in making the government reconsider. Consequently, *Sianel Pedwar Cymru* (S4C) broadcast for the first time on 1 November 1982.

In contrast, the equivalent process in Scotland reached a culminated in an upbeat announcement from BBC Director General Tony Hall, in February 2017, of a dedicated digital channel for Scotland. Named 'BBC Scotland' the channel will broadcast from 7pm to midnight from autumn 2018. It will begin life with a budget of £30 million and include a 9pm news hour backed by 80 journalists who will be able to draw on the full resources of the BBC network. On announcing details of the 9pm programme, Hall said 'it could teach a few lessons to news broadcasters around the world' (Miller, 2017a).

On the one hand, the contrast between these two processes seems simply to highlight the differing trajectories and focal concerns of Scottish and Welsh nationalism. For example, the concept of any leading Scottish nationalist politician going on hunger strike would be considered by most people to be absurdly unlikely.

Methods aside, the question of language warrants brief consideration in this regard. In Scotland, unlike in Wales, minority language activism has generally stood apart from the constitutional question. The Gàidhealtachd's record in winning pragmatic concessions on a non-partisan basis is evidenced by the fact that Secretary of State for Scotland, George Younger, was a personal enthusiast and increased funding for Gaelic broadcasting, despite his party's hostility towards devolution and Scottish nationalism (Hutchinson, 2005). The launch in 2008 of a joint effort between the BBC and Scottish Government funded MG Alba, BBC Alba, can be seen as the culmination of a long tradition of Gaelic media's effectiveness at cross-party lobbying.

Yet the Gaelic case is exceptional in the UK context. The struggle to align broadcasting policy in a manner that accommodates, rather than occludes, the various national and regional identities within the UK has often been a fraught and complex process.

Broadcasting Scotland, the BBC *and Scottish Nationalism*

But while Scotland's nationalism has not, on the whole, emphasised cultural or linguistic claims to the right to media representation, in recent years passions around the rights and wrongs of broadcasting in Scotland have intensified. Current affairs output in particular has come in for sharp criticism and there has been widespread controversy over the BBC's handling of the Scottish independence referendum. The protests that took place in front of BBC Scotland's headquarters at Pacific Quay on three occasions towards the end of the 2014 referendum campaign achieved a profile that transformed questions over the remit and conduct of the broadcaster in Scotland into a pressing political concern.

However, it is too easy to overstate the novelty of the anti-BBC sentiment that arose during the referendum. In fact, controversies around the BBC's coverage of seminal political events stretch back to the corporation's infancy, when it worked closely with government during the 1926 General Strike. As Tom Mills has argued in *The* BBC: *The Myth of a Public Service* (2016), the organisation has seldom achieved balance when government policy or an established political consensus is challenged by insurgents. According to Mills, the invariably close relationship between the BBC hierarchy and the political elite has, 'shaped editorial policies and practices, making the BBC much more amenable to elites than democratic and egalitarian movements' (Mills, 2016: 35).

Examples of how the BBC is an integral part of the British establishment, with its own conservative internal cultures, can be seen in the Scottish context too. The side-lining of maverick BBC Scotland controller and former *Guardian* editor Alastair Hetherington, who sought more autonomy in order to align the BBC with the establishment of a Scottish Assembly in the 1970s, is a notable example of this tendency. The BBC's anxieties with regard to Scottish nationalism first emerged in 1932, with the removal of the first Scottish Regional Director, David Cleghorn Thomson, for suspected Scottish nationalism. After this incident the corporation conducted an investigation throughout its Scottish operation to weed out staff with sympathies to the cause (McKechnie, 2013).

The record of the SNP on broadcasting has to be seen in this wider, far from tranquil, context. Yet despite the intensity of focus on the role of the Scottish media after 2014, for much of the SNP's time in government, as in other areas, the party has been reluctant to step beyond its reformist comfort zone.

The inevitable tendency of politicians to focus on journalistic broadcast output has also diminished the prospects of a compelling and deliverable national broadcasting strategy. From the chimera of a Scottish film studio, to the country's meagre film budget, or Scotland's loss of HBO blockbuster *Game of Thrones* to Northern Ireland, when it comes to film and broadcasting, Scotland remains the poor relation in these isles.

Given the controversy around S4C in the 1980s it is somewhat ironic that the 'Welsh renaissance' in TV drama centred on Cardiff, has been based on the landing of big ticket productions, such as *Doctor Who*, for the BBC network. As the Screen Sector Leadership Group have identified: 95 % of the licence fee raised in Wales gets spent there, as opposed to 55 % in Scotland (Miller, 2017b).

Beyond Preserving the Status Quo

As I have argued elsewhere (Silver, 2015) the need for a critical mass of production skills and a mature screen culture cannot be walled off from current affairs coverage, where production values and cultural perceptions play a vital role in framing output. Thus the lack of a cohesive film and broadcasting strategy exacerbates a lack of progress when it comes to the remit, scope and quality of journalistic output.

As in a number of other policy areas, there is an element of the SNP's critique that actually seems more intent on preserving elements of post-war British social democracy than developing Scottish alternatives. This partly explains why, despite its contradictions, the BBC has been the overwhelming object of focus in media debates, to the exclusion of STV. As in the mantra voiced by many prominent SNP voices that 'Labour left me,' there is a language around the performance of the BBC in Scotland that frequently sounds orphaned.

This narrative should be challenged. Rather than harking back to a 'golden age' of public service broadcasting in Britain, we should understand that the BBC has been in ascendant during periods of economic growth. In simple terms, at moments when the overall base for the license fee has increased, as in the 1960s and the 1990s, this has created de-facto cultures of editorial independence and innovation, in alignment with increased funds (Mills, 2016: 24-26). At times of economic crisis, such as our own, the creeping exertion of government pressure to scale back operations becomes inevitable. This can be seen, for example, in the current UK Government's plan to pass on costs and responsibility to the BBC for administering free TV licences for over 75s, which in effect amounts to a cut in the corporation's budget of one fifth. Cuts to BBC Scotland, alongside controversial staffing decisions, were explained by former BBC Scotland Controller Ken MacQuarrie in the context of a frozen licence fee and 25 % cuts across the entire corporation (Scottish Parliament, 2012: 650-651).

However, the focus on the BBC and licence fee spending in Scotland did not define the SNP's initial approach to broadcasting when it gained power. One of the key planks of the SNP's first 100 days in office after forming a minority government in 2007 was to set up the Scottish Broadcasting Commission. Its key recommendation was a Scottish Digital Network with a mandate to provide competition to the BBC, while operating under a public service remit.

With echoes of the long running 'Scottish Six' controversy (over the case for a fully Scottish anchored prime-time news programme), the passage on broadcasting in the SNP's 2007 manifesto that preceded this move placed a specific emphasis on current affairs, 'As a very minimum we will demand the creation of a Scottish news service. Devolution has resulted in significant divergences in policy and practice north and south of the Border. This must be reflected in news coverage.'

The commission was not without its detractors from the outset. Early critiques saw ulterior motives behind the SNP's plans. Scottish Tory culture spokesman Ted Brocklebank contended, 'Influencing editorial policy is precisely the ultimate goal of the separatists.' David Cairns, minister of state at the Scotland Office, said Mr Salmond was intent on 'Denying Scots access to the world's most respected broadcaster by creating a parochial and narrow Scottish Broadcasting Corporation' (BBC, 2007).

However, the Commission was notable in managing to achieve cross-party support in the Scottish Parliament, an achievement that fits with the widely accepted account that the SNP was a more nimble, creative and effective force in minority government.

According to Blair Jenkins, the former BBC Scotland news chief who chaired the commission, this cross-party endorsement must have bolstered the BBC's confidence to commit to the new channel in 2017: 'the public service case we made for a dedicated Scottish channel has never been challenged (other than on financial grounds) and it has remained the key aspiration in Scottish broadcasting debates.'

This latest move from the BBC can be read as nod to the Scottish Broadcasting Commission's findings, although the new channel will operate with less than half the budget proposed for the Scottish Digital Network. Jenkins is sceptical on this point, 'I remain unconvinced that £30 million is a sufficient budget for the new channel, but at least we can now direct our attention to increasing that funding.'

Former BBC presenter Lesley Riddoch expressed suspicions that the 9pm news hour is 'destined to fail' (Riddoch, 2017). Yet, the move does re-frame the picture of the embattled BBC that emerged during the Scottish independence referendum and also validates the policy of cautious lobbying that the SNP have pursued since 2011.

Although Tony Hall is now the third Director General to reject plans for such a programme, the status of 'the Scottish Six' remains fundamental to the framing of the entire debate around broadcasting in Scotland since devolution. In response to news of the new BBC channel in Scotland, Nicola Sturgeon welcomed the proposed move, while also expressing dismay that the 'Six' has been shelved yet again.

The contours of the 'Six' debate are illustrative of a wider problem. When Director General John Birt rejected the concept out of hand in 1998, it revealed how closely intertwined broadcasting and nationalism are. As Birt explained in his autobiography,

> BBC *news was iconic. Opting out of the Six would be a powerful symbol of Scotland moving away from UK-wide institutions. Scottish viewers would be deprived of UK-wide and international news that formed the common knowledge underpinning a UK-wide democratic system. The end of a single, common experience of UK news, would, moreover, encourage separatist tendencies...*
>
> (Birt, 2002: 483)

In a move that then controller of BBC Scotland, John McCormack, later branded 'totally unacceptable,' Birt lobbied Tony Blair to prevent such a move and to supress any attempt to devolve control over broadcasting to the new Scottish Parliament. The legacy of Birt's uncompromising approach bears a significant level of responsibility for debates on Scottish media remaining BBC-centric. BBC Scotland has been trapped by demands to fulfil the role of a national broadcaster on the one hand, while battling successive waves of cuts, a crisis of morale and a tangible decline in production standards on the other.

The historic mishandling of 'the Scottish Six' question is also illustrative of how the debate around broadcasting has become something of a proxy war, with the 'Six' functioning as a 'nationalist shibboleth.'

For some media professionals in Scotland this has been the source of great frustration. As Robin Macpherson, Chair in Creative Industries at the University of the Highlands and Islands, said of the controversy:

The height of the debate about what might change in Scotland, represented by the Scottish Six, shows you just how appalling superficial, wafer-thin and unsophisticated our debate about what Scotland ought to expect from its media is. Because that something so pathetically small, as whether or not to have a Scottish six o'clock news, could become a touchstone for media change in Scotland, I think that tells you almost everything you need to know.

If the 'Six' has served to narrow the focus of Scottish demands, this stems in part from the fact that nationalist politicians have tended to present a moderate, common sense case for the BBC to 'catch up' with devolution. This stands in sharp contrast to the impetus behind the establishment of broadcasters in other small nations such as Ireland, Catalonia or Wales. Scottish nationalism has seldom claimed an existential right to the representation of a national culture and public life.

That said, the pragmatic case was central to the successful effort by SNP MP and former BBC and ITN journalist John Nicholson to persuade Westminster's Culture, Media and Sport Select Committee to back the 'Six' in 2016.

Following news of Nicholson's success in committee, the *Daily Record*'s Torcuil Crichton described the 'Six' as the 'Holy Grail of Scottish nationalism' (Crichton, 2016). When Tony Hall announced that a 'Six' was once again to be rejected in 2017, *Scottish Daily Mail* commentator Stephen Daisley noted, 'The Nats are apoplectic but can't say why because, in truth, the Scottish Six was all about boosting support for separation' (Daisley, 2017).

Though Daisley and Crichton's views are voiced in the shrill tone of tabloid newspaper columnists, their basic contention is well-founded. The fundamental link between nationalism and mass media was explicitly outlined by Ernest Gellner in 'Nations and Nationalism': 'it is the media themselves, the pervasiveness and importance of abstract, centralised, standardised, one to many communication, which itself automatically engenders the core idea of nationalism' (1994: 127).

As Nick Stevenson has pointed out, the frequently cited concept of the public sphere as outlined by Jürgen Habermas is 'explicitly connected to the nation state' (2002: 61) (see Gerry Hassan's chapter in this book on the contours of the public sphere in Scotland). The liberal media scholar Paddy Scannell, who has argued for the promotion of national public media amid the pressures of globalisation and commodification, sees a national broadcaster as 'perhaps the only means at present – whereby common knowledge and pleasure in a shared public life are maintained as a social good for the whole population' (1990: 26).

This serves to underline how questions of media representation and nationalism are not so much *related* as *inseparable*. This is why within Scotland the debate on broadcasting has been so circular. Every time the moderate case for 'catching up' with devolution is endorsed the debate returns once again to allegations of separatism, parochialism and nationalist illiberalism. The political potency of broadcasting is, like archaic geological formations, only occasionally visible on the surface, but absolutely fundamental to the shape of the wider landscape.

But tectonic shifts in media technology have seriously started to destabilise such accepted norms. For Michael Tracey the proliferation of media has led to a process of 'retribalisation' that is 'profoundly individualistic and definitely not collective, public, shared or coherent.' (1998: 264). These issues have become highly topical due to growing anxieties around the impact of social media, with the rise of clickbait journalism and 'fake news' throwing into doubt the capacity of any actor, even one validated by the nation state, to command trust and respect in a mediascape made up of constantly accessible conflicting narratives. The growing capacity of individuals to engage in what Manuel Castells describes as 'mass self-communication' renders national identities fluid and has challenged the nation state as the relevant unit to define public space (Castells, 2013).

Therefore, whatever Scotland's constitutional future, the development of an innovative and dynamic broadcasting culture in Scotland will have to transcend the national question one way or another. In this regard, the most prescient question for Scottish broadcasting to answer would be how to best remake public service broadcasting traditions at a moment of flux for the nation state. In a rapidly challenging world this will be a deeply necessary task if Scotland's political class are to live up to the aspirations of diversity, openness and tolerance they espouse when envisioning a new Scottish democratic settlement.

References

BBC (2007), 'Commission looks at broadcasting,' BBC *News*. Available at: http://news.bbc.co.uk/1/hi/scotland/6936082.stm [Accessed March 1, 2017].

Castells, M. (2013), *Communication Power,* Oxford: Oxford University Press.

Crichton, T. (2016), 'Scottish Six is the Holy Grail of nationalism, says Torcuil Crichton.' *Daily Record,* 5 August, Available at: www.dailyrecord.co.uk/ news/politics/scottish-six-holy-grail-nationalism-8562328

Daisley, S. (2017), 'Sturgeon dodged a banana skin flung down by NatBot 58', 24 February. Available at: https://stephendaisley.com/2017/02/24/sturgeon-dodged-a-banana-skin-flung-down-by-natbot-58/

Gellner, E. (1994), *Nations and Nationalism: New Perspectives on the Past*, Oxford: Blackwell.

Hansard (2016), 'Gwynfor Evans and Welsh Politics,' H.C. Volume 612 Column 254WH.

Hutchinson, R. (2005), *A Waxing Moon: The Modern Gaelic Revival*, Edinburgh: Mainstream.

McKechnie G. (2013), 'Nationalism and the BBC', *Scottish Review of Books*, Vol. 9 Issue 3.

Miller, P. (2017a), 'World will learn 'lessons' from new TV bulletin,' *The Herald*, 24 February.

Miller, P. (2017b), 'Scottish BBC licence fee money should be spent in Scotland, say screen experts,' *The Herald*, 21 February.

Mills, T. (2016), *The BBC: Myth of a Public Service*, London: Verso.

Birt, J. (2002), *The Harder Path: The Autobiography*, London: Time Warner.

Riddoch, L. (2017), 'Is new Scottish BBC channel destined to fail?', *Scotsman*, 27 February 2017, accessed at: www.scotsman.com/news/opinion/lesley-riddoch-is-new-scottish-bbc-channel-destined-to-fail-1-4377340

Scannell, P. (1990), 'Public service broadcasting: the history of a concept,' in Goodwin, A. and Whannel, G. (eds.), *Understanding Television*, London: Routledge.

Scottish Parliament. (2012), *Official Report Education and Culture Committee*, 29 May.

Silver, C. (2015), *Demanding Democracy: The Case for a Scottish Media*, Edinburgh: Word Power Books.

Stevenson, N. (2002), *Understanding media cultures social theory and mass communication*, London: Sage Publications.

Turner, A W. (2010), *Rejoice! Rejoice!: Britain in the 1980s*, London: Aurum Press.

Tracey, M. (2002), *The decline and fall of public service broadcasting*, Oxford: Oxford University Press.

The Importance of Arts and Culture: A Journey Over Devolved Scotland

Mark Fisher

Back to the Future: Labour and Culture

FIRST A LITTLE perspective. In 2006, I began an online article with the question: 'Why does the Scottish executive keep making such a pig's ear of its arts policy?' Fair to say I hadn't been impressed. The Labour administration had just put forward its draft culture bill proposing the abolition of the Scottish Arts Council and Scottish Screen to make way for a single body that would be called Creative Scotland. The arts community had reacted with widespread outrage, irritated by the draft bill's apparent erosion of the arm's-length principle, designed to ensure distance between funder and recipient, and its failure to take on board anything substantial from a recent £513,400 cultural report. The author of that report, James Boyle, told *The Scotsman* newspaper: 'The overwhelming judgment is of a weak document that hasn't been put together with any enthusiasm or determination. It just looks as if it was born to fail' (Boyle, 2006).

This was odd because Labour first minster Jack McConnell had made all the right noises, not least with his high-profile St Andrew's Day speech of 2003 in which he had promised to put culture at the heart of everything the government did. 'Each member of the Scottish cabinet will use the power of cultural activity to help them in their work – culture will not be an add on, it will be at the core of everything we do', he had said (McConnell, 2003).

It was hard to see this being borne out in practice. Although it was under Labour that the National Theatre of Scotland was brought into existence, bringing to an end nearly two centuries of campaigning and ushering in the single greatest cultural success story of recent decades, the administration gave few signs that it regarded the arts as a priority. How else to explain the merry-go-round of ministers in charge of culture in the first years of the decade? There were five of them in four years: Sam Galbraith lasted less than five months from November 2000; Mike Watson clocked up a year; Elaine Murray came and went in six months; Frank McAveety was a beacon of stability at eighteen months; and Patricia Ferguson a genuine stayer, remaining for almost two-and-a-half years after her appointment in 2004.

The Coming of the SNP

The SNP was duly condemnatory about the executive's cultural record, but it was by no means certain that it wouldn't go the same way. Linda Fabiani achieved a relatively respectable two years after her party's 2007 electoral win, but Michael Russell's tenure was just nine months. The administrative turbulence came to an end, however, in 2009 with the appointment of Fiona Hyslop who has been in post ever since. Even though her remit has been stretched across a composite portfolio of 'culture, tourism and external affairs', she has proved herself not only a stable presence but a dedicated, knowledgeable and passionate champion of the arts. Certainly, it is rare to find an arts minister willing, as she was in 2013, to go on record saying, 'I want us to embrace what's difficult, what's challenging and what's uncomfortable' (Hyslop, 2013). Her place as a cabinet secretary, since 2011, sends a signal that the government takes her, and her culture brief, seriously. Or that is at least how Hyslop's supporters see things.

Longevity, of course, is no measure of achievement, but on Hyslop's watch, the Scottish Government has, at the very least, shielded the arts from the worst cuts south of the border and, at best, shown genuine commitment. The past ten years have not been a period of plenty, but neither have they been the disaster a less diligent administration could have permitted. We should not take it for granted that entrance to Scotland's national collections is free and has been since 2001 in spite of pressure to introduce museum charges.

More easily open to question are the knock-on effects of central government cuts to local authorities, an important source of arts funding that has become increasingly stretched. Even a fortunate arts organisation in 2017 is likely to have suffered several years of stand-still council funding; others will have been saddled with outright cuts. In 2013, to cite an extreme example, Moray Council announced it would slash £30m from its budget for the following three years, promising to close seven libraries (it settled on four) and ending arts funding altogether. In 2016, the same council increased fees for music tuition by 20 % after deciding against an 18 % hike in council tax. Even if the council could have made a different set of decisions (by cutting the arts, it saved itself only £94,000 over three years), the initial pressure came from central government.

Also of concern is a centralising tendency in the administration which has made the arm's-length principle less certain. In 2007, stewardship of the national companies passed from the Scottish Arts Council to the Scottish Government. Since then the National Theatre of Scotland, the Royal Scottish National Orchestra, Scottish Ballet, the Scottish Chamber Orchestra and Scottish Opera have been directly answerable to Holyrood. On the one hand, this has helped ring-fence spending on the national companies and removed the necessity for other companies to compete for the same funds. On the other, it raises the possibility – if only in theory – of the national companies becoming an arm of government, embodying its political values and muting any criticism.

That is supposition, but there is also the strange case of Scottish Youth Theatre. When, in 2014, Creative Scotland dropped its regular funding of the company, whose patrons include prominent independence supporters Brian Cox and Alan Cumming, the outgoing First Minister Alex Salmond stepped in with a three-year rescue package of £1 million direct from government coffers. 'Now the Youth Theatre is in financial difficulty and we cannot in conscience have that, indeed I just won't have that', Salmond told his party conference in Perth (BBC, 2014). A complaint from Creative Scotland that the intervention undermined the 'entire regular funding process' led to the new money being shared among national youth performing companies and an end to the automatic entitlement of ministers to attend Creative Scotland board meetings. It took the stand-off to enshrine the funding body's arm's-length status, but it's odd that it happened at all.

Creative Scotland Stramashes and the Creative Industries

The biggest cultural headache the SNP Government has had to deal with is one effectively bequeathed to it by Labour. If the arts community was angered by the draft legislation to bring Creative Scotland into being, it was apoplectic about the reality when it emerged in 2010. Under the watch of chief executive Andrew Dixon and his second-in-command Venu Dhupa, the funding body lost the confidence of the sector to such an extent that both chose to resign at the end of 2012 after two-and-a-half years in post.

A couple of months earlier, 100 artists – including Liz Lochhead, AL Kennedy, James Macmillan, Peter Maxwell Davies, David Greig and John Byrne – had signed a letter complaining of the organisation's 'ill-conceived decision-making and a lack of empathy and regard for Scottish culture' (BBC, 2012). In May, Creative Scotland had caused widespread alarm by changing the way many companies were funded. It was prompted by a decision by the Scottish government to cut £2 million of support, intending the shortfall to be more than made up with funds from the National Lottery. As lottery funds could be used only for one-off projects, Creative Scotland's solution was to switch its support of 49 arts organisations from the relative security of two or three-year funding to the insecurity of project grants.

In addition to the uncertainty, artists worried the shift put too much control in the hands of the funding body. An organisation funded for two years would be free to follow its artistic instincts; an organisation funded a project at a time could do only what its paymasters allowed. It was a system that could have turned Creative Scotland into the country's de facto artistic director. It was if the funding body were becoming more important than the artists. That's why Hyslop stepped in to declare: 'It is not for administrators, bureaucrats or governments to tell artists what to do.'

An internal report concluded that relationships with artists had become 'fractured' and those between staff and senior management were little better. Staff felt 'undervalued and underutilised'. Just as concerning was the importing of business jargon into the funding body. In post-Blairite style, Creative Scotland would talk about 'strategic commissioning' and 'investment' in the arts without specifying what the return on such an investment would be. The protesting artists demanded an end to 'business-speak and obfuscating jargon'.

Hyslop duly raised concerns, but it is also possible to frame the crisis as a product of the Scottish Government's own legislation. As the pugnacious editorials in *Variant* magazine pointed out, the government had stated that Creative Scotland should aim to provide: 'not only personal enjoyment of aesthetic quality and the enjoyment involved in cultural participation, but also benefits in terms of unlocking creative and entrepreneurial potential and enhancing well-being and community pride.'

The government's blurring of the arts into the more vaguely defined 'creative industries' exacerbated the tension between art for its own sake and art as a tool of economic policy. This was especially the case given the legislation allowed the possibility but not an obligation for Creative Scotland to support such areas as 'advertising; architecture; crafts; design; designer fashion; film; interactive leisure software; music; performing arts; publishing; TV and radio; and visual arts' (see Creative Scotland, 2016). The implication was that a poetry festival in St Andrews was somehow doing the same thing as a video games company in Dundee. Even if that argument could be made, the government did not provide the money to enable Creative Scotland to fulfil such a broad brief. Those in the film sector where similarly disgruntled by the amalgamation of Scottish Screen into the wider remit Creative Scotland. You could make the case that Dixon fell on his sword for doing the job he'd been contracted to do.

The Role of Arts and Culture

In general, however, what the SNP government appears to have recognised is that for relatively little expenditure, it can achieve many of its goals through support of the arts. For a party with a vested interest in sustaining the idea of a national identity at home and abroad, and a political interest in promoting social cohesion and a communal sense of belonging, cultural spending looks like a good deal. This was all the more the case when the cultural budget was one of a limited range of devolved powers the government had at its disposal. Through art, it could not only make a difference, but make that difference apparent.

To present culture as an instrument of government in this way can make you feel uneasy. There is a line in T.S. Eliot's play 'Murder in the Cathedral' in which Thomas Becket is weighing up the pros and cons of becoming a martyr. He's approached by a series of tempters who urge him first to change tack and finally to accept martyrdom for a chance of selfish glory. 'The last temptation is the greatest treason', he says, 'to do the right deed for the wrong reason.'

Those who value the arts will be happy the government looks favourably on culture. But what is its motivation? Does it value culture regardless of whether it achieves its instrumental aims? Or is it interested only to the extent that culture can project an attractive image to the world and play a part in urban regeneration projects – art as social work? Is it, in other words, doing the right deed for the wrong reason?

From this point of view, Scottish Government thinking echoes the views of Peter Bazalgette, the outgoing head of Arts Council England. In January 2016, he wrote in the *Observer* about what he thought was a 'sterile' debate between those who believed in arts for art's sake and those who took an instrumental approach. His organisation, he said, had decided, 'It's both, stupid.' He continued: 'We gathered together the inspiring evidence: urban regeneration and talent development, the fundamental but threatened role of the arts in schools, the amazing programmes in prisons and health care. But we were careful to articulate the intrinsic benefits too – the art-for-art's-sake folk had a point.'

Here in Scotland, Hyslop takes a similar line. On the one hand, she recently set up a creative industry advisory group 'to discuss how to make the sector stronger and enhance support'. Its 26 members represent organisations ranging from Canongate Books to the Royal Incorporation of Architects in Scotland, and are on a mission to determine 'what targeted support is needed to achieve a more strategic approach to take our creative industries to the next level'. That level is couched in terms of 'scale, employment and growth' and the economic value of the sector, which explains why Paul Wheelhouse, minister for business, innovation and energy, is also part of the group.

On the other hand, countering the business-speak tendencies has been Hyslop's genuine commitment to the arts as articulated in her powerful 2013 speech at Edinburgh University's Talbot Rice Gallery. The UK Government's culture secretary Maria Miller had recently caused alarm by insisting arts leaders must prioritise the case for 'culture's economic impact'. It was a view Hyslop rejected. 'We do not measure the worth of culture and heritage solely in pounds and pence', she said. 'I don't need or want the culture or heritage sector to make a new economic or social case to justify public support for their work. I know what these sectors can deliver because I see it in action.'

She agreed with Miller that culture and heritage had economic benefits, but denied that was their most important function. Much as Bazalgette would say some years later, she asserted: 'We do not need to choose between culture for its own sake, or for wider benefits. We can do both.'

Perhaps it's a have-your-cake-and-eat-it philosophy, but it would be consistent with, for example, the Scottish Government's Expo Fund, introduced in 2008 to allow Edinburgh's twelve major festivals to maintain their 'global competitive edge'. The fund has totalled upwards of £2 million a year and has been spent on everything from science exhibitions to short films. The Edinburgh Festival Fringe uses its award to fund Made in Scotland, a showcase of home-grown theatre, dance and music. The Edinburgh Art Festival has supported projects including Martin Creed's recladding of the Scotsman steps in marble extracted from quarries around the world. And Edinburgh's Hogmanay has put the money to use in SCOT:Lands, a free programme of poetry, music and performance on 1 January.

Talk to the performing arts companies who've been given the chance to tour internationally as a direct consequence of the Expo Fund, as well as to audiences who have enjoyed the work, and it is hard not to treat this as a good thing. At the same time, from the Scottish Government's point of view, you can see the soft-diplomacy appeal of a scheme that spreads an image of Scotland as a culturally vibrant place. It knows too that the capital's festivals bring £261m in additional tourism revenue to Scotland every year. The support is not entirely philanthropic. Both sides gain from the deal, but it's convenient for the arts to have a government with an interest in promoting Scotland as a distinct and distinctive nation.

Many see this as the result of having a minister and, indeed, an administration that takes culture seriously. Yet the SNP's have-your-cake-and-eat-it approach brings together promotion of Scotland and a championing of culture, while attempting to mitigate the worst excesses of significant financial constraints. It does so with a pragmatism that is pick and mix – rejecting the onslaught of business speak, but embracing such notions as the 'creative industries'. Perhaps that tension will be addressed by the drafting of the government's culture strategy, an SNP manifesto commitment, but then again, this mixture is the way some people regard the wider story of the SNP in office over the past ten years.

References

BBC (2012), 'Creative Scotland 'crisis' slammed by leading artists', *BBC News*, 9 October, accessed at: www.bbc.co.uk/news/uk-scotland-19880871

BBC (2014), 'SNP Conference: Alex Salmond unveils Scottish Youth Theatre funds', *BBC News*, 14 November, accessed at: www.bbc.co.uk/news/uk-scotland-scotland-politics-30052178

Boyle, J. (2006), quoted in 'Former arts chief Boyle attacks arts bill as weak and 'born to fail'', *The Scotsman*, 15 December, accessed at: www.scotsman.com/lifestyle/culture/former-arts-chief-boyle-attacks-bill-as-weak-and-born-to-fail-1-734308

Creative Scotland (2016), *Creative Industries: A Strategy for Creative Scotland 2016-17*, Edinburgh: Creative Scotland.

Hyslop, F. (2013), 'Past, present and future: Culture and heritage in an independent Scotland', Speech, 5 June, Edinburgh: Talbot Rice Gallery, accessed at: www.scotland.gov.uk/News/Speeches/Culture-Heritage05062013

McConnell, J. (2003), 'St Andrew's Day Speech', 30 November, Glasgow: Royal Scottish Academy of Music and Drama, accessed at: www.scotland.gov.uk/News/Releases/2003/11/4641

Begbie's Belief: Miserablism Behind Bars: No Longer a Nation of Trainspotters

Eleanor Yule

'I'M AFRAID IT'S A NO.' Fans of *Trainspotting* waited for two decades to hear these opening lines from *T2 Trainspotting*, the much-anticipated sequel to one of the most popular British films of the 1990's adapted from Scottish writer Irvine Welsh's both acclaimed and controversial best-selling book.

The 'No' in *T2* is appropriately addressed to the miserablist anti-hero of the piece, hard man Franco Begbie (Robert Carlyle). The 'no' to which Begbie responds with violent outrage refers, not as one might think to outcome of the 2014 Scottish indyref, but to Begbie's request for parole after two decades behind bars for a violent murder.

The irony is not lost. As an anti-hero locked into a miserablist paradigm, Begbie's bid for freedom, like the Scottish Nation's 2014 indyref, was destined to failure. The 'No' Vote on the 18 September that year seemed to reinforce for the devastated 'Yes' campaigners, Welsh's famous dictum that is was indeed 'shite being Scottish', and no matter how hard Scotland had attempted to alter its destiny the nation was locked into a cycle of failure and self-defeat. To many, at first, the results of the 2014 indyref appeared to perpetuate this enduring narrative and part of the narrative of miserablism is looking for someone to blame.

In *T2* inmate Franco Begbie blames his lawyer for the 'no' from the parole board. He is furious that his plea of 'diminished responsibility' was not supported by his justifiably suspicious lawyer. Like any cultural 'victim' Begbie believes his character defects are not his fault, but the fault of the society that created them, and not just in him but in his class and kin. As a member of the disenfranchised white, male, Scottish working classes Begbie chooses to carry a generational chip on his shoulders the size of the Queen Mary, even though his conception occurred decades after its masterly construction.

This arresting of reality began long before Begbie's birth and even before his father's descent into unemployment, alcoholism and homelessness. It started when a sizeable percentage of Scotland's skilled working men were dispossessed of their land and then their jobs. This left many feeling impotent, consigned to the industrial slag heaps and misguided modernist ghettos along with their long-suffering wives and their rudderless offspring. The only escape from this crushing fate was to either flee the fatherland, ironically on the boats they sweated to build, or lose themselves in football, knife crime, the needle or in Begbie's case the pub. *T2* indulges in a nostalgic flash back to Begbie's signature scene in *Trainspotting* where he lobs a pint glass into a crowd of drinkers in an Edinburgh pub, splitting open the head of a young woman in order to start a fight.

Begbie's twisted logic allows his to take no responsibility for his crimes that include pathological violence, sexism, racism, bigotry and homophobia and by denying responsibility he fails to change, fails to adapt or grow up. The prison system in which he has served a 20 year stretch reinforces this stagnation, perpetuating a generational miserablism with its own black economy, as Welsh acknowledged in 2005:

> *Scotland now having the highest prison population in Europe; this only serves to make things worse. By incarcerating so many of its citizens, the country has created a kind of jail culture in some areas. Prison is no deterrent to many disadvantaged young people from housing schemes; they will have friends or relatives who have served or are serving prison terms…It's very easy to get sent down these days: just being poor gives you an excellent head start.*
>
> (Welsh, 2005)

For Begbie then, stuck in this time warp of 'jail culture' and in a generational miserablist cycle of poverty, addiction and violence creating a giant ego and no self-worth, it is not surprising that after two decades in the system he remains untransformed and unrepentant. Unlike his nemesis Mark Renton (Ewan McGregor) who fled to Europe for his transformation, Begbie is locked a miserablist paradigm where time stands still and the narrative remains unchanged.

Begbie blames 'the system' for his violent behaviour and Mark Renton (Ewan McGregor) for his prison sentence. By making off with his sizeable share of the drug money Begbie was 'forced' to take his anger out on his murder victim, which left him in jail and Renton a wealthy man living in Amsterdam scot free.

Since Begbie's deserved incarceration and Renton's exile to Europe in 1996 Scotland *has* finally been taking responsibility as a nation (the kryptonite to the deep freeze of miserablism) and evolved both politically, culturally and democratically. The last two decades have seen Scotland become a devolved nation under the leadership, firstly, of a gradually failing Labour Party and latterly under the rising power of the SNP, culminating in ten years of rule, three of which have been steered by a female first minister, unprecedented in Scottish politics.

The proliferation of higher education courses within Scotland has helped to decrease the polarisation of the classes and has encouraged a refreshing ethnic and cultural mix in the major cities. Scotland's recent pro-EU stance is evidence of the nation's awareness that being connected beyond the union has enriched the nation not just economically but helped diversify its culture. The combination of Scotland's increasingly autonomous and distinctive political scene, boosted by the high voltage experience of the indyref and Brexit, alongside a thriving cultural scene, point to a very different society than that portrayed in *Trainspotting* and *T2*.

Most of all Scotland has been taking responsibility for itself and its *own* identity reflected recently by the new Scottish TV Channel being established by the BBC. This victory after a long fought battle with the network to fairly reflect the Scots contribution to the license fee will hopefully allow Scotland to represent its inherent and growing diversity beyond the stark polarities of nostalgic 'tartanry' and 'kailyard' or the miserablism of 'Clydesidism' that film theorists Jane Sillars and Duncan Petrie have identified as historically dominant cultural tropes (Petrie, 2000; Sillars, 2009).

Although Begbie is stuck in this polarised past his ticket to freedom in *T2* arrives in the form of a cunning plan; a self-harming blade to his gut. Escaping the busy hospital where he is taken from prison to receive medical care Begbie's first place of refuge is his former family home and to a wife and a son who barely know him. Like Rip Van Winkle, Begbie has emerged into a Scotland that has moved on without him.

Despite his 20-year absence from the marital bed Begbie asserts his conjugal rights on his first night back only to discover he cannot rise to the occasion. His wife's relieved reassurance does not stop him from resorting to handfuls of stolen Viagra in a hilarious attempt to regain his former potency. Begbie is painfully crippled by the swelling that results. Like Punch, Begbie is Welsh's glove puppet, recast as a comedic satyr from antiquity. As a miserbalist anti-hero in a post–referendum Scotland, Begbie's brutal brand of masculinity is rendered impotent but is still stubbornly inflated, signalling that this transformation of Scotland is not entirely complete.

Crime still thrives in Auld Reekie, but the black-market economies have shifted away from hard drugs to sex. The boozer staggers onwards but under ten years of SNP rule with stricter drink drive policies and minimum unit pricing its clientele are migrating to coffee houses, bistros and Polish delicatessens. Begbie's old mate, Simon 'Sick Boy' Williamson (Jonny Lee Miller), finds it easier to sell Eastern European women than pints of heavy in his auntie's old Leith pub, which, like his ennui, he has inherited from a past generation. In what must be an ironic reference to The Proclaimers' iconic song 'Sunshine on Leith', Sick Boy's grim hostelry is named 'Port Sunshine'. Miserabalism may not be 'over and done with' as The Proclaimers' song might have us believe but the times they are a'changing.

Perhaps because *T2* took a long time to develop and is partially based on Welsh's 2002 sequel *Porno*, and was adapted by John Hodge who is less optimistic about Scotland's political progress the film fails to reflect the scale of Welsh's new optimism about his old nation post-indyref. In his by-line for *The Guardian* a day after the referendum results, Welsh was uncharacteristically hopeful, claiming that 'the glorious' failure' of the Yes campaign could be 'Scotland's finest hour' and an outcome which highlighted the 'compelling narrative of the post-devolution generation':

> *This country, when it was ever known on the global stage under the union, was associated with tragedy, in terrible events like Lockerbie and Dunblane; it's now synonymous with real people power. Forget Bannockburn or the Scottish Enlightenment, the Scots have just reinvented and re-established the idea of true democracy.*

(Welsh, 2014)

As in the famous Bruce and the Spider fable, failure is part of winning the battle, but only if you believe you are ultimately capable of victory. SNP support and the referendum results have demonstrated a marked increase in Scotland's self-belief but as an independent nation the country is still serving its apprenticeship.

Before his inevitable re-incarceration Begbie attempts to initiate his son, Frank Junior, into his life of crime. Begbie wants to pass on to his son, who he sees as a 'chip off the old block', the only thing he has to offer; the narrative of miserablism; a life of poverty, violence, bigotry, addiction and blame. Frank Jr., as part of the youth of an evolving Scottish culture, understands the hope invested in him and the responsibility he has been given for making for his own personal and political choices. Being a true democrat Frank Jr. tries to please his father by joining him on a heist but his heart is not in it. Instead Frank Jr. confesses to his disbelieving father that he is applying to go to college where if he works hard he will hopefully become a hotel manager.

T2 ends with Begbie back inside. This time he is locked up in the boot of a car, dumped by his old gang outside the prison gates, awaiting re-incarceration. Although he will end up back behind bars, he is still waiting to re-emerge when given half a chance.

Unlike his father, and as part of Scotland's new generation, Frank Jr. has chosen to break away from his ancestral cycle of being defined by a narrow definition of masculinity and a pattern of hopelessness and self-defeat. By choosing to go to college and work in the service industries he will have an opportunity to connect with and welcome outsiders who can enrich the Scottish nation financially and culturally. As long as he can afford to go to college and there are jobs available for him to apply to his break from miserablism may be complete.

Scotland is transitioning from a narrative of miserablism and dependence to one of inclusion, diversity and hope. No longer a nation of Trainspotters watching life pass by from a static platform, Scotland has boarded the train but the destination is something that the nation, the people and its leaders still need to choose.

References

Macnab, G. (2017), 'T2: Trainspotting's John Hodge Interview: 'I wouldn't rule out a Trainspotting 3 film I suppose'", *The Independent,* 23 January, accessed at: www.independent.co.uk/arts-entertainment/films/features/t2-trainspotting-john-hodge-danny-boyle-irvine-welsh-renton-sick-boy-ewan-mcgregor-a7542196.html

Petrie, D. (2000), *Screening Scotland,* London: British Film Institute.

Sillars, J. (2009), 'Admitting the Kailyard', in: Murray, J., Farley, F. and Stoneman, R. (eds), *Scottish Cinema Now,* Newcastle Upon Tyne: Cambridge Scholars Publishing, pp. 122-138.

Welsh, I. (2005), 'Scotland's Murderous Heart', *The Guardian,* 20 October, accessed at: www.theguardian.com/society/2005/oct/20/penal.crime

Welsh, I. (2014), 'This Glorious Failure Could Yet be Scotland's Finest Hour', *The Guardian,* 20 September, accessed at: www.theguardian.com/commentisfree/2014/sep/20/irvine-welsh-scottish-independence-glorious-failure

Yule, E. and Manderson, D. (2014), *The Glass Half Full: Moving Beyond Scottish Miserablism.* Edinburgh: Luath Press.

The Mongrel Nation of Scotland? Scottishness, Identities and Nationalism

Stephen Reicher and Nick Hopkins

Introduction

ON COMING INTO government in May 2007, the SNP administration identified 15 national outcomes aimed at making Scotland 'a better place to live and a more prosperous and successful country'. Objective 13 declares 'we take pride in a strong, fair and inclusive national identity' (see Reicher, McCrone and Hopkins, 2010). That is undoubtedly a noble aspiration, but is it even possible? And, if it is possible, has it been achieved?

For many, nations and national identities are, by definition, exclusive and unfair. Nationalism is portrayed as a toxic ideology that divides, grades and discriminates between people. Or, at the very least, nationalism has a pernicious aspect which all too easily comes to the fore. To cite George Robertson, Scottish MP, Labour Cabinet member and NATO General Secretary: 'when nationalist pride spills over into ethnic superiority then it becomes ugly and dangerous and we should all beware. Across Europe today we are seeing the dark side of nationalism: the hatred, the paranoia, the racialism' (cited in Reicher and Hopkins, 2001: 60). Robertson was speaking in 1994. Today, nearly a quarter of a century later, his words seem more pertinent than ever.

It follows that those who peddle nationalism are, whether they know it or not, dealing in dangerous stuff. As we write, a controversy is raging over the speech of Sadiq Khan, Labour's London Mayor to the 2017 Scottish Spring Conference in which, at least in draft, he argued that 'there's no difference between those who try to divide us on the basis of whether we're English or Scottish and those who try to divide us on the basis of our background, race or religion' (see The Guardian, 25 February 2017). Even if Khan and his party subsequently retreated from the charge that the SNP are racists, the argument still implies that any aspirations they have to inclusion and fairness are inherently at odds with their nationalism. Whatever their aspirations, the outcomes of their administration will be far less noble.

Others take a more nuanced view of nationalism. They suggest that there are many different forms of nationalist ideology, with more or less divisive implications. Often a division is made between two variants. The one, based on the ideas of German romantics like Herder, does indeed tend towards racism. It suggests that a nation is a matter of one's past lineage and that you cannot absorb nationhood by living in a country. Such an ethnic viewpoint would indeed question the Scottishness of those who have chosen to immigrate and make Scotland their home. And it was this that was implied when, during the 2014 referendum campaign, Alistair Darling appeared to endorse the idea that the SNP subscribed to a 'blood and soil nationalism' (Ponsonby, 2014).

But there is another view, the so-called 'civic' approach, which suggests that nationhood is more about one's future than one's past and that anyone who lives in a country and commits to that country deserves national status. Such a view would indeed include migrants, even as it excludes emigrants, whoever their parents might be. This, as far back as 1853, Patrick Dove declared to the National Association for the Vindication of Scottish Rights that 'whether he be black, white, red or yellow, the moment [a man] identifies with the institutions of Scotland, that moment he becomes a member of the Scottish nation, and Caledonia must throw around him the mantle of protection' (cited in Morton, 1996: 270).

A Positive Record

So which is it? Is Scottish nationalism, civic or ethnic, inclusive or exclusive, compatible or incompatible with the idea of a fair and inclusive society (although, as we shall see in due course, all these distinctions may be a little simplistic)? Well, the SNP clearly articulates a civic position. At the SNP Conference in 1995 Alex Salmond famously declared 'we see diversity as a strength not a weakness of Scotland and our ambition is to see the cause of Scotland argued with English, French, Irish, Indian, Pakistani, Chinese and every other accent in the rich tapestry of what we should be proud to call, in the words of Willie McIlvanney 'the mongrel nation of Scotland'' (cited in Reicher and Hopkins, 2001: 164). More concisely, but less poetically, the SNP General Election Manifesto two years later pledged that 'citizenship will be established on the basis of residency or birth' (SNP, 1997: 7). Far from being exceptional, such a view is consistently expressed both in SNP documents and by SNP representatives (Leith and Soule, 2012).

It isn't just words. As Hepburn and Rosie (2014) catalogue, the SNP has taken highly inclusive policies towards immigration, they have pursued a pro-active Equalities Agenda, they have passed hate crimes legislation and supported public campaigns to promote a 'One Scotland Many Cultures' agenda. Such policies seem to be reflected in the fact that ethnic minorities themselves tend to identify themselves as Scottish to some degree and also that the wider Scottish public accepts ethnic minorities as Scottish. They are also reflected in the fact that racial hate crimes in Scotland are falling (according to a Crown Office report, in 2015-16 they were at the lowest level since 2003-4) and, as reported in *The Scotsman* on 22 September, 2016, while hate crime as a whole rose markedly in England after the Brexit vote of June 2016 (as much as 68 % in Suffolk) it actually fell by 15 % in Scotland.

While it is hard to establish an overall causal relationship between SNP positions and these various social outcomes, there is at least some evidence that speaks to this matter. First, there is little to support the notion that the SNP's support for division with England links to support for ethnic division (as Sadiq Khan contends). Quite the opposite in fact. Thus a survey during the referendum campaign showed that 'opposition to immigration is noticeably lower among those intending to vote 'yes' for independence' (Oxford University Migration Observatory, 2014). Second, albeit not specifically related to Scotland, Pehrson, Vignoles and Brown (2009) find that an association between national identity and anti-immigrant prejudice is only found in countries where nationhood is defined ethnically, and not when it is defined civically. Third, our own experimental studies (Wakefield *et al.*, 2011) show that, when people are exposed to a civic as opposed to an ethnic definition of Scottishness, they are more likely to help and support an individual who is of Asian descent but who is committed to Scotland. It really does seem as if Salmond's words about the cause of Scotland being argued in a Chinese accent do make a difference.

Causes for Concern

We need to start this next section with a *caveat*. The issues we are discussing are so politically sensitive that there is tendency to polarise debate: either nationalism and nationhood are the best of worlds or they are the worst of worlds. A single positive or negative instance is then used to draw general one-sided conclusions. That makes it particularly hard to make balanced assessments of complex phenomena such as Scottishness. So, if we now raise some causes for concern it is not to reverse our broadly positive conclusions as outlined above. Nor is it to provide material for those who wish to distract from what has been achieved to date. Rather, it is to be constructive in determining in how we can progress still further in achieving the objective of a strong, fair and inclusive Scottish society.

The first thing to acknowledge, then, is that there is still progress to be made. There are a plethora of excellent studies into Scottish public attitudes towards Scottishness, and, more specifically, towards who is Scottish (e.g. Bond, 2017; Hepburn and Rosie, 2014; Hussain and Miller, 2006; McCrone, 2017). Together they tell a powerful and consistent story. They confirm that Scotland is distinctive compared to other parts of the UK in terms of the greater acceptance of ethnic minorities as part of the nation. But they also show, first, that certain minorities – notably those born in England with English accents resident in Scotland – have a hard time being accepted; second that it remains harder for someone non-white than someone white to be accepted as Scottish – what Hepburn and Rosie, 2014 call the 'ethnic deficit'; third, that in some ways things are getting worse – over the last decade Muslims are seen as more of a threat to Scotland.

Such survey findings are corroborated by our own experimental work. This shows that, when someone makes a claim to Scottishness based on civic criteria ('I live in Scotland and am committed to Scotland') as opposed to ethnic criteria ('I was born in Scotland of Scottish parents') it is less persuasive and leads them to be less persuasive (Hopkins, Reicher and van Rijswik, 2015). They are also corroborated by Leith and Soule's (2012) analysis of online discussions which show a preponderance of ethnic criteria in defining Scottishness. So yes, Scotland is more inclusive than England or Wales, and yes, things are largely moving in the right direction, but nonetheless, it is reasonable to accept Leith and Soule's conclusion that there remains a considerable gap between the position of the SNP and popular conceptions of nationhood.

In this context, it becomes particularly important that the SNP is vigilant and consistent in promoting an inclusive vision of Scottishness across the range of government activities – any failure to challenge lapses (irrespective of whether these lapses originated with the Government or not) runs the risk of bolstering existing ethnic exclusivism. For instance, in 2009 (the 250th anniversary of Robert Burns birth), Event Scotland organised the Scottish Homecoming, primarily as a tourist initiative. It was initially an appeal to those whose ancestors had left the country to come back for a visit. However, it appealed to them as Scots. This was echoed by Alex Salmond who called on 100 million people with 'blood links' to Scotland to return 'home' (reported in *The Scotsman* on 16 June 2008) – as if Scottishness is indeed linked to blood and soil and is entirely white (as were those who left generations back). Such ethnic conceptions of nationhood were compounded by a promotional poster showing 'a crowd of stereotypical, white kilted Scots' (Morrison and Hay, 2010).

To be fair, these problems were noted and addressed. But the cure was arguably worse than the original complaint. As for the poster, a solitary Asian man was electronically added to the image. As for Salmond, he dropped the term 'blood Scots' and while he still appealed to those of Scottish ancestry to come home, he additionally appealed to so-called 'affinity Scots': 'we also want anyone who has an interest in Scottish culture and history to come and visit too' (reported in *The List*, 1 December, 2008). This echoed the Minister for Enterprise, Energy and Tourism who, back in 2007, had declared: 'Whether you are Scottish or simply love Scotland, you are invited to come home – home to the land of your ancestors so you can experience a living culture.' The problem here is that, rather than including those with an affinity to Scotland with those of Scottish ancestry in the Scottish nation, these declarations seem to distinguish them, to indicate that affinity is trumped by ancestry and hence to reinforce an ethnicisation of nationhood. At best (and being generous) the statements are ambiguous. They certainly do not constitute an acknowledgement that a mistake has been made and a clear repudiation of the initial lapse.

So far we have been arguing, as many others argue, on the basis that ethnic and civic versions of national identity are opposed poles of a single dimension, the one being unambiguously bad and the other being unambiguously good. The implication is that our task is to move from ethnic Scottishness towards civic Scottishness. But, as we have already intimated, such stark oppositions are simplistic. It may be better to see the ethnic and the civic as separate dimensions (so more of the one does not necessarily mean less of the other) or even as interdependent dimensions of nationhood. The question is then how they work together in producing political and civil society.

Peukert (1987), for instance, shows how ethnic exclusion of Jews in Nazi Germany, combined with an ambiguity as to who was Jewish, led to a situation where anyone who did not show sufficient commitment to the Nazi order could be accused of also being a 'community alien' and subject to the appalling consequences. On an analogous (but less extreme) level, writers like Stuart Hall showed how, in the UK of the 1970s and 1980s, notions like crime were racialised such that those who violated the social order were understood as being inherently 'other' and hence repressed rather than reintegrated into society (Hall, Critcher, Jefferson, Clarke and Roberts, 1978).

Equally, ethnic and civic criteria may work together when defining who belongs in the first place, and this may play out unequally for different groups. Thus, on the whole, civic criteria – to the extent that they are employed at all – complement rather than replace ethnic criteria. The Scottishness of some-one born in Scotland of Scottish parents and with a clear Scottish accent is rarely if ever questioned. It is only if you don't have these attributes that you have to prove your commitment to the nation (McCrone, 2017).

That in itself is fundamentally discriminatory. Only ethnic minorities have to be constantly jumping through hoops, affirming their loyalty (and having to condemn those of their ethnicity who are disloyal or even dangerous). But worse still, this is often a game that ethnic minorities can never win. The very fact that they have to try so hard to demonstrate their national credentials serves to mark them out as not really of the nation (cf. Joyce, Stevenson and Muldoon, 2013). The ethnic minority member ends up as Sisyphus, forever undertaking onerous tasks in order to arrive at nationhood but doomed never quite to get there.

Moreover, what exactly is it that one has to demonstrate to claim nation-hood? What is it that constitutes commitment under civic nationalism? Our attempts to pin that down in the case of Scottishness show the answer to be particularly elusive. Is it a matter of feelings – of cheering when Scotland score a goal? Is it a matter of holding particular values and beliefs? Is it a matter of doing things like serving the community? There is no clear answer. There is no agreed checklist. And this is dangerous. For it becomes possible to elaborate criteria of belonging which are restrictive, oppressive and even totalitarian.

In particular, commitment can be equated with particular political posi-tions, such that dissent from these positions serves to exclude one from the national community. In this way civic nationalism can be just as exclusive as ethnic nationalism. There were certainly elements of this in the 2014 referen-dum debate. To cite the BBC Scotland correspondent, James Cook, writing for the BBC *News* website on 17 September 2015: 'Scotland's most successful mod-ern author J.K. Rowling and its greatest Olympian Sir Chris Hoy were both abused online, as were thoughtful pro-Union commentators such as David Tor-rance, Chris Deerin and Alex Massie, painted not just as political opponents or sceptical journalists but as enemies of Scotland, traitors, Quislings and so on.' The same was certainly true of the 'Better Together' standard bearer, Alistair Darling (Watt and Carrell, 2014)

It is important, again, to get this in balance. Such attacks did not ema-nate from the SNP leadership. Even among activists, they were far from a dom-inant trend. According to polling, only a small minority of people suffered any abuse during the debate and then, there was considerably more online abuse against 'Yes' supporters than 'No' supporters (Campbell, 2015). So, overall we tend towards the position that the referendum debate was a genuine and open national conversation in which unprecedented proportions of the population participated in a debate about who we are and where we want to go.

Nonetheless, to advance the cause of inclusiveness, it is particularly important that such attacks on the Scottishness of one's opponents are decisively repudiated by the leadership, whenever and wherever they occur. It was – and it remains – a matter of some controversy as to whether there was a willingness to do so. Our point is that exclusive versions of nationhood need to be challenged whether they take an 'ethnic' or a 'civic' form. There is no room for ambiguity and for responses which allow the exclusivists to believe that their positions are condoned or even endorsed. Ambiguity here has the potential to function like indifference in the face of evil.

Conclusion

Back in 2010 we wrote a report for the Equalities and Human Rights Commission (EHRC) on Scottish Government Objective 13, to take pride in a strong fair and inclusive Scottish identity. We concluded that such an aspiration is realistic, that the Scottish Government was committed to this goal both in words and actions. At the same time, we argued that there is still some way to go in terms of the policies and practices through which Scottishness is defined and different groups are made to believe that they do (or don't) belong in Scotland. We said: 'that making Scottish identity (and hence Scottish society) fairer and more inclusive depends upon a systematic programme of action that would interrogate the way identity is defined through our public discourse and educational texts, the ways we mark and celebrate our national story, and the practices of all our institutions' (Reicher, McCrone and Hopkins, 2010: 23). Now, some seven years later, where do things stand?

Overall, we suggest, the balance sheet remains broadly positive. The SNP has worked hard to fashion a sense of Scottish identity which is not associated with exclusion and may even be linked to inclusion. This is clearly bearing fruit. Minorities are part of the nation to a greater extent than before (and probably more than elsewhere in the UK). But at the same time, there is still a long way to go before we could rest on our laurels.

The population certainly have not kept pace with the politicians. Those not born in Scotland of Scottish parents still have to work harder at acceptance, they still have to do more to prove their credentials, and they still can't be sure of acceptance however hard they work (or perhaps, precisely because they have to work so hard). Moreover, what people have to do to prove their Scottishness may infringe on their rights and liberties as much as being excluded.

Progress depends upon bringing these failings into the open, upon acknowledging these failings, and upon acting robustly to deal with them. In sum, we are becoming Willie McIlvanney's mongrel nation. To go further, we need to be clear that we are not there yet.

References

Bond, R. (2017), 'Minorities and diversity in Scotland: evidence from the 2011 census', *Scottish Affairs, 26 (1)*, 23-47.

Campbell, S. (2015), 'The abusers and the abused', *Wings over Scotland*, 29 July, http://wingsoverscotland.com/the-abusers-and-the-abused/ (accessed 27 February 2017)

Hall, S., Clarke, J., Critcher, C., Jefferson, T., and Roberts, B. (1978), *Policing the Crisis: Mugging, Law and Order and the State*, London: Macmillan.

Hepburn, E. and Rosie, M. (2014), 'Immigration, nationalism and politics in Scotland', in Hepburn, E. and Zapata-Barrero, R. (eds.), *The Politics of Immigration in Multi-Level States*, Basingstoke: Palgrave Macmillan, pp. 241-60.

Hopkins, N., Reicher, S. D., and van Rijswijk, W. (2015), 'Everyday citizenship: Identity claims and their reception', *Journal of Social and Political Psychology, 3*, 84-106.

Hussain, A.M. and Miller, W.L. (2006), *Multicultural Nationalism: Islamophobia, Anglophobia and Devolution*, Oxford: Oxford University Press.

Leith, M.S. and Soule, D.P.J. (2012), *Political Discourse and National Identity in Scotland*, Edinburgh: Edinburgh University Press.

McCrone, D. (2017), *The New Sociology of Scotland*, London: Sage

Morrison, A. and Hay, B. (2010), 'A review of the constraints, limitations and success of Homecoming Scotland 2009', *Fraser of Allander Economic Commentary, 34*, 44-54.

Morton, G. (1996), 'Scottish rights and 'centralisation' in the mid-nineteenth century', *Nations and Nationalism, 2*, 257-279.

Oxford University Migration Observatory (2014), *Scottish Public Opinion*, accessed at: www.migrationobservatory.ox.ac.uk/resources/reports/scottish-public-opinion/

Peukert, D.J.K. (1987), *Inside Nazi Germany*, Batsford: London.

Ponsonby, G.A. (2014), 'Darling under pressure to apologise after recording casts doubt on 'Blood and Soil Nationalism' denial', accessed at: www.newsnet.scot/nns-archive/index.php?option=com_content&view=article&id=9306:darling-under-pressure-to-apologise-after-recording-casts-doubt-on-blood-and-soil-nationalism-denial&catid=6:general&Itemid=89

Reicher, S.D. and Hopkins, N.P. (2011), *Self and Nation*, London: Sage.

Reicher, S.D., McCrone, D. and Hopkins, N.P. (2010), '*A strong, fair and inclusive national identity: A viewpoint on the Scottish Government's Outcome 13*, Equalities and Human Rights Commission Research Report 62. EHRC: Manchester.

SNP (1997), *Yes we can win the best for Scotland*, Edinburgh: SNP.

Wakefield, J. R., Hopkins, N.P., Cockburn, C., Shek, K. M., Muirhead, A., Reicher, S.D., and van Rijswijk, W. (2011), 'The impact of adopting ethnic or civic conceptions of national belonging for others' treatment', *Personality and Social Psychology Bulletin*, 37, 1599-1610.

Watt, N. and Carrell, S. (2014), 'Alistair Darling: 'You can be patriotic and so no to independence', *The Guardian*, 12 September, accessed at: www.theguardian.com/politics/2014/sep/12/alistair-darling-patriotic-no-independence-scotland-referendum

Section Six: The Wider World and Context

Scotland International

John MacDonald

BEFORE 2007, SCOTLAND'S capacity as an international actor had not been greatly explored. The practice of international affairs wasn't well embedded in the machinery of government, nor was it particularly well understood by Scotland's political parties. Domestic issues dominated the political agenda.

The SNP entered government in 2007 fully aware of this. Yet its independence aspirations meant that it could not confine its focus to the domestic. The party knew that to lead Scotland to independence, it must develop a strong knowledge of international affairs so that it could argue convincingly why the status quo does not serve Scotland well. It knew it must also enhance Scotland's international profile, activity and networks with the aim of normalising – as much as possible – the sense that Scotland acts, and is accepted, as any other nation state.

One decade on, the SNP has undoubtedly made progress on both these fronts. It has expanded Scotland's international activity and profile. Its international affairs programme, although modest, has brought recognition and some prestige to Scotland internationally. Through the course of the 2014 Scottish independence referendum, the SNP's vision for how an independent Scotland would provision itself and act on the world stage attracted praise from many quarters. The peaceful, democratic nature of the referendum process enhanced Scotland's international reputation.

Yet for all of Scotland's growth in international affairs over the past decade, the constitutional realities of 2017 remain much as they were in 2007. While sovereignty remains in London, Scotland has negligible capacity to impact the big international issues which affect it. This is demonstrated vividly by current events: at the time of writing, Scotland's government has virtually no influence over how the UK government is handling a European Union (EU) exit that Scotland did not vote for.

This chapter charts the evolution of Scotland's international affairs under ten years of SNP government. It highlights the major dynamics and developments through this period, and illuminates how the SNP has emerged as the most fluent, active and well-connected of all Scotland's political parties when it comes to international affairs. The chapter concludes by considering how the 2016 UK vote to leave the EU – popularly known as Brexit – might influence Scotland's thinking about its place in the world. The international dimension was not a decisive issue for voters in the 2014 independence referendum. Will Brexit change this in Scotland's next referendum?

Scotland and International Affairs: A Brief Overview

Significant parameters impact Scottish Governments where international affairs are concerned. It is worth briefly exploring them. The Scotland Act (1998) dictates that 'UK foreign policy' and 'defence' are reserved to the UK government (Scotland Act, 1998). Scottish Governments thus cannot involve themselves with 'hard' military, security or territorial issues. They cannot pursue membership of the inter-governmental bodies most heavily involved in international rule-making. Nor can they ratify international treaties.

There are four key mechanisms which can facilitate Scotland's international activity and enhance its international profile:

1. Develop a strong international reputation – a 'brand' – based upon the distinctiveness and success of domestic Scottish policies.
2. Initiate international activity based upon devolved policy areas such as economic development.
3. Optimise Scottish participation in EU programmes.
4. Promote trade and culture through high-level visits and other exchanges (Bailes, 2014).

An SNP goal while in government has been 'to place Scotland as a responsible nation and partner on the world stage' (Scottish Government, 2008b). In looking to achieve this, the party has adopted all four of these approaches.

Hello World (2007 – 2011)

The SNP's early efforts to enhance Scotland's international profile were something of a mixed bag. It looked to existing mechanisms such as the EU-funded Northern Periphery Programme, aiming to position Scotland 'as an equal partner' to other programme participants such as Finland, Iceland and Norway (EPRC, 2012). Yet there were difficulties getting the party – including First Minister Alex Salmond – 'sufficiently engaged' with European Union affairs more broadly during its first term in office (Author interview 1).

The 2008 'International Framework' (Scottish Government, 2008b; 2015) was the boldest statement yet of devolved Scotland's international ambitions.

Yet question have been asked over how effectively it has mobilised engagement across Scottish Government departments in the way that, for example, the Malawi Development Programme has (Author interview 1).

Far less ambiguous was the 2009 Climate Change (Scotland) Act. Described at the time as 'world-leading' climate change legislation (SCCS, 2009), it represents a significant landmark in Scotland's growing international reputation for 'climate leadership' (Aberle *et al.*, 2015). However, it also provided a platform for exposing tensions between the political centre in London, and an independence-seeking government in Edinburgh intent on promoting Scotland more boldly on the world stage. Keen to publicise his government's new legislation, First Minister Alex Salmond requested to attend the 2009 Copenhagen Climate Conference as part of the UK government delegation. The request was refused. One senior SNP source describes the refusal as 'the UK Government cutting off its nose to spite its face... unwilling to showcase Scotland's good international showing on climate change' (Author interview 2).

The SNP also increased Scotland's International Development Fund during its first term, from £6 million to £9 million (Scottish Government, 2008a). This prompted questions – and some derision – from within the Department for International Development (DFID) as to why the Scottish Government was seeking greater activity in this sphere, commanding a budget which was a fraction of DFID's own (Author interview 1).

While there are certainly questions to be asked over the aims and effectiveness of Scotland's international development work, the notion that Scottish Governments might wish to engage with the world on Scotland's terms on some issues remains a poorly understood curiosity at the UK Government level.

2011 – 2014: Scotland as 'good global citizen'

Scotland's 2014 independence referendum elevated questions over Scotland's place in the world to a new level. International affairs were never going to be a decisive issue for voters yet it was incumbent upon the SNP to articulate a clear and credible vision of how an independent Scotland would provision itself, and act, internationally. Alex Salmond synthesised this vision in 2013, when he declared: 'An independent Scotland would not be a global superpower. But we would be a good global citizen' (Salmond, 2013).

The 'good global citizen' theme was evident in the Scottish Government's independence white paper. It stipulated that an independent Scotland would:

- Be a global leader in the field of international development;
- Spend less annually on defence, maintaining a military model based upon territorial protection and peacekeeping;

- Have a written constitution enshrining – among other things – Scotland's status as a nuclear-weapons-free-zone;
- Seek membership of the United Nations, the European Union, the Organisation for Cooperation and Security in Europe, and the North Atlantic Treaty Organisation (NATO) (Scottish Government, 2013).

The SNP's abandonment of its longstanding opposition to NATO disappointed many independence supporters. Yet it was regarded by others as a maturing of the SNP's worldview, a well-judged signal to Scotland's transatlantic neighbours that independence wouldn't undermine the status quo and should not be regarded with trepidation.

During the campaign, Scottish-Nordic synergies were repeatedly emphasised to illustrate how an independent Scotland could do better. Ahead of the referendum, the Scottish Government launched a Nordic-Baltic statement aimed at further strengthening Scotland's relations with those nations (Scottish Government, 2014). Senior SNP figures declared that an independent Scotland would prioritise the 'Northern dimension' and 'co-operate with the Arctic Council, with Nordic and other northern neighbours' (Robertson, 2014).

These ideas found considerable support. Dominic Hinde observes that the Nordic region 'loomed large' in the independence campaign, 'with meeting rooms around the country filled with talk of Nordic prosperity and new northern horizons' for Scotland (Hinde, 2016). However, it is important to note that this was not purely a Scottish discussion. Some Nordic commentators themselves depicted Scotland as a 'new Nordic state' in the making which could 'reinvent Nordic co-operation' and 'the very notion of what being Nordic means' (Settle, 2014).

The 2014 Scottish independence campaign revealed a vast appetite for reimagining Scotland and its place in the world. Amid a frustrating debate in which much was misinterpreted, over-sold or ignored, by both sides, it has been somewhat overlooked that the SNP's vision of 'good global citizen' Scotland was entirely credible (Bailes, 2014). It may even have been attractive to many Scottish voters who rejected independence. Ultimately, the international dimension was not decisive in influencing Scotland's vote.

2014 – 2016: Consolidation

The resettling of Scotland's political landscape after the 2014 referendum has resulted in a high degree of polarisation along constitutional lines. SNP membership has soared, the party made startling gains in the 2015 UK general election, and it secured a third successive term in government after the 2016 Scottish parliamentary election.

With Scotland's constitutional question still looming large, the SNP continues to consolidate its knowledge of, and networking in, the spheres of international affairs and security. It is in London where we see this most vividly. Having returned 56 of Scotland's 59 MPs to Westminster in 2015, the SNP Westminster group's allocation of 'short money' has soared from £187,000 in 2014-15 to £1.22 million for the 2016/17 period (Kelly, 2016). These funds have already supported a substantial increase in research and activity on international affairs.

With its new numbers, the SNP is now represented on Westminster's Foreign Affairs and International Development Committees. An SNP MP chairs the International Trade Committee. Representation on these committees gives the SNP considerable policy insight, as well as new connections and contacts. The party is active within the Westminster Foundation for Democracy which supports democratic development programmes across the world. In Brussels, Alyn Smith MEP has sat on the EU's Foreign Affairs Committee since 2014.

What this means is that the SNP now has access to platforms, information, activities, contacts and funding which would have been unthinkable back in 2007. Its parliamentarians and their staff travel the world on committee-related work, on various projects and fact-finding trips. They meet with, and learn from, foreign government ministries and organisations such as NATO. Activity at Westminster feeds up to colleagues at Holyrood, where international affairs opportunities are less substantial.

If an SNP aim since 2007 has been to bolster Scotland's international activity and profile, and strengthen the party's proficiency in international affairs with an eye on independence, it cannot be denied that considerable progress has been made. However, as things stand, Scotland's status as an international actor continues to be defined by the fact that the big international decisions affecting Scotland are taken in London. This has been exemplified by the UK government's decision to hold an 'in-out' referendum on EU membership, and what we have witnessed since.

Brexit: Scotland at the Crossroads

In 2016, the UK voted to leave the EU in the face of a strong Scottish vote to remain (BBC, 2016). Scotland now contemplates once more the question of independence from the UK, while trying to factor in how the Brexit process fits into the equation. It is profoundly confusing.

What is perfectly clear is that when viewed through an international affairs prism, Brexit is not good for Scotland. Constitutionally restrained from feeding into UK foreign policy, EU membership provides Scotland a crucial 'passport' for collaborating with other European nations. EU funding has supported key Scottish policy initiatives – notably in renewable energy – which have raised Scotland's international profile. EU funding would also be important in supporting greater involvement in spheres of growing interest to Scotland, such as Arctic affairs.

Scotland's status as an international actor is central to much of the uncertainty over what Brexit negotiations may yield. For example, UK government assertions that full fisheries powers will be 'repatriated' to Scotland appear dubious since this would entail giving Scottish Governments the capacity to negotiate and ratify international fisheries treaties (Brooks, 2016). While former Prime Minister Gordon Brown has recently called for this to happen, London has never shown enthusiasm for granting Scotland such 'sovereign' powers (*The Telegraph*, 2017).

For all that Brexit seems likely to damage Scotland, the Brexit process is entirely in the hands of the UK government. This is to be expected. The UK is the sovereign state and EU member. It was never realistic to think that Scotland might somehow be treated as an equal partner in the negotiating process. However, it is a situation which illustrates starkly the SNP's contention that Scotland cannot control its own affairs while it is in the UK.

The SNP's decade in power will coincide with a political climate of unprecedented complexity. A second Scottish independence referendum is on the cards at some unspecified future date (Smith, 2017). Scotland's First Minister contends that Scotland will seek EU membership after a vote for independence (Cowburn, 2017). However, it remains unclear whether Scottish voters will support Scottish independence in Europe over remaining within a UK which has relinquished EU membership.

The debate to come will coalesce around the issues which dominated the previous debate; notably an independent Scotland's economic prospects and its currency. However, other questions will be interrogated this time around. How is Scotland likely to be impacted by the UK government's post-Brexit international relations and trade deals? Will a Scotland residing within the post-Brexit UK manage to maintain a meaningful relationship with Europe? If Scotland simply has a deeper sense of *Europeanness* than England and Wales, should it remain within a political union which has rejected the European project and what it stands for?

These questions may make the international dimension more influential in the next Scottish independence referendum than in the last one. Whether this will prompt a different result remains to be seen.

References

Author interview 1: author interview with retired senior Scottish Government civil servant. 20 February, 2017.

Author interview 2: author interview with current senior SNP official. 22 February 2017.

Aberle, N., Martinelli, A., Roberts, N. Wakeham, M. and Foyster, G. (2015), 'Six Steps to Climate Leadership, Environment Victoria, accessed at: http://environmentvictoria.org.au/wp-content/uploads/2016/06/Six-steps-to-climate-leadership.pdf

Bailes, A., (2014), 'The Scottish Independence Referendum', *Kutafin University Law Review*, Volume 1, Issue 1, September 2014, pp. 36-37.

BBC (2016), 'EU referendum: Scotland backs remain as UK votes Leave', *BBC News*, 24 June 2016, accessed at: www.bbc.co.uk/news/uk-scotland-scotland-politics-36599102

Black, A. (2012), 'Scottish independence: Cameron and Salmond strike referendum deal'. BBC Scotland, 15 October, accessed at: http://www.bbc.co.uk/news/uk-scotland-scotland-politics-19942638

Brooks, L. (2016), 'Scotland stands to gain 'significant powers' from Brexit, claims minister', *The Guardian*, 29 November, accessed at: www.theguardian.com/politics/2016/nov/27/scotland-gain-significant-powers-brexit-claims-david-mundell

Cowburn, A. (2017), ''Nicola Sturgeon says Scotland will pursue EU membership after independence', *The Independent,* 19 March, accessed at: www.independent.co.uk/news/uk/politics/nicola-sturgeon-scottish-independence-referendum-eu-membership-back-of-queue-spain-a7638101.html

Daily Telegraph, 'Gordon Brown lays out third option for Scotland to avoid "bitter division and Whitehall "power grab"', *Daily Telegraph*, 18 March 2017, accessed at: www.telegraph.co.uk/news/2017/03/18/gordon-brown-lays-third-option-scotland-avoid-bitter-division/

Ehrenberg, B. (2014), 'Who won? How Edinburgh voted in Scotland's independence referendum', *City AM*, 19 September, accessed at: www.cityam.com/1411119101/who-won-how-edinburgh-voted-scotlands-independence-referendum-results-map-and-charts

European Policies Research Centre (EPRC) (2012), *The Evaluation of the Northern Periphery Programme: Draft Final Evaluation Report*, pp. 16-17, accessed at: www.lansstyrelsen.se/vasterbotten/SiteCollectionDocuments/Sv/om-lansstyrelsen/upphandlingar/Ex-Ante%20Evaluation%20of%20the%20Northern%20Periphery%20Programme%202014-2020/Enclosure%203%20EPRC_Draft_Final_Evaluation_Paper.pdf

Freeman, T. (2017), 'Heriot-Watt job losses blamed on Brexit', *Holyrood*, 6 March, accessed at: www.holyrood.com/articles/news/heriot-watt-job-losses-blamed-brexit

Hinde, D. (2016), *A Utopia Like Any Other: Inside the Swedish Model*, Luath Press.

Kelly, R. (2016), *Short Money*, House of Commons Briefing Paper, 19 December.

Robertson, A. (2014), 'Independence essay: supporting our northern allies', *The Scotsman*, 7 May, accessed at: www.scotsman.com/news/opinion/independence-essay-supporting-our-northern-allies-1-3400832

Salmond, A. (2013), 'Scotland as a good global citizen', Address to the Brookings Institute, Washington DC, 9 April, accessed at: www.scotland.gov.uk/News/Speeches/scotland-global-citzen

'Copenhagen: Salmond throws a lifeline to sinking Maldives', *The Scotsman*, 15 December 2009, accessed at: www.scotsman.com/news/copenhagen-alex-salmond-throws-a-lifeline-to-sinking-maldives-1-783037

'Brexit: Maintaining freedom of movement "vital" to Scotland', *The Scotsman*, December 2016, accessed at: www.scotsman.com/news/politics/brexit-maintaining-freedom-of-movement-vital-to-scotland-1-4311535is

Scottish Government (2008a) *Scottish Government Development Policy*, accessed at: www.gov.scot/Publications/2008/05/06144819/1

Scottish Government (2008b), *Scottish Government International Framework*, accessed at: www.gov.scot/Publications/2008/04/23150847/1

Scottish Government (2009), *Climate Change (Scotland) Act 2009*, www.gov.scot/Topics/Environment/climatechange/legislation

Scottish Government (2013), *Scotland's Future: Your guide to an independent Scotland*, Edinburgh: Scottish Government.

Scottish Government (2014), *Nordic Baltic Policy Statement*, accessed at: www.scotland.gov.uk/Resource/0044/00445851.pdf

Scottish Government (2015), *Scottish Government International Framework*, accessed at: www.gov.scot/Publications/2015/03/3466_

Scotland Act (1998), accessed at: www.legislation.gov.uk/ukpga/1998/46/contents

Stop Climate Change Scotland (SCCS) (2009), 'Scots climate bill on verge of leading the world, says SCCS', accessed at https://unison-scotland.blogspot.co.uk/2009/06/scots-climate-bill-on-verge-of-leading.html

Settle, M. (2014), 'SNP to make common cause with our neighbours to the north', *The Herald*, 10

February, accessed at: www.heraldscotland.com/news/13144987.
    SNP_plan_to_seek_common_cause_with_our_neighbours_to_the_north/
Scottish National Party (2017), '5 ways Scotland is a good global citizen',
    accessed at: www.snp.org/scotland_international_development
Smith, P. (2017), 'Nicola Sturgeon: There will be a sec-
    ond Scottish independence referendum'. ITV News, 18
    March, accessed at: www.itv.com/news/2017-03-18/
    nicola-sturgeon-there-will-be-a-second-scottish-independence-referendum/
Vevers, D. (2016), 'Scotland backs Remain in EU vote in every coun-
    cil area', STV News, 24 June, accessed at: https://stv.tv/news/
    politics/1358464-eu-referendum-scotland-votes-remain/
Walker, W. (2014), 'Foreign Reactions to the Referendum in Scotland', Scottish
    Global Forum, 15 September, accessed at: www.scottishglobalforum.net/
    walker-foreign-reactions.html

Defence and the SNP

William Walker

SCOTLAND WAS BORN fighting, as the saying goes, in centuries of internal strife and resistance to conquest. Even after Culloden and the Union's consolidation, Scotland's fighting traditions were sustained by its regiments' prominence in the 19th and 20th centuries' imperial and great wars.

Warfare is therefore woven into the stories told and retold about Scotland's past. Yet it is striking how little military affairs, and concerns about the nation's security, featured in the emergence of Scottish nationalism as a political force in the 20th century. There is only passing reference to defence issues in histories of the SNP (Lynch, 2002: Hassan, 2009).

Although opposition to conscription, the presence of nuclear weapons and the UK's foreign adventures played their parts, the SNP's advance was not driven to any significant degree by military concerns. Furthermore, unlike in Ireland, the use of violence to achieve political goals was considered out of bounds at every level of society and in every part of the country. Billy Wolfe tells the story in his memoir of an SNP meeting in Bathgate in 1962 when 'a stranger to the rest of us exhorted us to choose the road of violence and what he, and others, call 'action'... He was politely but firmly shown the door' (Wolfe, 1973: 16). Ambitions must be realised by peaceful means and through the ballot box.

Military men and women were also largely absent, even in retirement, from the groups that promoted Scottish nationhood. Especially within the officer class, loyalty to the Crown, the British state and London's command did not diminish with the SNP's rise. The armed forces' allegiance to the Union was implicit in the devolution settlement of 1998, whereby defence policy was reserved to London, and in its revision after the 2014 referendum. While Scotland's martial traditions were maintained and admired in the British Army, the strong sense of Scottish identity within it did not extend to political identity even when the fourteen Scottish regiments were amalgamated into a single regiment in 2006, pointedly called the Royal Regiment of Scotland rather than the Scottish Regiment or Army.

A Defence Policy in Embryo

This is not to say that defence was absent from the SNP's policy debates. It received attention as a natural consequence of the quest for self-government and in the Party's imagining of the stance that a sovereign Scottish state would adopt on defence. A resolution passed at the SNP's annual conference in 1968 asserted that:

> The primary responsibility for the defence of Scotland must rest on the Government and citizens of Scotland; that the Government shall hold available such forces as may be required to honour Scotland's obligations to the United Nations Organization; that the Government shall not permit the existence of foreign bases on Scottish soil or on Scottish waters; and shall become signatory to a Treaty to limit the spread of nuclear weapons.

The SNP was determined at this stage to avoid any whiff of militarism. It was strongly opposed to NATO membership and to the stationing of other states' military forces – especially British and American nuclear forces – on Scottish territory. Often looking to the Republic of Ireland's example, it presumed that a friendly, neutral Scotland would need comparatively little to defend its territory and support its foreign relations.

The 1968 Resolution held, more or less, for the next forty years. It could not suffice, however, after the SNP's success in the 2007 and 2011 Holyrood elections and announcement that a referendum would be held in 2014. The Party's leadership found itself having to consider – seriously for the first time – how Scotland could function as a state within the state system, how to establish the kinds of relations with other states that would secure its legal recognition and provide entry to international organisations, and how to frame its policies and shape its military forces so that others would regard it as a useful and reliable ally rather than as a source of disruption.

This was not a simple task. Enunciation of a defence policy for the referendum was preceded by a drive to embrace NATO after decades of antagonism towards it, a shift that proved more difficult to secure than the Party's earlier volte-face on membership of the European Communities. 'Scotland in Europe' could become a slogan in a way that 'Scotland in NATO' could not. The debate culminated in approval of a motion at the 2012 Party Conference confirming that 'An SNP Government will maintain NATO membership subject to an agreement that Scotland will not host nuclear weapons and NATO continues to respect the right of members to only take part in UN sanctioned operations'.

With this major change in the bag, the SNP and Scottish Government set out to formulate a defence plan to take into the referendum that would be sufficiently detailed and coherent to earn respect. Outcomes were lengthy sections on defence and security in the 2013 White Paper covering, among other things, Scotland's main ambition and priorities, the size and shape of military forces, the future of bases and defence industries, levels of expenditure, and involvement in intelligence gathering. The 'priorities for action' included maintaining a budget of £2.5 billion for defence, 'securing the safest and speediest withdrawal of nuclear weapons from Scotland', strengthening maritime capabilities, and building a defence force of 15,000 regular and 5000 reserve personnel within ten years of independence (Scottish Government, 2013: 232-251; 261-267).

Despite the effort, the Scottish Government found itself vulnerable to criticism of its defence proposals on several fronts including their costing, claims on future work for shipyards on the Clyde, the compatibility of the SNP's anti-nuclear stance with NATO membership, and London's willingness to agree to a favourable division of military assets. In the event, however, defence did not figure prominently in the referendum. Furthermore, the future of Trident, an issue that was bound to trouble an independent Scotland's relations with the rest of the UK, France and the US, was a dog that barked but feebly. Unlike with the currency, the UK Government could not proclaim the benefits that the Union's survival would bring to Scotland through Trident's retention. Nor was the Ministry of Defence (MoD) keen to reveal its befuddlement over how to respond to Faslane and Coulport's loss, should it happen (there was no contingency planning). For its part, the Scottish Government was happy to stick to generalities and avoid detailed discussion of the means by which Trident and its large and dangerous paraphernalia would be removed.

Brexit and the General Election's Ironic Consequence

The 2014 Scottish referendum's defeat appeared, in its immediate aftermath, to have put paid to independence a decade or more, postponing the need for further detailed consideration of a Scottish defence policy. In addition, the granting of additional powers over fiscal and other matters after the referendum did not extend to defence and foreign policy that remained stubbornly reserved to London. Just two years later, the situation is very different. The Brexit vote has reignited the debate about Scotland's constitutional future and place in the world, and the general election of 2015 has strengthened the Party's ability to engage with defence issues at a political level by dramatically increasing the SNP's representation in the UK Parliament.

On 13 March 2017, Nicola Sturgeon announced that preparations would be made for a second referendum on Scotland's independence to be held, she proposed, in Autumn 2018 or Spring 2019. It remains to be seen whether, when and on which and whose terms the referendum will be held. If it does go ahead, the Scottish Government is committed to providing the electorate with a fresh analysis of Scotland's future and the policies that would follow independence. A second White Paper, probably shorter than its predecessor in 2013, would cover defence, security and foreign affairs along with the other areas of policy.

The ideas and proposals on defence in this White Paper would probably be quite similar, in broad terms, to those set out in 2013. A Scottish state would not take part in the UK's great power games. It would focus instead on defence of the nation and its adjoining region, notably performing a maritime role in Europe's northern waters. It would be a dependable member of NATO and active participant in Europol and the EU's Common Defence and Security Policy when EU membership had been achieved. It would acquire necessary military assets and support the industrial capabilities pertinent to its defence needs. It would honour its longstanding pledge to remove nuclear weapons from Scottish territory and convert the nuclear bases to conventional purposes. It would increase the priority given to cyber security, in cooperation with others, acknowledging its emergence as one of the 21st century's great concerns.

The most significant change since 2014 has occurred in the SNP's ability to formulate defence and security policy and provide closely reasoned support for its positions at home and abroad. This is an ironic consequence of the election in May 2015 of 56 SNP MPs to the UK Parliament. A group of five Scottish MPs with a research staff now attends to defence affairs, its members able to join in foreign visits, use the House of Commons Library, and join gatherings at London's various think tanks. The Party is also represented on the Defence Select Committee. Restrictions imposed on the Scottish Government and Parliament by the Scotland Act's reservation of defence and foreign policy to London do not apply with the same force to the SNP's contingent at Westminster.

In addition, most foreign embassies and governments, and international organisations, have become more open to dialogue with the SNP now that it is well represented in the UK Parliament, and have become more sympathetic to Scotland following the Brexit vote. As a result, the SNP finds itself better prepared than in 2014 for engaging in debates about defence policy, and better connected abroad.

There is a further irony. If successful in a second referendum, the SNP would find itself detached from the sources in London of information, expertise and institutional support that have been so valuable since 2015. Implementation would require their transfer to and reconstruction within Scotland, to the extent possible for a small state with relatively few resources.

Uncertain Foreign Attitudes in a Volatile International Environment

The Scottish Government would be launching another referendum in a period of great international volatility: tension between great powers, anxiety and instability in Europe, violence in the Middle East, economic insecurity, unsettling technological dynamics, and division within the United States under an administration that is mistrusted and untutored in world affairs.

The SNP may consider that Brexit has given the case for Scottish independence extra legitimacy and sympathy abroad. This may be true. The injustice of Scotland's removal from the EU against its democratic will is widely acknowledged, and a UK Government that is doing injury to the EU and its member states will be less able to draw on their support when campaigning against Scotland's independence. In European capitals, London apart, there may also be attraction in welcoming a country led by experienced politicians that is espousing a pro-EU cosmopolitanism against the trend.

The UK's allies in Europe and elsewhere would be less enthusiastic, however, if Scotland's ambitions were seen to be threatening more instability and insecurity in dangerous times. They would need persuasion that their security would not be weakened by the various adjustments to British policies, capabilities and bases that would follow a successful Scottish referendum. The Scottish Government may now be able to produce a narrative on defence and security that is more convincing than the narrative contained in the 2013 White Paper. But it would have to indicate flexibility in its positions, and willingness to depart from the ideal, to prevent attitudes hardening against it.

The SNP-led Scottish Government has made strides since 2007 in its understanding of military affairs and formulation of defence and security policies, as well as in developing contacts with individuals, governments and agencies that would matter if independence were achieved. But it has yet to cross – of course – the crucial threshold to implementation involving, among many other things, the reconfiguration of armed forces and their equipment, creation of a Scottish defence ministry and associated institutions, conversion of bases, and establishment of working relations with other states' military forces and bureaucracies inside and outside NATO.

Both London and Edinburgh would also have to confront the issues, ducked for so long, surrounding the UK's nuclear deterrent and its location in and removal from Scotland. The UK Parliament's approval of the submarines' manufacture in July 2016, followed by the award of contracts, has added to the difficulties of altering the status quo. Where else might the submarines and their armaments be based? How and when would they be removed if they were removed? What would the transition entail? How would American and NATO interests be satisfied? (Walker, 2015).

As in 2014, it is unlikely that the result of another Scottish referendum would be much influenced by voters' views on the SNP's defence policies. Their credibility abroad might, however, have greater significance than in 2014 if – as seems likely – voters' willingness to follow the Scottish Government's lead depended more heavily on confidence that Scotland would be admitted to the EU, NATO and other international organisations without great fuss. If foreign governments decided that their core security interests would be injured by the UK's break-up, their concerns might reverberate within Scotland's electorate, increasing fears that an independent Scotland would be excluded from the mainstream despite recognition of its unjust treatment.

If there is no second Scottish referendum, or if a referendum is held and lost, London will retain its hold on defence policy. The SNP's grasp of the issues will have increased, but its influence over policies that affect Scotland will remain marginal.

References

Hassan, G. (ed.) (2009), *The Modern SNP: From Protest to Power*, Edinburgh: Edinburgh University Press.

Lynch, P. (2002), *SNP: The History of the Scottish National Party*, Cardiff: Welsh Academic Press.

Walker, W. (2015), 'Trident's Replacement and the Survival of the United Kingdom', *Survival*, vol. 57, no. 5, pp. 7-28.

Wolfe, B. (1973), *Scotland Lives: The Quest for Independence*, Edinburgh: Reprographia.

The Meaning of Independence

James Mitchell

EDMUND MORGAN, EMINENT historian of the American revolutionary era, wrote a short book on 'The Meaning of Independence' (Morgan, 1978: 4) focusing on the thought of three 'architects of independence'. He remarked, 'Independence meant many things to many men.' (This was not a revolutionary generation when it came to gender.) One reviewer of the book noted how little attention had been paid to the meaning of independence amongst historians (Greene, 1978: 1087). In outlining the thinking of his three subjects, Morgan describes these architects' evolving understandings of independence. Morgan's expansive interpretation of independence incorporated the operation of the American constitution (Adams' bicameralism with a strong executive), the America's external relations (Washington's suspicion of foreign entanglements), and the relationship between the citizen and the state (Jefferson's reverence for the individual over the nation).

He noted how each architect interpreted independence differently and how independence affected and helped define each of them. Much that would subsequently be taken for granted – including those 'truths we hold to be self-evident' – was highly contested at the time and changed in meaning over time (Ellis, 2002). The clear message from these Founding Fathers from over two centuries ago remains relevant today. Independence is not immutable nor can it be defined in one-dimensional terms.

A similar picture emerges when considering an independence movement as articulated by the Scottish National Party. While the party might insist that its aims and objectives remain the same as when it was founded, consistency of language is not the same as consistency of meaning. The short two clause objectives written at the SNP's foundation have been open to interpretation. The 'restoration of national sovereignty' lay at the core and was assumed to mean the creation of a state operating as an actor in a Westphalian world order. But in recent times, the SNP's understanding of the context in which states operate has undergone significant change. The party has long attempted to articulate its view of the kind of society and economy that should accompany independence.

Just as any identity – national or any other kind – is partly defined in contradistinction to an 'Other', so understanding Scottish independence requires an understanding of independence's 'Other', the nature of the UK state. The most common sense in which independence has been imagined has been in contradistinction to the contemporary UK but in one sense it mirrored the UK's self-image. Scotland would become an independent equal member of the Westphalian state system. The reality, of course, is that no two states are equal but national 'sovereignty' was important to Scottish and British nationalists. However, over the last generation, a key difference has emerged in Scottish and British nationalisms, culminating in the Brexit referendum in understandings of sovereignty. While the SNP clings to the language of the old order, notably independence and sovereignty, it has abandoned or at least diluted these ideas to a remarkable extent in its understanding of Scotland's constitutional future.

Pivot to Europe and Devolution

One of the most significant changes that led the SNP on the path to post-sovereignty constitutionalism occurred in the late 1980s. The party had receded into a constitutional foetal position following the defeats of 1979. It opposed devolution and was hostile to the European Community. Sovereignty would reside exclusively in Scotland. Constitutional power would not be shared. Over time, the party accepted, and in time embraced, both devolution and Europe with a mixture of pragmatism and principle. Without abandoning the rhetoric of the Westphalian system of states, the party's thinking edged towards a very different understanding of Scotland's external relations. Its opponents maintained that 'independence in Europe' was oxymoronic but the idea signalled a shift in thinking.

Devolution was different. Support for a devolved Parliament was a stepping stone in the direction of independence and did not involve, until after the new millennium, any long-term intention to share power with London, though the party had always accepted that special institutional arrangements with the rest of the UK would be required. In the 1970s, the SNP had argued that a social union would continue to exist and occasionally referred vaguely to some kind of Council of the British Isles.

The pivot to Europe was not about supporting a United States of Europe on a federal model but was an ill-defined understanding of Europe as a kind of confederation. In essence, the vision of Europe was one closer to De Gaulle's *Europe des Patries* than Jean Monnet's federal union. But SNP thinking continued to evolve, in fits and starts, reflecting its wider context. It followed Labour in its attitude to the Euro. And as with Labour, SNP attitudes towards European integration tended to wax and wane with the rhythms of European politics.

If the late 1980s marked a key juncture in SNP thinking then another significant moment, and the most important in the party's history, was the establishment of the Scottish parliament. The party was transformed from being an amateur activist party into a professional Parliamentary party with the real prospect of gaining governmental power. Every national movement defines itself against what is perceived to be inhospitable rule. Seeking to break free of this rule is the common goal and mobilising force. Such goals are articulated in general terms, allowing scope for different interpretations and building alliances. Detail detracts from vision but gives opponents scope to fill in unhelpful detail. There is little incentive for a party to offer detail when its goal remains a distant prospect. A fringe party, as the SNP was for most of its history, might work up a detailed prospectus that would be duly ignored.

But when the SNP became a credible electoral threat, whether or not its goal of independence seemed imminent, it came under pressure to outline and defend a more detailed account of its goal. Visions which may mobilise support require translation into meaningful, even banal, details if ever to be realised but this creates tensions.

Devolution brought the real prospect of governmental power and the possibility of independence a step closer. But otherwise it did not affect the SNP's understanding of independence. Little work was done on the detail as winning power at Holyrood was the main focus. Support for independence would drag SNP support down. Independence was tenth in a list of ten SNP commitments in the first elections to the Scottish Parliament. In an attempt to assuage criticism, the party replaced 'self government' with 'independence' in its aims in a major overhaul of the party constitution in April 2004. But this was a superficial change. More important, the party abandoned its pre-devolution claim that a majority of Scottish Parliamentary seats would be a mandate for independence. Instead, it proposed a referendum, the more obvious institutional manifestation of popular sovereignty. But what was meant by independence remained vague as the leadership continued to focus on becoming a credible alternative party of government.

The SNP struggled with this in the early days of devolution but intimations of future thinking began to emerge within a few years of devolution. Kites were flown. As the 2007 election approached, two senior members made significant contributions. Kenny MacAskill raised questions which now seem unexceptional but at the time marked a significant challenge to the SNP:

> *Is there a need for a separate DVLA or even Ordnance Survey? ... Does a bureaucracy need to be created in Saltcoats as well as in Swansea? Can we not simply pay our share as well as our respects? Do we need to reinvent the Civil Aviation Authority or other such Institutions as opposed to exercising control from north of the border even if the Institution remains located in the south of it... There are numerous other organisations and Departments where separation is not necessary but the right to direct and instruct is.*
>
> (MacAskill, 2004: 29-30)

In a co-authored book, Mike Russell, suggested that what was needed was a 'new union' (MacLeod and Russell, 2006: 125) advised some constitutional continuity that would be anathema to party hard liners, implying that there would continue to be some kind close relationship with rUK.

In 2007, support for independence was half that for *more powers* and almost 10 % below support for the status quo. The lack of an overall majority ensured that there would be no referendum had the SNP Government really wanted to fulfil its commitment to a referendum. Instead, the Government launched its 'national conversation' with a White Paper, 'Choosing Scotland's Future' three months after the election. The White Paper was a timid document, with 88 references to independence and 92 to devolution, reflecting the limited support for independence. The aim was to keep the issue of Scotland's constitutional status on the agenda without pushing independence hard and focus on presenting the party as competent. The success of this strategy was evident at the 2011 elections when the party won an overall majority but support for independence remained at the same level that it had been four years before. But the success of the strategy of demoting independence resulted in an overall majority making a referendum on independence almost inevitable.

Citizenship

The party had long elected representatives to the House of Commons and councils across Scotland so it needed policy positions on the vast array of matters that would come before these institutions. It had developed a clearer public policy platform than it previously had, and also a better understanding of its key policy objective of independence. The SNP had always leaned to the left. Like others, it was affected by changing contexts and its competitors. Adaptation and a willingness to compromise are key to electoral success and the powers of the Parliament limited ambition, though would also be an excuse for political timidity.

The SNP needed to cut out a distinct profile on everyday public policy, different from Labour but not so different that it could not convert Labour voters. For many years, the SNP had simply mimicked Labour, giving the impression that an independent Scotland would simply be a place governed according to a Labour programme. It struggled to identify a message that differed from Labour other than on the constitution and 'standing up for Scotland' but Labour's drift rightwards opened up opportunities.

In the early days of devolution when public spending was rising on average annually by 5 % in real terms, the parties competed in promising generous welfare policies. All or most supported universalist policies, but over time the SNP would stand alone in support of many of these policies. The SNP had become the party of universalism by default. An independent Scotland would have, by implication, a distinct form of citizenship.

But the most notable aspect of citizenship developed by the SNP was its multiculturalism. The SNP well understood what it was like being in a minority. There was also a less principled basis to support for multiculturalism. The party wanted to distance itself from any association with the kind of nativist nationalism that opposed immigration. It was also keen to show its support for existing minorities including Scotland's Catholic community. The constitution of an independent Scotland envisaged by the SNP was a classic example of multiculturalism with the kinds of checks and balances, rights and obligations found in any modern constitution. It was also another way of distinguishing Scotland from its 'Other'.

Conclusion

The SNP Government's White Paper on independence was a remarkable document and its contents would have been inconceivable a generation before. What was on offer would likely have been criticised as too modest, not 'real' independence by a generation of nationalists and left open much for further development. Independence is not immutable and the probability must be that any future white paper will be different in some, possibly important respects just as the reality of the UK's independence is about to change dramatically. An independent Scotland within the EU might end up have more autonomy than the UK outside in some important respects.

References

Ellis, J. (2002), *Founding Bothers: The Revolutionary Generation*, New York: Vintage Books.

Greene, J. (1978), 'The Meaning of Independence', *Journal of American History* vol.64, pp. 1087-1088.

MacAskill, K. (2004), *Building a Nation: Post Devolution Nationalism in Scotland*, Edinburgh: Luath Press.

MacLeod, D. and Russell, M. (2006), *Grasping the Thistle*, Glendaruel: Argyll Publishing.

Morgan, E. S. (1978), *The Meaning of Independence: John Adams, George Washington and Thomas Jefferson*, New York: W.W. Norton & Co.

The Evolution of the European Dimension: Where Next?

Michael Keating

Europeanism and Nationalism

AT FIRST SIGHT, support for European integration and for national self-determination may appear at opposite ends of the political spectrum, given the purpose of the European project as being to transcend the nation state. It is indeed true that some stateless nationalist movements are opposed to the European Union. Others, however, were early adopters of the European idea. The Basque Nationalist Party was for European unity as far back as the 1930s, when it participated in various European Christian Democratic movements. Catalan nationalism has long seen Europe as representing progress and emancipation, against a backward-looking Spanish state. Partly this is to do with ideological positioning. Nationalist movements close to the political mainstream of Christian Democracy, Social Democracy and Liberalism are more pro-Europe than those on the extreme nationalist right or the anti-capitalist left. The pro-European nationalists, in turn, divide into two streams. Some aspire to become full member states of the European Union, insisting that membership is not incompatible with national sovereignty. Others go further, seeking to transcend the nation-state model altogether in a Europe of the Peoples on post-sovereigntist lines.

The SNP from Euroscepticism to Europeanism

The SNP has always had a pro-European wing but, during the 1960s as the UK moved closer to the European communities, the issue became contested with increasingly hostility. To concerns about the loss of sovereignty, and about Brussels being even more remote than London, were added worries about the impact of European agriculture and fisheries policies, which were especially sensitive in some of the parliamentary seats the party won in the elections of 1974. During the 1975 European referendum the SNP called for withdrawal, although the pro-European minority were allowed to dissent. Jim Sillars and his short-lived breakaway Scottish Labour Party were lonely voices in the late 1970s in making the link between Europe and independence.

This all changed in the mid-1980s, at the same time as the Labour Party swung to Europe. Jacques Delors' vision of a social Europe swung Labour, the trade unions and the growing social democratic tendency within the SNP towards Europe, helped by the increasingly strident Euroscepticism of Margaret Thatcher. Europe was now presented as a framework for independence, especially after Jim Sillars joined the SNP and rode to victory in the Govan by-election of 1988. The SNP's vision, however, was of an intergovernmental Europe of nation-states, rather than the federalist ideals of their Basque, Catalan and Flemish counterparts.

There was a post-sovereigntist tendency, the position of which was articulated by Neil MacCormick, Edinburgh law professor and MEP (1999-2004), but these remained a minority. A continuous presence in the European Parliament from 1975 has meant regular exposure to Europe and the party has cultivated links with like parties through the European Free Alliance and bilateral relationships, while taking pains not to become embroiled in the domestic politics of other countries.

The connection between European integration and national independence appears logical in theory. Europe provides an external support system, securing market access, and lowers the cost of independence. It also allows the party to rebut accusations of being inward-looking and to present itself as more open and internationalist than the main UK parties. Yet over 30 years the theme has not had great resonance with the voters.

Successive surveys have shown almost no connection between support for independence and for the EU. There is a connection between moderate pro-Europeanism and support for devolution, representing the middle points on the Europhile-Eurosceptic and unionist-nationalist spectra. This is evidence of extensive support for the idea of multilevel government and divided authority, perhaps reflecting Scotland's long experience of union and divided authority. Those voters who feel only Scottish and support independence on the other hand, and those who feel only British and are against devolution (this is a small minority) are rather more Eurosceptic than those in the middle. This is perhaps not so surprising, as these are the most attached to the sovereign nation-state.

The party was also conscious about the Euroscepticism of a sector of its voters. It long insisted that it wanted to abolish the Common Fisheries Policy (CFP) and would make this a condition for joining the EU, although it is in practice not possible for new member states to opt of existing policies.

Into Government

The SNP came to government in 2007 as an unashamedly pro-European party. Alex Salmond made a well-publicised trip to Brussels shortly after assuming office, aiming to position Scotland as a European nation and actor. In speeches he struck a pro-European pose that very few UK party leaders felt able to match. The commitment to get rid of the CFP was downplayed, helped by recent reforms in the policy itself, although the matter remained sensitive in some constituencies in the North East.

There was strong support for the social dimension in Europe, which provided another means of distancing Scotland from the UK line, especially after the return of the Conservatives (initially in coalition with the Liberal Democrats) at Westminster. The SNP, like its predecessors in the Labour-Liberal Democrat coalition, also took a notably pro-immigration line, arguing that this is a demographic and economic issue and that Scotland needs more people. This has led it to support free movement of labour within the EU at a time when that was becoming a focus for growing Euroscepticism in much of England and Wales.

The SNP Government has issued a series of statements about Europe. 'Scotland's Agenda for Reform' (2014) supported the overall reform agenda but differed from the UK Government in calling for better regulation rather than deregulation, in view of the importance of regulation to the social dimension. 'The Benefits of Scotland's EU Membership' (2015a) made a strong case for continued involvement in Europe. There is an 'Action Plan for EU Engagement' (2015b), promising a commitment to partnership and reform. All of this contrasts with the cautious and critical line on Europe taken at the same time by the UK Government.

The opportunities for the Scottish Government to take its own line in Europe are, in practice, limited. Scottish ministers can, by invitation, join the UK delegation in the Council of Ministers where devolved matters are concerned but must agree in advance to a common UK line and cannot dissent in the course of negotiations. Scotland's input is provided through the Joint Ministerial Committee (Europe) and through the linked civil service networks. The SNP position has always been that these arrangements are inadequate and that there should be 'direct' Scottish representation. In fact, only member states can participate in the Council as of right and represent themselves (Scottish ministers thus represent the UK).

The demand for direct representation has seemed therefore to boil down to a demand that Scottish ministers should be present in the Council as of right, rather than by invitation, but this would not change the basic position that there is a single UK delegation and a single UK negotiating line. In spite of the potential for EU issues to provide break points between Scotland and the UK, European policy on matters covered by the devolved institutions tends to be low-key and uncontentious except, from time to time, in fisheries and has provided few occasions for advertising a clash of interests.

Representation of 'regions' and local governments in the EU is provided by the Committee of the Regions (CoR), which is consulted by the main institutions in the course of making policy. In practice, it has been a disappointment, as it lacks powers and its membership is too heterogeneous to present a common line on many issues. The Labour-Liberal Democrat coalition did invest a certain amount in the CoR, which First Minister Jack McConnell would attend. It has not been a priority for the SNP and MSPs no longer sit on it, leaving the seats to local government (the same is true in Wales and Northern Ireland).

The SNP in government largely continued its predecessors' efforts in para-diplomacy, working with devolved governments around Europe on matters of common interest. There was some tilt towards areas with national aspirations, comparable to Scotland but no concerted effort to promote a Europe of the Peoples against the nation-states. It is, rather, that the SNP aspires to make Scotland a state itself, alongside the existing members. While there are good relations with parties in the Basque Country, Catalonia and Flanders, the SNP in government has been conscious that, in the event of a successful independence referendum, it would need at least the neutrality, if not the sympathy, of member state governments with their own restive minorities.

Even the Spanish Government has at times recognised that the case of Scotland differs from that of Catalonia in that the UK unwritten constitution allows independence referendums should Westminster do decide. So in times of stress, such as the Scottish referendum or Catalonia's repeated clashes with the Spanish Government and courts, the SNP has kept a certain distance from other nationalist parties. It also takes pains to avoid any association with parties of the extreme right or tainted with violence.

The Independence Referendum

Membership of the EU was a central part of the SNP's independence prospectus in 2014; there was no question of independence outside Europe. This provided some credibility to the independence case, avoiding difficult issues such as customs posts, access to the single European market, global trading relations and a range of policies including the environment. It is notable that few people on either side actually questioned the desirability of EU membership. Rather, the debate hinged on whether a Yes or a No vote would best secure Scotland's position in Europe. The No side chose to suggest that an independent Scotland would be excluded from the EU and so lose out.

After some suggestions that Scotland would automatically remain in the EU, the SNP position was that membership could be secured either through the accession process (Article 49 of the treaty) or by treaty change (Article 48), with the latter being its preferred option. The No side adopted a variety of tactics. They suggested that Scotland's application might be vetoed by another member state (by which they clearly meant Spain). They argued that, even if Scotland were allowed to join the EU, it would have to spend a period outside and then re-join. They said that Scotland would have to join the Euro and the Schengen area of passport-free travel.

Commission President José Manuel Barroso even said in a television interview that it would be 'difficult if not impossible' for Scotland to be in the EU, although without giving any treaty-based argument. The strategy here was to increase the level of uncertainty, in the knowledge that this was the best way to sway cautious voters. The Yes side argued that, given the rise of Euroscepticism in England, and proposals within the Conservative Party for a referendum on Europe, the only way to guarantee Scotland's place in Europe was to vote for independence.

The SNP, however, took a rather cautious line on Europe during the independence referendum campaign. Its independence White Paper was strongly pro-EU but it proposed to retain the UK opt-outs, including on the Euro, the Schengen area and Justice and Home Affairs. This amounted to a very 'British' form of EU membership, rather than a strategy to use Europe to break out of the British mould, as Ireland has or to join with enthusiasm in new measures of integration.

With the UK already semi-detached from the EU and political opinion opposed to further union, following the UK line could have meant that Scotland would be dragged in the British Eurosceptic wake. Given the commitment of the SNP to a stronger social dimension in Europe and to the Common Foreign and Security Policy, this might have caused tensions. The commitment to Europe was tempered by the recognition that in future Scottish election campaigns would see 'some arguing for a looser form of partnership' (Scottish Government, 2013: 216). The most important passage, however, stated that 'We will not be taken out of the EU against our wishes as may turn out to be the case if we are not independent' (Scottish Government, 2013: 217).

The SNP's enthusiasm for Europe was thus balance both by the knowledge that a section of its own supporters are Eurosceptic and by the need to remain aligned with the UK across key areas, notably its preference for retaining the

Pound sterling after independence. There was an acknowledgement that small states can succeed in Europe were they focus their efforts, set priorities and forge alliances. There was less recognition that small states may do best where they place themselves at the heart of Europe, rather than adopting the aloof role of a large state like the UK, or seeking to pick and choose which policies to adopt.

In the event, the European issue did not prove decisive in the referendum outcome. The EU issue was not particularly salient during the campaign but did contribute to the uncertainty. While this may have favoured the No side, the Yes side also sought to take advantage over the uncertainty about the UK's membership.

Our pre- and post-referendum surveys show a small fall in the numbers of people who thought that nobody knew whether Scotland could have become part of the EU although they still amounted to 51 % of respondents. The numbers believing that Scotland would have been able to retain EU membership on the same terms as the UK went up slightly, from 27 % to 29 % while the numbers doubting it went down from 45 % to 41 %.

This suggests that considerable uncertainty remained at the end of the campaign. The EU issue may have been marginal and was certainly less significant than the issue of the currency but the research does show that, if the EU had made it clear that Scotland would be a member, Yes and No would have been level. The argument of the Yes side that the risk lay in staying in the UK and been dragged out of Europe seemed to gain little traction. The hypothesis that the UK might withdraw from the EU depressed both the Yes and No vote by similar amounts and increased the Don't Knows, suggesting that the argument was too complex and speculative.

A month before the vote, an ICM poll tempered the picture of Scots as Europhiles, showing that while 59 % of Yes voters wanted Scotland to apply to join the EU, 27 % disagreed. There was a more longstanding scepticism about claims that Scotland would have to join the Euro, with three quarters of voters rejecting this claim already in 2013 (What Scotland Thinks/Panelbase). Overall, the evidence is that the EU issue did contribute to risk and uncertainty, to playing to the advantage of the No side and vindicating their strategy of emphasising doubt, but that its role was less than that of other factors, notably the currency (Liñeira *et al.*, 2017).

The EU Referendum

The SNP came out of the 2015 UK election enormously strengthened, winning all but three of the Scottish seats at Westminster. Conservative Prime Minister emerged, ironically, weakened by winning a surprise (albeit small) majority. This obliged him to carry out his promise to renegotiate the UK's terms of EU membership and hold an in-out referendum. The SNP opposed the whole idea of a European referendum as unnecessary and its position during the negotiations was to restate its support for the EU, including the free movement of workers, a major target of Cameron and the UK Conservatives. SNP support for welfare also put them at odds with the Conservative desire to curb welfare benefits for migrant workers.

The Conservative commitment to simplification and deregulation also pitched them against the SNP line, although this commitment itself was dropped in advance of the negotiation in order to keep Labour voters on side in the future EU referendum. When Cameron completed his negotiations with the Brussels agreement of February 2016, the SNP came out in favour of a Remain vote in the referendum, while arguing that the agreement itself was unnecessary since they would have voted to remain in any event.

During the referendum campaign, SNP leaders including Nicola Sturgeon played a prominent role, not only in Scotland but as part of a wider Remain coalition. It was suggested that the result that would have suited the SNP best would be a Remain vote in Scotland but a Leave majority across the UK as a whole, since this could provide the pretext for another referendum. This was far from the case. SNP strategy for 30 years had been predicated on both Scotland and the rest of the UK being within the EU, so avoiding difficult issues about market access and borders. The circumstance of the UK leaving the EU was not a propitious one for the independence case, since with Scotland in and the UK out of Europe, there would be a hard border between the two. It was not at all clear that, given the choice of remaining in the UK or the European single market, voters would choose the latter. The SNP was very conscious of this and the risks of a second independence referendum so soon after the last. A Remain vote, on the other hand, would allow them to postpone the independence issue to a better time.

The result of the Brexit referendum was even more dramatic than most observers had anticipated. While England and Wales voted leave by 53 %, Scotland voted 62 % for Remain. Indeed Remain were ahead in Scotland in all local government areas and nearly all social categories, although those with minimal education did support Leave. On the other hand, around a third of SNP voters had opted for Leave, representing persistent Eurosceptic tendency, and these could not be counted on to support independence next time if this were explicitly tied to Europe. It is likely that these were disproportionately represented among the working class voters who at elections had deserted Labour for the SNP. This provided a severe test of the SNP's European commitment.

In the aftermath of the Brexit vote, the party (and so the Scottish Government) faced a series of difficult choices. They could join a pan-UK effort to block Brexit but, while there was a nominal Remain majority at Westminster, nearly all Conservative and most Labour MPs (eying the results in their own constituencies) were minded to vote to leave the EU – if such a vote were even permitted by a government committed to give notice to leave using the royal prerogative. A second option was to join a coalition for a soft Brexit, remaining within the single market.

Initially, the Scottish Government laid down a series of strict conditions, including not only the single market with free movement of labour, but the social dimension of Europe and continued influence in Europe, amounting to little short of membership. If this were to fail, they would fall back on a differentiated solution for Scotland, initially expressed as Scotland remaining in the single market even if the rest of the UK left, a proposal that presented so many practical obstacles that it is better understood as a negotiating gambit. Failing that, it reserved the right to call another independence referendum.

The obstacles to such a referendum are many. The SNP argued, with some justice, that Scotland was in danger of being dragged out of the EU against its will. In its programme for the Scottish elections of 2016 it had mentioned precisely this as one of the material changes in conditions that would legitimate a second independence referendum. After all, the unionist side in the 2014 referendum had warned that the only way for Scotland to remain in the EU was to vote No, and this had been disproved. On the other hand, the SNP Government did recognise that such a referendum would require Westminster's consent. Winning a referendum would require citizens effectively to choose the European Union over the UK union, a dilemma they had avoided in 2014. Moreover, some major difficulties that had pulled down support for independence in 2014 were now even more acute. The fall in the oil price had worsened the finances of a putatively independent Scotland. Sharing the Pound would be impossible with Scotland in the EU and the UK outside; the provision secured by David Cameron to recognise the EU as a multi-currency union fell automatically with the Leave vote.

To add to its difficulties, a Leave element emerged within the SNP itself. During the referendum campaign, Jim Sillars, who had played a key role in converting the SNP to Europe, called for a Leave vote, citing the EU's neo-liberal and pro-austerity turn and the hostile attitude of EU leaders during the 2014 independence referendum. After the Brexit referendum, Alex Neil, SNP MSP and former minister, who had been Sillars' right-hand man in the Scottish Labour Party initiative in the 1970s, revealed that he, too, had voted Leave. Now he presented Brexit as an opportunity for the Scottish powers to repatriate powers back from Europe and take Scottish self-government a step further without the need for another referendum.

How European is Scotland under the SNP?

Survey evidence shows that Scots are not committed Europhiles and, on many measures, rather resemble the English. On the other hand, the old 'permissive consensus' on Europe, whereby people allow their leaders to build European institutions and policies, has persisted longer in Scotland than any other part of the UK except London. The issue of migration, too, has been handled by the parties in a largely consensual manner, and framed as an advantage rather than a threat. This has drawn the sting of Euroscepticism and created a space for an openly pro-European nationalist party.

On the other hand, the SNP lacks the pro-European passion found, for example, in the Basque Nationalist Party (as opposed to the more radical nationalists) or the Catalan self-determination movement, for whom Europe is the essential counterpoint to Spain. Europe was initially a useful space for the deployment of Nationalist strategy but was gradually incorporated into the party's ideological portfolio, but it is not a defining feature of the party. It featured more prominently in the rhetoric of Alex Salmond than in that of his successor Nicola Sturgeon.

Given the political balance in Scotland, the SNP has not had to invest a lot of political capital to create a pro-European environment and this shows in the failure to link independence more tightly to the parallel process of Europeanisation. The travails of the EU itself have not helped. Had the Euro been more successful, the SNP would have had a politically convincing alternative to its policy of keeping the Pound sterling after independence. Had Europe forged a common policy in response to the migration crisis, Scotland's efforts to present a more humane face and accept its humanitarian obligations would have found a stronger support framework.

The SNP's European strategy faced serious challenges in the face of a faltering European project and the momentum in England and Wales to leave the EU. In the referendum of 2016, while England and Wales voted narrowly to leave, Scotland voted decisively to remain. At the Scottish election of 2016, the SNP had flagged this as a circumstance that would justify another independence referendum. Yet matters are not as simple. Analysis of the vote showed that voters still did not make the connection between independence and Europe, with around a third of SNP voters choosing Leave. Faced with the choice of the UK or the European Union, it was not clear that Scots would choose Europe.

References

Liñeira, R., Henderson, A. and Delaney, L. (2017), 'Public Opinion and the Issues', in Keating, Keating (ed.), *Debating Scotland: Issues of Independence and Union in the 2014 Referendum,* Oxford: Oxford University Press.

Scottish Government (2013), *Scotland's Future,* Edinburgh: Scottish Government.

Scottish Government (2014) *Scotland's Agenda for Reform,* Edinburgh: Scottish Government.

Scottish Government (2015a), *The Benefits of Scotland's EU Membership* Edinburgh: Scottish Government.

Scottish Government (2015b), *Action Plan for EU Engagement,* Edinburgh: Scottish Government.

The State of Social Democracy and the Scottish Nationalists

Ben Jackson

DURING THE 1980s and 1990s, the SNP sought to position itself as a social democratic party. This was a significant and consequential strategic shift from a party that had previously styled itself as rejecting conventional left-right polarities in favour of the defence of Scottish interests. The rise of a more discernibly left-wing SNP leadership – personified above all by Alex Salmond and, more briefly, Jim Sillars – led the party to make a more determined effort to market itself as a left-wing alternative to the Labour Party. The most developed ideological rationale for this shift was offered by Stephen Maxwell in a pamphlet issued by the '79 Group, the SNP faction formed precisely to push the party in a more socialist direction and in which both Salmond and Sillars played important roles.

In 'The Case for Left-wing Nationalism' (1981), Maxwell argued that a Scottish cultural nationalism would be a dead end for the advocates of Scottish independence, since Scotland's history of a non-coercive political union with England and subsequent integration into British imperialism and capitalism meant that Scottish cultural identity was 'too weak to serve as the basis for modern political nationalism'. Instead, Maxwell proposed that the SNP should focus on Scotland's growing economic and social problems, which offered 'an opportunity to create a new, aggressive sense of political nationality to challenge the traditional defensiveness which ties the working class to Labour.

The SNP's target should be to establish itself as the radical Scottish alternative to the Labour Party' (Maxwell, 2013 [1981], p. 99). The '79 Group's version of this novel direction for the SNP focused overwhelmingly on the Scottish working class as the key political constituency for this new Scottish nationalism and used the more traditional (and thus politically authoritative) language of socialism rather than social democracy. Neither of these approaches were to be straightforwardly applied by the SNP in subsequent years, but the underlying point – that the SNP's aim should be to link Scottish nationalism to economic and social grievances and hence to win over Labour supporters – became fundamental to the SNP's political identity and ideology as the Thatcher years and the Labour Party's shift to the centre created new opportunities for such a case to gain a hearing.

Yet it would also be fair to say that there has always been some ambiguity about the relationship between independence and left-wing socio-economic objectives in this political case for Scottish nationalism. Maxwell's pamphlet offered an illuminating example of this: on one reading, his case was simply that a pre-existing nationalist commitment to Scottish independence can only be made electorally viable if it is cloaked in a suitably social democratic garb. On another interpretation, it is the commitment to a more egalitarian Scotland that comes first, with independence seen as the most plausible route to bringing about such social change. In one formulation, social democracy is an instrumental means to independence; in the other, it is independence that is the means to achieve social democracy. This might seem like an abstract theoretical point, but in this chapter I want to suggest that this ambiguity in the relationship between the SNP and social democracy helps us to understand the character of its governing record after 2007.

What is Social Democracy?

Before I turn to the SNP's time in office, however, it is first necessary to define more precisely what is meant by 'social democracy'. In its broadest sense, social democracy is the use of gradual and democratic, rather than revolutionary, means to create a more egalitarian society, and it is accordingly the ideology associated with the family of socialist and Labour parties that emerged in the course of the 20th century as competitors for political office in the advanced industrialised democracies.

Yet it is also an ideology that changed a great deal across that period. From an initial belief in the necessity of the collective ownership of capital to ensure a just society, social democrats shifted to the argument that corporatist bargaining, an activist state, public spending, and progressive taxation could in fact significantly reduce class inequality and pluralise democratic decision-making. This classical mid-20th century version of social democracy, which, as the exponents of Scottish independence often note, reached its fullest fruition in Scandinavia, relied on strong trade unions, the welfare state, and Keynesian economic management to maintain full employment.

This model of social democracy was itself subject to considerable pressure and rethinking after the 1970s, as social democrats sought to recast their ideas in the face of a resurgent economic liberalism and changes in the class structures and economies of the industrialised nations. Somewhat schematically, it can be said that social democrats became more accepting of the deregulated markets that had become a predominant feature of capitalism in the late 20th century but sought to protect and enhance the role of the state in equalising access to those markets and in reducing the economic and social inequalities that resulted from this deregulation. The 1997-2010 Labour Government in Britain provided a clear example of this pattern, and exercised a considerable influence (both positive and negative) over the leaders and strategists of the SNP.

If we return to the SNP's version of social democracy, it is apparent that a parallel political journey to the one undertaken by Blair and Brown characterised the SNP during the long road to taking power at Holyrood – and indeed has characterised their period in government since 2007. Stephen Maxwell's 1981 vision of a left-wing nationalism was premised on the assumption that the Scottish private sector was an economic failure and therefore required extensive state support and control in order to revive manufacturing industry and reduce foreign (non-Scottish) ownership of the nation's economic assets. Maxwell proposed a revival of Scotland's economy via a programme of radical social democracy, including 'a major extension of the public sector in the form of improved public services, increased public finance for industry conditional on the adoption of co-operative ownership and other forms of industrial democracy, and public control of Scotland's financial institutions' (Maxwell, 2013 [1981], p. 94).

By 2008, when Alex Salmond gave a speech about Scotland's economic prospects as Scottish First Minister at Harvard University, he lauded Scotland as an example of the kind of 'small, open and dynamic economy' that could prosper in the new era of global capitalism. Salmond set out the importance of state support for economic growth by investment in 'human capital', inducing greater inward investment from places such as the United States, and learning from the competitive strategies undertaken by other small European economies, notably Ireland (with its low corporate taxation) but also Iceland and Norway (Salmond, 2008).

The form of social democracy that had been placed at the heart of the SNP's political identity by 2007 was therefore one that sought to yoke together economic efficiency and social justice by stressing the importance of public investment in raising economic performance and the need for lower levels of poverty and inequality to build a productive and cohesive society. It was also a form of social democracy that emphasised the crucial role of wealth-creation by the private sector. As Nicola Sturgeon put it: 'I am a social democrat, I believe in pursuing greater equality... but... you can't do that unless you have a strong economy, unless you have got a vibrant business base earning the wealth that makes that possible' (quoted in Torrance, 2015, p. 202).

Social Democracy and the SNP in Government

But while there are important substantive parallels between the policies of the SNP and New Labour in this period, the SNP has also achieved some success in defining its social democracy as more authentic than Labour's under Blair and Brown. In part this achievement is rhetorical – in the more welcoming environment of Scottish public debate, Alex Salmond, Nicola Sturgeon and their colleagues have been more forthright in their public statements of their social democratic governing philosophy, whereas Tony Blair and Gordon Brown, hemmed in (they believed) by the febrile London-based media, were always considerably more reserved in their articulation of their egalitarian objectives (their successors have obviously, and in different ways, felt less constrained in this respect).

But it is also in part a result of decisions taken by the SNP in office, which has introduced certain key symbolic policies designed to differentiate their Scottish Government from previous Labour Governments at Westminster and Holyrood. Foremost among these has been the abolition of tuition fees for Scottish students attending Scottish universities, but other measures such as the abolition of prescription charges and the introduction of a Scandinavian-style 'baby box' for new-borns have played a similar role. The SNP in government has also sought to preserve Labour policies scrapped in England by the Conservatives after 2010 such as the Educational Maintenance Allowance and to oppose new Conservative measures such as the bedroom tax or the raising of the income threshold for paying the higher 40p tax rate.

How social democratic is the policy record of the SNP in government? This is a harder question to answer than partisans on both sides of this argument will admit. On the one hand, the distinctively social democratic understanding of the welfare state is one that emphasises universal, high quality services and benefits, as well as in certain cases earnings-related social insurance, on the grounds that the welfare state serves as a mechanism of cross-class social integration and that support for the welfare state can only be maintained politically if both working and middle class voters feel that they gain something from it (Esping-Andersen, 1990; Korpi and Palme, 1998). This suggests that some criticisms of the SNP are misguided insofar as they argue that only policies targeted specifically at the worst-off can be classified as egalitarian or social democratic.

On the other hand, the reason that quintessentially social democratic welfare states such as Sweden produce such impressive outcomes in terms of reducing poverty and income inequality is that they form part of a broader, relatively coherent social model rather than being made up of ad hoc individual decisions about government spending. In particular, fundamental to the success of Swedish social democracy has been the combination of a universal welfare state with strong corporatist wage bargaining (which has, among other things, narrowed the range of income inequality in Sweden before redistribution); economic and social policies designed to maintain high levels of employment; and relatively high levels of direct and indirect taxation.

Nothing like this level of systematic thinking appears to have characterised the SNP's policy record. Of course, one reason for this (as the SNP's supporters would be quick to observe) is that the powers of the Scottish Parliament are not equivalent to the powers exercised by independent nation states and the SNP is therefore constrained in the policies it can introduce. However, even taking into account the inability of the Scottish Government to influence key domains of economic and social policy, it is nonetheless the case that considerable scope for political action exists within the devolution framework, scope that has been significantly enhanced with the sweep of new powers granted to the Scottish Parliament in recent years.

But there seems to have been as yet little debate within the SNP about how these new powers might be used as part of a wide-ranging, coherent effort to advance egalitarian social democratic objectives. Indeed, the high profile policy of free university tuition has been introduced while at the same time cuts have been made to student grants for disadvantaged students and to further education, thus undermining the impact such a policy might have had in reducing debt burdens on the worst-off and widening educational access (Hunter Blackburn, 2014).

Here we return to my earlier observation about the relationship between independence and social democracy in the SNP's ideology. Defenders of the SNP's record in government would argue that it will only be through the achievement of independence that public policy in Scotland can be decisively realigned in a social democratic direction. But there is nonetheless in the meantime plenty of scope for a more integrated social democratic approach in a devolved Scotland. The intellectual founder of social democracy, Eduard Bernstein, faced an analogous debate in the socialist movement in the late nineteenth century about whether socialists should look to make gradual improvements within the capitalist system as it existed or hold out for a larger-scale, qualitative transformation in society after the revolution. Bernstein's view was that evolutionary and piecemeal reform would be a more legitimate and effective way of proceeding. As a result, he famously said, 'what is usually termed 'the final goal of socialism'... is nothing to me, the movement is everything' (Bernstein, 1898: 168–9).

A similar argument might be made in the context of contemporary Scottish nationalism about the status of 'independence' as a final goal – if a commitment to social democracy is simply an instrumental means of mobilising political support for the larger end of Scottish independence, then there will be little impetus to make concrete policy changes within the framework of the powers currently enjoyed by the Scottish Parliament. However, if the ultimate goal is a more social democratic Scotland, and demands for greater Scottish democratic autonomy are the means by which this goal will be realised, then it will seem more urgent to begin building that social democratic Scotland right away. The SNP's record in government so far suggests that it is in fact the former rather than the latter view which predominates within the party.

References

Bernstein, E. (1898), 'The Theory of Collapse and Colonial Policy', in H. Tudor and J. M. Tudor (eds.), *Marxism and Social Democracy: The Revisionist Debate 1896–1998*, Cambridge: Cambridge University Press.

Esping-Andersen, G. (1990), *The Three Worlds of Welfare Capitalism*, Princeton: Princeton University Press.

Hunter Blackburn, L. (2014), 'The Fairest of Them All? The Support for Scottish Students in Full-Time Higher Education in 2014-15', working paper, Centre for Research in Education Inclusion and Diversity, University of Edinburgh.

Korpi, W. and Palme, J. (1998), 'The Paradox of Redistribution and Strategies of Equality: Welfare State Institutions, Inequality, and Poverty in the Western Countries', *American Sociological Review*, 63 (1998), pp. 661-87.

Maxwell, S. (2013) [1981], 'The Case for Left-Wing Nationalism', in S. Maxwell, *The Case for Left-Wing Nationalism and Other Essays*, Edinburgh: Luath Press.

Salmond, A. (2008), 'Free to Prosper: Creating the Celtic Lion Economy', speech at Harvard University, 31 March 2008, at http://www.gov.scot/News/Speeches/Speeches/First-Minister/harvard-university.

Torrance, D. (2015) *Nicola Sturgeon: A Political Life*, Edinburgh: Birlinn.

Making the Scotland of the Future: A Time for Boldness and Honesty

Joyce McMillan

IT IS A Thursday morning, and on the radio, BBC Radio Four 'Today' presenter Jim Naughtie is talking to the leaders of Scotland's two main unionist parties about how to combat the dominance of the SNP. The Conservatives' Ruth Davidson is perched on the Cairngorms, while Labour's Kezia Dugdale has failed to provide herself with any such memorable setting. But all three are happy to discuss the problems that arise when, as Naughtie puts it, an over-bearing government always 'gets its own way'.

No one uses the phrase 'one party state' – which is just as well, since the phrase clearly bears no relation to the multi-party rammy that is Scottish electoral politics. Yet still, it remains true that the sight of a dominant SNP Government often (but not always) 'getting its own way' at Holyrood – often with little effective opposition, thanks to the weakened state of the three main UK parties in Scotland – has aroused some parts of the British establishment to levels of concern about the state of our democracy that they have rarely if ever expressed before – not in the years when an increasingly moribund Labour Party totally dominated municipal and parliamentary politics across large swathes of Scotland, or during the long periods since the 1970s when Westminster governments elected on quite a modest minority of votes have acquired enough power, through the First Past the Post system, to impose hugely unpopular policies, ranging from the poll tax of the 1980s to the recent privatisation of the Royal Mail.

For democracy campaigners, of course, the irony is that there certainly are democratic issues that need to be addressed, eighteen years on from the election of the first devolved Scottish Parliament in 1999. At the beginning of 2016, the Convention of Scottish Local Authorities called for a new Constitutional Convention, to address issues around the failing structure of Scottish local government, and its clearly broken relationship – both financial and constitutional – with central government. Beyond these urgent questions around local government and its role, there is also a whole range of pressing issues around the operation of the Scottish Parliament, and the level of democratic accountability it is able to provide.

It is increasingly clear, for example, that the Parliament's committees are far weaker than was envisaged back in 1999, that their success in improving the quality of legislation is very limited, that they too often vote along party lines, and that the Parliament has failed to develop the cadre of powerful long-term committee chairs that has emerged at Westminster in recent years. The link of accountability between Parliament, people and Scottish Government has been further weakened by the extension of the Scottish Parliamentary term from four to five years, a move made by both Parliaments, almost without debate, in order to fit in with Westminster's new five year fixed term; the absence of a second chamber makes these weaknesses the more urgent.

Although no elected politician would dare say it, there is, in my view, mounting evidence that the Scottish Parliament is perhaps slightly too small, at 129 members, to provide both a full complement of government ministers across the range of powers it now has, and the kind of rigorous independent supervision of government policy that is necessary in a healthy democracy.

It is not an interest in these vital practical details of a working democracy, though, that seems to motivate the people who complain most about 'SNP dominance' of Scottish politics. Instead, the implication is rather that something has gone wrong in Scotland; that the people – or around half of them – have given up on 'normal' politics and parties, have thrown reason to the winds, and are now so irrationally wedded to the SNP that nothing can shift them from their unreasonable prejudice against all things UK.

And of course, there are elements among those supporting the SNP of whom that might be true. As a general account of the reasons for the recent rise of the SNP, though, this narrative is both immensely patronising and dangerously incomplete; and it is difficult to avoid the conclusion that it owes some of its popularity to the fact that it lets a whole generation of unionist politicians off the hook, when it comes to recognising, analysing and dealing with the reasons why around a million Scots, over three decades, have abandoned the UK parties, and switched allegiance to the SNP.

The Scots' Unionist Crisis of Confidence

For in the end, it is not that difficult to identify the points at which those three parties began to lose touch with mainstream Scottish opinion, and to haemorrhage support. The Scottish Tories blew it in the 1980s and early 1990s, when they failed to distance themselves from the worst excesses of Thatcherite neoliberalism. Labour blew it in the mid-2000s, when Scots voters began to register the depth of Tony Blair's flirtation with the same ideology, and the reckless foreign policy into which it was leading him. And the Liberal Democrats finally blew it in 2010, when they entered into a full-blown coalition with a Tory party that enjoyed very little support in Scotland. If those three parties were fully to acknowledge that they have lost support for perfectly legible and rational reasons, though, they would be faced with a series of difficult political tasks and decisions which they seem strangely reluctant to undertake.

It's the reluctance of those three parties to face up to these fundamental questions about their future direction, and the future of Scotland, that has left them so enfeebled in their appeal to Scottish voters. It is their poor political performance, more than anything else, which has left the independence parties – the SNP and the Scottish Greens – looking like the ones who still understand the potential of politics to catch voters' imaginations. Although the first instinct of the British establishment is always to talk as if the SNP must have achieved its current dominance by nefarious means, in truth the party is guilty of nothing but of winning elections – winning them, too, under a system that sets a much higher bar for that achievement than the Westminster one.

The unionist parties in Scotland will begin to fight back effectively on the day when they finally acknowledge that simple truth, and get to work on offering an inspiring future vision of their own. In the meantime, there is a corresponding need for the Scottish Government to be pressed towards a clarity of vision which is not simply mired in caution-based, pragmatic decision-making.

For example, when the Finance Secretary, Derek Mackay, announced Scotland's first annual budget since the Scottish Government received new tax powers under the post-referendum Smith Commission measures, it soon became evident that the main public debate would be over a few small variations in income tax that could result from that change. The Conservatives want lower taxes wherever possible, in order to make Scotland 'more competitive' — although recent economic history suggests that there are better competitions to join than the one to attract the kind of high earner who resents paying a few extra quid to support the country's basic physical and social infrastructure. xxx

Labour, by contrast, wants a 50p tax rate on the top one % of earners, and a one penny rate increase all round, mainly to help boost Scotland's struggling local services. But the SNP, it soon became apparent, could only dip a timid toe into the stormy waters of differential tax rates between Scotland and England by raising the level at which the higher tax rate kicks in only in line with inflation, rather than giving those earning more than £43,000 a year the small extra boost signalled by the Westminster government.

The Conservatives and *The Telegraph*, of course, called this 'clobbering hard-working families', and attacking the living standards of 'middle-class Scots'. Yet in fact, people earning at this level are in or close to the top 10 % of earners, far above the 'middle' of society. And the additional sum they were being asked to pay is about £6.50 a week, roughly the price of a single large glass of wine in a pub; I would be interested to see substantial evidence, after the fact, that any of them will miss the money at all.

It is, in other words, something of a pity that this exaggerated yowling and breast-beating about very minor tax-rises for the better off has become such an ideological fixation in UK political debate; for if the case for some higher taxation is almost unanswerable, after eight years of austerity, there are many other aspects of the SNP's current programme that need the sharpest scrutiny, and betray the party's apparently almost infinite capacity for ideological inconsistency and confusion.

This is a party for, example, that says it wants to reduce tax breaks for the well-off; but is apparently determined to cut Air Passenger Duty, a measure which is not only environmentally questionable, but also disproportionately benefits Scotland's tiny minority of affluent frequent flyers. This is a party which talks the talk on workers' rights, and a decent living wage; but also cultivates friendly relations with companies like Amazon – with the shocking revelation in December 2016 that some of its Dunfermline warehouse workers were living in tents at the site, rather than attempting the impossible feat of working long hours, and commuting to and from their homes in Perth on the minimal wages they earn (Carter, 2016). This is a party which talks about empowering Scottish communities, but has presided over a further drastic decline in the financial autonomy and status of Scottish local government; this year, Scotland's capital is apparently so cash-strapped that it cannot even afford any significant Christmas lights outside the city centre. Numerous other such contradictions are explored further in this book: the product of the SNP's 'Big Tent' political coalition.

Above all, this is a party that constantly trumpets its green credentials; but which seems incapable of developing a policy on transport, and particularly on new roads and bridge construction, which bears any relation to its low-carbon commitments. And its relationship with the North Sea oil industry suffers from the same ambiguity. As Bank of England governor Mark Carney pointed out this week, carbon reduction targets dictate that most hydrocarbons now still underground will have to remain there. Yet in December 2016 in the Scottish Parliament, climate change champion and First Minister Nicola Sturgeon was to be heard heartily agreeing with one of her own MSPs that there are still massive untapped reserves of oil in the North Sea, and that the industry must be supported in exploiting them.

The Dominance of the SNP

The Scottish Government is not alone, of course, in sending out such mixed signals; they are the depressing common currency of western politics. There are two reasons, though, why this failure of clarity on the part of the Scottish Government is particularly frustrating.

The first concerns its very strong political position. Even with the worst possible political luck, the SNP has another four years of government ahead of it at Holyrood, and is likely to be the largest party there until at least 2026. Under these circumstances, it has no excuse for the kind of short-termism that plagues democratic government across the West.

It could afford to take long views, to set up think tanks and research institutes to develop serious strategic policies, and to demand consistency in pursuing those strategic goals across all departments of government – yet still it does not do so, in ways that could cost us all dearly over time.

Secondly, this failure is frustrating because Scotland's potential, in these years of transition away from a carbon-based economy, is so obvious, and so vast. The truth is that if we seize the global opportunities that are emerging now, and use all our expertise to invest in an industrial and energy infrastructure that serves that new low-carbon economy, this country could be looking at an immensely exciting and prosperous future, generating sustainable jobs and an ever-higher quality of life for a growing population who have chosen to make their lives here.

Yet instead, we waste time bickering over the remnants of a neoliberal low tax ideology that has had its day, and over the prolonging of the most recent wave of hydrocarbon exploitation to come into Scottish communities for a few decades, and then disappear again, leaving them for dead. To say that this is not the way of the future is to state the obvious.

The greatest gift Nicola Sturgeon and her government could give Scotland now would be to lift their eyes for a moment from the detail of day-to-day policy, and start drawing a clearer picture of the future to which they want to take us; and of how the paths they are pursuing now will lead us, in time, from here to there.

The above compromises are the realities of modern politics we are continually told by so-called 'realists'. But realism hasn't got us very far these last few decades, as it has continually compromised with the powerful forces of corporate capitalism and neoliberalism.

Instead, the SNP a decade into office, with the potential of a second decade in office, need to mark out a route map to a future Scotland. That entails doing the detailed work and aiding new institutions – think tanks, research institutes and independent expert bodies. All of these would contribute towards the common goal of charting a course to that destination – one which lays out choices, obstacles, resistance and trade-offs – and which treats people as adults, citizens and active partners in this project. Such a politics is tantalisingly within our grasp.

References

Carter, G. (2016), 'Amazon workers roughing it in tents to hold down seasonal jobs at Fife warehouse', *Daily Record*, 12 December, accessed at: www.dailyrecord.co.uk/news/scottish-news/amazon-workers-roughing-tents-hold-9428522

Time to Party? Politics and Energy Inside and Outside the SNP

Simon Barrow

WHAT DOES IT mean to belong to a political party in Scotland in 2017? In particular, what does it mean to belong to the SNP – a party governing in a devolved administration, wanting to strengthen that institution's power, and simultaneously seeking its transformation into a sovereign parliament in a newly independent nation? These questions are interlocked but distinct. The first is important for understanding the overall political, social and cultural terrain of Scotland. The second revolves specifically around the choice that continues to haunt and entice the country in terms of whether is can or should be a sustainable, independent nation.

Until recently it has been a commonplace of the dominant commentariat that the political party as a form is in crisis in modern, western democracies. Ingrid van Biezen, Peter Mair and Thomas Poguntke charted this phenomenon in their analysis of party membership across contemporary Europe (Biezen *et al.*, 2012). There has been a slight upswing in party membership Britain since the low of 2013 (Nardelli, 2014). The House of Common library noted that the Conservatives, Labour and the Liberal Democrats have increased their size to around 1.6 % of the electorate in 2016, compared to a historic low of 0.8 % in 2013 (Keen and Apostolova, 2017). In the same time, Labour Party membership almost doubled from 0.6 % in 2013 to 1.1 % in 2016.

Membership of 'other' parties has also changed markedly in recent years. In July 2016 SNP membership was around 120,000, compared to 25,000 in December 2013. In July 2016 Green Party (England and Wales) membership was around 55,000, compared to 13,800 in December 2013. UKIP's membership increased from 32,000 in December 2013 to around 47,000 in May 2015, though it then fell to 39,000 by July 2016.

This factors shaping this broader context for examining what has happened to the SNP and what that means for people inside, outside and on its edges are twofold. On the one hand, mainstream politics has increasingly looked like an epiphenomenon of corporate and economic power, nationally and transnationally. The perceived ability of a party to change things significantly looks to have diminished correspondingly. On the other hand, the more fluid (sometimes fleeting) affiliations spawned by consumerism, digital culture and a sense of deep domestic disempowerment within an irreversibly complex world have led to more people feeling that 'joining' no longer matters in the way it once might have done.

The Party Isn't Over: The Case of Corbyn's Labour and the SNP

The two big recent exceptions to the overall pattern of decline in membership have been British Labour and the SNP. These two are, however, remarkably different cases. Labour's surge in members, fuelled by the unexpected advent of Jeremy Corbyn, the activism of the Momentum group and bitter competition between opposing wings of the party, has produced a situation where the staple party of British social democracy appears strong on paper (and at public meetings) but still struggles to convince that it can both win an election and govern. Moreover, the impact of the Labour membership surge has been negligible in Scotland, where decades of presumption and the dogged determination of the Scottish portion of the party to pursue strategies which show little sign of succeeding has produced a crisis its leaders still seem not fully to comprehend.

The SNP, on the other hand, has grown its membership beyond all expectations on the back of the 2014 independence referendum – a defeat for the party's central and guiding ambition which has, in key respects, only fuelled the appetite for its message, following what was nevertheless an upsurge in support for a self-governing Scotland on 45 % of the vote. This popular growth has come at a time when the SNP has been returned to a governing role at Holyrood for a third successive term, has a leader in Nicola Sturgeon who retains incredibly high popularity ratings, and has virtually swept the board in the Westminster elections in 2015.

Nothing succeeds like success. That has been one reason for people joining the SNP in drives, for sure. Another is that those who backed independence but who may have been in other parties or none decided in the wake of 2014 (and perhaps Sturgeon's arrival as leader and First Minister) that the SNP's strength was crucial to any chance of securing the dream of full self-government. A third reason has been the undeniably effective organisation and communication that has delivered the party a positive image and solid achievements, despite the fact that most of the mainstream media in Scotland and beyond remains sceptical or critical of it.

The Personal, the Political and the Four Dimensions of SNP Success

The key question, of course, is whether or how the SNP can maintain anything like the 125,000 level of membership it now claims through to a possible second independence referendum in the next few years or the Holyrood elections in 2021. The 2017 council elections are another (perhaps underestimated) marker in this evolving story. In the meantime, four factors will clearly play a major role in how things pan forward. First, the ability of the SNP to persuade people that it can govern well and consensually overall. Second, its ability to tap into a huge membership practically and financially. Thirdly, continued electoral success (particularly in the wake of the comparative 2017 General Election setback). And fourth, how it handles the massive challenges of Brexit and what the party leadership wisely wish to call #ScotRef rather than #indyref2.

It is not immediately evident that those four challenges all point in the same direction. Elements of them also inevitably look different from inside, outside and on the edge of the SNP as a political culture, a political machine and a political movement – since it is seeking and needing to be all three at once in order to achieve its historic aim. I find myself in a curious position of being, in a certain way, an insider, an outsider and an 'edger' simultaneously. That is, I am invested differently in the three 'rings of influence' which the party needs to hold together in strategic terms. First, I took the decision to join the party in November 2014, though not to seek office or power in any way. Second, I run a small think tank, Ekklesia, which is not affiliated to any party and firmly wishes to maintain its own critical independence. Third, I actively work with friends and allies across the progressive political spectrum, all of whom have to rub up against the SNP as a dominant part of the terrain they operate on.

Notwithstanding an understanding of the social, economic and cultural roots of current political tensions within Scotland, one of the most curious aspects of the scene for someone who moved to Edinburgh from England in June 2010 is that if I got all my SNP, Labour, Green and non-aligned radical friends in one room, I am pretty sure that they would agree instinctively on the great majority of policy trajectories. Yet this overlap in outlook is not reflected in administrative and electoral politics, especially because of the deep hostility between Labour and the SNP, who now compete for the same vote on the same territory with similar (disputed) claims to being left-of-centre parties for much of the time.

My own wish is to see the greatest possible collaboration between progressive forces against the alarming and overlapping rise of a hegemonic Conservative Party in England, reductive and reactionary populism, and the deep poison being released by Brexit, the alt right, Trumpism, racism and anti-migrant sentiment. From where I stand and engage, the project of an independent, forward-looking Scotland depends at least in part on the ability to galvanise political aspirations which cannot by definition be confined to any one political party, but which need to find expression in systems of power which inextricably depend on parties, no matter what their form or fortune (Barrow & Small, 2016). That, along with the need for forms of democratic renewal which threaten the settled interests of the protagonists they have to get onside, is one of the defining paradoxes of contemporary political debate.

On the other hand, in order to do this, it is necessary to capture affiliation and consent across an increasing diversity of civil society. This is an extremely difficult trick to pull off, as Labour's ruptures and the wider challenge to social democratic parties across Europe illustrates. It has long been argued that the single imperative of independence, along with the shift towards power in urban areas and the ability to present yourself as both a governing party and an insurgent force, is what has given the SNP the ability to succeed in building a 'broad church' in a way that other centre-left parties have failed to do. But the tensions represented by 'broad church' polarities are equally a challenge moving forward. How do you please enough of the people enough of the time in order to win self-government for a small nation, while maintaining a meaningful political direction outwith the simple question of who governs?

Part of the answer, of course, is that the SNP cannot hope to win independence and govern alone (with the 2011-16 period of majority government likely to be the exception). To succeed in its principle aim it needs an effective alliance between those inside and outside the party. In particular it needs to bring together those for whom independence will remain a defining issue, alongside a winning proportion of those for whom it remains a matter of uncertainty. The need to hold together and appeal to such a wide cross-section of Scottish society, together with the success of an inherited top-down culture, is what makes for understandable caution within the SNP. This is buttressed by an appeal to party loyalty which can readily squash the boldness of vision and policy outlook which is also required.

Different Locations for Viewing and Engaging the SNP

It is fascinating to view these tensions at work from within the SNP, to comment on them from the outside, and to work with them in relation to the processes of progressive allying – which is what I find myself doing, much of the time. Since 2014 I have been somewhat involved in a local branch, attended five party conferences, promoted several policy changes, got elected to the national council (the twice yearly SNP policy discussion body) and formed friendships and relationships across the party. Equally, I find myself invested in the post-carbon and more radically redistributive politics embodied by the Scottish Greens and others, and part of various social and policy initiatives which are pressing the SNP hard from boundary positions. It is also the case that my option for (and way of) belonging to this particular party could have led me to make a different choice.

For example, with a background of trade union activity and an interest in rethinking democratic socialism, the traditions of the Labour Party and the wider left have in the past created a strong sense of affinity for me. As someone reshaped by environmental and feminist concerns, the imperative of a post-carbon economy and a critique of masculinist politics, the Greens also have an obvious appeal. It is a fact that I have used my vote to support particular candidates from several different parties over the years. That makes me, in principle, a rather different kind of 'floating voter'. I am the kind of committed political operator that, at one level, a party like the SNP can only attract by being sufficiently coherent and effective to be able to succeed. Yet I am also looking for a party form sufficiently open, progressive and flexible to be able to attract and retain support in the face of the inevitable compromises that a winning party has to make.

Value-driven political activists in search of a place to locate themselves are also highly unrepresentative. Most people in Scotland or in any other modern democracy do not spend much or most of their time thinking about politics or being politically active. Indeed, as is the case with an impending second independence referendum, they may find the colonising of news and social life by political concerns grating or tiring after a time, rather than energising and inspiring. What all this illustrates is that the process of political formation in and around parties is frighteningly complex, especially near the tipping points of political change and power. So what, in temporary conclusion, are some of the signs and symbols of the way the SNP has been handling these tensions and opportunities within the terrain the party seeks both to operate on and to shape? Three indicators stand out for me. The variability and significance of branch life, the tensions between institution and movement, and the balance between background support and practical engagement.

More Than A Branch Office

Branches remain important organising units for any political party. At their best they maintain political interest and debate, create social bonds, recruit other supporters, work as springboards for campaigning, provide a point of contact with elected politicians, act as a political barometer within the party, operate the infrastructure needed to win elections. Those are all important tasks. Dysfunctional or low functioning local units can impede or inhibit some or all of these requirements.

In those terms, I belong to a good branch in Leith. The story within the SNP is not necessarily so positive in other areas. Maintaining local infrastructure and relating it to the wider structure of a party is difficult but necessary work. A sense of momentum and direction is vital. Overall, the SNP looks and feels to be doing that. Coming in from the outside you can rapidly sense the balance of dynamism, stasis or atrophy of a political party from its local expression. Would you actually encourage a friend you wanted to persuade to come along? Or is the culture inward looking and resistant to change? These are the questions that have to be negotiated practically for the SNP as part of a social force for progressive independence, not just a party seeking to use electoral power responsibly and effectively.

Party Conference and Leadership

If local party life provides one kind of barometer for both the politics and operational temperature of a party, the annual and spring national conference provides a different view. These events are showpiece gatherings of 'the faithful' which offer an opportunity for some elements of policy-making or policy advertising, inner networking, and external visibility and promotion. In the case of the SNP they are extremely well managed affairs which have an increasingly 'corporate' dimension, but which still feel more open and accessible than the security-centred, image-driven beasts of the UK-wide party conferences – as I know all-too-well from my journalistic forays down south.

That said, the attempt from the centre to restrain and channel the more radical instincts coming up from the grassroots of the SNP (on fracking and land reform, for example) is noticeable. On the one hand, delegates to an SNP conference can seem less overtly ideological in received (left-right/green-carbon) terms than, say, those attending Labour, Conservative and Green events. On the other hand, the dominant left-of-centre ethos and assumptions are strong, at least at a rhetorical level. Those coming in to the SNP from what can broadly described as the left of the political spectrum will feel pretty comfortable most of the time, at least in the Central Belt and urban areas. How that translates into governing imperatives is more complex, as this book illustrates, but the formation of a small ginger groups (like SNP Socialists) and the flexing of muscles from the branches are factors to watch (Gray, 2017).

One defining (or, at least, clarifying) moment for the party as a nationally gathered assembly was perhaps the minor disturbance caused by the IdeaSpace 2016 SNP conference fringe festival. This was organised independently of the party and ran concurrently with the conference and its 'official fringe' in an adjoining venue in Glasgow. At first, the reaction from the SNP centrally was not positive. Fringe meetings not run by the party itself were seen as competitive and potentially disruptive. They also acted as a focus for intense criticism of the formal fringe programme, where corporate interests loomed large (Ineos and Gatwick, for example) and charities and pressure groups were being charged a small fortune to host events or stalls. To many onlookers this reaction seemed suspiciously like a centralist routinisation of political charisma, and the rejection of movements for change in and around the party. At first MPs and MSPs appeared to have been urged only to speak at 'official' fringe events. But that was clearly not going to work, either practically or at a PR level. In the end, there was peaceful co-existence and a fruitful degree of cross-fertilisation.

This temporary clash may seem a tiny issue in the overall political framework of Scotland in 2016. But it sent out important signals about the tensions within Scotland's governing party. The first response of the SNP as a party machine was one of control and suspicion. Then there was a growing recognition (no doubt reluctant in some parts of the party) that such instincts can easily feed that which they are intended to resist. By contrast, many grassroots delegates saw IdeaSpace as an opportunity to open up debate about everything from progressive alliances to green politics in and around the SNP. Movements and parties are to some extent in inevitable tension, but the two forms can also overlap and ally in the creation of a process of change and mobilisation (in this case for progressive independence). Perhaps it is stretching too much to theorise all of that from the IdeaSpace controversy, but the signs of what may or may not happen in the future could be detected in that brief moment.

Equally, the 2016 SNP Depute Leader campaign and ballot was an important barometer on where the SNP is as a party and where it might be going. The poll contained warnings about the problems of success in abundance. First, the actual turnout was remarkably low – at 34 % – after what had been a well-publicised roadshow of exemplary, comradely debates (on the surface, at least). It reminded me of an acute observation Iain Macwhirter made about the 2014 referendum: words to the effect that the Yes campaign was like a festival, but the question about festivals is always, at the end of the day, 'how many have actually bought tickets?'

In the case of the referendum, the answer from the Yes side was 'not enough to win'. In the case of the 2016 SNP Depute Leader contest, the answer was not enough to mobilise even half of the party's vast incoming membership to spend a minute or two voting online. That is a clear sign of how membership of political parties has become increasingly symbolic rather than functional in recent years, returning to my opening portrait of the ambivalent situation for parties in both the UK and Scottish landscapes.

The result of the Depute Leader poll also contains interesting clues about political culture. In the end, with four good candidates and a proportional voting system, the election did not even go to a second round, such was the scale of victory of the 'establishment candidate', Angus Robertson. It was clear that the party at the highest level wanted Robertson to win. He has been a highly effective operator, part of the old guard and a 'safe pair of hands'. Equally, at the time, he had three existing and demanding jobs (constituency MP, leader of the SNP Westminster group, and member of the House of Commons Security Committee) and was unlikely to take the symbolic role of Depute Leader in new or galvanising directions. Yet that is what the other candidates (left-leaning Tommy Sheppard MP, Euro-expert Alyn Smith MEP, and socialist councillor Chris McEleny) were all arguing strongly for in different but coinciding ways. Robertson also echoed some of this rhetoric, but from a grassroots perspective little seems to have happened with the Depute role since his election. That may change following his defeat in the 2017 UK General Election.

The good news for the SNP in the depute contest is that it displayed a depth of talent, a sense of unity, a good quality of debate, and the ability to pick a winner. The difficult news was that all candidates were male (in contrast to the undoubted progress the party has made on gender equality), the status quo looked unassailable, voter participation was low (reflecting real difficulties in mobilising the larger membership) , and fresh currents of thought and action struggled to make a wider impact. That, together with the reversal of an upward electoral tendency in 2017, may reflect a rather cautionary picture of the way things look within the party at the moment.

Can the overall tension between effective central organisation and restless grassroots aspiration can be brought together with the kind of synergy required for the SNP to be seen as a truly progressive force? Can it continue to succeed not just as a governing party, but as a key part of a movement aiming to persuade a majority in Scotland to opt for independence? All this remains to be seen. It is a huge task. In the meantime, it is clear that the known challenges the SNP faces are significant and strategic. They will require a different set of practices from the ones which got the party to where it currently is. The SNP has, in the last decade, undertaken a journey from being an outsider to an insider within the political system it is both operating in and trying to replace. More functionally, it is a party that exemplifies an outsider ethos, with insider practice at the top. How the party navigates the balance between mechanism and movement will be one of the key determinants of its future prospects. It has to learn and adapt the skills of statecraft, while not losing the political edge which questions the status quo and cosy arrangements of too much of modern Scotland. In any event, the jury remains intriguingly out on the SNP's future – while the terrain of Scottish politics moves forward in exciting, ground-breaking and frequently unpredictable ways.

References

Barrow, S. and Small, M. (eds.) (2016), *Scotland 2021*, Edinburgh: Ekklesia/ Bella Caledonia.

Biezen, I., Mair, P. and Poguntkle, T. (2012), 'Going, going... gone? The Decline of Party Membership in Contemporary Europe', *European Journal of Political Research*, 51: 24-56.

Gray, M. (2017), 'SNP conference shake up as branches set new agenda with real debates', *CommonSpace*, 27 January, accessed at: www.commonspace.scot/articles/10197/ exclusive-snp-conference-shake-branches-set-new-agenda-real-debates

Keen, R. and Apostolova, V. (2017), *Membership of UK Political Parties*, London: House of Commons Library Briefing Paper, No. SN05125.

Nardelli, A. (2014), 'Party membership in the UK' is tiny, *The Guardian*, 29 September, accessed at: www.theguardian.com/news/datablog/2014/sep/29/ labour-conservatvies-uk-party-membership-is-tiny

Facts and Figures Over Ten Years: An Overview

Andrew Conway

Introduction

IF YOU SEE a circular shadow on the ground but cannot see the object itself, what can you conclude? Most would assume it's a sphere but it might be a cone, a cylinder, a rugby ball or one of a great many other shapes aligned in just the right way. Without seeing the object itself, the only way to learn more from its shadow is to illuminate the object from different directions.

I would urge you to think of the following graphs in this way. Each one is a shadow of Scottish society – incomplete and conflated. If you form an impression from a particular one, hold it with a certain element of doubt until after you've inspected the others and perhaps considered information from elsewhere too. Also guard against actively looking for a particular meaning based on whatever convictions you hold. Let the data speak to you, even – and especially – if it tells you something you do not like.

To find out more about each graph you can visit the web link mentioned on each page or consult the list of references at the end.

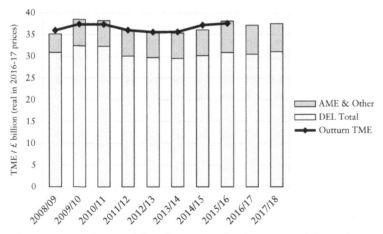

Figure 1 Level 1 and level 2 SPICe budget spreadsheet from parliament.scot HM Treasury GDP deflators from gov.uk

Figure 1 – Scotland's Budget for financial years (April-March). The bars show the total planned spending in budgets proposed by the Scottish Government and passed by vote in the Scottish Parliament. DEL stands for Departmental Expenditure Limit totals that are set in spending reviews spanning several years for costs that can be planned in advance, such as building a hospital or paying teachers. AME stands for Annual Managed Expenditure that cannot be planned in advance, such as for unemployment benefit following the 2008 financial crisis. DEL plus AME equals TME or Total Managed Expenditure which is the legal limit on what the Scottish Government can spend.

The Outturn TME shown by the line is what was actually spent in each year. Note that the budget was significantly exceeded in 2008-09 by £0.8 billion (during the recession), and in 2014-15 by £1.1 billion (for NHS and teachers' pensions shortfall) requiring amendments to the Budget Act in the Scottish Parliament and an extra transfer of funds from the UK government.

www.activecitizen.scot/p/budget.html

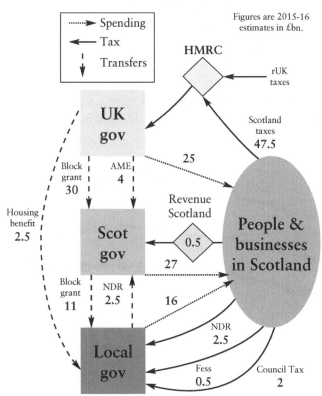

Figure 2 Level 1 and level 2 SPICe budget spreadsheet from parliament.scot General Expenditure and Revenue Scotland from gov.scot Quarterly National Accounts from gov.scotLocal Government Finance Statistics from gov.scot

Figure 2 – Fiscal flows. This diagram shows movements of money for 2015-16 through Scotland's three levels of government and its economy. Spending represented by dotted arrows is controlled by the level of government shown, with just over 60 % of spending controlled either by the Scottish or Local Government (councils). Although HMRC collects the majority of Scotland's taxes, following the Scotland 2016 Act (Smith Commission), 40 % of Scotland's total tax revenue is devolved or assigned to the Scottish Government's budget.

The block grant from the UK to the Scottish Government is determined by the Barnett formula whereas the one received by the councils, which is called the General Revenue Grant, is decided by the Scottish Government in its budget. NDR stands for non-domestic rates which are collected by councils and redistributed back to them by the Scottish Government inside the block grant.

If you add up total public expenditure into Scotland it comes to £68 billion and the tax revenues total to £53 billion. The £15 billion difference is the fiscal budget deficit. This figure does not appear in the Scottish Government's budget, which must be balanced by law, but is instead handled at the UK level where the overall deficit is matched by borrowing.

www.activecitizen.scot/p/fiscal-flows.html

Figure 3 – Income inequality. This graph shows measures of household income adjusted for inflation to be in 2014-15 prices. In 2014-15, the median income was £24,900, which means that half of households had more than this

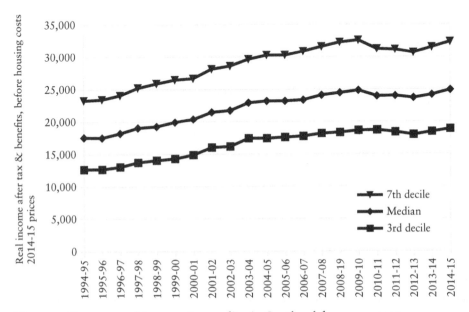

Figure 3 Poverty and income inequality in Scotland from gov.scot

income, and half had less. In a similar way we can talk of deciles so that 30 % of households have an income below the third decile and 70 % below the seventh decile. The data is drawn from annual surveys and adjusted according to the make up of individual houses (called equivalisation).

Everyone's incomes rose in real terms until 2009-10. Compared to 1994-95 values, the third decile increased by 47 %, the median by 41 % and the seventh decile by 40 %. Although these percentages appear to suggest that inequality lessened over this time, it is also true that inequality increased in absolute terms with the gap between the seventh decile and third decile widening from £10,600 in 1994-95 to £14,000 in 2009-10. Income inequality has decreased slightly since the pre-recession peak with the third decile rising by one % and the seventh decile falling by one %.

Statistics on wealth inequality are much more uncertain because there are few wealth taxes, but it is clear that wealth inequality is much larger than income inequality.

www.activecitizen.scot/p/inequality.html

Figure 4 – Scotland's population. Scotland's population had been in long-term decline until the mid 2000s when it began to rise. This was mainly due to immigration from newly admitted EU states. Since 2000, the population has grown at an annual rate of about 0.4 %, which is below the UK's growth rate of 0.7 %.

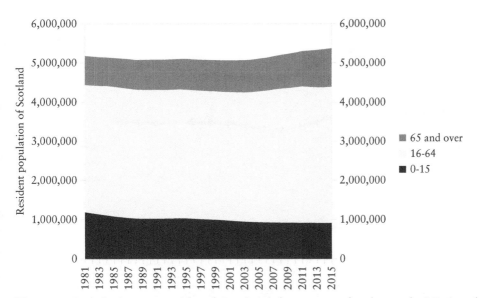

Figure 4 Population pyramids of Scotland from nrscotland.gov.uk (National Records of Scotland)

Those aged 65 and over have increased in number by 33 % between 1981 and 2015. This is not simply due to increased life expectancy but is instead mainly explained by the so-called post-war baby boomers entering this age group. The decline in numbers of children has slowed in recent years and 2015 saw its first increase in many decades. This is possibly related to the recent increase in immigration. Overall though, the number of under-16s has decreased by 23 % between 1981 and 2015.

It seems likely that future years will continue to see a rising elderly population and that will place a greater demand on the NHS and social care (Figure 10). Also a rise in the number of children will need to be factored into planning for schools (Figure 5).

www.activecitizen.scot/p/population.html

Figure 5 – School statistics. The number of pupils in Scotland divided by the number of teachers is shown for the three types of schools funded by the public sector.

In general, it is considered desirable for the pupil to teacher ratio to be as low as possible. This ratio decreased to reach a minimum in 2007 and 2008 for all types of schools, but it has since increased. For primary schools this is in part caused by a rise in number of pupils since 2010, though this is not true for secondary schools, which have continued their long term decline in pupil numbers. This will of course change in the next few years as the rise in primary

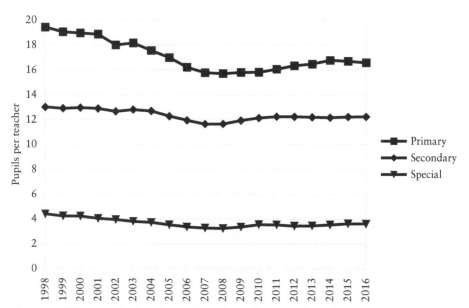

Figure 5 Historical school, pupil and teacher numbers from scot.gov

pupil numbers feeds through to secondaries. The change in number of children in Scotland can be seen in Figure 4.

Between 1998 and 2016, the number of primary schools has decreased from 2291 to 2013 (11 %), secondary schools from 392 to 359 (10 %) and special schools from 185 to 141 (24 %).

www.activecitizen.scot/p/schools.html

Figure 6 – Energy. Energy consumption has been steadily decreasing due to increased efficiencies of central heating boilers and car engines, and to a lesser extent improvements in electrical devices such as TVs and light bulbs. The reduction in 2009 was caused by the recession. The amount is 'gross' because it includes losses such as those in transmitting electricity on power lines. One TWh is a billion kWh (kilowatt-hours).

Renewable energy has increased from 4 % of the total in 2005 to 15 % in 2014. This is in part because the total has decreased, but also due to the rapid growth of onshore wind farms which have tripled renewable energy's contribution between 2005 and 2014.

By final use, 53 % of energy consumption involves burning fuels directly for heating, 25 % is burned for transport, and 22 % is used as electricity.

www.activecitizen.scot/p/energy.html

Figure 7 – Employment rate. The employment rate is the percentage of people aged from 16 to 64 who are in work.

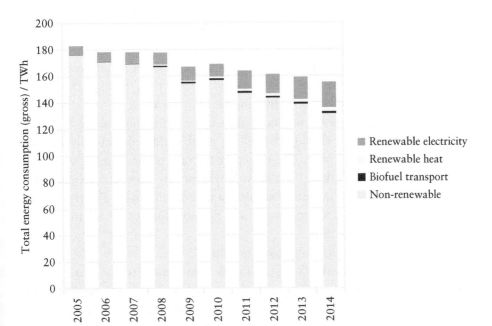

Figure 6 Energy in Scotland from scot.gov

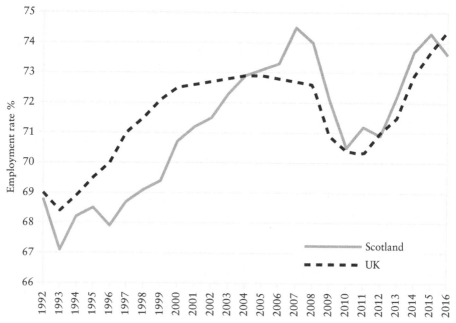

Figure 7 Employment series LF42 (Scotland) and LF24 (uk) from ons.gov.uk

Scotland's employment rate rose from 67 % in 1993 to peak at 74.5 % in 2007. It fell after the 2008 financial crisis to a low of 70.5 % in 2012 and recovered to near its pre-crisis peak in 2015. The slight fall in 2016 is likely due to the impact of the oil price crash of 2014-15 on companies serving the oil and gas industry (see Figure 8).

The uk shows a similar pattern but until 2004 its employment rate was as 1 to 2 percentage points higher than Scotland's. Since then, Scotland's employment rate has mostly remained slightly higher than the uk's.

Each person aged 16-64 is placed into three categories in the statistics: employed (has a job), unemployed (seeking a job) and economically inactive (no job and not seeking one). The employment rate is the number employed divided by the sum of all three. The unemployment rate however is the number unemployed divided by the sum of employed and unemployed. For this reason the two rates do not add to 100 % and it is possible for both rates to increase (or decrease) at the same time.

www.activecitizen.scot/p/employment.html

Figure 8 – GDP growth. Gross Domestic Production (GDP) is a measure of activity in an economy. Here 'real' means that adjustments are made for inflation. The growth rate is calculated as the percentage change between one quarter (e.g. January-March is Q1) and the same quarter in the previous year.

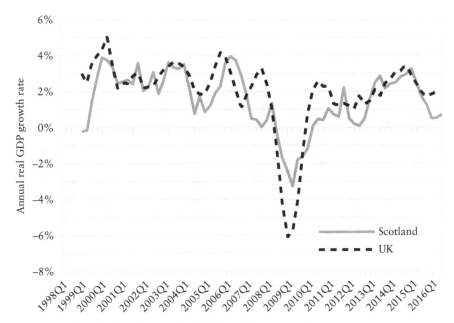

Figure 8 Scotland's Quarterly National Accounts from gov.scot GDP CVM series ABMI from ons.org.uk

Scotland's main GDP figure published by the Scottish Government excludes economic activity in the North Sea; in contrast, it is included in the UK's GDP. (This is a consequence of the EU's ESA10 national accounts system.) If a geographic share of North Sea GDP was included in Scotland's GDP, then the growth rate shown in this graph would be more variable and would have been negative since 2015Q1. By this measure therefore, Scotland has been in recession since early 2015.

Scotland's GDP growth (without the North Sea) has been broadly similar to that of the UK for most of the time shown on the graph. The shallower recession experienced by Scotland in 2008-09 is probably due to the oil price remaining high in 2008 which benefited onshore companies serving the North Sea. However the oil price crashed in 2009, which explains why Scotland's recovery after the recession was weaker than the UK's.

Growth recovered for Scotland and the UK to around two % in 2013-14, which is a poor recessional recovery by historical standards. Scotland's growth has suffered since the 2014-15 oil price crash and there is evidence in the national accounts that this is due to the slowdown in the North Sea industry affecting onshore service industries.

www.activecitizen.scot/p/gdp.html

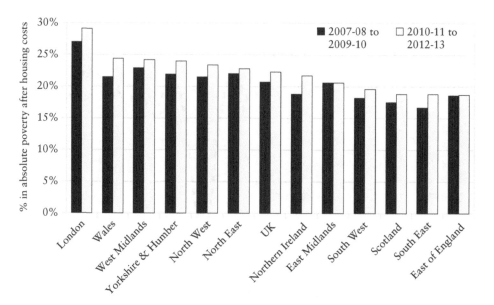

Figure 9 Living standards, poverty and inequality in the uk from ifs.org.uk
Households below average income (HBAI) from gov.uk

Figure 9 – Absolute poverty. A household is classed as being in absolute poverty
if its income with taxes deducted and benefits added is below 60 % of the median
for a given recent reference year (2010-11 being such a year). All houses in the
first income decile (see Figure 3 for an explanation of deciles and the median)
and most of those in the second will be in absolute poverty. Housing costs are
deducted from household income in this dataset.

London has by far the highest rates of absolute poverty due to its very high
housing costs. Scotland's poverty rate is amongst the lowest in the UK, comparable to that of the South East and East of England regions.

Scotland, in common with all parts of the UK, saw a few percentage points
rise in absolute poverty across the 2008-09 recession.

www.activecitizen.scot/p/poverty.html

Figure 10 – Main expenditure areas. This graph shows inflation-adjusted
totals for public spending by all levels of Government. Social Protection is by far
the largest area of spending and so uses a separate scale shown on the right axis.
The largest part of Social Protection is spending on state pensions with most
of the rest being on various benefits. Much of this is by the UK Government,
though councils spend significant amounts on social care.

Health, Education and Training, Public Order and Safety, and Transport are
devolved and so budgeted for by either the Scottish Government or councils.
All show a clear increasing trend until 2006-07, which was only continued by

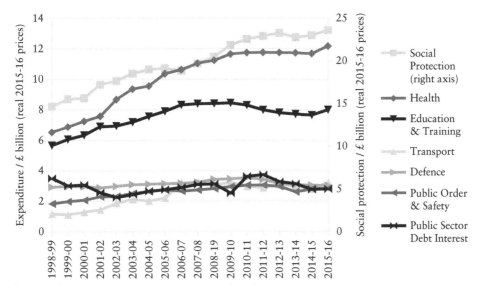

Figure 10 General Expenditure and Revenue Scotland from gov.scot

health thereafter. Education spending in particular dropped from a high of £8.4 billion in 2007-08 to a low of £7.6 billion in 2014-15 though it increased to £8.0 billion in 2015-16.

Public Sector Debt Interest is a population share (currently 8.3 %) of the UK's total and is the only area to show a real terms fall in the last 20 years, dropping by 20 %. Even though public debt increased significantly since 2008, this was offset by a larger proportionate fall in interest rates (gilt yields).

www.activecitizen.scot/p/expenditure.html

The 2017 UK General Election: All Change for Scottish Politics and the SNP?

Simon Barrow and Gerry Hassan

THE RESULT IN Scotland of the general election on 8 June 2017 came a few weeks after the SNP formally marked ten years of ascendancy, following the formation of a minority administration at Holyrood in May 2007. Inevitably, it produced a welter of justification, speculation and assertion, as well as, from some, denial or doom-laden soothsaying.

There is obviously a relationship between these two events – the record of the SNP in office in Holyrood, the long-term effects of incumbency, and a whole set of political targets for opposition parties to attack and use. There was also the manifestation of the 'British effect' of Westminster elections which has historically worked in such contests against the SNP, focusing on Tories and Labour, but which was put on hold by the tsunami of the SNP 56, but which is clearly now back in play, much to nationalist discomfort. All of this has to be taken into account along with noting the distinctions between the SNP's ten-year rule at Holyrood becoming such an important factor in what were Westminster elections. Clearly, Scottish politics have changed dramatically, with implications for the SNP, independence, and the other political parties (Hassan 2017).

A Changing Electoral Landscape

In recent history, the SNP has both pitched and performed differently in Westminster, Scottish Parliament and local authority elections. But as the question of independence has come to dominate the domestic political landscape since 2011, so the distinct issues which should characterise the powers of these three different areas of jurisdiction have been elided. The Scottish Conservatives chose to fight both the May local elections and the June Westminster election almost entirely on this terrain – while the SNP found itself heavily scrutinised for its performance in Government in both polls, even though this was not within the remit or power of the candidates contesting these two sets of elections.

The result was a degree of uncertainty within the SNP campaign in June 2017. Having secured an increase in local representation (though not as great as some had predicted, and constrained in outcome by the proportional system that means few councils end up in anyone's overall control), the party set out to win votes on the basis of three overlapping claims. A vote for the SNP, it declared, would prevent the Tories gaining a blank check for a hard Brexit, create solid opposition to Westminster austerity, and give Scotland a strong voice in a parliament that still holds the purse strings and maintains overall power. The mandate for calling another independence referendum, Nicola Sturgeon stressed, came from the Holyrood elections and a majority in the Scottish Parliament. But the campaign was lacklustre and there is little evidence that these messages got across. 'Stronger for Scotland' is getting as tired as it is vague.

Given the exceptional and monumental success of the SNP in the 2015 UK general election, a fall from 56 out of 59 available Scottish seats was inevitable, all but the most hardened optimists recognised. Polling and punditry suggested that holding between 40 and 50 constituencies was possible. In the end the SNP achieved 35 seats: a loss of 21 (a loss of 37.5% of their 2015 tally). The outcome left the SNP with more seats than the other three parties (Conservatives on 13, Labour on 7 and Liberal Democrats on 4). Critically, the SNP won 36.9% of the vote — winning the popular vote and finishing 219,620 votes ahead of the second place Tories on 28.6% (compared to a 1,020,309 gap in 2015), with Labour finishing in third place for the first time in a post-war Westminster election. Yet, the party lost 476,867 votes and 13.1% of their support.

The Reversal of a Winning Trajectory

Predictably, some claimed 35 out of 59 seats as a great victory, pointing out that the SNP had won its seventh election in a row, and nine out ten over the past ten years, despite being a minority or majority administration at Holyrood during that period. This was the second best ever SNP Westminster result in its history, they declared. Others pointed, more realistically, to recognition of a steep decline from 'peak SNP' in 2015, and the intense vulnerability of the party in Westminster seats across Scotland.

For the truth is that nine of the SNP's 35 seats now have majorities under 1,000. Indeed, four have majorities under 100 – Fife North East (2), Perth and North Perthshire (21), Glasgow South West (60) and Glasgow East (75). A total of seventeen – almost half the party's seats – have majorities under 2,500. Not one of the six SNP Glasgow seats looks impregnable. The only formidable SNP majorities appear to be Dundee West and East, Kilmarnock and Loudoun and Ross, Skye and Lochaber – the only seats with majorities over 5,000. In not one of the SNP's seats held did the party win over half the vote, making it highly vulnerable to continued tactical voting (Hassan, 2017).

Alastair Meeks has noted that the new political environment leaves the SNP particularly vulnerable across huge swathes of the country:

> For now, the SNP still hold a majority of the seats in Scotland. Beneath the surface the position looks considerably worse than that suggests. 22 of the SNP's remaining 35 seats are held by a margin of 7% or lower. In almost all of those seats, the SNP faces a clear unionist challenger. The omens for the SNP in the next general election look grim. Even if their vote share stays the same, they might lose a lot of seats simply from increased tactical voting by better informed electorates in each constituency. The safest SNP seat in Scotland would fall to a swing of under 8%. They suffered swings against them of more than twice that in some constituencies last week. The volatility that worked so well for them in 2015 has left them looking potentially vulnerable everywhere.
>
> (Meeks, 2017)

Just as all the major parties that contested the 2017 UK general election can be said both to have won and to have lost, so the competing narratives around the significant fall in the SNP Westminster vote continue. Tactical voting against independence and for Brexit (some 30 % of previous SNP voters backed exiting the EU, despite the party's strongly pro-Europe position) was one factor.

So was the momentum that gave the Tories their best result in Scotland since 1983 (seats won) and 1979 (votes gained). Likewise, Labour took left wing and pro-independence votes from the SNP on the basis of Jeremy Corbyn's unexpectedly strong showing and more radical manifesto, rather than the disarray of Scottish Labour.

Virtually all the opinion polling also shows that some 75 % of those who voted Yes in 2014 supported the SNP. But this is significantly down from 89 % in 2015. Among the factors that merit close examination in relation to this decline are the criticism the SNP's Holyrood record received, the impact of a late youth surge to Corbyn, and a resurgence of the difficulty the party has persuading people to vote for them when the UK election can still only be won by the Tories or Labour.

Facing Multiple Political Challenges

While pro-SNP media tended to underestimate the severe damage inflicted on the party in 2017 (which included the dramatic loss of the 'big beasts' Alex Salmond and Angus Robertson), sceptics have not always acknowledged two other factors. First, as we have noted, the SNP has historically performed less well at Westminster compared to Holyrood — although this distinction may be eroding. Second, and more importantly, the 2017 UK general election constitutes a degree of 'rebalancing' in spite of a deeply non-proportional First Past the Post voting system. It was always unfeasible and unfair that the SNP should hold over 90 % of seats on 42+ % of the popular vote. Even 35 seats overstates their proportional vote size by around seven seats.

Nevertheless, the 2017 election leaves the SNP with a major challenge of renewal and refocusing. Neither an unqualified victory nor a total disaster, it is undeniably a reversal and a watershed. At every level the party's ultimate vision (if it can be described as such) shows signs of needing serious revamping.

The SNP's dominance of the independence movement is healthy for neither. A fresh, clear and convincing offer, and a significant upswing in public support, will be needed before a new referendum can come back onto the agenda. At Holyrood, the party has often lacked radicalism and vision. Its political identity continues to be up for grabs – perhaps the essential transition to a post-carbon economy with a more northern European identity creates an opportunity here to break with being 'the party of oil'.

If the SNP still wants to replace Labour as the key social democratic standard-bearer in Scotland, it has much work to do in further mapping out its political vision. Policy-making also needs to draw far more on popular expression and expertise that is sympathetic, but independent, creative and forthright (Daley 2017). A genuine post-austerity economics must be articulated and demonstrated much more clearly. The large SNP membership needs to be strengthened and mobilised in ways that have evidently not been the case in recent elections. The myth of a 'strong party machine' should be seriously questioned and re-forged through significant internal reform. Far greater clarity is needed about the boundary and coincidence between a party and a movement.

An Absence of Strategic Vision

These are not so much conclusions from an analysis of the June 2017 election as they are an invitation on that basis, and in terms of the other analyses highlighted in this book, to reconsider what the SNP is now, and where it is heading. Standing still is not an option. Nicola Sturgeon has in many respects provided that 'strong and stable leadership' for her party that Theresa May promised the UK but was unable to deliver. However, stability and strength is not enough for a forward-moving and successful party. Organisation, imagination, a convincing offer, the capacity to review and change, are, and will remain, essential. Above all, there is a need for strategic vision.

The SNP now has to re-examine its record, style of performance and intention as a party of government. It also needs to take the opportunity to review its relationship to the larger independence movement and its place in the wider, changing identity of Scottish politics. It has become clear that the last ten years, and the thwarted hope of the 2014 referendum, have disguised the absence of a long term SNP political strategy.

This has also begun to hinder the cause of independence, which was significantly more popular than the party in the 2017 elections. The cumulative effect of no post-mortem on the 2014 defeat and no revision of a detailed independence offer is taking its toll. The party leadership has not confronted hard truths in the peak period of 2014-17. It will now find that, in more difficult circumstances, it will have to make big decisions, including what to do about a second independence referendum. The choices will be parking it explicitly, leaving it on the table but inactive, or advancing it post-Brexit. While the latter looks extremely unlikely, for all the noise and denial of some independence supporters following the 2017 election, all of the options are fraught with risk.

For most of the last decade the party has been aided by the continued weakness and ineptitude of their political opponents. That is no longer the case. Alex Salmond and Nicola Sturgeon were for the most part brilliant tacticians during this period. The 2007 victory and minority government, the 2011 Holyrood landslide, and the 2015 peak of 56 SNP MPs were very significant achievements. But recent events following the 2014 indyref campaign have included the 2016 loss of the Scottish Parliament majority, a qualified endorsement of the 2017 local elections, and the 2017 UK general election reverse. The last three elections illustrate not just a temporary blip in an upward trajectory but a stalling and reversal of that trajectory. It shows the limits of political leadership based on short-term tactical manoeuvring and positioning. In a more competitive political environment, defined by unpredictability and uncertainty, the lack of a considered overall strategy – as a government, a movement, a party and an advocate for independence – has become more telling and more critical.

References

Daley, S. (2017), 'Where the SNP has gone wrong and how it can turn things around', *Common Space*, 14 June: https://www.commonspace.scot/articles/11168/steve-daley-where-snp-has-gone-wrong-and-how-it-can-turn-things-around

Hassan, G. (2017), 'Build it and they will come: Scotland and independence after the election', *Bella Caledonia*, 13 June: http://bellacaledonia.org.uk/2017/06/13/build-it-and-they-will-come/

Meeks, A. (2017), 'The biggest loser: How Nicola Sturgeon did even worse than May', *Political Betting*, 15 June: http://www2.politicalbetting.com/index.php/archives/2017/06/15/the-biggest-loser-how-nicola-sturgeon-did-even-worse-than-tmay/

APPENDIX

Scotland 2007-2017: A Chronology

Gerry Hassan

2007

3 May: SNP finish one seat ahead of Labour in Scottish Parliament elections. SNP win 32.9% of the constituency vote and 31.0% of the regional vote. Labour win 32.2% and 29.2%; Conservatives 16.6% and 13.9%, Lib Dems 16.2% and 11.3% and Scottish Greens on 4.0% of the regional vote. The SNP wins 47 seats, Labour 46, Conservatives 17, Lib Dems 16, Scottish Greens 2, independent 1.

3 May: In local government elections the SNP win 363 councillors to Labour's 348, in the first election to be held under the Single Transferable Vote (STV).

11 May: SNP and Scottish Greens sign a working agreement with the Greens backing Alex Salmond for First Minister in return for a climate change bill and one committee chair.

16 May: Alex Salmond elected First Minister with 49 votes to Labour's Jack McConnell's 46 with Conservatives and Lib Dems abstaining.

14 June: Fiona Hyslop, Education minister, announces the abolition of student fees.

24 June: Gordon Brown elected unopposed leader of the British Labour Party. Harriet Harman elected deputy leader with 50.4% against Alan Johnson's 49.6% in the fifth round.

27 June: Gordon Brown becomes UK Prime Minister.

28 June: Des Brown becomes Secretary of State for Scotland while also holding the post of Secretary of State for Defence.

14 August: Alex Salmond and Nicola Sturgeon launch the Scottish Government's 'national conversation' on independence and publish the White Paper, 'Choosing Scotland's Future'.

3 September: Scottish Executive is rebranded and renamed as the Scottish Government.

14 September: Wendy Alexander is elected unopposed leader of Scottish Labour.

15 October: Menzies Campbell resigns as UK Lib Dem leader.

15 November: John Swinney, Finance minister announces first SNP budget including a council tax freeze.

29 November: Aberdeenshire councillors reject Donald Trump's golf course and development on the Menie estate.

30 November: Wendy Alexander sets out argument for review of Scottish devolution and the case for an independent commission to create detailed plans which became the Calman Commission.

6 December: Scottish Parliament votes to create the Calman Commission on Scottish Devolution by 74 to 46 with three abstentions.

2008

8 February: Tavish Scott becomes leader of the Scottish Lib Dems winning 59.0% of the vote, defeating Ross Finnie on 21.3% and Mike Rumbles on 17.9%.

11 February: Bridge tolls abolished over the Forth and Tay Road Bridges.

25 March: Calman Commission on Scottish Devolution formally announced by Des Browne, Secretary of State for Scotland.

4 May: Wendy Alexander declares 'Bring it on' in relation to an independence referendum.

28 June: Wendy Alexander resigns as Scottish Labour leader.

24 July: John Mason wins Glasgow East for the SNP in a Westminster by-election defeating Labour's Margaret Curran by a majority of 365 votes.

21 August: Alex Salmond says, in an interview with Iain Dale about Scotland's view of Thatcherism, 'It didn't mind the economic side so much. We could see the sense in some of that. But we didn't like the social side at all.'

8 September: Scottish Broadcasting Commission publishes its final report 'Platform for Success' making the case for a digital public service TV channel for Scotland.

13 September: Iain Gray becomes Scottish Labour leader defeating Cathy Jamieson in the second round of voting by 57.8% to 42.2%; in the first round Gray won 46.0% to Jamieson's 33.3% and Andy Kerr's 20.7%. Johann Lamont becomes deputy leader after defeating Bill Butler by 60.2% to 39.8%.

3 October: Jim Murphy becomes Secretary of State for Scotland.

13 October: The UK Government takes a 58% stake in the Royal Bank of Scotland to recapitalise the bank. Alistair Darling, Chancellor, injects a total of £37 billion into RBS, Lloyds TSB and HBOS plc.

3 November: Scottish Government gives approval for Donald Trump's golf course and development in the Menie estate, Aberdeenshire.

6 November: Labour's Lindsay Roy wins Glenrothes Westminster by-election with a 6,737 majority over the SNP's Peter Grant.

24 November: Patrick Harvie elected unopposed co-convenor of the Scottish Greens.

2009

28 January: Scottish Government budget defeated after 64-64 tied vote on the casting vote of Presiding Officer.

4 February: Scottish Government revised budget passed 123 votes to two.

8 May: *Daily Telegraph* begins publishing parliamentary expense claims of MPs.

19 May: Michael Martin, Speaker of the House of Commons, announces his resignation following criticism; a parliamentary motion calling on him to resign is signed by 22 MPs.

4 June: European elections see SNP win 29.1% to Labour's 20.8% with the Conservatives on 16.8%, Lib Dems on 11.5% and Scottish Greens on 7.3%.

15 June: The cross-party Calman Commission involving Labour, Tories and Lib Dems, 'Serving Scotland Better: Scotland and the United Kingdom in the 21st century' calls for significant new tax powers for the Scottish Parliament published.

16 June: Jim Devine, Labour MP for Livingston is deselected from the party over parliamentary expenses.

25 June: Scottish Parliament debate on Calman Commission proposals votes to support it by 69 votes to 49 with one abstention.

4 August: Climate Change (Scotland) Act gains Royal Assent.

20 August: Abdelbaset al-Megrahi, convicted of the bombing of Pan Am flight 103, is released by Kenny MacAskill, Justice minister, on 'compassionate grounds'.

12 November: Labour's Willie Bain wins the Glasgow North East Westminster by-election with a majority of 8,111 over the SNP's David Kerr.

25 November: UK Government White Paper, 'Scotland's Future in the United Kingdom: building on ten years of Scottish devolution' is published.

30 November: Scottish Government publishes the White Paper, 'Your Scotland, Your Voice' after the 'national conversation' on Scotland's future.

2010

22 January: Anne Moffat, Labour MP for East Lothian is deselected over her travel expenses.

22 February: Scottish Government publishes 'Scotland's Future: Draft Referendum (Scotland) Bill Consultation Paper'.

6 May: UK general election sees the Conservatives win 306 seats to Labour's 258. In Scotland, Labour win 42.0% to the SNP's 19.9%, Lib Dems 18.9% and Conservatives 16.7%. Labour win 41 seats, Lib Dems 11, SNP 6 and Conservatives 1.

11 May: Five days after the election Gordon Brown resigns as Prime Minister. David Cameron enters Downing Street and announces a Conservative-Lib Dem coalition.

11 May: Danny Alexander becomes Secretary of State for Scotland.

25 May: UK Government's Queen's Speech announces legislation to implement recommendations of the Calman Commission.

29 May: Michael Moore becomes Secretary of State for Scotland, replacing Danny Alexander, after David Laws is forced to resign from the Treasury.

22 September: Ed Miliband is elected Labour leader, defeating his brother David Miliband by 50.65% to 49.35%.

30 November: Michael Moore, Secretary of State for Scotland publishes the Scotland Bill 2010 proposing new powers for the Scottish Parliament, based on the recommendations of the Calman Commission.

11 December: Stewart Stevenson resigns as Transport minister following his handling of transport problems caused by heavy snow; the next day he is replaced by Keith Brown.

23 December: Tommy Sheridan, former leader of the Scottish Socialist Party, is found guilty of perjury.

2011

17 January: TNS-BMRC poll shows Labour with a 16% constituency vote and 14% regional vote lead over the SNP: 49% to 33% in the former and 46% to 33% in the latter.

26 January: Tommy Sheridan is sentenced to three years imprisonment after being found guilty of perjury.

31 March: Former Labour MP Jim Devine is sentenced to sixteen months imprisonment after being convicted of false accounting.

1 April: Prescription charges are abolished in Scotland.

5 May: SNP win an overall majority in the Scottish Parliament winning 45.6% of the constituency vote and 44.0% of the regional vote. Labour win 31.7% and 26.3%; Conservatives 13.9% and 12.4%, Lib Dems 7.9% and 5.2%, with the Scottish Greens on 4.4% in the regional vote. In parliamentary seats, the SNP win 69, Labour 37, Conservatives 15, Lib Dems 5, Scottish Greens 2, independent 1.

5 May: UK-wide referendum on Alternative Vote sees proposed change defeated with 67.9% voting against change and 32.1% for change on a 42.2% turnout.

17 May: Willie Rennie is elected leader of the Scottish Lib Dems unopposed.

18 May: Alex Salmond is re-elected First Minister with 68 votes to none against, and 57 abstentions.

29 June: Christie Commission on the Future Delivery of Public Services is published, stressing the need for 'preventive' focus.

30 June: Labour holds Inverclyde in a Westminster by-election following the death of David Cairns. Labour's Iain McKenzie wins with a 5,838 majority over the SNP's Anne McLaughlin.

10 September: Publication of the Sarah Boyack-Jim Murphy review into Scottish Labour proposes that the post of leader of Scottish Labour is created replacing the previous post of Leader of the Labour Party in the Scottish Parliament.

15 September: Fixed-term Parliaments Act receives Royal Assent, creating a UK parliamentary fixed term of five years and moving the date of the next Scottish Parliament election to 5 May 2016.

4 November: Ruth Davidson is elected leader of the Scottish Conservatives defeating Murdo Fraser by 55.2% to 44.8%. In the first round Davidson won 40.3%, Fraser 36.9%, Jackson Carlaw 14.6% and Margaret Mitchell 8.3%. Turnout was 63.8%.

17 December: Johann Lamont becomes leader of Scottish Labour winning 51.8% to Ken Macintosh's 40.3% and Tom Harris's 7.95%. Anas Sarwar wins the deputy leadership with 51.1% to Ian Davidson's 33.3% and Lewis MacDonald's 15.6%.

2012

19 January: Offensive Behaviour at Football and Threatening Communications (Scotland) Act receives Royal Assent.

14 February: Glasgow Rangers FC goes into administration.

23 February: Eric Joyce, Labour MP for Falkirk West, is suspended from the party after being arrested over a House of Commons assault.

1 May: Scotland Act 2012 receives Royal Assent.

3 May: Local government elections sees the SNP win 425 seats to Labour's 394. Against expectations Labour hold on to control of Glasgow City Council.

25 May: Yes Scotland, the cross-party body for a Yes vote in the independence referendum, is launched.

14 June: Charles Green buys Glasgow Rangers FC assets and business, setting up a new company.

25 June: Better Together is launched: the cross-party body for a No vote in the independence referendum.

4 July: An application by Rangers to transfer their membership of the Scottish Premier League to a new company is rejected; Rangers eventually start again in the fourth tier of senior football.

27 July – 5 August: London 2012 Summer Olympics.

25 September: Scottish Labour leader Johann Lamont delivers her 'something for nothing' speech.

15 October: Edinburgh Agreement is signed between UK and Scottish Governments, agreeing framework and principles of the independence referendum.

19 October: SNP conference votes 426 to 332 to overturn the party's traditional policy of opposition to NATO membership.

23 October: SNP MSPs Jean Urquhart and John Finnie resign from the party over its NATO conference decision and become independents.

2013

30 January: Scottish Government announces, after testing with the Electoral Commission, that the referendum question will be: 'Should Scotland be an independent country?'

25 February: Cardinal Keith O'Brien resigns as head of the Catholic Church in Scotland over allegations of sexual misconduct.

4 March: Bill Walker, SNP MSP for Dunfermline is suspended from the party following allegations from three of his ex-wives of violent behaviour.

21 March: Alex Salmond announces the date of the referendum will be 18 September 2014.

1 April: Police Scotland and Scotland Fire and Rescue Service come into operation.

20 June: Aberdeen Donside Scottish Parliament by-election is held by SNP's Mark McDonald with a reduced 2,025 majority over Labour's Willie Young.

23 June: *Sunday Herald* reveals that some in Better Together refer to their campaign as 'Project Fear'.

27 June: The Scottish Referendum (Franchise) Bill which gives 16 and 17 year olds the right to vote passes its final vote in the Scottish Parliament.

7 July: Andy Murray beats Novak Djokovic to win Wimbledon for the first time.

23 September: Bill Walker, former SNP MSP for Dunfermline, is sentenced to twelve months imprisonment for domestic violence and resigns as an MSP.

7 October: Alistair Carmichael becomes Secretary of State for Scotland.

23 October: Ineos, owners of the Grangemouth petrochemical plant, announces its closure with the loss of 800 jobs. Two days latter the plant is reprieved after management and the Unite union accept a 'survival plan'.

24 October: Dunfermline Scottish Parliament by-election is won by Labour's Cara Hilton with a 2,873 majority over the SNP's Shirley-Anne Somerville: a Labour gain from the SNP.

26 November: Scottish Government White Paper on independence, 'Scotland's Future' is published.

29 November: A police helicopter crashes into the Clutha Vaults bar in Glasgow killing ten people.

2014

23 January: Cowdenbeath Scottish Parliament by-election is won by Labour's Alex Rowley, defeating the SNP's Natalie McGarry by 5,488 votes.

13 February: George Osborne, UK Chancellor of the Exchequer, says that an independent Scotland cannot use the UK pound as its currency. He is supported by Danny Alexander, Chief Secretary to the Treasury, and Ed Balls, Shadow Chancellor.

12 March: Marriage and Civil Partnership (Scotland) Act receives Royal Assent.

27 March: Children and Young People (Scotland) Act receives Royal Assent.

28 March: 'Crisis at Better Together' *Daily Mail* story with Alastair Darling's leadership of the campaign is criticised.

4 April: Margo MacDonald, independent MSP for the Lothian Region and former SNP MP and MSP, dies.

22 May: European elections sees SNP win 29.0% to Labour's 25.9%, with
the Conservatives on 17.2%, UKIP 10.5%, Scottish Greens 8.1% and Lib
Dems 7.1%. UKIP win the overall UK contest in seats and votes and take
one Scottish seat, its first ever north of the border representation.

23 July – 3 August: Glasgow hosts the Commonwealth Games.

7 September: YouGov opinion poll put Yes ahead for the first time in a public
poll: 51% to 49%.

8 September: Former UK Prime Minister Gordon Brown says that, with a
No vote, further devolution will be delivered on a clear timescale, with
a broad plan published by the end of November and final agreement by
January 2015.

14 September: The Queen, leaving Crathie Kirk, near Balmoral, says to a
group of well-wishers about the referendum: 'Well, I hope people will
think very carefully about the future.'

16 September: *Daily Record* publishes 'The Vow', signed by the leaders of the
three main UK parties – Prime Minister David Cameron, Deputy Prime
Minister Nick Clegg and Labour leader Ed Miliband – promising substantive more powers to the Scottish Parliament.

18 September: Scotland votes 55.3% to 44.7% against independence, with a
84.6% turnout.

19 September: Alex Salmond announces his resignation as First Minister and
SNP leader.

19 September: David Cameron announces cross-party Smith Commission on
further powers for the Scottish Parliament.

23 September: SNP MSP John Wilson resigns from the party over NATO policy.

24 October: Johann Lamont resigned as Scottish Labour leader, saying that
some of her colleagues in Labour's Westminster leadership treat the Scottish party 'like a branch office of London'.

14 November: Nicola Sturgeon is elected unopposed as leader of the SNP.
Stewart Hosie elected deputy leader with 55.5%, defeating Keith Brown
with 44.5%. In the first round Hosie wins 42.2%, Brown 34.2% and
Angela Constance 23.5%. Turnout was 55.7%.

19 November: Nicola Sturgeon is elected First Minister, with 66 votes to Ruth
Davidson's 15.

27 November: 'Report of the Smith Commission for further Devolution to the
Scottish Parliament' is published.

13 December: Jim Murphy is elected as Scottish Labour leader with 55.8% of
the vote, with Neil Findlay winning 35.0% and Sarah Boyack 9.2%. Kezia

Dugdale is elected deputy with 62.9% of the vote, defeating Katy Clark, who won 37.1%.

22 December: Six people die when a Glasgow City Council refuse lorry crashes into crowds in George Square.

31 December: First same-sex marriages take place in Scotland.

2015

1 January: Revenue Scotland is created.

3 April: *Daily Telegraph* publishes story with headline – 'Sturgeon's secret backing for Cameron.' It claims that Nicola Sturgeon told the French ambassador that Ed Miliband wasn't 'Prime Minister material' and she would 'rather see' David Cameron in office. Within one hour Sturgeon refutes the story.

7 May: UK general election sees David Cameron returned as head of Tory majority government. In Scotland the SNP win 56 out of 59 seats with Labour, Lib Dems and Tories reduced to one each. In votes the SNP win 49.97% to Labour's 24.3%, with the Conservatives on 14.9% and Lib Dems 7.5%.

11 May: David Mundell is appointed Secretary of State for Scotland.

16 May: Jim Murphy announces he will stand down as Scottish Labour leader, following a 17-14 vote for him to remain in post by the Scottish Labour Executive.

22 May: Liberal Democrat Alistair Carmichael admits he leaked the Nicola Sturgeon memo.

1 June: Former Liberal Democrat leader Charles Kennedy dies.

24 July: Community Empowerment (Scotland) Act receives Royal Assent.

15 August: Kezia Dugdale is elected Scottish Labour leader, defeating Ken Mackintosh by a margin of 72.1% to 27.9%. Alex Rowley is elected deputy leader, with 55.5% against Gordon Matheson's 44.5%. In the first round Rowley wins 37.4% to Matheson's 33.2% and Richard Baker's 30.4%.

12 September: Jeremy Corbyn is elected Labour leader, winning 59.5% of the vote, defeating Andy Burnham with 19.0%, Yvette Cooper on 17.0% and Liz Kendall on 4.5%. Tom Watson is elected deputy leader with 50.7% of the vote, defeating Stella Creasy with 26.4% and Caroline Flint with 22.8% on the third ballot.

29 September: Michelle Thomson, MP for Edinburgh West, resigns the SNP whip after the police announce an investigation into alleged irregularities in relation to property dealings.

24 November: Natalie McGarry, MP for Glasgow East, resigns the SNP whip
while police investigate financial irregularities in the pro-independence
group Women for Independence.

27 November: Maggie Chapman is re-elected co-convenor of the Scottish
Green Party, winning 57.7% of the vote to Zara Kitson's 42.3%.

9 December: Alistair Carmichael election court case finds he told a 'blatant
lie' when he denied leaking Sturgeon memo, but it is not proven that he
committed an 'illegal practice'.

2016

23 March: Scotland Act 2016 receives Royal Assent.

30 March: Scottish Elections (Dates) Act receives Royal Assent, extending the
term of the Scottish Parliament from four to five years with the elections
after 2016 held on 6 May 2021.

22 April: Land Reform (Scotland) Act receives Royal Assent.

5 May: Scottish Parliament elections sees the SNP win 63 seats to the Conservatives 31, Labour 24, Scottish Greens six and Lib Dems five. In constituency votes the SNP win 46.5% to Labour's 22.6%, Conservatives 22.0%
and Lib Dems 7.8%. In the regional vote the SNP win 41.7% to Conservatives 22.9%, Labour's 19.1%, Scottish Greens 6.6% and Lib Dems 5.2%.

17 May: Nicola Sturgeon is re-elected First Minister, with 63 votes to Lib Dem
Willie Rennie's five.

22 May: Stewart Hosie announces he will not stand again for SNP depute
leader post.

23 June: UK votes for EU withdrawal by margin of 51.9% to 48.1% on a
72.2% turnout. Scotland votes 62% to 38% against withdrawal on a
67.2% turnout.

24 June: David Cameron announces his resignation as UK Prime Minister.
Nicola Sturgeon says that a second independence referendum is 'highly
likely'.

28 July: Supreme Court rules against aspects of the Scottish Government's
named person scheme in the Children and Young People (Scotland) Act.

31 July: Council house sales end.

24 September: Jeremy Corbyn is re-elected British Labour leader, defeating
Owen Smith by 61.8% to 38.2%.

13 October: Angus Robertson wins the SNP depute leadership with 52.5% of
the vote on the first ballot, defeating Tommy Sheppard on 25.5%, Alyn
Smith on 18.6% and Chris McEleny on 3.4%. Turnout is 33.9%.

20 December: Scottish Government White Paper, 'Scotland's Place in Europe', is published.

2017

1 January: First baby boxes in Scotland pilots start in Clackmannanshire and Orkney.

22 February: BBC announces new BBC Scotland TV channel to begin broadcasting autumn 2018.

13 March: Nicola Sturgeon calls for a second independence referendum in light of UK EU withdrawal.

16 March: Theresa May says that 'now is not the time' for a second independence referendum.

28 March: Scottish Parliament votes 69-59 for a second independence vote.

29 March: UK triggers Article 50 to begin process of leaving the EU.

4 May: Local government elections sees SNP and Tories make gains and Labour finish third. SNP wins Glasgow from Labour.

8 June: UK general election sees Theresa May returned as leader of a Tory minority government. In Scotland the SNP win 35 out of 59 seats, with the Tories on 13, Labour on seven and Lib Dems on four. In votes the SNP win 36.9% to the Conservatives on 28.6%, Labour on 27.1% and Lib Dems on 6.8%.

8 June: Conservative Rachael Hamilton wins Ettrick, Roxburgh and Berwickshire Scottish Parliament by-election, increasing the party's majority from 7,736 to 9,338 votes over the SNP's Gail Henry.

8 June: Tory Rachael Hamilton win Ettrick, Roxburgh and Berwickshire Scottish Parliament by-election increasing the party's majority from 7,736 to 9,338 votes over the SNP Gail Henry.

Contributors

SARAH ARMSTRONG is Director of the Scottish Centre for Crime and Justice Research and a Senior Research Fellow at the University of Glasgow.

SIMON BARROW is Director of the beliefs, ethics and public policy think-tank Ekklesia. He has edited, written and contributed to numerous books, most recently *Scotland 2021*, with Mike Small (Ekklesia / Bella Caledonia, 2016).

SARAH BEATTIE-SMITH is a Green activist, writer and artist based in Dunbar, East Lothian. She works as a policy and communications consultant on energy and climate change.

JOHN CARNOCHAN retired from Strathclyde Police in 2013 as a Detective Chief Superintendent after almost 39 years service. He was the co-founder of the Scottish Violence Reduction Unit.

PAUL CAIRNEY is Professor of Politics and Public Policy at the University of Stirling. He advised the Scottish Parliament's Commission on Parliamentary Reform, but these are his views, developed before the appointment.

ANDREW CONWAY is a writer, scientist, coder, data-wrangler and erstwhile entrepreneur with interests in economics and philosophy and how they may be applied to improve or, at the very least understand, society.

JOHN CURTICE is Professor of Politics at Strathclyde University and Senior Research Fellow at ScotCen Social Research. Chief Commentator at whatscotlandthinks.org, he is a regular media commentator on Scottish politics.

JIM CUTHBERT lectured in Statistics at Glasgow University, before joining the government statistical service. He worked in the Treasury and in the Scottish Office, where he was latterly Chief Statistician. He has since engaged in consultancy and research, particularly into Scotland's public finances.

MARGARET CUTHBERT was a lecturer in economics at the Universities of Glasgow, Strathclyde and Heriot Watt, before taking up economic consultancy. She has researched extensively on the Scottish economy and public finances.

MIKE DANSON is Professor of Enterprise Policy, Heriot-Watt University. He has researched and advised governments, public agencies, international organisations, and civic institutions on local and regional economic development, with more than 13 books, 100 book chapters and 250 papers and reports.

KATE DEVLIN is UK Political Correspondent for *The Herald*, covering Westminster politics in particular. She has previously covered the Scottish Parliament and health policy.

ALISON ELLIOT is Associate Director of the Centre for Theology and Public Issues at the University of Edinburgh. She was previously Moderator of the General Assembly of the Church of Scotland and the first women elected to the post. She chaired the Land Reform Review Group of the Scottish Government.

MARK FISHER is the Scottish theatre critic for *The Guardian*, a former editor of *The List* magazine and a freelance contributor to *Variety*, *The Scotsman* and many other publications. He is the author of *The Edinburgh Fringe Survival Guide* (Bloomsbury) and *How to Write About Theatre* (Bloomsbury).

DOUGLAS FRASER has been business and economy editor at BBC Scotland since 2008. He was previously based at Holyrood as political editor of *The Herald*, and of *The Sunday Herald* and he covered education, the Highlands and the arts for *The Scotsman*.

KATIE GALLOGLY-SWAN is a researcher and campaigner with a degree in social anthropology from Harvard University. She works for a wide range of projects including Common Weal, Our Land, Govanhill Baths, Glasgow Pound Working Group, and a range of deliberative research projects.

DANI GARAVELLI is a journalist and columnist for *Scotland on Sunday*. She spent seven years working for English regional newspapers, including the *Newcastle Journal*, before heading back north. She now writes for a variety of publications including *The Herald Magazine*, *Scottish Review of Books* and *Holyrood*.

PETER GEOGHEGAN is a writer, broadcaster and lecturer in journalism at the University of the West of Scotland. His most recent book is *The People's Referendum: Why Scotland Will Never Be the Same Again* (Luath Press 2015).

GERRY HASSAN is a writer and researcher. He is author of *Scotland the Bold* (Freight Books, 2016), *Independence of the Scottish Mind* (Palgrave Macmillan, 2014) and *Caledonian Dreaming* (Luath Press, 2014) and edited *Scottish National Party Leaders* with James Mitchell (Biteback Publishing, 2016).

WILLIAM HENDERSON is Lecturer in Law at Glasgow Caledonian University, specialising in international law and human rights. His work both domestically and internationally has included statehood, institutions, and governance.

NICK HOPKINS is Senior Lecturer in Psychology in the School of Social Sciences at University of Dundee. He is co-author with Stephen Reicher of *Self and*

Nation (Sage Publications, 2001) and co-edit the journal the *British Journal of Social Psychology*.

LUCY HUNTER Blackburn worked for 20 years in public administration, mainly in the civil service. She is now an ESRC-funded doctoral student at the University of Edinburgh, specialising in student finance, on which she has published extensively. She blogs at adventuresinevidence.com and is a board member of Sceptical Scot.

BEN JACKSON is Associate Professor of Modern History at Oxford University and the co-editor of *Political Quarterly*.

DAVID JAMIESON is a staff journalist with *CommonSpace*. He writes on social movements, politics, history and economics for a range of national and international publications.

ANUJ KAPILASHRAMI is a Lecturer in Global Public Health policy in the University of Edinburgh. She convenes the People's Health Movement Scotland and is a Steering group member of the UK PHM.

MICHAEL KEATING is Professor of Scottish politics at Aberdeen University. He is author of numerous books including *Small Nations in a Big World: What Small Nations Can Learn* (with Malcolm Harvey) (Luath Press, 2013) and edited *Debating Scotland: Issues of Independence and Union in the 2014 Referendum* (Oxford University Press, 2017) and *A Wealthier, Fairer Scotland: The Political Economy of Constitutional Change* (Edinburgh University Press, 2017).

SUE LAUGHLIN has worked for the NHS in Glasgow for 30 years. She is now exploring the impact of equality legislation on city life in Glasgow for a PhD.

JOHN MACDONALD is Director of the Scottish Global Forum.

LESLEY MCARA is Professor of Penology at the University of Edinburgh and Co-Director of the Edinburgh Study of Youth Transitions and Crime.

NEIL MCGARVEY lectures Scottish and local politics at the University of Strathclyde. He has published widely in these fields. He is co-author (with Paul Cairney) of *Scottish Politics* (Palgrave), which will be published in its third edition in 2018.

JAMES MCENANEY is a former secondary school English teacher now lecturing at Glasgow Clyde College. He is a writer with an interest in Scottish education and Freedom of Information. He is a columnist with *CommonSpace* and also written for the *Daily Record*, *The Times Educational Supplement Scotland* and *The Ecologist*.

JOYCE MCMILLAN is a columnist and theatre critic for *The Scotsman*. She is author of *Theatre in Scotland: A Field of Dreams* (Nick Hern Books, 2016), a collection of her cultural reviews covering more than 30 years.

SARA MARSDEN researches public health policy at the University of Edinburgh and previously worked at the Care Quality Commission.

JAMES MITCHELL is Professor of Public Policy at the School of Social and Political Science at the University of Edinburgh. He is author of *Takeover: Explaining the Extraordinary Rise of the SNP*, with Rob Jones (Biteback Publishing, 2016), *The Scottish Question* (Oxford University Press, 2014) and *The Scottish National Party: Transition to Power*, with Rob Jones and Lynn Bennie (Oxford University Press, 2012). He edited *Scottish National Party Leaders* with Gerry Hassan (Biteback Publishing, 2016).

MARY MUNRO is Editor of *Scottish Justice Matters* and Senior Visiting Fellow at the University of Strathclyde.

KEN NEIL is an artist, academic and writer with an interest in the ways in which culture has informed and has been adopted by the Yes movement and the politics of nationalism in Scotland. He is a professor of art and design and works at the Glasgow School of Art.

VÉRÈNE NICOLAS supports leaders, teams or organisations in their efforts to nurture collaborative, values driven and blame-free cultures. She is based in Glasgow and works primarily with civil society organisations and activists in Scotland and abroad. Further details can be found at: www.verenenicolas.org

RICHARD PARRY is an Honorary Fellow in the Centre on Constitutional Change at the University of Edinburgh. He was previously Reader in Social Policy and has published widely on Scottish government issues since the 1980s.

STEPHEN REICHER is Professor of School of Psychology and Neuroscience and former Head of the School of Psychology at the University of St. Andrews. He is co-author with Nick Hopkins of *Self and Nation* (Sage Publications, 2001).

LESLEY RIDDOCH is a writer, broadcaster and organiser of Nordic Horizons. She is author of *Blossom: What Scotland Needs to Flourish* (Luath Press, 2013) and co-edited with Paddy Bort: *McSmorgasbord: What post-Brexit Scotland can learn from the Nordics* (Luath Press, 2017).

TONY ROBERTSON is Lecturer in Public Health at the University of Stirling, having previously worked as a post-doctoral researcher in Edinburgh and Glasgow. He is also a member of the steering group for the People's Health Movement Scotland.